Time Out

Mumbai

timeoutmumbai.net

Time Out Guides Ltd
Universal House
251 Tottenham Court Road
London W1T 7AB
United Kingdom
Tel: +44 (0)20 7813 3000
Fax: +44 (0)20 7813 6001
Email: guides@timeout.com
www.timeout.com

Published by Time Out Guides Ltd, a wholly owned subsidiary of Time Out Group Ltd.
Time Out and the Time Out logo are trademarks of Time Out Group Ltd.

10 9 8 7 6 5 4 3 2

This edition first published in Great Britain in 2011 by Ebury Publishing.
A Random House Group Company
20 Vauxhall Bridge Road, London SW1V 2SA

Random House Australia Pty Ltd 20 Alfred Street, Milsons Point, Sydney, New South Wales 2061, Australia

Random House New Zealand Ltd 18 Poland Road, Glenfield, Auckland 10, New Zealand

Random House South Africa (Pty) Ltd Isle of Houghton, Corner Boundary Road & Carse O'Gowrie, Houghton 2198, South Africa

Random House UK Limited Reg. No. 954009

Distributed in the US and Latin America by Publishers Group West (1-510-809-3700)
Distributed in Canada by Publishers Group Canada (1-800-747-8147)

For further distribution details, see www.timeout.com.

ISBN: 978-1-84670-212-9

A CIP catalogue record for this book is available from the British Library.

Printed and bound by Butler Tanner & Dennis, Frome, Somerset.

The Random House Group Limited supports the Forest Stewardship Council® (FSC®), the leading international forest-certification organisation. Our books carrying the FSC label are printed on FSC®-certified paper. FSC is the only forest-certification scheme supported by the leading environmental organisations, including Greenpeace. Our paper procurement policy can be found at www.randomhouse.co.uk/environment.

Contents

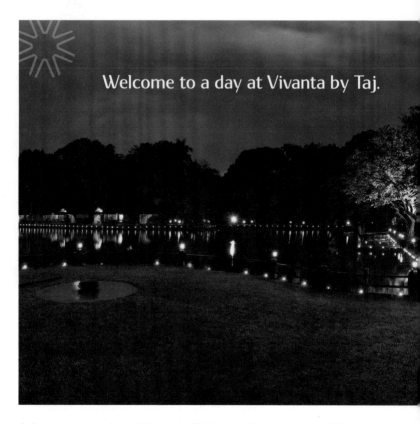

Welcome to a day at Vivanta by Taj.

A day is not just a day at Vivanta by Taj, but a million moments waiting to surprise you. Vivanta is designed for the new-age traveller who seeks heightened experiences in living spaces, gourmet dining, health and wellness, and a spirited nightlife.

Introduction

Visitors often dismiss Mumbai as not being representative enough of 'the real India', accusing the city of being too urban, too Western, too unlike what they want India to be. The fact is that Mumbai is India on steroids: 435 square kilometres (168 square miles) bursting at the seams with the hopes and dreams, cultures and cuisines, languages and races, petty quarrels and disgruntled compromises of a billion people. Appropriately, Mumbai is the economic engine that drives India's growth; home to the country's central bank, two stock exchanges, the commodities markets and the headquarters of thousands of companies. More wealth is created and very conspicuously spent in Mumbai than anywhere on the subcontinent. It's not just commerce that keeps Mumbai on the move: the city is India's biggest manufacturer of popular culture – film, television, music, dance and fashion. It has dominated the popular Indian imagination through the hundreds of books, movies and songs it has inspired, its headline-grabbing gangsters and supercops and some of the country's greatest cricket heroes.

But if the 'real' India is supposed to be shockingly poor, with appalling living conditions and a gross neglect of basic human rights, then Mumbai is disastrously real – too real for the 55 per cent of its population that lives in slums. The city's infrastructure is crumbling, property prices are too high for the lower and middle classes to afford proper housing, the roads are too narrow and battered to handle the exploding traffic, clean water is scarce and the electric supply is dwindling. After decades of civic mismanagement, misappropriation of funds and widespread corruption, the citizens of Mumbai are paying the price for the short-sightedness of their elected officials.

Yet, Mumbaikars rarely seem to do anything more than complain about the conditions in which they live. The city carries on with its day-to-day business as though the floods, religious riots, nativist demonstrations and occasional terrorist bombings are little more than traffic diversions. Disruptions are forgotten quickly and life goes on as normal. On 11 July 2006, when seven bombs went off on commuter trains across the city during the evening rush hour, services were up and running again the same night. People were back at work the next day.

As much the real India but thoroughly unreal in every way is Goa, 595 kilometres (370 miles) south of Mumbai. The former Portuguese colony was folded into India in 1961, 14 years after the rest of the country achieved independence from the British, and it retains a Latinate character to rival any Mediterranean or South Atlantic destination. Though it is no longer the untouched paradise discovered by the original flower children of the 1970s, packed as it is with the burgeoning Indian middle class, British charter tourists and neo-hippies, Goa remains charmingly relaxed and thankfully unspoiled away from the main tourist areas.

Neither Mumbai nor Goa can claim to be all of India but they make up two ends of the spectrum – one a too-real adrenaline shot of urbs in extremis, the other an unreal promised land where the party never stops. *Bijal Vachharajani, Mumbai Editor.*

Mumbai in Brief

IN CONTEXT

The guide's opening section introduces you to the history of Mumbai – the story of how the seven islands came together to form the bustling metropolis it is today. Just over three centuries old, it doesn't bear the burden of history like the rest of India but it is beleaguered with civic and infrastructure problems. Yet Mumbai manages to stand on its own as a thriving cultural hub.

▶ *For more, see pp17-46.*

SIGHTS

Mumbai doesn't reward tourists who come armed with checklists. It is a city that is fascinating not for its museums, nor for its architectural heritage; no, it's in the people of Mumbai, the hectic activity of its streets and the ridiculous contrasts of appalling poverty and overblown wealth – and the complete indifference with which Mumbaikars deal with them – that the appeal of the city lies.

▶ *For more, see pp48-65.*

CONSUME

In this section of the book, you'll find a selection of the best accommodation options that will fit most budgets – from swish five-star hotels to tiny heritage ones. Mumbai has expanded to accommodate scores of cafés, restaurants and pubs, which offer a variety of cuisines. For your convenience, we have categorised the Indian restaurants separately from international ones.

▶ *For more, see pp75-134.*

ARTS & ENTERTAINMENT

Here we cover the city's vibrant festivals and give you a lowdown on Mumbai's performing arts scene – where to see the best dance performances, catch plays, see art, unwind over a drink and listen to music. If you're travelling with children, we give you a quick guide on family outings. We also tell you where to go to relax after a day of sightseeing and shopping.

▶ *For more, see pp135-168.*

GOA

Mumbai is beguiling and and exhilarating, for sure, but it's also exhausting. Which is why we suggest that while you're here, you do as locals do and get out; after all, there's plenty to see. Whether you want to search for crocodiles, potter around Portuguese colonial towns or kick back on one of Goa's balmy beaches with a plate of fish curry and an ice-cold beer, we'll point you in the right direction.

▶ *For more, see pp169-226.*

Mumbai in 48 Hrs

Day 1 Colaba, Colonial Charm & Cricket.

8AM Take a stroll down **Colaba Causeway**, then sidetrack down to the harbour to the **Gateway of India** (*see p49*) and the nearby **Taj Mahal Palace Hotel** (*see p77*).

10AM From here, stroll back down to the **Regal Cinema** (*see p143*) and take in the **National Gallery of Modern Art** (*see p149*), and the impressive domes and balconies of the **Chhatrapati Shivaji Maharaj Vastu Sangrahalaya**, formerly the Prince of Wales Museum (*see p53*), across the street.

1PM If you're feeling peckish, walk up to **Kala Ghoda** past a stretch of colonial-era buildings and the landmark **Jehangir Art Gallery** (*see p149*) and tuck into some first-class curries at **Khyber** (*see p101*) or try the outstanding South Indian seafood at nearby **Trishna** (*see p101*).

3PM Close by is the faded but beautiful **Kenneseth Eliyahoo Synagogue** (*see p53*) and the cool clothes store **FabIndia** (*see p125*). From here, it's a quick stroll to the **Bombay High Court**, the **University of Mumbai** and the cricket at **Oval Maidan** (*see p51*).

5PM It's tea time and you're in India, so Replenish yourself at the **Tea Centre** (*see p101*) next to Churchgate station. For the real deal, plump for hot apple butter tea and chilli garlic potatoes. Still got some energy?

7PM Then walk up to **Flora Fountain** (*see p56*) and wander the hawker-packed pavement arcades nearby.

10PM It's a short walk down Veer Nariman Road to **Horniman Circle** and the **Asiatic Society** (*see p54*).

GETTING AROUND

The intense traffic, crowds, noise, heat, shocking poverty and poor infrastructure can make Mumbai an exhausting and overwhelming city. Be gentle on yourself and don't try to do too much at once. Drink plenty of water. Some areas are best appreciated on foot, but most of the time you'll find taxis much easier and a relatively cheap way to get around. Getting out to the suburbs is almost always faster by train, but if you can't face those packed carriages, you'll find it isn't that expensive to go by cab. Many street and place names have been officially changed in the last 20 years but most locals still use the old names. New names are often not recognised, even by taxi drivers, so in our listings and maps we've given both where appropriate and a prominent nearby landmark to aid navigation.

TOUTS AND SCAMS

Mumbaikars are warm and welcoming to foreign visitors, but around tourist-heavy

Day 2 Marine Drive, Babulnath Temple & Cocktails.

8AM You can't leave Mumbai without a taxi ride down the three-kilometre **Marine Drive** (*see p65*) for a stroll on **Girgaum Chowpatty** (*see p65*).

10AM From here it's another short taxi ride to **Walkeshwar** for the ex-colonial enclave of **Malabar Hill** and the holy and serene **Banganga Tank** (*see p62*).

1PM On the way back south, drive up Balbunath Marg past the **Babulnath Temple** (*see p65*) to nearby **Soam** (*see p104*) for some fabulous vegetarian Gujarati food. Then it's off to the old **Crawford Market** (*see p59*) for a wander around the city's liveliest and oldest food market.

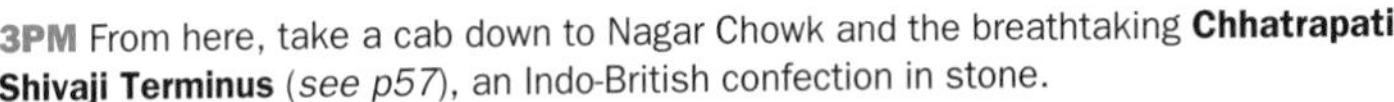

3PM From here, take a cab down to Nagar Chowk and the breathtaking **Chhatrapati Shivaji Terminus** (*see p57*), an Indo-British confection in stone.

5PM By now you're probably beginning to feel a little hot and bothered. Rest your feet and cool down by popping into the Barista across the street for an iced coffee. Feeling suitably refreshed, amble down Waudby Road to the lawns of **Azad Maidan** past the elite **Bombay Gymkhana** (*see p57*) to **Mahatma Gandhi Road** and the open-air **Fashion Street** clothes market (*see p132*).

6PM By this time head back to **Marine Drive** for fabulous cocktails and views from the **Dome bar** (*see p117*) on the roof of the **InterContinental Marine Drive**.

10PM Stroll down the road past **Not Just Jazz by the Bay** (*see p117*) for some live music. Then, if you're still hungry – and who wouldn't be after a day like this? – head to **Ziya** (*see p98*) for a taste of nouvelle Indian cuisine.

sites like Colaba Causeway and the Gateway of India you're likely to be zeroed in on by persistent hawkers, beggars and the odd hashish dealer, especially in winter – peak tourist season. Some visitors find being repeatedly offered drums and oversize balloons for a 'very good price' distressing and tiresome, but be philosophical and just accept it as the price of admission. Scammers and con artists do operate but muggings – of either tourists or locals – are very rare. You might be ripped off by a cute 12-year-old asking you to buy her some powdered milk at a hugely inflated price, or an aspiring shoe-shine boy who just needs a hundred rupees to buy some polish and brushes, but you're unlikely to be robbed at knifepoint. Colaba is by far the worst spot for foreigner-focused hawkers and hustlers. If it's all getting a bit much, get out of Colaba for instant relief. If you go to Bandra, however, do watch out for the fake nuns 'collecting for the orphans'.

Mumbai in Profile

South Mumbai

The Southern part of Mumbai is steeped in history – it's the area where guided historical walks begin, taking you through the bustling **Crawford Market**, past the iconic **Chhatrapati Shivaji Terminus** and to the historical Fort area. Visit the **National Centre for the Performing Arts**, a great destination to soak in some culture, or simply to watch the sunset at **Marine Drive**.

► *For more, see pp48-65.*

CHURCHGATE

One of the busiest stations in the city, Churchgate is replete with iconic heritage buildings such as the **Eros Cinema**, the **University of Mumbai** and the **Rajabai Clock Tower**. Take a stroll down to the Oval Maidan, an area which used to be edged by the Arabian Sea and is now a popular venue for children and adults to play cricket.

COLABA

From pavement stalls selling clothes and accessories to swanky restaurants and bars, **Colaba Causeway** is tourist haven. Stroll down the road for bargain buys or catch a film at Regal, one of the city's oldest cinema halls. Go gallery hopping and then round it off with a visit to the **Chhatrapati Shivaji Maharaj Vastu Sanghralaya**.

LOWER PAREL

Earlier local trains, packed with commuters, would empty at Dadar and Churchgate stations. Now with offices moving away from South Mumbai, Lower Parel is the hub for media offices. It's also home to defunct mills that have been converted into luxury malls such as **High Street Phoenix** and lounge bars like **Blue Frog**.

The Suburbs

Mumbai's suburbs have grown organically over the years and are crowded with apartment blocks, offices and places to eat and drink. The **Bandra Kurla Complex** is now a busy office enclave, home to the headquarters of many multinationals.

► *For more, see pp66-70.*

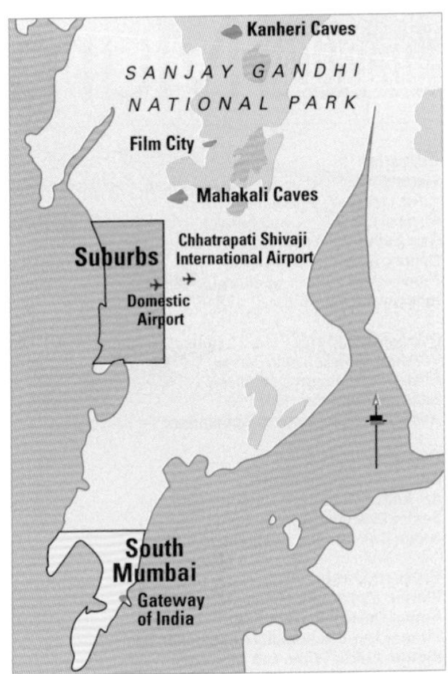

ANDHERI

Andheri has nine pin codes and more people than any other suburb. From bungalows to high-rises, mangroves to malls, hipsters to eclectic restaurants, it's all here. Catch a glimpse of the geological marvel **Gilbert Hill** in this suburb and dine at one of the funky eating joints. The eastern side of Andheri is where you'll find the **Mahakali Caves**.

BANDRA

While John Fryer's 1675 description of Bandra as a large village, with tiled-roof houses and land 'that yields as good cabbages, colewort and better radishes than ever I yet saw', is one of the oldest portrayals of the area, today Bandra is one of Mumbai's hippest suburbs with swish restaurants, pubs and stores. It also has **Band Stand** and the **Carter Road Promenade**, which offer spectacular views of the Arabian Sea.

Time Out Mumbai

Editorial
Editorial provided by Time Out Mumbai, Paprika Media Pvt Ltd, www.timeoutmumbai.net
Mumbai Editor Bijal Vachharajani (Time Out Mumbai)
Goa Author Vivek Menezes (Time Out Mumbai)
Deputy Editor Patrick Welch
Proofreader Tamsin Shelton
Indexer Alice Harman

Managing Director Peter Fiennes
Editorial Director Ruth Jarvis
Business Manager Dan Allen
Editorial Manager Holly Pick
Assistant Management Accountant Ija Krasnikova

Design
Art Director Scott Moore
Art Editor Pinelope Kourmouzoglou
Senior Designer Kei Ishimaru
Group Commercial Designer Jodi Sher

Picture Desk
Picture Editor Jael Marschner
Acting Deputy Picture Editor Liz Leahy
Picture Desk Assistant/Researcher Ben Rowe
Picture Editor (Time Out Mumbai) Chirodeep Chaudhuri

Advertising
New Business & Commercial Director Mark Phillips
International Advertising Manager Kasimir Berger
International Sales Executive Charlie Sokol
Advertising Sales (Time Out Mumbai) Vishwanath Shanbhag, Nakul Puri and Renuka Rangachari

Marketing
Sales & Marketing Director, North America & Latin America Lisa Levinson
Senior Publishing Brand Manager Luthfa Begum
Group Commercial Art Director Anthony Huggins
Marketing Co-ordinator Alana Benton

Production
Group Production Manager Brendan McKeown
Production Controller Katie Mulhern

Time Out Group
Chairman & Founder Tony Elliott
Chief Executive Officer David King
Group Financial Director Paul Rakkar
Group General Manager/Director Nichola Coulthard
Time Out Communications Ltd MD David Pepper
Time Out International Ltd MD Cathy Runciman
Time Out Magazine Ltd Publisher/MD Mark Elliott
Group Commercial Director Graeme Tottle
Group IT Director Simon Chappell

Contributors
Introduction Leo Mirani. **History** Jerry Pinto (*Who is Shivaji, Anyway?* Leo Mirani; *Mumbai or Bombay?* Iain Ball; *The Empire Strikes Out* Chetna Mahadik). **Mumbai Today** Leo Mirani (*Slumbai* Iain Ball). **Communities** Jerry Pinto. **Bollywood** Nandini Ramnath, Rachel Dwyer (*You Too Can Be a Star* Leo Mirani). **South Mumbai** Chetna Mahadik (*Munificent Mumbaikars* Rachel Lopez; *A Beatle in Bombay* Iain Ball; *Naval Display* Vidya Balachander; *Fortified Walls* Naresh Fernandes). **The Suburbs** Jerry Pinto, Iain Ball (*Local Heroes* Iain Ball; *Village Life* Rachel Lopez). **Day Trips** Naresh Fernandes, Jerry Pinto. **Hotels** Iain Ball, Leo Mirani (*Crowning Glory* Iain Ball). **Restaurants & Cafés** Iain Ball, Divia Thani-Daswani, Vikram Doctor, Roshni Bajaj Sanghvi, Neha Sumitran and contributors to Time Out Mumbai (*Vast Food Nation* Vikram Doctor; *Street Eats* Iain Ball; *Bombay Mix* Antoine Lewis; *Theme Perks* Neha Sumitran; *Thali-ho* Time Out Mumbai team). **Pubs & Bars** Leo Mirani, Ben Leahy and contributors to Time Out Mumbai. **Shops & Services** Divia Thani-Daswani (*Curio City* Roshni Bajaj Sanghvi; *Spend to Save* Time Out Mumbai team). **Calendar** Nikhil Subramaniam. **Children** Meher Marfatia, Amrita Bose, Bijal Vachharajani. **Film** Nandini Ramnath (*Metromorphosis* Chetna Mahadik). **Galleries** Srimoyee Mitra, Jerry Pinto, Deepanjana Pal, Zeenat Nagree. **Gay & Lesbian** Vikram Doctor. **Mind, Body & Soul** Tanvi Chheda, Divia Thani-Daswani, Vidya Balachander, Saumya Ancheri (*Press Here* Roshni Bajaj Sanghvi). **Music** Amit Gurbaxani, Aditya Kundalkar. **Nightlife** Leo Mirani, Ben Leahy. **Sport & Fitness** Jamie Alter, Che Kurrien, Vidya Balachander. **Theatre & Dance** Pronoti Datta (Theatre), Suhani Singh (Dance). **Goa** Vivek Menezes, Iain Ball (nightlife). **Getting Around** Deepanjana Pal, Leo Mirani. **Resources A-Z** Naresh Fernandes (media), Suhani Singh, Nikhil Subramanian, Neha Sumitran. **Further Reference** Naresh Fernandes, Nandini Ramnath.

Maps mapsofindia.com

Front cover photography eye ubiquitous/Robert Harding

Back cover photography Apoorva Guptay and Shutterstock

Photography pages 3, 6, 7, 10,11, 12, 13, 30, 43, 120, 165, 145, 253 Time Out Mumbai; pages 12 (centre left), 13 (centre), 17, 32, 35, 52, 73, 77, 151, 152 Amit Chakravarty; pages 17, 98 Tejal Pandey; pages 21, 38, 143 Janak Shah; pages 25, 29, 69, 163, 166 Chirodeep Chaudhuri; pages 33, 116 Poulomi Dey; pages 42 (bottom right), 75, 90, 113, 128, 245 Apoorva Guptay; pages 49, 140, 153 Hashim Badani; pages 67, 169, 171, 176, 177, 180, 185, 188, 189, 190, 191, 193, 194, 199, 200, 202, 203, 205, 206, 208, 211, 212, 215, 216, 219, 220, 223, 226, 227 Vivek Menezes; pages 68, 138 Tejal Pandey; pages 71, 81, 82, 109, 125, 157, 158 Vikas Munipalle; pages 72, 111, 135, 160, 162 Parikshit Rao; pages 76, 118 Poulomi Basu; pages 103, 108, 115, 137 Nishad Joshi; pages 119, 136 Janak Shah; pages 131, 154 Ashima Narain.

The following images were providedby the featured establishments/artists: pages 18, 27, 37, 41, 42,43, 44, 79,86, 89, 142.

The editor would like to thank Smiti Kanodia, Neelam Kapoor and all at *Time Out Mumbai*.

About the Guide

GETTING AROUND

The back of the book contains street maps of Mumbai, as well as overview maps of the city and its surroundings. The maps start on page 248; on them are marked the locations of hotels (❶), restaurants and cafés (❶), and pubs and bars (❶). The majority of businesses listed in this guide are located in the areas we've mapped; the grid-square references in the listings refer to these maps.

THE ESSENTIALS

For practical information, including visas, disabled access, emergency numbers, lost property, useful websites and local transport, please see the Directory. It begins on page 228.

THE LISTINGS

Addresses, phone numbers, websites, transport information, hours and prices are all included in our listings, as are selected other facilities. All were checked and correct at press time. However, business owners can alter their arrangements at any time, and fluctuating economic conditions can cause prices to change rapidly.

The very best venues in the city, the must-sees and must-dos in every category, have been marked with a red star (★). In the Sights chapters, we've also marked venues with free admission with a FREE symbol.

PHONE NUMBERS

The area code for India is 91. The area for Mumbai is 022; numbers usually have eight digits. The area code for Goa is 0832, usually followed by a seven-digit number. You don't need to use the code when calling from within Mumbai. From outside India dial your country's international access code (00 from the UK, 011 from the US) or a plus symbol, followed by the Indian country code (91), 022 for Mumbai (dropping the initial zero) and the number listed in this guide. For more on phones, including information on calling abroad from the UK and details of local mobile-phone access, see p235.

FEEDBACK

We welcome feedback on this guide, both on the venues we've included and on any other locations that you'd like to see featured in future editions. Please email us at guides@timeout.com.

Time Out Guides

Founded in 1968, Time Out has grown from humble beginnings into the leading resource for anyone wanting to know what's happening in the world's greatest cities. Alongside our influential weeklies in London, New York and Chicago, we publish more than 20 magazines and over 50 travel guidebooks and apps. In 2004, the fortnightly Time Out Mumbai magazine launched, followed by Delhi and Bengaluru titles. The company remains proudly independent, still owned by Tony Elliott four decades after he launched *Time Out London.*

Written by local experts and illustrated with original photography, our books also retain their independence. No business has been featured because it has advertised, and all restaurants and bars are visited and reviewed anonymously.

ABOUT THE TEAM

Bijal Vachharajani lives in Mumbai, edits the Kids section of *Time Out Mumbai* and works on environment and wildlife conservation campaigns. **Vivek Menezes** has covered Goa for Time Out since its magazines were first launched in India. He is a widely published writer and photographer and lives in Panjim.

A full list of the book's contributors can be found opposite.

In Context

Churchgate Terminus. See p52.

History

From Heptanesia to Mumbai, the city has come a long way.

Somewhere underneath the vast, overcrowded urban explosion that is Mumbai lies a cluster of seven disjointed islands, populated only by Koli fisherfolk and mosquitoes. The city that exists today is virtually unrecognisable from that landmass. But it's from this unremarkable archipelago that this modern metropolis grew – engulfing it as it expanded, first by building causeways to connect the islands, then by filling in the sea until only the names of these blobs of land remained. Over the last five centuries, the island that came to be known as Bombay underwent an extraordinary metamorphosis into the contiguous finger of land that now stretches south-west from the mainland. It is hard to imagine that it's from such mundane beginnings that the financial, media, glamour and film capital of India has arisen.

EARLY DAYS

All that remains of Mumbai's early history are occasional scraps of activity in between centuries filled with what we can only suppose was the incessant hiss of the Arabian Sea, the cursing of Kolis, the city's original inhabitants, and the thump of falling coconuts. There are almost no records of those times, but the channels between the islands were so deep they must have been often impossible to cross, with monsoon storms leaving each island isolated from the others. Despite their ordinariness, Ptolemy marked the islands in his maps and the ancient Greeks knew them as Heptanesia (literally, 'Seven Islands'). But even when the legendary warrior king-turned-Buddhist, Ashoka – ruler of the Mauryan Empire – turned his attention to the region in the third century BC, he ignored the islands, instead colonising areas located beyond the northern limits of modern Mumbai. In those days, Nalla Sopara (now a 15-second commuter stop for trains on their way north to the end of the line) was a bustling town, located at the crossroads of ancient trade routes, and became a patronage centre for magnificent Buddhist monasteries. You can still see the remnants of some of them in the Kanheri caves at Borivali.

What is known is that around the seventh century AD, a prince of the Chalukya Dynasty – a political dynasty that ruled large parts of the western and southern regions of the country – constructed the breathtaking cave-temples at Gharapuri, now called Elephanta Island, with an iconography that represents an early dialectic between Buddhism and Shaivism (the worship of Shiva). The Silhara kings of the Konkan region in the south moved north to take control of all seven islands in the ninth century; this was the first recorded instance of what was to be the first of many battles for control of the region, with the seven islands being batted between competing powers like a tennis ball over the next 1,000 years. Even with the Silharas in control, the islands and their Koli inhabitants remained undisturbed; the Silharas instead established their regional capital in Thane, on the northern limits of present-day Mumbai.

In 1127, the Walkeshwar Temple in what is now Malabar Hill, with its sacred Banganga tank, was constructed by Lakshman Prabhu, a minister in the court of the Silharas. It was an extraordinary achievement and a measure of the Silharas' devotion to Lord Rama, the Hindu god and hero of the epic *Ramayana*, who is supposed to have created the tank by shooting an arrow into the ground and bringing forth the waters of the Ganges. The terrain was difficult and required extensive infrastructure to transport masonry from one island to another. The Silharas managed to retain control of the islands until 1343, when the Sultan of neighbouring Gujarat took over and ruled it for the next two centuries.

IMPERIAL AMBITIONS

The story of the city's transformation begins with the Portuguese. The Portuguese explorers had already arrived in Goa in the 16th century, on a mission to wrest control of the near-priceless spice trade from the Arabs and win souls for Christendom. One of their first recorded visits to Bombay was in 1508, when a ship halted briefly at Mahim Island while travelling to an outpost at Diu in Gujarat. For the next two decades the Portuguese kept making short visits to the islands and in 1532 they finally seized Bassein (now Vasai, just north of Mumbai's municipal limits) from Sultan Bahadur Shah of Gujarat. From here the Portuguese took the entire region, including the seven islands. At that time, the Arabian coast was a bustling region of trading ships and seaside outposts. The Portuguese already possessed Goa, Daman and Diu, and Vasai became an important part of their maritime trade network.

To protect their shipping routes, the Portuguese fortified the islanded region, establishing cannon-equipped outposts at Mahim, Sion, Bandra and, of course, Bassein. It was around this time that the region got a new name – 'Ilha da Boa Vida', meaning 'the island of good life' in Portuguese. When the Portuguese first came to the place they called 'Bandora', now Bandra, they found an ideal spot: a strategically

'Apparently, Charles was not exactly sure where his wedding present was; he initially thought that the islands were somewhere in Brazil.'

important point overlooking the sea, amply supplied with drinking water from nearby freshwater springs. In 1640, they stationed a permanent garrison of troops here and built a small fort, which they called the Castella de Aguada ('the Water Point'). Armed with a pair of cannons, the garrison kept watch over sea lanes crucial to Portuguese trading interests. Anxious about the spiritual wellbeing of their troops, they also built the Chapel of Nossa Senora de Monte ('Our Lady of the Mount') nearby and cut a road linking it to the fort.

Over the next 100 years the region's social history was shaped by Portuguese religious, economic and political impulses and resembled other Portuguese outposts – including Goa and Daman in India and Malacca in Malaysia. Many village communities from Mahim to Vasai converted to Christianity and the landscape became punctuated with churches and chapels. The Portuguese destroyed the Walkeshwar Temple, which was eventually rebuilt in 1715 by a wealthy Hindu trader. Over 350 years later, the Nossa Senora de Monte church – now known as Mount Mary – is still a place of worship. At the fort, only ruins remain (now restored and home to a gorgeous amphitheatre). Thane, to the north-east of the islands, became an attractive township of villages, temples and churches nestled between lakes and coconut groves.

For all the development, the Portuguese still didn't see much trade potential in the area and it remained a backwater. Instead it was their rival, the British East India Company, who cast a covetous eye over the area from its headquarters in Gujarat. It considered it a perfect natural harbour for the Company's first Indian seaport. The main attraction, of course, was the deep bay on the eastern waterfront overlooking the mainland. The Surat outpost began pressing its London headquarters to purchase the islands from the Portuguese. It finally got its hands on them in 1661, when they were given to King Charles II as part of the dowry for his marriage to Portuguese princess Catherine de Braganza. Apparently, Charles was not exactly sure where his wedding present was; he initially thought that the islands were somewhere in Brazil. In 1668, he leased the islands to the British East India Company for the sum of £10 a year and the Company quickly established a colony in and around an existing Portuguese fort, which grew rapidly from 10,000 people in 1661 to 60,000 by 1675.

In 1687, the East India Company transferred its headquarters from Surat to what the British now called Bombay.

BIRTH OF A TRADE HUB

Bombay's early population mostly comprised Koli fisherfolk, East India Company officials and migrants from Gujarat who set up shop to service the outpost. Among the migrants were an émigré community of Iranian Zoroastrians known as Parsis (*see p40* **Communities**), who were to become a decisive commercial and political force in Bombay's development. That was foreshadowed earlier in the colony's history by the actions of a Parsi trader, Rustomji Dorabji: just two years after the Company moved to Bombay, the outpost was beset by a plague outbreak. At the same time, a nearby Africa-descended tribe called the Sidis launched an attack on the colony from their base down the coast in Janjira (near present-day Alibag). Despite the chaos caused by the plague, Dorabji managed to raise an impromptu army from the local Kolis and repelled the Sidis in a counterattack – saving the colony and killing the Sidi chief in the process.

That the size and influence of the Parsi presence was strong very early in Bombay's history is proved by the fact that a Tower of Silence – a traditional Parsi funeral place, where bodies are left to be consumed by vultures – was built on Malabar Hill in 1672.

In 1708, the first Parsi *agiary* (fire temple) was built – the Banaji Limji Agiary – with a second in 1733. Two years later, the Parsis set up a shipbuilding industry, which later became one of the largest suppliers of ships to the British Royal Navy. A young Parsi shipbuilder from Gujarat, Lowji Nusserwanji Wadia, was invited to Bombay by the East India Company to build it ships, an enterprise that led to the Wadia dynasty of shipbuilders.

Who Is Shivaji, Anyway?

Mumbai's favourite son.

When you land in Mumbai and go from the airport to your South Mumbai hotel, you will no doubt experience a sense of déjà vu. Getting into a cab at the Chhatrapati Shivaji International Airport, you pass Shivaji Park in the middle of the city before you arrive downtown, where you might drive by the magnificent Chhatrapati Shivaji Terminus and the Chhatrapati Shivaji Maharaj Vastu Sangrahalaya as you turn in on Chhatrapati Shivaji Marg towards Colaba. So who is Chhatrapati Shivaji?

The son of an officer in the court of Bijapur in Western India, Shivaji Bhonsle laid the foundations for the modern state of Maharashtra, of which Mumbai is the capital. In the late 17th century, Shivaji established a rebel fiefdom within Bijapur and by the age of 30 successfully gained control of a chunk of land around the Pune region, with 40 forts, 7,000 horsemen and 10,000 foot soldiers. As his power grew, he took on the mighty Aurangzeb, king of the most powerful empire in India at the time, the Mughals. Shivaji's battles against the Mughals have been widely recorded and retold in folk tales, books and Marathi performances and his legend continues to inspire Maharashtrians. But what makes his exploits useful to today's politicians is that he established a Hindu kingdom in a land then run by Muslims.

Scholars continue to debate whether Shivaji set out to be what historian James Laine calls a 'Hindu King in Islamic India'. Cambridge University Press's *The Marathas* contends that Shivaji was never one to propagate a Maharashtrian or Hindu state, nor that he discriminated against Muslims, instead welcoming them into his state and his army.

Not that the local right-wing nativist political party is concerned; Shiv Sena (Army of Shivaji) rode to power on a wave of anti-Muslim rhetoric following religious riots and bomb blasts in the city in 1992-93. One of its first acts in power was to rename the city from the colonial Bombay to the Marathi 'Mumbai'. It then renamed several landmarks after the warrior King who evoked native pride and anti-Muslim sentiment. The Shiv Sena hasn't been in power at state level since 1999, but it won the last municipal elections in 2007 and currently controls Mumbai's local government. Though the Shiv Sena has mellowed in recent years, a breakaway party, the Maharashtra Navnirman Sena, continues to harp on about 'outsiders'.

The Parsis remained at the forefront of the city's development and, in 1777, its first newspaper, the *Bombay Courier*, was published by Rustomji Keshaspathi. The city's main activity was as an import–export hub: diamonds, tea, paper, porcelain, raw silk, calicoes, pepper, herbs and drugs sailed out to Britain and lead, quicksilver, woollen garments, hardware and bullion sailed in. Bombay's status was further boosted by an increase in cotton trade with China after 1770, an exchange that continued over the next century.

During this period the city saw a continuous migration of traders from Surat, which further energised the economy. Some historians suggest that the rise of Bombay as a successful trading hub precipitated the decline of Surat, which soon lost its cherished status as a major port. In subsequent years, the islands began to attract many Gujarati traders (both Hindu and Muslim), including Parsi shipbuilders from the mainland. Most people lived in and around a fort at the heart of the colony, originally built by the Portuguese and further developed by the British. Known as Bombay Castle, it was essentially a walled township in the area of the city today known as Fort.

A fragment of the fort wall still exists next to St George's Hospital. By 1813, almost half of the 10,000 people who lived in the Fort area were Parsis. As it became more and more crowded and often prone to disease, its richer inhabitants began to move out to new townships beyond the walled city, building bungalows and mansions in the city's first suburbs: Byculla, Mazgaon and Malabar Hill.

SHAPING THE CITY

By the beginning of the 19th century, business in Bombay was booming, so much so that in 1801 the British Government sent a reporter to document the extent of the city's trade. His reports convinced the politicians to end the East India Company's monopoly on trade in 1813, encouraging even greater commercial expansion. A few years later, a massive civil engineering project to reclaim land from the sea was commissioned, its aim to fuse the disparate islands of Bombay into a single landmass. Over the next few decades, as the city took shape, a large middle-class population emerged that drove a huge demand for newspapers, schools and colleges.

In 1822, India's first Indian-language newspaper, the Gujarati daily *Mumbai Samachar*, was published in Bombay. Still running today, it's the country's oldest newspaper. The first copy of the *Bombay Times* (the forerunner of the *Times of India*) rolled off the presses in 1838. Grant Medical College was founded in 1845, and within another 15 years Wilson College and Bombay University were established. Other colleges like Elphinstone College and St Xavier's went up within a decade. Both the new media and colleges were largely patronised by children of Gujarati merchants and traders, the indigenous Christian populations and Maharashtrians. Middle-class suburbs sprang up in the new neighbourhoods of Kalbadevi, Girgaum, Gowalia Tank, Mohammed Ali Road, Thakurdwar and Walkeshwar.

By the middle of the 19th century, the knitting together of Bombay's islands through land reclamation was nearly complete. Causeways linked Bombay, Sion, Salsette and Colaba; Mahalaxmi and Worli were joined; and in 1845, Mahim and Bandra were connected by the Mahim causeway thanks to a rich Parsi – Lady Avabai Jamsetjee Jeejeebhoy – who paid Rs 157,000 for it. Legend has it that she prayed at several religious sites for the survival of a sick child. When the child recovered after she prayed at Mount Mary Church, Lady Avabai built the causeway to allow more devotees access to the Virgin Mother without having to take a ferry.

As the physical landmass came together, Bombay's political and commercial links with the Empire were tightened. A regular steamship service between the city and London was established in 1843; 15 years later, direct British Government control of the Indian colony was established after the First War of Indian Independence (the 'Sepoy Mutiny') in 1857, which led to all of the East India Company's formal political powers being handed to the Crown.

'A massive civil engineering project to reclaim land from the sea was commissioned, its aim to fuse the disparate islands of Bombay into a single landmass.'

URBS PRIMA IN INDIS

By 1845, the basis of a modern city had been created with land covering 440 square kilometres (170 square miles) – a complex landscape of fields, coconut groves and outsize colonial structures, of cosmopolitan enclaves and sleepy villages. Bombay was the starting point of India's first passenger railway line in 1853, connecting the city to Thane in Maharashtra.

In the 1860s, the British began a construction programme, erecting architecture that was designed to signal to the natives that they were here to stay – a direct response to the Indian uprising of 1857. Victoria Terminus, the Prince of Wales Museum, Bombay University, the General Post Office, the Old Customs House, Elphinstone College, the Public Works Department Building – all were begun in the 1860s. With typical imperial hyperbole, they began to refer to Bombay as 'urbs prima in Indis' – the first city of India.

In 1864, the Bombay, Baroda and Central India Railway (later merged with other railways to form what is now the Western Railway) was extended to Bombay, boosting the flow of cotton from the hinterlands. Cotton now dominated trade through Bombay. Raw cotton from Gujarat was shipped to Lancashire in England, processed into cloth and then shipped back via Bombay to be resold in the Indian market. Although cotton trading was the city's main activity, businessmen began to recognise that bigger profits could be made by spinning the cotton themselves. In 1854, the first cotton mill, the Bombay Spinning Mill, was opened by a Parsi, Cowasji Nanabhai Davar.

It was met by vociferous opposition from Lancashire mill owners anxious to avoid the 'outsourcing' of the cotton spinning business, and was only pushed through thanks to the influence of the British manufacturers of the cotton looms. In 1870, around 13 mills were in operation in Bombay. The shipping of raw cotton was still the main engine of the city's economy, however, and it received a massive boost when the American Civil War broke out in 1861. The war forced global markets to look for alternative sources of cotton for the booming textile industries of Britain and other countries in Europe. Bombay consequently became the world's foremost cotton supplier, with money pouring into the city until the war ended in 1865.

Within a year of the war's end, however, most of the companies were liquidated and many speculators went bankrupt. In spite of this, the city continued to grow, using the wealth generated during the boom to make itself over by shifting more and more into cotton spinning. The city's strategic location as a trade hub was given a further boost with the opening of the Suez Canal in 1869. By 1895, there were 70 mills in the city, rising to 83 in 1915 before stagnating in the global recession of the 1920s. Despite continued British political control, most of Bombay's cotton mills were owned by Indian families. In 1925, only 15 mills were British-owned, and even then the management was mostly Indian.

With the growth of the mills, Bombay's population rapidly increased as thousands of Maharashtrians migrated to the city to work the looms. The workers, usually male, initially lived in hostels and dormitories but eventually the *chawl* – a tenement still in use today in which each family has one room, with all sharing a common veranda and toilets – emerged as basic housing for workers and their families. The workers settled

'The British maintained control through a combination of fairness and a shameless policy of divide and rule.'

close to the mills, with new neighbourhoods springing up in Byculla, Lalbaug, Parel and Worli. These neighbourhoods were often referred to by one name – Girangaon – the 'Village of Mills'. It was a dynamic cultural space and spawned generations of writers, poets and dramatists in Marathi and Gujarati. As the city grew, more land was reclaimed and more roads, causeways and wharves were built. The population had already increased from 13,726 in 1780 to 644,405 in 1872. By 1906, it had become 977,822.

The British continued to develop the city's infrastructure, with innovations such as the drainage system that continues to serve the city today. It was in 1860 that piped water began to flow to the city from Tulsi and Vihar lakes, and in 1870, the Bombay Port Trust was officially formed. The Princess Dock was built in 1855, followed by Victoria and Mereweather Dry Docks in 1891 and Alexandra Dock in 1914.

TOLERATE THY NEIGHBOUR

From its early beginnings, Bombay had been a vibrantly diverse city of Europeans and Indians from across the subcontinent, and by the 19th century, the lines between communities had been drawn – but an uneasy tolerance prevailed. Europeans socialised among themselves in sports clubs, with cricket as the main recreation. The Bombay Gymkhana was set up in 1875, exclusively for Europeans, spurring other communities, including Muslim, Hindu and Parsi, to set up their own gymkhanas, all in a line by the sea along Marine Drive. A friendly rivalry developed between them, with a regular 'Pentangular' cricket tournament (the fifth team was called, and made up of, 'the Rest') never failing to make headlines in city newspapers.

The British maintained their control in the city through a paradoxical combination of a reputation for fairness and a shameless policy of divide and rule. In the 1880s, the commander of the Bombay police was a British superintendent named Charles Forjett, who was greatly admired by Indian residents for his harsh treatment of corrupt policemen and for conducting regular operations against the Parsi mafia who controlled the illegal liquor business in the Falkland Road region. The British were concerned about the power of religious festivals to encourage a desire for political independence, and tried to regulate them, albeit tentatively.

The nationalist and freedom fighter Lokmanya Tilak saw the same potential and transformed the Ganpati festival, once celebrated on a small, domestic scale across Maharashtra, into a large-scale, outdoor event. He brought his supporters to Bombay's beaches, ostensibly to immerse idols of the elephant-headed Ganesha in the sea as per tradition, and then gave fiery speeches about their political responsibilities and the dream of *swaraj* (self-government). The British were checked from interfering too much in religious issues by the lessons of 1857, in which a rumour about rifle cartridges being made with pig and cow fat (thereby offending both Muslims and Hindus) had sparked an army rebellion that nearly lost them the colony. The British left Tilak largely alone and mass immersions during the Ganpati festival continue to this day, with its freedom-movement origins mostly forgotten.

Instead of direct action, the British responded to such challenges to their authority with the same divide-and-rule policy they had used all over the country – by playing Hindus and Muslims off against each other. It was hardly difficult for the British in Bombay, a city where communities were already naturally divided into different

Model of **Gandhi** agitating against British rule at Mani Bhavan.

The Empire Strikes Out

The birth of Indian independence.

The political force that would shape India's destiny was born in Bombay on a mild December day in 1885. A delegation of 70 Indian lawyers, professors and journalists congregated at the Gokuldas Tejpal College to establish the Indian National Congress, India's first national political party, which is still in power today in Delhi.

Had he lived to see it, the Congress's founder would have been shocked. His name was Allan Octavian Hume, a retired civil servant from Kent. An ardent but puritanical social reformer, Hume served as the INC's General Secretary until 1908, when its stance was not outright opposition to British rule, but just a demand for a more of a say for Indians in government. It was only after repeated British refusals that its politics became radicalised.

Bombay remained at the centre of events throughout the Indian freedom struggle, despite being much younger and smaller than Calcutta or Delhi. Lacking the rigid social structures that prevailed in other cities, social reform was already under way in Bombay. The city admired ability and rewarded merit, attracting India's best and brightest. It also had a cosmopolitan and enlightened middle class and an array of colleges and cultural institutions.

Mohandas Gandhi, commonly known as the Mahatma ('Great Soul'), chose Bombay as his base upon his return from South Africa, living in the now-famous Mani Bhavan in Gamdevi. It was from here that Gandhi planned and co-ordinated civil disobedience movements, and introduced his revolutionary concepts of non-violence, *satyagraha* ('truth force') and *swadeshi* (loosely, 'buying Indian goods'). He found enthusiastic support from the people of Bombay, financially and by way of manpower.

When the fatal blow to British rule finally came, it was struck from Bombay. Gandhi launched the Quit India movement on 8 August 1942 at Gowalia Tank (now August Kranti Maidan), with Congress support. He urged Indians to act as citizens of an independent nation and use non-violent civil disobedience to frustrate British control. Hundreds of thousands across India responded. Just five years later, the British Empire fell in India.

'As the city became increasingly politicised, communal riots began to plague Bombay.'

enclaves. With so little official thought put into planning residential neighbourhoods for the poorer or even middle-class populations, the only support network for those looking for homes or the means to build them came from within their own ethnic groups. As the city became increasingly politicised, communal riots began to plague Bombay for the first time.

A NEW CENTURY

Bombay was still a city among other Indian cities. But in 1875, the basis for its current status as India's economic capital was established with the Bombay Stock Exchange – then referred to as the Native Share and Stockbrokers Association. As the cream of India's professional talent flooded into the city, political movements began to flourish (*see p25* **The Empire Strikes Out**). Political ferment saw the establishment of the Indian National Congress – the first Indian political party – in 1885 at the Gokuldas Tejpal College in South Bombay.

By this time a lack of adequate urban planning was causing large parts of the city to choke from over-congestion, a problem that became disastrous just a few years before the end of the 19th century, when bubonic plague broke out, possibly carried by rats on grain ships from Hong Kong. Thousands fled the city and Indian and foreign ports quarantined all goods arriving from Bombay, with ruinous consequences for the city's economy. The tragedy was compounded by the failure of the monsoon in 1899, leading to one of India's worst-ever famines. The British authorities responded to the catastrophe by setting up a City Improvement Trust to encourage the development of the suburbs and relieve pressure on the southern part of the city.

By the beginning of the 20th century, the first outlines of the character of modern Bombay had begun to emerge. By 1906, the city's population had topped one million. It quickly became a hotbed of the new politics that would lead to Indian independence,

Mumbai or Bombay?

What's in a name.

In 1995, the Shiv Sena, a far-right Maharashtrian political party, changed the city's official name from Bombay to Mumbai, the Marathi name for the city. It was the centrepiece of a drive to eradicate British Raj-era place names in the city, which included renaming the Victoria Terminus as Chhatrapati Shivaji Terminus. 'Mumbai' is derived from Mumba, a name for the Hindu goddess Mumbadevi, and aai, meaning 'mother' in Marathi, the language of Maharashtra.

Visitors often assume that it's politically incorrect to use the old name and are surprised to discover that the millions of English-speaker in Mumbai still call the city Bombay. The fondness for the old name is mostly just a case of old habits dying hard, but for some it's also a rejection of the Shiv Sena and its violent, anti-outsider politics. But it's even more complicated, as each name also carries distinct class connotations – 'Bombay' implies the English-speaking elite, 'Mumbai' the middle and working classes. Either way, as a visitor you're unlikely to upset anyone whichever name you use.

Mumbai's western bay in the 1880s...

...and in the 1990s.

fired up by Mahatma Gandhi's return from South Africa in 1915. Gandhi took a house called Mani Bhavan in Gamdevi, from where he began to rally citizens to the cause. Prominent Bombay businessmen, traders, workers and professionals became his votaries. Technological innovations that had slowly emerged in the West were implanted in Bombay in rapid order, with the first transmission lines of the Tata Power Company criss-crossing the city's skyline in 1915. In 1926, the first motorised bus service started between Afghan Church and Crawford Market. The first electric train started in 1927, an intercity service from Bombay to Pune and Igatpuri. A few years later the first electric commuter train (still known in Mumbai as 'EMUs' – Electric Multiple Units) rolled out. In 1932, the Parsi industrialist JRD Tata flew the first scheduled airmail flight from Karachi to Bombay via Ahmedabad, landing his single-engined de Haviland Puss Moth on a grass strip at Juhu Aerodrome.

The Lumière Brothers' Cinematographe showed four silent short films at the Watson's Hotel in Bombay in 1896, charging an entry fee of one rupee. It was a phenomenon that the *Times of India* described at the time as 'the marvel of the century', and quickly fired the imaginations of a generation of Indians. The Indian film industry was born in Bombay a few years later. A man named HS Bhatavdekar filmed the city's first documentary in 1899, of a wrestling match, which he showed across the city to general acclaim. The first full-length feature film, *Raja Harishchandra*, was made in 1913 by Dadasaheb Phalke and shown at Bombay's Coronation Cinematograph. By 1920, the Indian film industry was fully formed, with Bombay at its heart. By 1931, about 207 films were being made every year (but it wasn't until the 1990s that the term 'Bollywood' was coined).

GROWING PAINS

After 'freedom at midnight' gave birth to independent India on 15 August 1947, Bombay continued to expand beyond the suburbs of Mahim and Bandra – erstwhile Portuguese areas – swallowing up everything as far north as Mankhurd, Mulund and Dahisar. The city became the capital of Bombay State, a political creation that included the whole of what are now the two separate states of Gujarat and Maharashtra. In the following years Bombay became a battlefield for political movements based on language groups, mainly its Gujarati- and Marathi-speaking populations. The Samyukta Maharashtra Andolan was a major political force of socialists, trades unions and artists that fought fiercely for the formation of an independent state for Marathi-speaking people, with Bombay as its capital. They finally achieved their wish and Bombay State was split into two in 1960, but only after 105 of the movement's supporters had been shot dead by police during tumultuous political protests around Flora Fountain earlier the same year. A memorial at what is now called Hutatma Chowk commemorates the dead with an eternal flame.

Bombay's politics in the 1960s and '70s were dominated by the Left. But a splinter of the Samyukta Maharashtra Andolan morphed into a nativist movement – the Shiv Sena ('Army of Shivaji'), which won continued influence with its right-wing anti-outsider politics in the face of growing slum encroachment by immigrants from outside the city. During the 1970s, the city overtook Calcutta as the most populous city in India. A lack of political will, cushioned by a healthy economy benefiting from cheap labour, allowed slums to proliferate on a scale that had never been seen before (*see p33* **Slumbai**). Shiv Sena's founder, a former cartoonist named Bal Thackeray, came to dominate the city's political landscape using a combination of brutal mafia-like force and a string of local election victories. The decline of the textile industry contributed to this political shift and, after a catastrophic mill workers' strike in 1982-83, the century-old cotton-spinning industry effectively died in Bombay. With its passing, the mill workers lost their key position in the city's economy and politics.

The 1970s and early '80s were an exciting time in the city's cinematic history, with the emergence of filmmakers determined to set themselves apart from the mainstream Hindi film industry. They began to make realist and neo-expressionist films with strong elements of social commentary. Shyam Benegal's *Ankur* (*The Seedling*, 1974), introduced the stunning actress (and later MP) Shabana Azmi and was the first film to articulate the new conflict between India's educated, urbane city-dwellers and the feudal traditions of the countryside. Rabindra Dharmaraj's *Chakra* in 1981 was a searing look at the slums of Bombay, seen through the eyes of actress Smita Patil.

City authorities made few infrastructure improvements in the 1970s and '80s, despite the alarmingly rapid growth in the city's population. The largest was a plan to create New Bombay (now known as Navi Mumbai) – a parallel city across the harbour on the mainland, built to decongest the island city. It began slowly, faltered, and even today has yet to live up to its original aims.

The Shiv Sena continued to rise throughout the 1980s, thanks to the decline of the Left and increasingly visible corruption in the Congress. It was a political combination that proved to be lethal, culminating in the horrendous Bombay riots of 1992-93 – incidents that were in fact state-sanctioned and party-sponsored pogroms against Muslims. The violence erupted after the Babri Mosque was razed by Hindu militants in the city of Ayodhya, in the North Indian state of Uttar Pradesh. Hundreds of Muslims were killed by Hindu fundamentalists during the riots. On 12 March 1993 came 'Black Friday', when 13 bombs exploded in one day at locations across the city, including the Bombay Stock Exchange and the Air India Building. The bombs killed 257 people in what were revenge attacks by a Muslim group for the slaughter two months previously. The riots and bombings were a shattering blow to Bombay's self-image as a cosmopolitan, secular city that for years had avoided the communal violence that afflicts other Indian cities. It paved the way for the Shiv Sena's rise to power at both city and state levels and, in 1995, it changed the official name of the city to Mumbai (*see p26* **Mumbai or Bombay?**). Since then, Mumbai has been the victim of sporadic terrorist attacks. In July 2006, bombs tore through the first-class compartments of seven commuter trains on the Western Line, killing more than 200 people. More recently, on 26 November 2008, terrorists attacked iconic Mumbai landmarks including the Chhatrapati Shivaji Terminus, the Taj Hotel, the Oberoi Trident Hotel and Leopold Café, killing more than 100 people and holding the city hostage.

Since 1991, a series of economic reforms have liberalised India's economy, unleashing Mumbai's entrepreneurial energy. It aspires to become a new global city with a modern spirit close to that of its former identity as a trade hub. But while Mumbai may be the financial capital of a superpower-in-waiting, its citizens are still waiting for a transformation of its infrastructure, social housing and polluted air.

Mumbai Today

India's maximum city oscillates between the old and the new.

For all its chaos, Mumbai is a thriving and lively city, producing more wealth and culture than any other city in India. Perhaps thanks to the frantic energy of Mumbai, the rush to succeed in a traditionally business-oriented city or just a complete lack of introspection, Mumbaikars rarely do more than complain before getting on with life. There's no doubt that Mumbai in the 21st century is a tremendously exciting place to be; the city's stock index is soaring, business is booming and middle-class Mumbaikars now have access to goods and services they couldn't have imagined a few years ago.

Yet, the city is riddled with infrastructure and civic problems. Mumbai's binary nature – conspicuous consumption juxtaposed with starvation, apparent anarchy with a low crime rate, a thriving economy amid obvious poverty – has over the last few years been the source of increasing global interest. Everybody, it seems, is trying to figure out how Mumbai continues ticking despite all odds.

IN CONFERENCE

In November 2007, more than 300 urban planners, economists, geographers, anthropologists and architects from around the world assembled in Mumbai's posh Taj Mahal hotel for a conference called Urban Age. They hoped that studying the swirl of life outside the hotel's hushed confines would provide some clues about the potential problems the majority of the world's people will face in the 21st century – and how these pitfalls can be avoided. Already, more than half the world's population lives in cities and that number will rise to 75 per cent by 2050, according to experts at Urban Age. Mumbai and its sister megacities, said the organisers of the conference – the London School of Economics and Deutsche Bank – will 'provide the testing ground for our urban future'.

If this is the future, the world would have good reason to be a little alarmed. With the normal big city problems of overcrowding, strained water and sewage systems, almost no public housing, very few parks or open spaces, high levels of pollution and packed public transport, Mumbai is a perfect example of how not to do things.

All of this has turned Mumbai into a fertile field of study for academics from around the world. In fact, they've even coined a word for this new endeavour: 'Bombayology'. Dozens of seminars have been organised in the last few years to contemplate the future of the city, and it sometimes seems impossible to turn a corner in Dharavi, one of the city's most extensive slums, without bumping into Fulbright scholars, fellows from the American Institute for Indian Studies, PhD candidates, masters students and independent researchers collecting data on micro-finance schemes or women's organisations.

For students of urban planning, Mumbai is an endlessly fascinating challenge. A peninsula that extends south-west into the Arabian Sea, Mumbai is roughly one-third the size of Greater London. But with a population of 13 million within its city limits, it has nearly twice as many residents as Britain's capital. Another five million live in the suburbs and small towns in the hinterland, which puts the number of people in the Mumbai metropolitan region at just two million less than the population of Australia.

'Mumbai is roughly one-third the size of Greater London. But with a population of 13 million within its city limits, it has nearly twice as many residents as Britain's capital.'

Each day, six million of these people board Mumbai's intensely overcrowded suburban commuter trains and head into the city for work. Most businesses and government offices are concentrated at the southern tip of the city, leading to chronic traffic jams, overlong train journeys and carriages so packed that the railways had to invent a word to describe the situation: they call it the 'superdensecrushload'. At peak hour, trains meant for 1,700 passengers routinely carry 4,700 people, with 17 bodies crammed into a single square metre of space. Every day, eight people die while commuting, often from falling off the train or hitting a signal pole while hanging out the coach.

In an attempt to ease commuting woes, the Mumbai Metropolitan Region Development Authority, the government organisation that has the weighty task of guiding the city's growth, proposed a sea-link – a cable-stayed bridge off the western waterfront that will connect the suburbs and South Mumbai. The first section of the bridge was opened to traffic in August 2009 five years behind schedule, and is an attempt to reduce commuting time between the western suburb of Bandra and the mid-town district of Worli from 40 to seven minutes. But this ambitious project, which cost Rs 1,600 crore ($317 million) instead of the original estimated Rs 300 crore ($61 million), benefits only the 1.6 per cent of Mumbaikars who travel to work by car. 29 out of every 1,000 Mumbaikars own a car, the lowest number of any Indian city, yet most transport projects in the city benefit this group of people.

CIVIC WOES

Yet, somehow the city keeps functioning. Mumbai's average population density is 27,348 per square kilometre. Higher than even New York (9,551) or Mexico City (5,877), this number rises to 113,605 in the most crowded areas. Roughly 55 per cent of the city lives in slums – eight to ten people sharing a home smaller in area than an SUV – occupying six per cent of the city's land.

Thanks to the problems peculiar to the island's geography, there is only limited space in which to build and only one direction in which development can continue: north. But the smart addresses are in the south and western suburbs, which means developers are always seeking out old bungalows and small buildings to tear down so that they can be replaced with 15-floor apartment blocks and commercial complexes. Zoning restrictions seem to have almost been abandoned and the new buildings often lack sufficient parking space for all the residents, so many Mumbai streets are clogged with stationary cars. Water shortages are a chronic problem, and in 2009, a meagre monsoon compelled the Brihanmumbai Municipal Corporation to impose 15-30 per cent water cuts throughout the metropolis. In the summer of 2007, for the first time ever, the city faced the prospect of power cuts. Though it didn't come to pass, it's only a matter of time before the only city in India without electricity problems ceases to enjoy uninterrupted supply.

The rampant construction has hurt Mumbai's fragile ecosystem. The Mithi River, which runs from the Sanjay Gandhi National Park in the north of the city to the Arabian Sea in the west, has been reduced to a sewage canal, and its once-wide mouth has been narrowed by decades of reclamation – to build the swanky business district of Bandra-Kurla in the 1990s and, more recently, for the construction of the Bandra-Worli

Rush Hour at Bandra Station.

sea-link. Mangrove swamps along the city's coast, which protect the shore from the battering of the monsoon, have been illegally reclaimed, uprooted and destroyed.

On 26 July 2005, a freak cloudburst caused nearly a metre of rain to fall on Mumbai in 24 hours, flooding the entire city and killing 452 Mumbaikars. The deluge shut the city down – phones stopped working, power supply was cut, trains stopped – and cost Mumbai an estimated $3.5 billion in damage and lost business hours. The worst affected were the poor: in the northern suburb of Andheri, a landslide killed 72 slum-dwellers. In the days that followed the flood, they were the ones most susceptible to the waterborne diseases floating around the city.

CULTURAL RENAISSANCE

Faced with a looming economic crisis in 1991, India began the process of dismantling its protected economy, the results of which are apparent in the country's new-found reputation as an emerging giant. Already the home of Indian popular culture, with the film, TV and advertising industries based in Mumbai, the city's culture and media are flourishing in sync with the economy. Perhaps that's why as many students of 'Bombayology' spend their time researching Bollywood orchestras or the art district of South Mumbai as they do slum economies and urban planning.

Over the last few years, a high-profile magazine has launched every couple of months, three newspapers have been set up since 2005, dozens of new television channels have started operations and voluminous books about the city have invigorated international interest in Mumbai. A dozen new art galleries have opened over the last few years and well-established Indian artists are increasingly using Mumbai as an element in their works. The city's nightclubs bypass the global cool of house and trance to play a home-grown mishmash of remixed Bollywood meets electronica via hip hop. The country's first symphony orchestra was formed in Mumbai in 2006, and two years later the city hosted a full-fledged locally produced opera – Giacomo Puccini's *Madame Butterfly*. In 2010, Puccini returned with *Tosca*. New clubs that fly down international acts are packed every night and major pop and rock stars have started including Mumbai on their world tour schedules.

For the middle-class and upper-class Mumbaikar, there has never been a better time to live in the city, and for the visitor Mumbai has never been more attractive.

Slumbai

How the other half live.

Roughly 55 per cent of Mumbai's citizens live in *zopadpattis* – slums of varying sophistication. Some are little more than bamboo-and-tarpaulin shacks; others are three-storey brick-built rooms stacked precariously on top of each other and supplied with electricity and water connections. Slum-dwellers perform vital roles in Mumbai's economy, working as labourers in the city's booming construction sector or as domestic servants in wealthier households. A staggering 40 per cent of Mumbai's police officers live in slums. Slums are everywhere in Mumbai, and it has the dubious distinction of being home to Dharavi, Asia's largest slum and the location of Danny Boyle's Oscar-winning film *Slumdog Millionaire.* But it wasn't always like this. Slums first started appearing in Mumbai in the 1950s, as immigrants from other parts of Maharashtra state, and from poor rural states across India – particularly Uttar Pradesh and Bihar – began to arrive in search of work in a city seen as a land of opportunity. With no low-cost housing available, they began building shanties on patches of empty land.

It was the beginning of Mumbai's transformation into what locals ruefully call 'Slumbai', greased by gangsters, corrupt officials and conniving politicians. As immigration accelerated, the Mumbai mafia muscled in as slumlords, charging rents to slum-dwellers and threatening the private landowners whose land they had stolen. Police, bureaucrats and politicians were paid to look the other way as public land was grabbed. Politicians quickly realised they could benefit from these vast new additions to their electorates and used their clout to protect slums from demolition and provide them with some basic amenities. The slum-dwellers became 'vote banks' – blocks of support for any politician who would protect them from the law. By the 1970s, the slums had made a major impact on the character of the city, swallowing up many of its green spaces. The smallest patch of land is a potential slum, with shanties along roads, on bridges and even lining the city's railway lines. Every year, around 1,000 slum-dwellers are killed crossing train tracks just getting to and from their homes.

Numerous slum rehabilitation schemes have been launched over the years, with little impact. In 1995, the Shiv Sena government promised all slum-dwellers free (21-square-metre (225sq ft) flats. Its called for a million homes in five years, built by private developers in exchange for lucrative development rights. Ten years later, the scheme was widely seen as yet another scam, allowing builders to grab prime public land for a pittance, while building fewer than 40,000 homes.

The most ambitious scheme is the Dharavi Redevelopment Project, which aims to raze the homes of 350,000 residents, and erect a warren of skyscrapers in its place. The plans are to rehabilitate only those residents who settled before 1995 in eight-storey blocks, while using the rest of the area for large-scale commercial development. Despite huge concerns about its sheer unworkability, the Maharashtra governmentis determined to see the project go through.

Slums at Bandra station.

IN CONTEXT

Free of the clinical sterility of other Asian megacities, but safer and friendlier than metropolises like Lagos or São Paulo, Mumbai offers the unique experience of being not one city but many worlds: equal parts exhilarating, disheartening, charming, revolting, addictive, unfathomable and uncontrollable, but never boring.

IN A BAD STATE

After all, the city's difficulties with overcrowding, poverty, infrastructure, open spaces, public transport or a shattered ecosystem aren't insurmountable. Instead, Mumbai's biggest problem is bad governance. Local politicians seem to spend more time debating issues of language and culture than how to fix the housing crisis. In 1995, the city's name was changed from Bombay to Mumbai by the Shiv Sena, a nativist political party on the far right (*see p26* **Mumbai or Bombay?**). In the decades before that, scores of streets shed their colonial names and took on the names of local figures. Since then, the names of the airport, the city's biggest railway terminus and the museum have all been homogenised with a single name (*see p21* **Who Is Shivaji, Anyway?**). Yet, the problems that plague Mumbai are the same as those that afflicted Bombay.

Even when it had opportunities to attempt to solve Mumbai's problems, the government managed to let them slide. Mumbai's mills, once the engine of its economic prosperity, fell into disuse after disputes between management and trades unions in the 1980s. Located in the heart of the city, 54 mills occupy 243 hectares (600 acres) of prime land worth roughly Rs 210 billion ($5.2 billion), of which the government owns 115 hectares (285 acres). According to a 1991 state law, the land was meant to be divided in three equal parts for public housing, open spaces and commercial development. But the state government altered the law in 2001 to allow large-scale private development, and when a high-court ruling reinstated the law, the state went to the Supreme Court of India to have it overturned. An opportunity to regenerate the city with open spaces and low-cost housing was squandered by greedy politicians and builders.

Like other emerging cities in Asia, there is a plan. In fact, there are numerous plans, including the Mumbai Urban Transport Project, the Mumbai Urban Infrastructure Project, the Mumbai Metropolitan Region Development Association plan 1996-2011 (with a sequel that stretches from 2011 to 2021 reportedly in the works) and the catchily titled Vision Mumbai drawn by the consulting firm McKinsey for Bombay First, a business lobby. There are also plans for a second airport outside city limits, for the Mumbai metro rail, and smaller in size but as ambitious in scope, plans to rebuild all of the 2.23-square-kilometre slum known as Dharavi (*see p33* **Slumbai**) and perhaps all of C Ward, a 1.78-square-kilometre neighbourhood with a population of 202,216 people, located a couple of kilometres north of downtown. Yet, on its third birthday in 2007, the government of the state of Maharashtra, of which Mumbai is capital, boasted only of starting some projects.

If Mumbai is to change, it will be because citizens' groups are becoming increasingly vociferous about the city's chaotic administration. For instance, in 2007, Mumbai's municipal corporation announced a plan that amounted to giving the city's parks away to private organisations – 'caretakers' would be allowed to maintain the city's parks and playfields in return for which they would be allowed to build a clubhouse. But heated public protests killed the plan. Some of the city's nicest open spaces – including Bandra's Carter Road and the fort at Land's End – were created thanks to local citizen's groups, with the help of the local members of parliament.

Like Mumbai's problems, the solutions are age old. Bombayologists point out that Mumbai has been complaining about extreme congestion, flawed drainage systems and corrupt administrators for the last 350 years. But each crisis, these historians emphasise, has been overcome because citizens' groups and philanthropists have ensured that Mumbai continues to not just survive but thrive.

Communities

An identity crisis is gripping Mumbai.

TEXT: JERRY PINTO

Jerry Pinto is a well-known Mumbai journalist and author. His work includes Helen: The Life and Times of an H-Bomb, *on racial and community stereotypes in Hindi cinema.*

For decades, Mumbai was perceived as one of the most secular cities in India. The city had dismantled the barriers of caste simply by making it impossible to follow traditional proscriptions about purity and avoiding pollution. On the train and on the bus, in the mill and in the canteen, at the mess and on the cricket field, it was impossible to worry too much about who ate beef and who didn't, who was 'clean' and who was 'unclean'. Cram millions of people on a patch of land and they must either learn to co-exist or kill each other. Mumbaikars did not learn the virtue of tolerance on their own; they were forced into it by the congestion of the big city. Yet, in 1992 the city was shaken by communal violence, religious tolerance became a thing of the past as riots broke out, and today, caste and regional identities continue to plague the city.

'Mumbai's cosmopolitan façade went up in flames, riots took over the city… and we put to rest the idea of the national melting pot.'

IN CONTEXT

SEEING EYE

First the ABC charts in primary school did their dirty work, introducing us to apples and zebras. Then the Good Habits chart told us that we should brush our teeth, not with neem twigs but with toothbrushes and toothpaste. Next we were shown a 'People of India' chart and we struggled to find ourselves reflected in it.

As a Roman Catholic, I remember being slightly surprised to find that my father's native dress was supposed to be a suit and my mother was supposed to have bobbed hair and wear a dress.

I went home from school that day and asked my father why he didn't wear a suit.

'In this heat?' he asked.

I showed him the chart.

He laughed. 'Well, they couldn't put us in loincloths, could they?'

A cold thrill ran down my snobbish little spine. Yes, my father had been a tiller of the soil in his native Goa. Yes, he had walked 13 kilometres to school and back after he had watered the red bananas of which his village, Moira, was proud. I remember thanking my stars that we were once removed from the loincloth and that the chart of the communities of Mumbai had chosen to put us into double-breasted suits.

Today, of course, many years later, it is the height of chic to be the son of a farmer who actually carried his wares to the market and clawed his way out of poverty. The stereotyped representations on that chart no longer have the power to astonish/amuse/offend us. With our kitsch-tinted glasses, we can see ourselves as others see us and laugh in our new-found confidence as one of the largest consumer markets in the world, as the economic driver of the subcontinent, as the city where the stock market only has to cough for the national antibiotics to be trotted out. But like this city, built on rotting fish-heads and palm leaves, retrieved from a history of mosquitoes and amnesia, it is a shaky self-confidence.

THE MUMBAI MYTH

The urban myth of Mumbai's secular and classless self-image reads roughly like this: it was inherited from the older urban history of Surat, a port city in Gujarat situated on ancient trade routes that attracted settlers from across the Asian and African continents. As Surat declined, Mumbai emerged as a regional player and people migrated here in large numbers. Since they had already rubbed shoulders with the world, they brought with them their tolerance.

We were also in the habit of saying that there was only one god in Mumbai and his name was Mammon. No one was sure who actually had ever worshipped Mammon but we were proud of his classicism and, like the penguin-shaped dustbins that the municipality put on our streets because penguins are the only creatures with no religious associations, he was secular. We had not Kuber, the Hindu god of wealth, or even a Calvinist god of capitalism. He was just that ugly monster to whom we could all pretend allegiance so that we could laugh at the rest of the country when it went mad over symbolic acts of desecration – the slaughter of a cow near a temple, the mosque bedaubed with pig's blood. We were far too busy, far too intent on the good life, far too Western-looking, to bother about that kind of thing. As Bombayites, we left that to the excitable natives of the subcontinent. Our little finger of land was, we believed, too busy making money.

In 1992, we found that we weren't quite so different after all. Far away, in Ayodhya, in Uttar Pradesh, the forces of the Hindu Right went on a rampage and destroyed a mosque that they claimed stood on the birthplace of Lord Ram, the ninth avatar of Vishnu, the Purushottam or perfect man, the hero of one of India's seminal epics, the *Ramayana*. No one ever believed that the mosque would be demolished. Even when the mosque came down, no one believed that the rage and the despair would come home to us. It did.

Mumbai's cosmopolitan façade went up in flames. Riots took over the city, hundreds were murdered, and we put to rest the idea of the national melting pot, the *bhelpuri* city, the idea that Mumbaikars had voluntarily exiled themselves from their roots to float free in the city. The next state election returned a coalition government between two right-wing Hindu parties. The city was renamed Mumbai, another symbolic act of reversal.

But Mumbai is endlessly volatile and we want to go back to that prelapsarian age when the question 'What's your caste?' was not about whether you were going to be burnt alive or not. In the old days, that question wasn't even about caste. It was about identity, an attempt to place you, geographically, psychologically, socially, sometimes even politically.

Declare that you are a Pinto, which puts you firmly into a supposedly casteless religion like Roman Catholicism, and your fellow Catholics will ask you your village. This will help them discover exactly what kind of Pinto you are: whether you are from upper-caste stock or a convert from the lower orders.

As a Pinto, I might be a Goan, one of a large wave of migrants washed in from Goa who settled around the port areas, especially Dhobi Talao (the long-since drained 'Lake of the Laundrymen'). I would speak Konkani at home and the rice cooked in my home would have salt in it.

Or I might be an 'East Indian' Pinto, even though Mumbai is on the west coast. The term applies to the many converts the Portuguese made when they arrived here and who chose that name for themselves over the term 'Bombay Portuguese' by which they had been known. 'East Indians', they thought, would endear them to the East India Company, which until 1857 was the representative of colonial British power. As an East Indian Pinto, I would speak Marathi at home.

I might even be a Pinto of Koli origin, fiercely proud of being one of the first inhabitants of the islands, perhaps a generation away from fishing, but still offering coconuts to the sea on Nariyal Poornima, to appease the waves after the storms of the monsoon.

For in Mumbai, as in India, no community is solid, no religious persuasion unites all its members. Thus the Mumbai Hindu is subdivided according to caste (which still

Saraswati Chitra Kala's People of India educational picture chart.

IN CONTEXT

Stuck In the Caste

Complex class divides.

Caste is an uncomfortable phenomenon that most Mumbaikars just don't want to acknowledge. The word 'caste' is derived from the Portuguese word *casta*, meaning 'category'. The Portuguese and, subsequently, the British saw caste as a way of organising communities on a hierarchy based on the *varna* system. The *varna* system is derived from classical Hindu texts that divide societies into four parts: **Brahmins**, the highest group, represented by priests and teachers; **Kshatriyas**, warriors and kings; **Vaishyas**, who are the merchants and traders; and **Shudras** (also known as Dalits), at the bottom of the hierarchy as labourers and peasants. Some texts hold the '**untouchables**' (later referred to by Gandhi as the Harijan – the 'children of God') as a fifth caste who did jobs considered polluting: handling corpses and collecting excrement from homes without a sewage system.

However, many sociologists believe that explanations of caste that rely on the *varna* system are flawed. They argue that castes are not discrete but themselves divided into numerous sub-categories. Even people of the same caste may be forbidden from marrying because of these divisions. Brahmins may be ritually superior, but in wealth and status they may actually be dependent on other castes below them on the *varna* scale.

According to some social historians, the caste system has served mainly to perpetuate the domination of elite priests, rulers and merchants. Those now regarded as the lower castes may have originally been forest tribes absorbed into larger kingdoms. The theory of *karma*, in which people are doomed to their status in life by their deeds in past lives, can be seen as an ideological tool that helped suppress desires for political change. But caste can also be seen in other ways, for example as a means of organising a division of labour that gave rise to highly productive economies in India's past.

In Mumbai, caste still connects the modern city to the ancient history of the subcontinent. The city still relies to a large extent on 'scavengers' – known as ragpickers – to deal with waste. Most of these scavengers belong to castes that have always been scavengers. Look harder and you'll find a city in which the majority of its teachers still come from the upper castes, and most businessmen belong to communities that have dominated business for centuries. Caste even shapes where people live: over 75 per cent of slum-dwellers are from lower castes. That's a far cry from Mumbai's self-image as a meritocratic city of opportunity. No one talks of the slums of Dharavi as a Dalit colony but, effectively, they are. In many ways, Mumbai does not encourage casteism. Many Dalits see the city as a place that frees them from the oppression of rural caste politics. Mumbai is a major centre of Dalit art and literature, and plays an important role in Dalit politics. In the 19th and 20th centuries, it was a centre of Indian social reform and helped weaken caste-based politics. But Mumbai continues to struggle with caste and with those who see advantage in dividing people on the lines of their birth.

'The term Hindu may be seen as a misnomer, an inclusive term created by the British.'

persists) but is also acutely aware of his or her family origins. Village life may be a distant memory for many Mumbai residents but it still, in many ways, determines identity.

In any case, even if the large majority of the city is Hindu, that's not much of an identity at all, except for outsiders. You have only to read the matrimonial columns of the local newspapers to see how many different ways the term can be sliced, with caste only one of them.

MUMBAI MASH-UP

The very term Hindu may be seen as a misnomer, an inclusive term created by the British as a bureaucratic convenience to make their censuses easier. Hinduism itself is difficult to define as a religion because it has no single defining text. There are hundreds of Hindu texts of different importance to different communities. The four Vedas (ancient religious texts dating back to around 1,800 BC, but this is a contested date) are often held to be central, but the epics, the *Ramayana* and the *Mahabharata*, constitute the core of most Hindus' connection with their religion.

Hinduism has been called a way of life but this is also misleading about a deeply complex and seemingly self-contradictory religion. Hinduism offers a dualistic path in which God and Man are separate entities and a non-dualistic one in which Man's only duty is to recognise the godhead within him. It sanctions great excess as a route to the divine but encourages great asceticism as well. It has 330 million gods, with their own distinct identities; and a single deity into which all of them can be collapsed. It is possible, as one observer remarked, to say two completely opposing things about Hinduism and find scriptural support for both.

No one ever answers 'Hindu' to the question of caste. One might say 'Saraswat' and straight away that answer would suggest that the speaker is from Goa, migrated to Mumbai and belongs to the Brahmin orders. Or one might say 'Pathare Prabhu' and evoke a group that came to Mumbai in the 13th century with the king Raja Bhimdev from Patan in Gujarat. Or one might say 'Tamilian Dalit' and order up another lineage of social revolution, of an underclass that is beginning to be mobilised by affirmative action, of the tanneries in what is often (mistakenly) called Asia's largest slum, Dharavi. Or one might say 'TamBram', meaning 'Tamilian Brahmin', and another set of images – of classical Carnatic music concerts and tight-lipped morality – would be set into play. All these are stereotypes and as soon as you bump into the real human being behind them, they begin to fade. But they are, nevertheless, a legacy of that school chart.

Islam, you might think, would be easier. Muslims are supposed to be one people in their submission to Allah, their adherence to the Koran, right? But beyond the obvious Shi'a and Sunni divide there are regional differences as well. There are 'Dawoodi Bohras' from Gujarat, 'Memons' from Kutch and from Halai, 'Khoja Ismailis' (also called 'Aga Khanis'), 'Konkani Muslims' from the Konkan coast, 'Irani Shi'as' who trace their lineage to Iran, 'Manilas' and 'Khoyas' from Kerala.

Walk down Mohammed Ali Road and you'll see an enormous variety of mosques and Muslim groups running businesses, groups who share very little except their submission to Allah. A Muslim from the Malabar coast will not speak the same language as a Muslim from the northern plains of India. They may eat together (each thinking very little of the other's food) but they will not inter rmarry.

THE ARCHIVE OF IDENTITIES

But if you're walking around South Mumbai, the imprint of another migrant tribe, the Parsis, will be dominant. The Parsis are Zoroastrians, followers of the prophet Zoroaster, who were driven out of Iran by Muslim persecution. They arrived in Gujarat in the eighth or ninth century and sought asylum from the local king. He is said to have sent them a glass of milk full to the brim – his way of saying that his kingdom was full. The Parsi elders conferred, added some sugar to the milk and sent it back – to suggest that they would mix thoroughly and sweeten the life of the community. Thus the Parsis, true to their word, still speak Gujarati at home. And though, as good businessmen, they have been involved in a fair share of dirty dealing (the opium trade, for one), they have done their civic duty as well. Many of Mumbai's public institutions were built by the Parsi tradition of community service (*see p51* **Munificent Mumbaikars**).

Today, the Parsi population has tragically declined, with no more than 50,000 left in the city, and a mere 120,000 worldwide. I would often suggest to a Parsi friend that I was going to start Project Parsi, much like Project Tiger.

'Yes, with radio collars to track us wherever we go,' he would retort, with the trademark good humour that gave us Parsi theatre, one of the grand-daddies of the Bollywood film.

'And report on mating habits,' I would add.

'If mating was a habit among us, would you need a project?' Few communities can take so much slander with such good humour.

The decline of the Parsis has found a sad parallel in the sudden decline of the white-backed vulture in South Asia and beyond. The vulture plays a crucial role in traditional Parsi funerals, in which the body is left at the top of the Towers of Silence where vultures pick it clean. This tradition is endangered because the vultures are dying out.

Mumbai's communities define and redefine themselves and each resident can be seen as a moving archive of identities. That taxi driver may be from the northern state of Uttar Pradesh, but to most of his passengers he is a 'bhaiyya', a word that used to mean 'brother' but now means a northerner. That nurse may see herself as an Orthodox Syrian Christian but to most of her patients she is a 'Mallu' (someone who speaks Malayalam, the language of Kerala) or just an 'Anda-Gundu' (a name intended to evoke hilarity at the supposedly muddled sounds of a Dravidian language).

For this is a city that has had many visitors. It has been home to groups like the Sidis (with roots in Africa), many of whom still live in Dongri; the Iranis, who created the glorious institution known as the Irani restaurant; the Chinese, who were a significant presence in Mazgaon before the 1962 Indo-China War; along with Anglo-Indians and Armenians.

And there were Jews from the Maharashtra coast – referred to as 'Bene Israelis' – believing they were among the lost tribes who arrived in India before the destruction of Jerusalem's Second Temple. They moved to Mumbai in the early 19th century, but today they number less than 5,000; many have moved to Israel since 1947. In the 19th century, Bombay played host to a wave of Jews from Baghdad. The most famous family among them were the Sassoons, who built some of the city's major landmarks.

But if there is one space where Mumbai's ethnic diversity is represented in its full glory, it is the Hindi film industry. It may be a little puzzling that Mumbai should be home to a cinema whose language it does not speak very well. Most northerners flinch at the sound of a Mumbaikar speaking Hindi, as well they might. We mangle the language, throw in words from every tongue (including English) and don't bother with honorific or subtlety. But then that's why this city created a cinema that was so easily portable. Largely cosmopolitan and secular, Bollywood is truly representative of the city's diversity, even if much of it is behind the camera. When communities are caricatured and stereotyped, it is usually done with an insider's sanction. It was this that ultimately made the Hindi film such a mobile force that spread a little of the spirit of Mumbai across India.

Bollywood

Hindi cinema rules the roost.

No one knows for sure who coined the term 'Bollywood', which first gained currency in the early 1990s, though there are several candidates – mainly journalists and movie producers – vying for parentage. However, it's a neologism that's spread through the subcontinent like wildfire. The Bengali film industry, based in the Calcutta (now Kolkata) district of Tollygunge, is now commonly referred to as 'Tollywood', movies made in Madras (now Chennai) are said to come from 'Mollywood', while 'Lollywood' is used to describe the Pakistani film industry centred in Lahore. The term Bollywood is despised by many in the Hindi film industry, not least for defining Hindi films in relation to Hollywood, but it remains an unrivalled catch-all phrase for describing the farrago of emotion, action, song, dance and humour that animates almost every Hindi film.

Star Cast

A guide to the Bollywood A-list.

AAMIR KHAN
Aamir Khan hit gold with his second starring role in the teenage romance *Qayamat Se Qayamat Tak*. After a series of flops in the 1990s, Khan bounced back with scene-stealing performances in films like *Raja Hindustani*, *Rangeela* and the Oscar-nominated *Lagaan*. Adored by fans for his attention to performance over preening, Khan has often been described as a director's nightmare for the extraordinary interest he takes in the making of his movies. In 2007, he finally went ahead and directed and produced his first feature, *Taare Zameen Par*, which opened to widespread acclaim. He is now among Bollywood's most powerful producers, with such successes as *Jaane Tu... Ya Jaane Na* and *Peepli [Live]*.
Definitive films *Lagaan, Rangeela, Taare Zameen Par.*

AISHWARYA RAI BACHCHAN
A former Miss World, born in Mangalore, Aishwarya Rai has had an indifferent box-office track record but her looks and recent wedding to Abhishek Bachchan, the son of Amitabh Bachchan, ensure lifelong membership of the A-list. Rai entered films after a successful modelling career, and acted in Tamil movie *Iruvar* before moving into Hindi films. Rai has since packaged herself as an Indian crossover actress, in the mould of *Memoirs of a Geisha* star Zhang Ziyi, but hasn't managed to work her charms on the North American box office.
Definitive films *Devdas, Hum Dil de Chuke Sanam, Josh.*

DEEPIKA PADUKONE
The latest dream girl made a dream debut with Shah Rukh Khan in *Om Shanti Om back* in November 2007. Her classic Indian looks, used to great effect in *Om Shanti Om* where she played a 1970s Bollywood star, and her easygoing charm, have helped her carve a niche for herself in a very short time.
Definitive film *Om Shanti Om, Love Aaj Kal.*

HRITHIK ROSHAN
The son of director Rakesh Roshan, Hrithik Roshan is India's answer to Brad Pitt. His good looks, superb physique and ample acting talent place him squarely in the superstars' gallery. After a debut in *Kaho Naa... Pyaar Hai*, Roshan went through a lean patch before bouncing back with a bang with *Dhoom 2* and the superhero-themed *Krrish* in 2006.
Definitive films *Dhoom 2, Jodha Akbar, Kaho Naa... Pyaar Hai.*

KAREENA KAPOOR
The younger sister of actor Karisma Kapoor and a member of one of the oldest and most influential Bollywood families, Kareena Kapoor is the most camera-friendly of her generation. Blessed with strong movie genes, a confident face and tons of ambition, Kapoor's has found succes in a number of Bollywood movies and is now a household name. Noteworthy roles include *Chameli, Kabhi Khushi Kabhie Gham, Asoka* and *Jab We Met.*
Definitive films *Chameli, Jab We Met, Refugee.*

PRIYANKA CHOPRA

This former Miss World has worked very hard on her looks and her career, and the results are there for all to see. The twentysomething Chopra has worked in several A-list projects such as *Krrish* and *Don*. If there's any actor who can give Kareena Kapoor a run for her money, it's Chopra.

Definitive films *Don (2006), Kaminey.*

RANBIR KAPOOR

The cousin of Kareena Kapoor, Ranbir Kapoor is one of Bollywood's fastest-rising talents. He has clambered to the A-list on the strength of merely a handful of films. His ability to get under the skin of his roles and his appeal among younger audiences ensure that he is going to be around for a long, long time.

Definitive films *Wake Up Sid, Ajab Prem Ki Ghazab Kahani.*

SAIF ALI KHAN

Even though he came from good, media-friendly celebrity stock – his grandfather played cricket for England and then for India, and his parents were actor Sharmila Tagore and cricketer Mansoor Ali Khan Pataudi – Saif Ali Khan's career still took forever to kick-start. But once he got going with films like *Dil Chahta Hai* and *Ek Hasina Thi*, there's been no stopping him. He has evolved into a versatile actor who can switch effortlessly from buffoonery to baseness. He also now runs his own production company.

Definitive films *Dil Chahta Hai, Ek Hasina Thi, Omkara.*

SALMAN KHAN

The son of Salim Khan, the ace scriptwriter who co-wrote some of Bollywood's most iconic films in the 1970s and '80s, Salman Khan established his credentials as a romantic hero with *Maine Pyar Kiya* in 1989. His career has rollercoastered since then as he has gone from lover-boy to macho action hero with some comedy thrown in for good measure. However, most of the drama has been off-screen: Khan has been in court for killing two endangered blackbuck, and for drunkenly running down and killing a homeless man in Mumbai. On-screen, Khan is often portrayed as a toughie who's a fool for love. His *Dabanng* is one of the biggest hits of the decade.

Definitive films *Dabanng, Aran Arjun, Maine Pyar Kiya.*

SHAH RUKH KHAN

Shah Rukh Khan is the only modern actor to command a guaranteed box office opening and worldwide fan following, and with a fanbase of billions, he's considered by many to be the most successful actor in the world. Born in 1965 in Delhi, Khan studied theatre and acted in television serials before making the leap to Bollywood. A regular at film festivals all over the globe, Khan has experimented with several images through the past decade – anti-hero, common man, wealthy businessman – but will forever be remembered as the lover-boy extraordinaire, thanks to blockbusters like *Dilwale Dulhania Le Jayenge*.

Definitive films *Baazigar, Dilwale Dulhania Le Jayenge, Swades.*

TOTAL RECALL

Ever since films by the Lumière Brothers were first screened at the Watson's Hotel in Kala Ghoda in 1896, Mumbai has remained at the heart of the Hindi film industry. The first talkie in Hindi, *Alam Ara*, emerged in 1931 from the traditions of the city's theatre circuit. *Alam Ara* was directed by theatre director Ardeshir Irani, and established two unshakeable pillars of Hindi cinema: it had over ten songs mimed and enacted by the movie's cast, and its plot was drawn from a play – an early indication of how Hindi cinema would evolve its form and language from Indian dramatic traditions, from classical Sanskrit theatre to folk forms.

The melodramatic style that defines the Hindi film industry hasn't changed fundamentally over the past half-century: Sturm und Drang interspersed with song and dance. The 1970s and '80s saw action movies, multi-starrers and family weepies. With the 1990s came the rise of the so-called multiplex film, which refers to a movie that is produced with a relatively small budget, has an urban theme and actors who speak an urbanised Hindi that often weaves in English and slang. But the big-budget Hindi movie continues to thrive. Today, Bollywood continues to outperform Hollywood at the Indian box office. Bollywood has borrowed extensively from Hollywood's desire for punchy, slickly written films, and song-and-dance routines now resembles MTV – some sequences in Hindi movies now (intentionally) look like hip hop videos.

Spiced-up versions of Hollywood movies have always been a Bollywood staple, but there's now a marked tendency to borrow extensively from other movies right down to

You Too Can Be a Star

Bollywood bit part, anyone?

It's surprisingly easy to get cast as an extra in a Bollywood movie. Most big-budget films are now set (and shot) in foreign countries to appeal to the Indian diaspora, who pay many pounds or dollars for the pleasure of watching their countrymen gambol in the middle of Times Square. But since bits of the film are still shot at Mumbai sets – nightclub scenes or dance numbers, for example – directors need a crowd of foreign faces in the background to make it look like New York or London or wherever is the flavour of the month. Take a walk down Colaba Causeway (*see p48*), or generally loiter around the bars and cafés in Colaba and, if you're clearly not Indian, a casting agent may well approach you. Though it may sound sleazy at first ('Excuse me, do you want to be in a Bollywood movie?'), nearly all of them are above board. Often, though, they might be also be casting for advertisements instead of movies. These are usually last-minute things, and you will be expected to be free either immediately or the following day. For your efforts, which is mostly standing around and dancing a little, you get lunch, a few hundred rupees and, if you're lucky, the chance to meet a famous star. As with any activity while travelling, use common sense: ask for a business card or some sort of credentials and don't go off alone with strange men. Away from the camera, it's often possible to spot stars and starlets shaking their stuff at select expensive nightspots, among them Olive in Bandra (*see p118*), and Aurus in Juhu (*see p119*).

the last frame. The movie *Kaante* (2002) was a remake of Quentin Tarantino's *Reservoir Dogs* and was set in Los Angeles; the same director remade Chan-wook Park's *Oldboy* as *Zinda* (2005). A great deal of importance is now given to production design – sometimes at the cost of the plot, another tendency borrowed from Hollywood. Most movies are now shot on sets and in foreign locations. There's a veneer of modernity and urbanity in new Hindi movies. Actors now actually kiss, as they did before a puritanical streak hit the movies between the 1950s and late '90s, when the camera would cut away as their faces moved closer. But the basic values remain the same: the family is the core unit of stability and identity; marriage is the goal of romance; women look best when they're standing by their men; and wealth is sexy.

This new love for slickness means that Mumbai is increasingly losing its once-central role in Hindi films. For decades, the city was an evergreen star of Bollywood movies. The Marine Drive promenade in South Mumbai plays a role as the frontier of journey, hope, liberation and solace, as have the city's industrial zones, including its mills, factories and docks, the bustling streets and flyovers, the beaches, the brothels, bars and nightclubs. Mumbai's unique character types have influenced and shaped Hindi movies: the smuggler, the industrial worker, the bar dancer/prostitute, the industrialist, the dreamy-eyed migrant, the street-smart small-time criminal, the cop. It's difficult to judge who influenced whom: was the typical swagger associated with Mumbai characters picked off the streets, or do citizens learn their strut from the movies? It's hard to tell any more, but Mumbai's people are a bit like characters from their movies: loud, brash, romantic, anxious, hot-headed, money- and glamour-hungry, foolish at times, but always entertaining to watch.

INDIAN EMOTION

Unlike Hollywood, mainstream Hindi movies have always fused fancy with realism to the extent that descriptions of them as 'unrealistic' become almost meaningless. Instead, Hindi cinema employs melodramatic conventions that are close to those of opera. Just as in, say, *La Traviata*, a woman with an obviously fine pair of lungs can sing about dying of consumption, the lack of Western-style realism in Bollywood is beside the point; what Hindi films seek to convey is emotional realism, taken to its purest form through the use of music. A good Hindi film may lack a logical or original narrative but it will make perfect sense to the emotionally literate. Hindi films are not just about romantic love but family love and friendship; the dramatic tension on screen often arises from conflict between romantic love and family duty. Often, such conflicts are pushed to melodramatic extremes, so the family will only accept the couple when death threatens, such as in *Bobby* (1973), when the couple seem headed for a Romeo and Juliet-style tragedy.

Hindi film stories also often revolve around the breaking and restoration of the moral order. A woman who has sex outside of marriage may do so in an irresistibly erotic moment, but she will have to pay for her sin. One of the many reasons for the enduring popularity of actor Amitabh Bachchan is his talent for conveying moral outrage; his characters are determined to restore the moral order, even if that means breaking the law or dying in the process.

Unlike Hollywood, Hindi cinema isn't ruled by genre, although many films have elements of multiple genres rolled into one – the *masala* (mix of spices) summed up by the word 'Bollywood'. You could argue that the typical leading man in a Hindi movie must be more versatile than his Hollywood counterpart – he needs to know how to cry buckets as well as land a punch.

Hindi films are often dismissed as escapist entertainment, but there's nothing trivial about that. Turkish writer Orhan Pamuk wrote that the rest of the world will only understand the changes in India when 'we have seen their private lives reflected in novels'. But it's more likely to be in Bollywood that the fantasies and fears of modern India will find their clearest expression.

Offset you
flight wit
Trees for Citie
and make you
trip mea
something fo
years to com
www.treesforcities.org/offse
Trees for Cit
Charity registration number 103

Sights

Malabar Hill. *See p62.*

South Mumbai

Mumbai's oldest district is also its most charming

South Mumbai, also known locally as 'the town', is where you'll find most of the city's architectural and historical sites, including Colaba Causeway, the city's main tourist drag. It's also where Mumbai's wealthy work and play, and even though Bandra and Andheri are now the city's hottest nightlife hubs, die-hard South Mumbai snobs wouldn't dream of going anywhere else.

Among the south's sites you'll find the Fort, named for the long-since demolished fortress established by the British in the 17th century that became the nucleus of the city. The British influence is everywhere. The **University of Mumbai** looks like an Oxford college with palm trees, while **Chhatrapati Shivaji Terminus** bears more than a passing resemblance to London's St Pancras station.

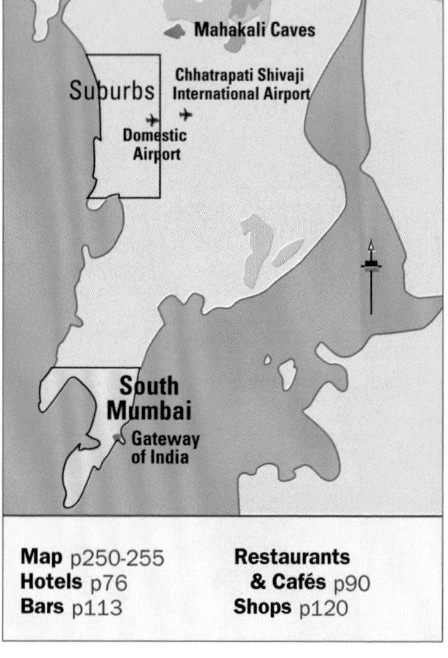

Map p250-255
Hotels p76
Bars p113
Restaurants & Cafés p90
Shops p120

SIGHTS

COLABA

Colaba Causeway – the city's prime tourist stretch – was once a strip of land that connected the islands of Bombay in the north with Colaba (named for the Koli fisherfolk who inhabited the seven islands before Portuguese colonists arrived) in the south. Home to some of the most expensive real estate in India, the Causeway today has shopping arcades, hotels, restaurants and bars on either side, but the island of Colaba sits just south of the causeway and goes on to the very edge of Mumbai, at Navy Nagar.

A recreation area for the British throughout the 18th century and populated solely by large numbers of deer released by the East India Company, Colaba changed dramatically after the British constructed the Causeway in 1838. The island was initially developed as a military cantonment, which is what it remains today. Green, well-maintained and quiet, it is still one of the most pleasant parts of the city, thanks to the army and navy installations (all of which are off-limits to civilians) and the sprawling campus of the Tata Institute of Fundamental Research, which is well regarded for its work in the fields of maths and physics.

In 1847, work began on the Church of St John the Evangelist. Known locally today as **Afghan Church**, it was built to commemorate the hundreds of British and Indian soldiers from Bombay who died in the disastrous First Afghan War of 1838-42. Horse-drawn trams followed a few decades later, lending the island a romantic charm.

Cuffe Parade was once one of the city's most desirable addresses, with mansions and bungalows – many owned by Parsi families – overlooking a genteel seafront promenade. Some of the mansions remain but the promenade has gone, as has the sea, pushed back over a kilometre and a half by land reclamation in the 1970s. It was quickly built over with apartment blocks, a shopping arcade, the twin towers of Mumbai's own World Trade Center and a large slum. But, look closer and it's not all 21st century metrpopolis: a few minutes' walk north is Gita Nagar at Back Bay, where the brightly painted wooden boats of Koli fisherfolk, the descendants of the city's original

Oval Maidan. See p51.

inhabitants, line the beach just as they did for centuries before the Portuguese came.

Colaba also possesses one of the city's finest public parks, the **Mumbai Port Trust Garden** (5.30am-11am-4.30-8pm daily), where Colaba residents go jogging and take in a stunning sea view. A little further north and you hit Colaba Causeway. Once a bridge connecting two islands, it is now the city's equivalent of Oxford Street. It's crammed with clothes shops, restaurants, bars, cafés, trinket stalls, wandering salesmen and, of course, tourists. The side streets here abound with mid-range hotels, handicrafts and jewellery shops, and some of South Mumbai's classiest bars, like perennial favourite Indigo (*see p115*), on Mandlik Road. At the southern end of the Causeway there's Sassoon Dock, a hectic wholesale fish market where the local Koli fisherfolk bring in the night's catch at around 5am. If you can get up, it's an experience (and smell) you won't forget in a hurry. Go north and the entrance to Colaba Market appears on the right – an open and lively produce market crowded with fruit and vegetable stalls and a line of jewellery shops. Also on the Causeway stands the massive, arched entrance of Cusrow Baug, a housing colony built in 1934 and reserved for members of the city's dwindling Parsi community. A watchman guards the gate, but if you ask nicely he might let you take a peek at its spectacular art deco-style *agiary*, or fire temple (from the outside only; non-Parsis are not admitted). *Baugs* (literally, 'gardens') were built for community living, and with its neat, geometrical buildings and gardens, Cusrow Baug has since catapulted into a prime Mumbai address.

A right turn at Electric House on the Causeway leads you to the back of the **Taj Mahal Palace hotel** (*see p77*), which dominates the seafront. The city's most famous hotel, it was built by Parsi industrialist Jamsetji Nusserwanji Tata in 1903 (*see p51* **Munificent Mumbaikars**). Built in a blend of Moorish and Florentine Renaissance styles, it's worth visiting even if you're not planning on staying. The Taj is just yards from the waterfront **Gateway of India**, an impressive, towering archway of yellow basalt built by the British to commemorate the visit of King George V and Queen Mary to India in 1911, the only visit of a reigning British monarch to the jewel in the Empire's crown. Designed by architect George Wittet, it provided a ceremonial entranceway to the subcontinent for George and his queen after stepping onto dry land, but that one was made out of papier-mâché – the stone version wasn't completed until 1927. In 1948, the last British troops to leave Indian soil exited through the Gateway.

Overlooking the Gateway and its garden is the elegant **Royal Bombay Yacht Club** (Apollo Bunder, 6752-7200, www.royalbombayyachtclub.com), established in 1846 and still one of the city's most exclusive private members' clubs, steeped in colonial-era atmosphere – but you'll need permission from the club secretary to step inside. At the end of Colaba Causeway is **SP Mukherjee Chowk** – a traffic roundabout

INSIDE TRACK TAJ TIMING

The best time to see the **Gateway of India** is one hour before sunset. You can check out the monument and take photos in daylight, watch the sun set behind the **Taj Mahal Palace hotel** (*see p77*) and see how different everything looks at night, when the lights come on.

with an ornate stone fountain. Under British rule it was named Wellington Circle, after the Duke of Wellington, and the base of the fountain is inscribed with an inventory of the Iron Duke's battles. Locally, the roundabout is known as **Regal**, after the striking art deco cinema (*see p143*) built in 1934 that sits at the end of the Causeway.

OVAL MAIDAN & CHURCHGATE

The Arabian Sea lapped at the edge of **Oval Maidan** (*maidan* means 'ground') until a land reclamation project in the 1920s extended the peninsula nearly 750 metres westward to Marine Drive. As a result, there's a notable contrast between the Victorian Gothic buildings on the *maidan*'s eastern side and the art deco apartments to the west. This 750-metres-long recreation ground between Maharshi Karve Marg (Queen's Road) and Karmaveer Bhaurao Marg (Mayo Road) was once a venue for dog-and-horse shows for the entertainment of British colonists in the 19th and early 20th centuries, before falling into disrepair. Now lovingly restored by residents of Queen's Road, it is the city's premier venue for impromptu cricket matches. On weekends there are dozens of games taking place simultaneously, overlapping to the point where it's almost impossible to tell where one ends and another begins. Visitors are very welcome to join the mêlée. On the Oval's eastern side is a row of some of the city's most impressive Victorian buildings. Next to the **Old Secretariat** and the **Sessions Court** at the southern end of Mayo Road are the curlicued stones and spiral staircases of the **University of Mumbai**, built in 1874 in the style of old English universities. Attached to the University Library and looming over the Oval is the **Rajabai Clock Tower**, constructed in 1878. To the left is the **Bombay High Court**, outside which down-on-their-luck itinerant lawyers in threadbare black suits tout for work. Visitors are allowed inside, which is highly recommended for courtroom scenes straight out of Dickens' *Bleak House*. Inside,

Munificent Mumbaikars

Local legends who left their mark.

Tourists, and indeed Mumbaikars, often think that all of South Mumbai's buildings of interest were made by the British. But while they may have been designed by architects from the Isles, neither the East India Company nor Queen Victoria herself can claim credit for commissioning the historical heart of the city. A clutch of local businessmen, nearly all of them Parsis (*see p35* **Communities**), believed in the early years of Bombay's economic prosperity in giving something back to society and so funded the construction of hospitals, schools and infrastructure. Not altogether selfless, they also built wonderful mansions for themselves.

The creamy-brown Fort House on Dadabhai Naoroji Road, which, as trivia buffs will tell you, was the site of the first party in Mumbai at which iced drinks were served, was originally the home of **Sir Jamsetjee Jeejeebhoy**. Not one to let a good business opportunity pass him by, he made his fortune from the opium trade with China. He then used all his money for good, funding the **JJ Hospital**, the **JJ School of Art**, the **JJ College of Architecture** and the establishment of the *Times of India*.

The other great Mumbai University building and Fort's most iconic structure, the **Rajabai Clock Tower** (*see above*), was financed by stockbroker and cotton merchant **Premchand Roychand**. He named it after his mother. Roychand made early money when he joined the Native Share and Stockbrokers Association (later Bombay Stock Exchange) at the age of 18 as the first trader who could read and write English. In seven years, he created a near monopoly on shares, stocks and bullion. Roychand also made money on the back of the cotton booms, thanks in no small part to practices that weren't altogether legal.

The blindingly white neo-classical building, which houses Deutsche Bank, next to the Sterling Cinema on Hazarimal Somani Marg, is one of two mansions owned by industrialist **Jamsetji Nusserwanji Tata**, the founder of the Tata Group of Companies, which today makes everything from cars to tea. An urban legend states that a tunnel runs between his two houses – the other is Esplanade House, the one with the statue of a dog at the entrance, opposite the Bombay Gym. Tata was a dazzling figure of staggering importance at the beginning of the 20th century who also built the **Taj Mahal Palace hotel** (*see p77*) and, in 1901, became the first Indian to own a car.

Bombay Stock Exchange. *See p54.*

look out for the satirical animal sculptures, like the monkey judge holding a hopelessly unbalanced scale, and foxes and wolves in lawyer's outfits. Across the street from the court is the **Bhika Behram Well**, built in 1725. It's a sacred well for the Parsi community (*see p35* **Communities**), surrounded by green benches where elderly Parsis read their holy book. The canopy above the well features vivid stained glass depicting the winged Ashofarohar, a Zoroastrian divine messenger. Only Parsis are allowed in. Westward along Veer Nariman Road sits the **Western Railway Headquarters**, built in 1899, with white domes rising above dark stone minarets. The staid concrete structure opposite is the **Churchgate Terminus** where the suburban Western Railway line ends. Opposite Churchgate is the **Eros Cinema** (*see p143*), another art deco gem built in 1938, now run-down but as busy as ever.

Rajabai Clock Tower

Mumbai University, Karmaveer Bhaurao Marg, next to High Court, Oval Maidan, Churchgate (www.mu.ac.in). Churchgate station. **Open** 10.30am-6.30pm Mon-Sat. **Admission** free. **Map** p250 F7.

The chimes of the Rajabai Clock Tower, which rises 85m (280ft) above the Mumbai University Library, have been sounding across the Oval Maidan every half-hour, with a few interruptions, since 1880. Modelled on London's Big Ben, the tower was built with a Rs 400,000 donation from Mumbai's first rogue trader, Premchand Roychand. In return, the clock tower was named after his mother, Rajabai. It was designed by Sir Gilbert Scott in Gothic Revivalist style and features stone heads of Shakespeare and Homer peering out from the crossed arches under the main spiral staircase. While you're here, look out, too, for the pretty stained-glasswork around the staircase, and the flower-like teakwood library ceiling.

INSIDE TRACK
CHHATRAPATI GUIDEBOOK

At the **Chhatrapati Shivaji Maharaj Vastu Sanghrahalaya**, opt for the museum guidebook (Rs 150) over the audio guide. It's more detailed, lets you navigate faster and doubles up as a souvenir.

KALA GHODA

South Mumbai's art district, **Kala Ghoda** (which means 'Black Horse') sits off the intersection of K Dubash Marg (Rampart Row) and Mahatma Gandhi Road. It's one of the city's most attractive areas, with some well-restored heritage buildings. Kala Ghoda owes its name to a four-metre bronze equestrian statue of King Edward VII (he reigned 1901-10), which was installed here in 1879 in what is now a car park, to commemorate his visit three years earlier. Edward sat there for the next 86 years, surviving long after the last British troops departed in 1948. The statue was finally removed in 1965 in a government drive to eradicate British-era statues from public places. Edward, unlabelled and stuck on a patch of grass, now greets visitors to the Byculla Zoo (*see p60*).

Since independence, the area has evolved into Mumbai's premier art district, with a number of galleries nearby. The largest are the **National**

Gallery of Modern Art (*see p149*) which stands off the Regal Circle, and the **Jehangir Art Gallery** (*see p149*). Artists also display their work on the pavement outside the Jehangir, which stands on one corner of the sprawling compound of the **Chhatrapati Shivaji Maharaj Vastu Sangrahalaya** (*see p53*), once known as the Prince of Wales Museum, on Mahatma Gandhi Road. A stroll around the area's galleries is a pleasant way to spend a few hours. For more on Mumbai's art scene and galleries in Kala Ghoda; *see p147* **Follow Your Art**.

Overlooking Kala Ghoda on the western side of the street is the **David Sassoon Mechanical Institute and Library**, built in 1870 and named after its founder, a renowned Jewish businessman and philanthropist from Baghdad whose family built many of the city's civic and cultural institutions. Sassoon's face peers out of the building's façade above its arched entrance and there's a life-size statue of him in traditional Jewish robes inside. Upstairs, a peaceful balcony overlooking Kala Ghoda is a popular spot for readers to while away the afternoons. To the institute's left stands **Elphinstone College**, Mumbai's oldest college, instituted in 1835 and taking up residence in this beautiful building in 1888. The college building had been a dark grey mess until renovation restored the exquisite golden stonework a few years ago. Similar magic was worked on the **Army & Navy Building** to its right, named for the Army & Navy Departmental Store it once housed. The Army & Navy recently became a department store once again, named Westside. Next door is the decrepit **Esplanade Mansion**, once the city's poshet hotel, Watson's.

Rampart Row, officially named K Dubash Marg, runs along the site of one wall of the 17th-century British fort that became the city's nucleus and was finally demolished in the 1860s. On the other side of the popular **Rhythm House** music store (*see p133*) the narrow Dr VB Gandhi Road (Forbes Street) leads to the sky-blue **Kenneseth Eliyahoo Synagogue**. Another Sassoon family-funded institution, it was built in 1884 for the city's once-thriving Jewish community. It's faded but still beautiful, especially in the afternoons when its tall, stained-glass windows cast a rainbow of light across the prayer hall. Before independence, the prayer hall benches were packed elbow-to-elbow for Saturday services; these days only a handful of people come to worship, as most of Mumbai's Jewish community migrated to Israel and elsewhere after 1948.

From the synagogue, the narrow Saibaba Lane leads back to Rampart Row, which is now lined with a stretch of smart restaurants, shops and art galleries. While you're here, keep an eye out for two mahogany trees in front of **Ador House** – legend has it that they were planted by the famous British explorer and missionary Dr David Livingstone in 1865. At the end of Rampart Row rises the tall spire of **St Andrew's and St Columba's Church**, built in 1819 and modelled on St Martin-in-the-Fields in London's Trafalgar Square. Mumbai's first Scottish church, St Andrew's massive doors open on to a carefully preserved interior of Burmese teak and shining brass, surmounted by an antique pipe organ. St Andrew's only opens for Sunday services at 6.30pm. Opposite the church, along Rampart Row, stands the **Bombay Natural History Society**, hidden behind thick foliage at Hornbill House. The members' society was formed by naturalists in 1884 to document the rich flora and fauna around Mumbai. Today, it conducts environmental projects and is at the forefront of efforts to save India's endangered species including the tiger and the great Indian bustard. Every February, Rampart Row is closed to traffic for the two-week Kala Ghoda Arts Festival (*see p139*), when art installations, photographs, multimedia works and paintings spill out from the neighbouring galleries on to the pavements. Theatre, music and dance shows are performed on a makeshift stage on the road, which is lined with stalls selling street food, ethnic clothes and jewellery.

★ Chhatrapati Shivaji Maharaj Vastu Sangrahalaya

159 MG Road, Kala Ghoda, near Regal Circle (2284-4519/www.bombaymuseum.org). **Open** 10.15am-6pm Tue-Sun. **Admission** Rs 300 including audio tour in English, French & Japanese; Rs 5 reductions; free under-5s. **Map** p250 G6.

The city's largest museum, the Chhatrapati Shivaji Maharaj Vastu Sangrahalaya was built in 1914, and originally called the Prince of Wales Museum of Western India. The building is a fusion of British, Hindu and Mughal architecture – a style called Indo-Saracenic – pioneered by British architect George Wittet in the early 1900s. The domes are from Mughal architecture (its sculpted windows resemble those of traditional Rajasthani dwellings) while the balconies and façade are typically British. The museum has over 30,000 artefacts including bronze and stone sculptures, miniature paintings, arms and armour, as well as Far Eastern art. Don't miss the only Assyrian frieze in India, on display in the Pre- and Proto History Gallery. The explanatory labels are poor, but there is a 45-minute audio tour.

▶ *Liked this? Check out the Bhau Daji Lad Museum; see p60.*

SIGHTS

FORT & BALLARD ESTATE

Under the Mumbai stink of petrol, dust and spices is that all-pervasive smell of fast money, and nowhere is it stronger than in Fort, the city's banking district, and Ballard Estate, the old shipping and finance district. The epicentre of Fort is the 28-storey **Bombay Stock Exchange**, which stands at the junction of Mumbai Samachar Marg and Dalal Street. The word *dalal* means broker, and Bombay's – and Asia's – first exchange was established here in 1875, then called the Native Share and Stockbrokers Association. The new building was built in the 1970s. On 12 March 1993, around 50 people were killed by a car bomb in the exchange's basement during Mumbai's worst-ever terrorist attack, now known as 'Black Friday' (*see p28*). The narrow lanes around the exchange are lined with brokerages, banks, insurance and other financial institutions, and bulls and bears dominate the conversation at local *chai* stalls.

Mumbai Samachar Marg leads to **Horniman Circle**, a fenced circular garden surrounded by elegant heritage buildings, including the imposing neo-classical **Asiatic Society of Mumbai** (*see right*). The circle was the heart of the city's cotton trade during its early boom years, and there's still an old trough near the western gate that was used to water the cattle carrying cotton bales to the market. After 1863, the cotton market moved to Colaba, but profits from the boom paid for the Horniman Circle Garden and the buildings around it.

Ahead of the Asiatic Society, Shahid Bhagat Singh Road curves into Mint Road, site of the imposing **Reserve Bank of India**, the regulating bank. Hidden behind a wall next to the RBI is the **Bombay Mint**, built in 1827 to produce gold and silver coins and still pumping out the steel rupee coins used today. Close by is the **Monetary Museum**, on **Sir Pherozeshah Mehta Road**.

On Modi Street, parallel to Mint Road, stands the **Maneckji Nowroji Sett Agiary**, Mumbai's oldest Parsi fire temple, first built in 1733 and rebuilt in 1891. You'll have to admire it from outside, though, as only Parsis are allowed to enter. Inside burns an eternal flame, believed to have been carried by Parsi refugees from Persia to India when they fled Muslim persecution around AD 800.

Ballard Road leads to the business district of **Ballard Estate**, a neat grid of refined office buildings designed by George Wittet (the designer of the **Gateway of India**). The area was reclaimed from the sea around 1910 with material excavated for the building of the access-restricted **Indira Docks** that stand beyond. The buildings here housed shipping offices and hotels for arrivals at the docks. Most have closed down, replaced by some of India's biggest corporations, like **Reliance House**, the corporate office of Reliance Industries, a Fortune 500 company. Today, the office of the **Mumbai Port Trust**, which regulates all port activities and is the city's biggest landowner, and the **Customs House** remain the Estate's most important administrative centres. A **War Memorial** for Mumbai Port Trust employees who died in World War I stands at the junction of Ballard Road, Sprot Road and Narottam Morarji Marg. The tiny **Ballard Bunder Gatehouse Navy Museum** on Ballard Road is a recent addition to the landscape.

FREE ★ Asiatic Society of Mumbai

Shahid Bhagat Singh Road, opposite Horniman Circle, Fort (2266-0956). CST or Churchgate stations. **Taxi** Monetary Museum. **Open** 10am-7pm Mon-Sat. **Map** p250 H8.

This milk-white neo-classical building with sweeping steps and imposing pillars has starred in numerous Bollywood films, usually masquerading as the Bombay High Court. The Asiatic Society was formed in 1803 with the purpose of 'studying the Orient', although 'Orientals' themselves were excluded. It remained a Europeans-only club until Sir Cursetji Maneckji was admitted in 1840, after he pointed out the stupidity of banning Indians when they were free to join the Royal Asiatic Society of Great Britain, its sister organisation. Inside, the library's curving stone staircases and cosy alcoves are filled with life-size statues of British-era governors, officials and philanthropists. The library is a repository of rare books, including an original manuscript of Dante's *Divine Comedy*, though sadly it's not on display.

FREE Ballard Bunder Gatehouse Navy Museum

Ballard Road, Ballard Estate (no phone). CST station. **Taxi** Ballard Pier. **Open** 9am-7pm daily. **Map** p253 J8.

This tiny museum was long overdue when it opened in 2005 – the first modern museum dedicated to Mumbai's illustrious maritime history. It's housed in a yellow stone gateway that was once lost behind a high wall after the Indian Navy took over the dockyards. The museum is filled with old black-and-white photographs, compasses, and intricate wooden models of ships and boats built by the Wadia family, which was once a famous Bombay shipbuilding dynasty.

FREE Monetary Museum

Amar Building, Sir Pherozeshah Mehta Road, Fort (2261-4043/www.rbi.org.in/scripts/ic_museum.aspx). CST or Churchgate stations. **Taxi** RBI. **Open** 10.45am-5.15pm Mon-Sat. **Map** p253 H8.

A Walking Tour of Fort

From hawkers to freedom fighters, students to rope makers – Fort has it all.

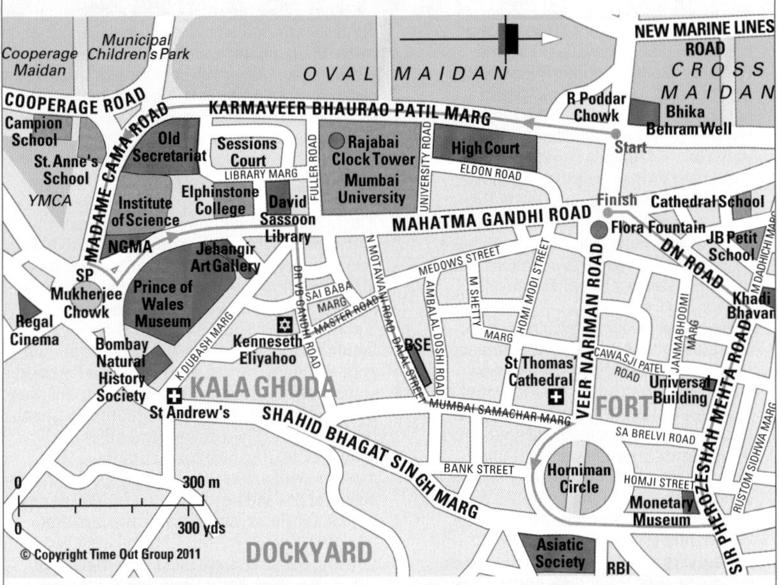

This tour of the area around the south-western part of the site of the old Bombay Fort takes about two hours. Start off at R Poddar Chowk, across from the **Bhika Behram Well** (*see p52*), situated between **Oval Maidan** (*see 51*) and **Cross Maidan** (so named for the cross put there by the Portuguese). Proceed down Karmaveer Bhaurao Patil Marg, lined with beautiful heritage buildings, including the **Bombay High Court**, the **University of Mumbai** (see p51) and the **Old Secretariat**, once the house of the British Governor of Bombay.

Turn right on to **Madame Cama Road**, named for Bhikaiji Rustom Cama, a Parsi feminist and freedom fighter made famous when she unfurled a prototype of the Indian flag at a socialist conference in Germany in 1907. At **SP Mukherjee Chowk** (*see p48*), better known as the Regal Circle, stands a fountain, built in 1865 and dedicated to Arthur Wellesley, the Duke of Wellington. On the southern side of the circle stands the art deco **Regal cinema** (*see p143*). Turn right on to Mahatma Gandhi Road, which runs along what was the western wall of the Bombay Fort. On the left are the exhibition halls of the **National Gallery of Modern Art** (*see p149*) and on the right the impressive **Chhatrapati Shivaji Maharaj Vastu Sangrahalaya**, formerly known as the Prince of Wales Museum (*see p53*). Continue down past the **Elphinstone College** (*see p53*) and the **David Sassoon Library** (*see p53*) and take a right into **Kala Ghoda** (*see p52*). Keep the **Rhythm House** (*see p133*) music store on your right and head down into the narrow Dr VB Gandhi Road, once a covered gully called Ropewalk Lane, filled with cable makers for the city's docks. Just one rope shop remains. On the right is the charming **Kenneseth Eliyahoo Synagogue** (*see p53*). Cut left on to the narrow Master Road into the heart of the finance district on Dalal Street, near the **Bombay Stock Exchange** (*see left*). Take a left on to Mumbai Samachar Marg past **St Thomas' Cathedral** (*see p56*) to the grand Horniman Circle and **Asiatic Society** (*see left*). Turn right on to Shahid Bhagat Singh Marg past the **Monetary Museum** (*see left*) and left on to the hectic **Sir Pherozeshah Mehta Road**, lined with shops and stalls. From here dive left into the hawker-infested arcades along the pavements of **Dadabhai Naoroji Road** to **Flora Fountain** (*see p56*).

A Beatle in Bombay

The Mumbai Album.

At 10am on 9 January 1968, a long-haired Englishman walked into the Universal Building on Sir Pherozeshah Mehta Road in Fort (*see p54*) and bounded up the stairs to the third-floor HMV recording studio. He was George Harrison, in Mumbai to record a soundtrack for an avant-garde movie, *Wonderwall*, starring Jacqueline Bisset. The recording sessions lasted five days, with contributions from some of India's most outstanding classical musicians, including *santoor* player Pandit Shiv Kumar Sharma.

Universal Building remains but the recording studio was long ago replaced by an insurance office. Derek Taylor, press agent for the Beatles for most of the 1960s, later wrote in his notes for a reissue of the *Wonderwall* soundtrack what Harrison remembered of the Bombay recordings. 'I decided to do it as a mini-anthology of Indian music because I wanted to help turn the public on to Indian music,' Harrison told him. 'It was fantastic really. The studio is on top of the offices but there's no sound-proofing. So if you listen closely to some of the Indian tracks on the LP you can hear taxis going by.'

'Every time the office knocked off at 5.30pm we had to stop recording because you could just hear everybody stomping down the steps. I mixed everything as we did it there, and that was nice enough because you get spoiled working on eight and 16 tracks.' *Wonderwall* premiered in London on 20 January 1969, but never got a general distribution deal. However, some of the music Harrison recorded in Mumbai made it on to the B-side of 'Lady Madonna' as 'The Inner Light'.

Did you know that the world's smallest coins were panams from Kerala, with a diameter of less than 1/16th of an inch? If not, you need to educate yourself at the Reserve Bank of India's compact Monetary Museum, which offers a short, stimulating history of Indian money, from barter to credit cards. Crisp and informative text accompanies the displays, and colourful infographics deconstruct complex concepts for kids. It has an impressive collection of old Indian coins, and a thorough guide to spotting counterfeit notes.

FLORA FOUNTAIN

The hectic Flora Fountain intersection at the junction of Mahatma Gandhi Road, Dadabhai Naoroji Road and Veer Nariman Road is now officially known as Hutatma Chowk (Martyrs' Square), but locals still just call the area 'Fountain', referring to its central ornate fountain mounted with a statue of the Roman goddess Flora, carved from imported Portland stone and erected in 1864. Before that, this was the site of one of the three gates of the original Bombay Fort. There are several other public artworks nearby, including a statue of two martyrs with a flame built in memory of the 105 people shot dead here by police in 1960 during a protest for the creation of Maharashtra state (*see p27*). Commerce of all kinds keeps Fountain flowing; the streets are lined with the offices of the Hong Kong and Shanghai Banking Corporation, Standard Chartered Bank, the Central Bank of India and Bombay House, the corporate office of the Tatas, one of India's oldest and most respected business houses. Under Fountain's shaded pavement arcades hawkers peddle everything from second-hand books and T-shirts to bootleg software, Bollywood posters and cheap Chinese vibrators.

The façade of the **Pundole Art Gallery** (*see p150*) is faced with a mural of black horses by the renowned Mumbai artist MF Husain, but even more impressive artwork graces the frontage of the 1930s-built **New India Assurance Company Building**, which has a unique art deco-style depiction of rural Indian workers. Along Veer Nariman Road, just before Horniman Circle, stands **St Thomas' Cathedral** (*see right*), the first Anglican church in Mumbai, built in 1718. On Medows Street, which also runs into the Flora Fountain junction, stands the blue **St Stephen's Armenian Church**, originally built in 1876 for what was once the city's flourishing Armenian community, of whom just three members are left.

Further along Dadabhai Naoroji Road sits the JN Petit Library, which features rare stained glass depicting Parsi philanthropists of the late 1800s. Nearby is Khadi Bhandar (286 Dadabhai

Naoroji Road, 2207-3208), a handicraft store dedicated to Gandhi, selling handmade ornaments, furniture and traditional Indian clothes made from homespun cotton.

A little off Dadabhai Naoroji Road along Sir Pherozeshah Mehta Road is the **Universal Building**, where, in 1968, George Harrison spent five days recording a soundtrack for the avant-garde film *Wonderwall* with Indian classical musicians (*see left* **A Beatle in Bombay**).

There's a stark contrast between the crowded, tangled bylanes to the east of Dadabhai Naoroji Road and the smart, broad roads to the west. Its eastern flank is known as **Bazaar Gate**, a market area dating back to the early 18th century, when the British Fort enclosed the area. Its character hasn't changed much since then, with teeming alleys filled with shops, tailors, fruit stalls and the occasional massage parlour. The area is dominated by Gujarati Jains, and many of the buildings have Gujarati-style wooden balconies and awnings, now hidden under years of dirt. Clearer evidence of the longstanding Jain influence can be found on Maruti Lane at the 200-year-old **Shantinathji Jain Derasar**, a multi-coloured Jain temple with two stone guards manning its entrance.

The area of the city to the west of Dadabhai Naoroji Road was developed after the fort walls were demolished in the 1860s to make room for urban expansion. This area now has some of Mumbai's most exclusive schools and colleges, including **Cathedral and John Connon School**, **JB Petit High School for Girls** and the **Alexandra Girls' High School**. It's also home to **Siddhartha College**, set up by Dr BR Ambedkar, the architect of India's Constitution and a champion of the country's lower castes, revered by the city's Dalit community (*see p38* **Stuck in the Caste**).

FREE St Thomas' Cathedral

Veer Nariman Road, near Horniman Circle. **Open** 10am-5.30pm daily. **Services** 7am & 8.45am Sun. **Map** p253 H8.

The Churchgate area is so named because of this church, built in 1718 near one of the gates of Bombay Fort, where Flora Fountain now stands. It was the first Anglican church in Mumbai and contains memorials to British colonists, many of whom seemed to have died from malaria before the age of 30. The names include Katherine Kirkpatrick, mother of James Achilles Kirkpatrick, who scandalised colonial-era India by marrying Hyderabadi beauty Khair un-Nissa, and whose story is told in William Dalrymple's *White Mughals*. The church was recently restored to its former impressive state, which led to it winning the UNESCO Asia-Pacific Heritage Award in 2004.

NAGAR CHOWK

Dominating Nagar Chowk (meaning 'City Square' in Hindi) is the spectacular **Chhatrapati Shivaji Terminus** (*see below*), Mumbai's main railway station and still known to many as 'VT' for its old name, Victoria Terminus. This area marks the northern boundary of the old British Fort; the last remnant of the fort wall still stands behind the terminus near **St George's Hospital**, unmarked and hidden behind a public toilet around the corner from the **General Post Office**. Across from the terminus on the corner between Mahapalika Marg and Dadabhai Naoroji Road stands the grand headquarters of the **Municipal Corporation of Greater Mumbai** – first set up in 1872 to take care of the city's upkeep, now a byword for inefficiency and corruption. In front of the building stands a statue of Sir Pherozeshah Mehta, the Corporation's creator. The Corporation is the favourite punch bag of most local newspapers, one of which is right next door at the **Times of India Building**, built in 1903 and home to the world's largest-selling daily English-language paper. Down Marzban Road, past the Barista café, sits the ever-popular **Sterling Cinema** (*see p143*).

Next to the Sterling Cinema stands **Tata Palace**, once the residence of India's foremost business family, now the offices of Deutsche Bank, mounted with circular galleries, stone lion heads and mock classical columns in the form of Greek virgins. Nearby on Waudby Road stands the 135-year-old **Bombay Gymkhana**, once a whites-only colonial enclave, now a private sports and social club for the city's elite, not open to visitors. On the other side of Azad Maidan, opposite the gymkhana's front entrance on Mahatma Gandhi Road is the vibrant **Fashion Street** (*see p130*), an open-air clothes market selling piles of fake Levis and reject export clothing to college students.

Chhatrapati Shivaji Terminus

Nagar Chowk. **Open** 4.30am-1am daily. **Map** p253 H10.

If the central suburban railway line is Mumbai's main artery, then Chhatrapati Shivaji Terminus, built in 1808 and formerly known as Victoria Terminus, is its beating heart. Along with the western suburban railway line, which terminates at Churchgate (*see p51*), CST is the city's main transport hub and the busiest train station in Asia, with around three million people passing through on 1,350 suburban and intercity services every day. The building was designed by FW Stevens, who also designed the offices of the Municipal Corporation of Greater Mumbai facing the station. CST was declared a UNESCO World Heritage Site

Quay to Development

What does the future hold for Mumbai's docks?

For a port city, the docklands play a surprisingly minor role in Mumbai's daily life. The port, along with the mills, made Mumbai the economic powerhouse it is today. But whereas the mills are part of the city's daily routine – covered in glass and home to shopping malls – the docklands, on the other hand, remain largely off-limits to the public, despite making up one-eighth of the total area of the island city.

The docklands have long been considered the last chance for urban renewal within Mumbai, but their potential seems to elude many of those in control of city planning. They are owned and administered by the 134-year-old Mumbai Port Trust, which is the single largest holder of property in the Mumbai Metropolitan Region, with roughly 7.5 square kilometres of land stretching from Sassoon Dock in the south to Wadala in the north. Yet, port activity and infrastructure take up less than two square kilometres – essentially, 75 per cent of the Trust's land lies unused.

In 2007, the Port Trust mooted the idea of filling in two of the city's oldest docks, Victoria Dock and Prince's Dock, to construct a container terminal and boost the port's cargo traffic. The Mumbai Docklands Regeneration Forum, a non-governmental body, said the idea had 'little merit', citing the increased vehicular traffic that would run through the city, and the availability of ports on the mainland across the harbour. Instead, the Forum has suggested a regeneration of Mumbai's docklands along the lines of cities like London or Melbourne, where once down-and-dirty industrial areas are attempting to be entertainment, dining and recreational districts.

Given the government's apathy towards public space – a similar battle saw 2.4 square kilometres of defunct mill-lands in central Mumbai sold off to developers in the face of stiff public opposition – the Forum's suggestions seem idealistic at best. Still, the Port Trust seems occasionally willing to give the green light to some public projects: the possibility of an expressway over its land, say, or the idea of allowing ferry terminals along the eastern waterfront. If nothing else, at least Mumbaikars will finally get a chance to see an integral part of the city.

in 2004 for its blend of 'Victorian Italianate Gothic Revival architecture and Indian traditional buildings'. The ornate exterior is a jungle in stone, with a life-sized pair of lions guarding the doors to its administration offices, and peacocks, monkeys, owls, chameleons, rams, elephants and other beasts peering down on commuters from the façade. After the Taj Mahal in Agra, CST is the most photographed building in India. The terminus also houses a small gallery on the history of the Central Railway. The CST was also one of the terror targets on 26/11 (*see p28*).

► *Find out who Shivaji is; see p21.*

AROUND METRO

Mahapalika Marg is bordered by numerous Raj-era buildings and the sprawling **Azad Maidan**, or 'Freedom Ground', so named for being the site of many anti-colonial rallies during India's freedom struggle. It remains a popular site for political protests today. Past the Municipal Corporation headquarters is the **Presidency Magistrate's Court** (also known as Esplanade Court), which was completed in 1889, and the Gothic façade of the **Cama & Albless Hospital**, built in 1886. Ahead is **St Xavier's College**, established in 1891, now the city's best arts college. Around the corner of Lokmanya Tilak Marg is the **St Xavier's High School**, the courtyard of which displays a piece of a ship's propeller that landed here after an explosion in 1944.

The road ends at a square called **Dhobi Talao**, meaning 'Washerman's Pond' – once home to a community of workers who laundered the city's clothes in a lake that has long been filled in. The community now works at the Mahalaxmi **Dhobi Ghat** (*photo p62*). On the southern side of Dhobi Talao is the **Metro Adlabs cinema**, a landmark art deco cinema built in the 1930s and refurbished in 2006 (*see p144* **Metromorphosis**). It's so famous in the city that many locals call the area around it 'Metro' instead of Dhobi Talao. The cinema has been turned into a multiplex but it retains its original splendour.

On the corner between Girgaon Road and Kalbadevi Road is the triangular **Jer Mahal**, an early 19th-century *chawl* – one of the first examples of the tenements that were built to house the thousands of immigrants who came to Mumbai to work in its cotton mills, with one room for each family. Millions of Mumbaikars continue to live in *chawls*. Although dilapidated, Jer Mahal is more attractive than most, with ornate wooden balconies and trellises. The lanes north of Dhobi Talao – Girgaon Road, Kalbadevi Road and Lokmanya Tilak Marg – are densely packed with shops, particularly sports goods and music stores. Lokmanya Tilak Road leads up to Crawford Market.

CRAWFORD MARKET

Sculptures of vegetable vendors adorn the arched entrance to the noisy and colourful **Crawford Market**, the city's first municipal market, built in 1869 to sell what it still sells today – fresh fruit, vegetables, spices, meat, imported foodstuffs and, in the back, live animals. It takes its name from its creator, Arthur Crawford, Mumbai's first municipal commissioner, who later resigned in a scandal over the market's financial mismanagement. The first building in Bombay to be lit by electricity, the range of foods has recently increased as import tariffs have been slashed – California plums and Malta oranges now sit alongside Maharashtrian mangoes. There's an old sign asking visitors to only hire licensed porters but the wording is ambiguous and some porters like to suggest to foreigners that it's mandatory to hire them – it's not. Like so many of Mumbai's heritage buildings, Crawford Market is fraying at the edges, but Victorian touches survive intact, the most impressive being two elaborate fountains by J Lockwood Kipling, the father of Rudyard Kipling. Both have since been given a flamboyant multicoloured paintjob. From 1865 to 1875, Lockwood Kipling was the dean of the **Jamsetjee Jeejeebhoy School of Art**, close to the market on Dadabhai Naoroji Road. Established in 1857, it was the city's first art school and remains one of India's premier art colleges. Rudyard Kipling was born in a bungalow on the college campus in 1865 and spent his early childhood there.

A short walk through the crowded lanes across the road from Crawford Market is the pristine white **Jama Masjid** on Sheikh Memon Street. It's an unusual mosque, built on a pond of tranquil, green water that has been incorporated into the design. Don't miss the intricate mosaic work on the exquisite marble staircase. North on Sheikh Memon Street, is the **Moolji Jetha Cloth Market**, the oldest wholesale cotton market in Asia, built in 1881. It's a maze of 800 cotton shops, where shopkeepers and buyers lounge on white mattresses and pillows, negotiating the price of rolls of fabric over steaming glasses of *chai*.

MOHAMMED ALI ROAD

A warren of narrow interconnecting lanes spreads out on either side of Mohammed Ali Road, which bustles in the shadow of the JJ flyover for most of its length. The area is a commercial district dominated by the city's Muslim community, with numerous *dargahs* (tombs of saints), mosques and *burqa* shops along its length. A short distance up Mohammed Ali Road is the green-domed **Minara Masjid**, one of the city's oldest mosques, and closed to all but Muslim men. During Ramzan, or Ramadan, every year the lane next to the mosque turns into a hectic open-air barbecue in the evenings as thousands gather to break their fast. A narrow lane to the left of the **Jamsetjee Jeejeebhoy Hospital** and **Grant Medical College** up ahead leads to **Irani Masjid**, a beautiful mosque covered in a mosaic of blue tiles. Again, only Muslims are allowed to enter.

In the days of the Raj, Mohammed Ali Road was known, along with the Hindu-dominated Kalbadevi area nearby, as the 'Native Town'. The stark divide between the Hindu and Muslim communities is most evident at **Null Bazaar**, marked by a Hindu temple named **Gol Mandir**: to its west extends the Hindu colony, and to the east the Muslim precinct, extending to Mohammed Ali Road. Near the temple is the famous **Chor Bazaar**, which means 'Thieves' Market' (*see p132*), once a place for fencing stolen goods. Now it's a perfectly respectable place selling everything from recycled car parts to old Bollywood posters and gramophones.

INSIDE TRACK
CANINE CARVINGS

Mumbai has a lot of pup-culture. Several of the city's iconic monuments honour dogs in stone. The University of Mumbai library has a staircase with a carved stone dog newel post, and Esplanade House on Hazarimal Somani Marg in Fort is guarded by a St Bernard dog statue, erected in memory of a beloved pet of the Tata family. At the Chhatrapati Shivaji Terminus, dog gargoyles leap out from the building's main façade. Opposite, at the headquarters of the Brihanmumbai Municipal Corporation, there's a white statue of a dog on the north-side pediment. And at the entrance of Crawford Market, on Lockwood Kipling's plaque of a market scene, there's the image of a stray dog observing the market's hustle and bustle.

Wander down **Mutton Street** and you'll come across old coins and postcards, dog-eared film posters and magazines, antique porcelain and furniture, and much more. Be ready for some intense haggling.

BYCULLA

Byculla, at the end of Mohammed Ali Road, was uninhabitable until 1793, after the Great Breach at Mahalaxmi was sealed and a new road constructed. It became the city's first real suburb, settled by the British after venturing out from the overcrowded walled city of Fort. They built new streets, lined with spacious bungalows, and the first European social club, the Byculla Club, in 1833. The rural character of the suburb changed dramatically with the opening of the city's cotton mills in the late 19th century. Byculla became part of Girangaon, the so-called 'Village of Mills', and home to a large migrant population of mill workers. As the area became increasingly congested, the British moved out to Malabar Hill (*see p62*). Nowadays, more than a few residents complain that it has returned to its old uninhabitable state: the mills are closed but Byculla is horrifically crowded and choked with traffic. Reminders of quieter times linger on in the form of the imposing **Gloria Church**, near Byculla Station, and **Magen David Synagogue**, near the police colony. Now fallen into disrepair and with a small tree growing out of its clock tower, the synagogue was built in 1861 by the Sassoon family – a philanthropic business family from Baghdad – for the large Jewish community that once lived here. A little ahead in a large compound, hidden behind a tall stone wall, is the **Christ Church**, the city's second Anglican church (after St Thomas' Cathedral at Churchgate), built in 1833.

Past Shepherd Road, the Sir Jamsetji Jeejeebhoy Road splits at a Y-shaped flyover. Stuck below the forking roads is the **Khada Parsi**, or the 'Standing Parsi', a bronze statue of the Parsi businessman and philanthropist, Sir Cursetji Maneckji (1863-1943), mounted on a 4.5-metre plinth. The right-hand road leads to the splendid **Bhau Daji Lad Museum** (*see below*), which stands in the grounds of the **Veermata Jijabai Bhosale Udyan** (*see right*), a park and zoo.

★ Bhau Daji Lad Museum

Veermata Jijabai Bhonsale Udyan (city zoo), 91 Dr Ambedkar Road, Byculla (E) (6556-0394). Byculla station. **Taxi** Rani Bagh. **Open** 10am-5.30pm Thur-Tue. **Admission** R100; R 50 under-12s; free under-5s.

The Bhau Daji Lad Museum was built in 1872 and originally named the Victoria and Albert Museum. As its more famous counterpart did for the Empire, the museum was built to showcase Mumbai's industrial skills and craftsmanship. The building was recently restored to its original Renaissance Revival splendour with intricate iron pillars, ornate chandeliers, exquisite gold railings, and a dramatic painted ceiling. It won a UNESCO heritage award in 2005. Displays include models and maps of the city as it was in the late 19th and early 20th centuries, and 1,200 original glass negatives that include rare images of the gates of the old Fort.

Veermata Jijabai Bhosale Udyan (Byculla Zoo)

91 Dr Ambedkar Road (2374-2162). Byculla station. **Open** 9am-5.30pm Mon, Tue, Thur-Sun. **Admission** Rs 10 adults, Rs 5 children.

The Veermata Jijabai Bhonsle Udyan, or Byculla Zoo, has for years been a prime example of how not to run a zoo: unhappy animals caged in tiny enclosures, with little or no information provided for visitors. It's locally known as Rani Bagh, meaning 'Queen's Garden', after its original name, Victoria Gardens. Formerly a 19-hectare (48-acre) 'pleasure garden', it became a zoo in 1873. The types of animal on display have not changed much since then: leopards, elephants, deer, crocodiles, tigers and hippos – although llamas and kangaroos are no longer in residence. The animal enclosures are often more depressing than educational; instead, the zoo's best features are its gardens and winding pathways, which are littered with Raj-era artefacts, like an ancient basalt elephant that the British recovered in pieces from Elephanta Island (*see p71*) and placed here. The first animal you encounter on entering is King Edward VII's horse. The statue was made in 1877 by JE Boehm, Queen Victoria's favourite sculptor, and once stood at Kala Ghoda (*see p52*).

BHULESHWAR & KALBADEVI

It's said that the Hindu pantheon has about 330 million gods. At first glance, it seems that each one has a temple somewhere in the crowded lanes of **Bhuleshwar** and **Kalbadevi**. In fact, some locals believe that Bhuleshwar is so named because even the gods lose their way in the area's labyrinthine alleys: bhula means 'to forget' in Hindi, and ishwar means 'god'. But actually the name just comes from the **Bhuleshwar Temple**, which was built by a wealthy fisherman by the name of Bhula. If you are ready to brave heaving crowds, get lost in the weaving lanes, evade wandering cows and leap over puddles of mud, then the area offers a wealth of colourful Hindu temples. The biggest is the **Mumbadevi Temple** (see below), named after the same goddess that Mumbai is named for. There's also the fuchsia-pink **Dwarkadheesh Temple**, nicknamed Monkey Temple by the British for the row of monkey

Profile Naval Display

The Marine Museum.

Since time immemorial, Indian seafarers have weathered stormy seas to reach distant parts of the world. Perhaps as sweet revenge, you have to endure what seems like an equally arduous journey to learn of their tales at the city's **Marine Museum** (TS Rahaman, Nhava, Panvel, Raigad, 2721-2236, open 8.30am-5.30pm Mon, Wed-Sun). To get to Mumbai's only museum dedicated to seafarers, you have to brave the stench of Bombay duck at Ferry Wharf, clamber on to a ferry to Uran and bump along winding roads for well over an hour to reach Nhava.

The museum, inside the verdant, 22-acre campus of the Training Ship Rahaman, is a two-storey, heritage structure, with a lotus pond at the entrance. The Gothic-style bungalow was originally the residence of Bomanjee Harmusjee Wadia, a member of the famous family of shipbuilders. The Wadias handed over the building to the Yusufs, a seafaring family that owned the Bombay Steam Navigation Company, in 1888. The Yusufs initially used the building as a residence, then as an orphanage for the wards of seafarers. It was converted into a museum in 1912.

The ground floor describes the robust maritime activity on the western and southern coasts of India. A noteworthy display is an Ashokan edict in the Brahmi script, which establishes that Sopara (near present-day Nala Sopara) was once a thriving port and a noted Buddhist centre. Intricate replicas show the difference between fishing boats (or *machua*), dhows that carry cargo and passenger traffic, and warships like the *HMS Minden*, a Wadia-built ship aboard which Francis Scott Key wrote the American national anthem, 'The Star Spangled Banner'.

The first floor tells the story of Training Ship Rahaman (Training Ship not being a ship at all, but the moniker given to institutions that prepare officers and crew for the Merchant Navy, even if they're on land.) TS Rahaman has provided pre-sea training since 1912.

The second floor of the museum contains personal artefacts – from fraying Persian carpets to ornate furniture. From the displays, it appears that the museum was intended more to be a showcase of family heirlooms (including original china from the ships of the Bombay Steam Navigation Company) than a modern museum. Don't come expecting state-of-the-art displays and you won't be disappointed.

GETTING THERE

Once off the ferry at Uran, take an autorickshaw to Nhava.

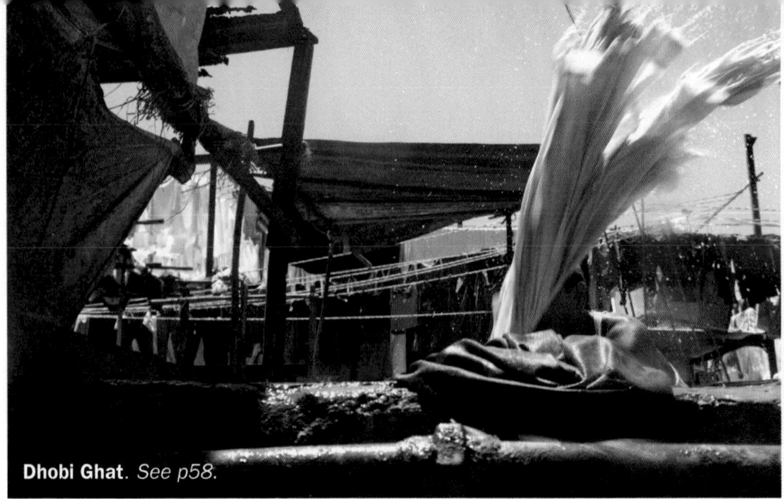

Dhobi Ghat. See p58.

statues across its façade; the **Ram Temple**, a one-stop shop for major gods, shared between Lord Ram, Ganesha, Maruti, Durga, Garuda, Vishnu, Laxmi and Hanuman; and the **Nar Narayan Temple**, where women peel peason the temple porch under delicate carvings depicting stories from Lord Krishna's boyhood (dancing on a serpent's head, flirting with milkmaids and stealing butter). All three temples stand close together on Kalbadevi Road. Apart from the temples, Kalbadevi is also home to numerous wadis (urban villages) with names like Gaiwadi (cow village) and Phanaswadi (jackfruit village).

The arched green doorway to the **Bombay Panjrapole** stands at the end of the Bhuleshwar Road behind a tight maze of stalls selling flowers, incense, coconuts, puffed rice, milk and other bric-a-brac used in temple rituals. Inside the Panjrapole are dozens of cows – sacred animals for Hindus – who graciously deign to eat the grass given to them by Hindu devotees. Bombay Panjrapole is run by a 170-year-old trust that operates five similar cow sanctuaries across the city.

FREE Mumbadevi Temple

Mumbadevi Road, near Zaveri Bazaar. CST station. **Taxi** Mumbadevi Temple. **Open** 5am-noon, 4-8pm daily. **Map** p255 G14.

If you should get lost searching for Mumbadevi Temple, look for long lines of flower-holding devotees snaking their way through the lanes and simply join them. Mumbadevi is the patron goddess of the Koli fisherfolk, the city's original inhabitants. The original temple stood at Azad Maidan near Nagar Chowk, but was demolished by the British along with a Roman Catholic church to make way for the city's expansion. The new temple was built in the 1830s and is one of the city's most popular. Generous devotees have provided the building with pure silver doors, while the walls teem with sculptures of vibrantly coloured gods and animals. Many temples have wishing wells, but Mumbadevi has wishing woodwork: devotees believe that the goddess will grant wishes if they embed a coin in the temple railings. The priests have recently banned the practice (it was wrecking the woodwork), but old coins still shine out from the beams.

MALABAR HILL

When you have the Governor of the state of Maharashtra as your neighbour, you know you're on the top rungs of Mumbai's lengthy social ladder. The upper-crust residents of **Malabar Hill** – sitting atop a green hillock at the end of Marine Drive – literally look down on the rest of the city. Until the early 1870s, the area was a dense jungle where British officers went fox hunting. But the coming of textile mills to once-posh Byculla (*see p60*) sent the British community scrambling for a new, unsullied suburb. The stretch between Malabar Hill and Worli is still speckled with British-era bungalows, though most have been demolished and replaced with high-rise apartment blocks.

The precinct of **Walkeshwar** at Malabar Hill is lined with temples and Gujarati-style homes that were rebuilt in the 18th century after being destroyed by the Portuguese the previous century. The largest temple is **Walkeshwar Temple**, dedicated to Lord Shiva, which was rebuilt in 1715. The *shivalingam* inside is made from sand, hence the name of the temple, which means 'sand god'. The district around the temple still has the feel of an older and slower Bombay, with doors to homes left open and women in colourful saris exchanging local gossip in the streets. Nearby is the holy lake, or 'tank' of **Banganga**, built sometime between the ninth and 13th centuries, and the oldest sacred Hindu site in the city. *Ban* means 'arrow' in Hindi and, according to legend, the water comes straight from the holy River Ganges some 1,600 kilometres (1,000 miles) away, brought forth by an arrow shot from the bow of Lord Rama. It's a place of rare serenity, with ducks gliding on the still, green waters and visitors relaxing on the worn basalt steps that lead down to them. Banganga usually becomes crowded in August, during the festival of Shravan, when Hindus come to pay their respects to deceased relatives by shaving their heads and purifying themselves in the tank.

There is also an unusual **Hindu graveyard** near the tank, notable because Hindus usually cremate their dead. But the Goswami community that lives here follows their own unique, centuries-old tradition of burying their dead in a sitting position. Men's graves are marked with a *shivalingam*, while the graves of women are marked with a footprint.

While most of Malabar Hill's greenery has been supplanted by concrete jungle, it still boasts one of the city's largest parks: **Kamala Nehru Park**, which provides a panoramic view of Marine Drive. Opposite the park are the **Hanging Gardens**, a spectacular viewpoint over Mumbai.

MAHALAXMI

Mahalaxmi, between Malabar Hill and Worli, takes its name from the **Mahalaxmi Temple** that stands here. It's an attractive temple, with bright exterior murals and carved wooden lintels. According to local folklore, Laxmi, the Hindu goddess of wealth, appeared in a dream to an engineer working on an ambitious land reclamation project to join the islands of Bombay and Worli in 1784. Laxmi revealed to him that an idol of her lay at the bottom of Worli Creek, which he recovered and later installed in a temple built on the reclaimed land. Close by is the spectacular **Haji Ali Dargah** (*photo below*), a beautiful shrine of white, windswept domes and minarets built on a tiny island off Worli Seaface, to a Muslim saint named Haji Ali. The causeway that connects the island to the mainland is lined with beggars and vendors selling toys and religious images.

Mahalaxmi is often referred to as the city's lungs, thanks to the greenery provided by the 26-hectare (64-acre) **Mahalaxmi Racecourse** (*see p165*), and the elite **Willingdon Sports Club**, which boasts Mumbai's oldest golf course. Both stand on either side of KK Marg, otherwise known as Racecourse Road. Entry to the uppity club, established in 1917, is restricted to members only, but the racecourse opens its 2,400-metre track to the public from November to May and is a popular walking spot. We recommend a quick visit to the **Mahalaxmi Dhobi Ghat**, on the left from the Mahalaxmi railway station exit, where over 200 *dhobis*, or laundrymen, wash clothes collected from local households in a maze of concrete wash pens. The *dhobis* then thrash the clothes on flogging stones, toss them into huge vats of boiling starch and hang them out to dry on long, criss-crossing clotheslines. It's a great place for taking photos and as such it's become a popular tourist attraction for foreign visitors, with a few vendors now selling trinkets and postcards on the bridge by the station. The whole thing is mystifying to locals, however, who wonder why foreigners should take so much interest in what they consider, essentially, an open-air laundromat.

Haji Ali Dargah.

Profile Fortified Walls

The Worli Fort.

Until recently, few Mumbaikars had ever seen Worli Fort, even if they'd actually heard about its existence. But since the Bandra-Worli Sealink bridge opened to traffic, tens of thousands of motorists approaching the bridge's southern end have been afforded an impressive aerial view of the square stone structure, perched at the end of a spit of land occupied by an ancient fishing village.

Looking westward from the battlements of the fort, the Sea Link dominates the skyline. But if you turn your back on the bridge, the traffic is inaudible. Enveloped by the smell of drying fish and the conversation of fishermen mending their nets, it's actually possible to imagine you're back in 1711, walking through Worli village with John Burnell, a sailor in the British navy. Burnell described Worli as 'the most airy point of land on the island' of Mumbai and was most appreciative of the views from the fort: 'You have a prospect of the ships sailing in the offing, the boats fishing in the Bay and opening of Mahem River.' Today the views remain impressive.

Worli Fort first finds mention in historical records in 1701, though the present structure seems to have been built perhaps a century or more later. When Burnell visited, it had a garrison of 12 soldiers who were supervised by a commanding officer.

Until 1910, the fort was used as a residence by junior officials of the Customs Department. Burnell noted that the men of Worli village went out fishing every day, while the women stayed home to sort, cure and dry the fish. That division of labour hasn't changed. But unlike in Burnell's day, when fishermen seldom returned empty-handed in the evening, catches off the Mumbai coast have been declining alarmingly. Still, that isn't immediately evident from the baskets of the women who sit at the street corners of Worli Koliwada, selling crabs, eels and mullet. In the distance, old men in white *kurtas* sing *kirtans* at the green-framed apavimochaneshwar temple. Someone beats a *dholak* and the whole neighbourhood seems to sway to a long-forgotten rhythm.

LOCATION
The Worli Fort is situated at the edge of Worli Koliwada, north of Worli seaface.

MARINE DRIVE & CHOWPATTY

Ask the average Mumbaikar where Netaji Subhash Chandra Bose Road is and he'll probably give you directions to Thane. Despite the change of name, Mumbai's most famous boulevard is still known as **Marine Drive** – a three-kilometre, palm-fringed arc sweeping along the western bay from the business district of Nariman Point to the wealthy enclave of Malabar Hill. For most Indians, Marine Drive is iconic shorthand for the city of Mumbai, made famous by appearances in numerous Bollywood films. The other unofficial name is the 'Queen's Necklace', coined by the British to describe the illuminated curve of the bayfront road at night. The seafront has a romantic, broad promenade that's a favourite walking and jogging spot. Marine Drive is lined with art deco buildings built in the 1920s and '30s, most of which are now in need of renovation. Still, this is Mumbai's most exclusive address. At the southern end stands the luxury **Oberoi hotel** (*see p83*), which was also one of the targets of the 26/11 terror attacks (*see p28*). Fabulous views of the bay and Marine Drive can be enjoyed over cocktails at the elegant **Dome** bar on the roof of the InterContinental Marine Drive hotel (*see p83*). The road extends past the lacklustre **Taraporevala Aquarium** and gymkhanas that host opulent weddings.

At the northern end of the promenade is the popular **Girgaum Chowpatty** (*chowpatty* means 'beach' in Marathi), a broad, curved beach where spectacular idols of the elephant-headed god Ganesha are immersed in the sea during the festival of Ganesh Chaturthi (*see p136*). The water is horribly polluted and people come to Girgaum Chowpatty only for a stroll on the sands, a head massage or the spicy snacks sold at the lines of stalls.

From Chowpatty, P Ramabai Marg runs north past Wilson College to **Mani Bhavan** (*see right*), once the Bombay home of Mahatma Gandhi, now a museum dedicated to his life. Nearby, at the western end of Laburnum Road is **August Kranti Maidan** (also known as Gowalia Tank) where Gandhi launched the Quit India movement on 8 August 1942, a mass movement that spread across India and brought British rule to an end five years later (*see p18*).

A little further ahead, past Chowpatty, Babulnath Marg leads to **Babulnath Temple**, dedicated to Lord Shiva and one of the city's holiest Hindu sites. The steps leading up to it are lined with traditional Gujarati houses for priests and temple employees. A short distance away on Hughes Road is the attractive **Khareghat Colony**, a Parsi housing complex. Behind the colony, higher up the hill, are the **Towers of Silence** – sprawling gardens that house a traditional Parsi funeral site, where bodies are left to be devoured by vultures. Rudyard Kipling, who spent his early childhood in Mumbai, once described finding severed human fingers near his house at the JJ School of Art (*see p51*); his mother believed they had been dropped by careless vultures returning from the Towers of Silence. Recently, the numbers of vultures have dramatically declined, and the traditional practice is under threat, but conservative members of the Parsi community refuse to consider any other means of disposing of their dead. The Towers are off-limits to non-Parsis, although visitors are allowed into the attractive gardens around it.

FREE ★ Mani Bhavan

19 Laburnum Road, off Ramabai Marg, Gamdevi (2380-5864, www.gandhi-manibhavan.org).
Open 9.30am-5.30pm daily.

Mani Bhavan was the home of the Mahatma (meaning 'Great Soul'), Mohandas Karamchand Gandhi, from 1917 to 1934, and the base for his civil disobedience movement that helped topple the British Empire in India. The museum contains many of his photographs, personal belongings and over 50,000 books and documents, including copies of his letters to figures such as Franklin D Roosevelt, Winston Churchill and Adolf Hitler. It also has a series of charming tableaux telling the story of Gandhi's life through clay models.

OPERA HOUSE

At the junction of Raja Ram Mohan Roy Road and Girgaum Road, the tranquil enclave of **Khotachiwadi** provides a snapshot of what much of Mumbai looked like before the coming of concrete. Once inhabited mainly by the East Indian community, it's a network of narrow, meandering lanes lined with pretty Portuguese-style bungalows with wooden porches, staircases, and balconies. Nowadays, the area's inhabitants are trying to hold out against pressure from developers to sell up.

The area around the junction of Girgaon Road and Sardar Vallabhbhai Patel Road is known as Opera House, after the once-magnificent **Royal Opera House** that stands on the crossroads. Built in 1925, the impressive frontage features neo-classical columns and elaborate sculpture-work of dancing figures playing musical instruments. The Opera House's timing was terrible, though – film was taking off and cinema became the city's great passion. It closed down to reopen as a cinema hall in the late 1930s, and ran for the next 60 years before shutting down in the 1990s. Now closed to the public, it has become dilapidated, with plants growing out of its crumbling stonework.

The Suburbs

Where Mumbai sleeps.

Like a tree that adds rings for each year of its growth, Mumbai's suburbs have grown organically, adding layer upon layer of humanity. Starting officially in Bandra, they were once farmland and forests, punctuated by villages or clusters of bungalows. No more. Today, the Western understanding of the word suburb has no place in Mumbai: there are no lawns and no backyards, no little semi-detached houses or cul de sacs; the suburbs are merely an extension of the city. This vast area is where most of Mumbai lives, and its sheer size ensures that the city's ever-present wealth contrast is visible here. So, while Bandra is a hit with the Bollywood set, Borivali, to the north, is home to a huge national park, in it yet another slum, one whose inhabitants occasionally fall prey to local leopards.

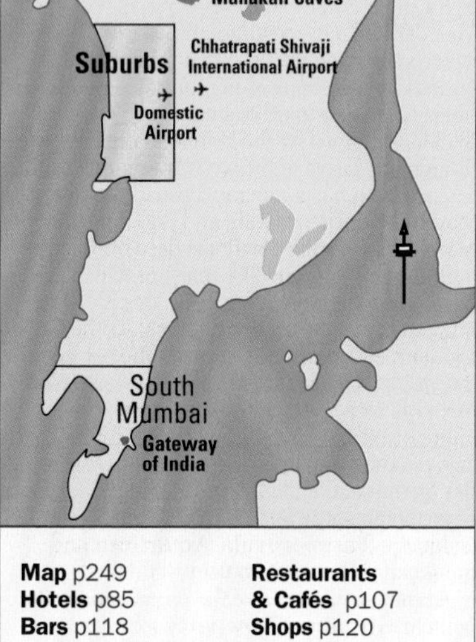

Map p249
Hotels p85
Bars p118
Restaurants & Cafés p107
Shops p120

SIGHTS

INTRODUCING THE SUBURBS

Because the buildings in the suburbs went up in an architectural era less interested in form than function, much of what you'll see here is none too pretty. Yet parts of it offer a hipper, younger, more chilled-out vibe than the south. Most notable among these is Bandra, home to Bollywood stars, bars, restaurants and hidden villages (*see p70* **Village Life**) and young professionals with money to burn. Also worth the trek are Goregaon and Borivali for their acres of greenery. Many sights close on public holidays so ring ahead to check.

DADAR

Though not technically a suburb, we have included the mid-town neighbourhood of Dadar in this section. Dadar station is a 25-minute train ride north from both Churchgate Terminus and Chhatrapati Shivaji Terminus. It was once an area for rice farming and became one of the first suburbs to be developed under the City Improvement Trust set up by the British after the city's bubonic plague outbreak and subsequent famine of the late 19th century. It's now a crowded and hectic heartland for the city's Maharashtrian community and site of the headquarters of the Shiv Sena, a right-wing nativist political party. If you go by train, you'll find a thriving and chaotic produce market as soon as you step out of the station on the west. But Dadar's greatest charm, a short taxi ride from the station, is **Shivaji Park**, a nearly three-hectare expanse of lawns that has been the training ground for some of India's greatest cricketers, including Sachin Tendulkar. It was created in 1925 by the British who, unusually for them, named it after the 17th-century Maratha warrior king Chhatrapati Shivaji, a hero to the Maharashtrian people (*see p21* **Who Is Shivaji, Anyway?**). The park became an important venue for political rallies in the Indian freedom struggle and, after 1947, a focal point for the Samyukta Maharashtra movement, which sought and finally won the creation of Maharashtra state. The park still plays host to scores of overlapping cricket games as well as giant rallies for the Shiv Sena and other political parties. Across from the park, off Swatantrya Veer Savarkar Marg, is the **Mayor's Bungalow**, an attractive colonial home closed to visitors. The mayor holds a merely decorative post in Mumbai and several mayors have complained about the poor state of the bungalow's interior; so much so that one even threatened to move into the zoo at Byculla.

BANDRA

Once a sleepy collection of mostly Roman Catholic hamlets (*see p70* **Village Life**) dismissed as parochial by the sophisticates who lived in the city to its south, Bandra has recently morphed into Mumbai's hottest area. Flat prices have skyrocketed from around Rs 50,000 per square metre ten years ago to current highs of around Rs 180,000 per square metre, and rural charm has been displaced by urban cool. A large part of Bandra's success is down to its location: it occupies a sweet spot between the south of the city and the new business districts in the north, with the sprawling business hub of the Bandra-Kurla Complex on its doorstep. There's something here for everyone: a tradition of communal tolerance that draws the Muslim community; the gravitational pull of movie-star glamour for hipsters, models and wannabe actors; and a diversity of restaurants, smart bars and nightclubs for young well-paid professionals. In a choking city, what once made it parochial is now part of its charm: tree-lined roads and public spaces like Jogger's Park, **Land's End** and the Carter Road Promenade.

But Bandra has been so successful that its appeal is beginning to eat itself; the new landscape of glass and aluminium-clad towers has little to do with the balconies and verandas of the old Bandra. Traffic and pollution levels are spiralling, with Bandra now claiming some of the worst air quality in the city. However, Bandrawallahs take some comfort from their tradition of civic pride – a rarity in Mumbai. Determined citizens greatly enhanced the suburb's charms with the restoration of Land's End, a small peninsula leading to the **Bandra Fort**. Named Castella de Aguada by the Portuguese, who built the fort in 1640, it was equipped with cannons to protect shipping routes and supplied fresh water from a nearby spring to trading vessels on their way to Goa or Vasai. The area behind the fort has been landscaped with palm trees and an attractive stone amphitheatre. Not far away, **Carter Road** was similarly restored with a promenade along the seafront. Local kids tend to race up and down the stretch and the other side of the street is a popular spot for teenagers to hang around, chat and smoke pot. At the end of Carter Road is Road No. 5, better known as just 'Off Carter Road' – a lively strip of shops and restaurants with tables out on the street.

Bandra has numerous churches, the most important of which is the **Basilica of Mount Mary**, on the hill along Mount Mary Road. A popular church, it brings thousands of devotees from across the city during the Mount Mary Fair in September. The original chapel was

INSIDE TRACK
DADAR FOR KIDS

If you are in Dadar with your family, head to Sant Dnyaneshwar Udyan and Baji Brabhu Udyan, two parks that offer a spectacular view of the sea and have separate kid's play areas. The parks, which have been recently spruced up, are opposite Shivaji Park, next to the Mayor's Bungalow.

Bandra.

Bandra-Worli Sealink.

built in 1640 and destroyed in a Maratha raid in 1738. The life-sized statue of the Virgin Mary was rescued from the sea by fishermen and housed in the attractive Portuguese-style **St Andrew's Church** on Hill Road while a new church was being built. It was returned in 1761. Until around 30 years ago, this was Bandra's highest point, visible from Mahim Beach. Also on Hill Road, **St Peter's Church** has some interesting frescoes and stained glass.

Many of the crosses that dot Bandra's streets are 'plague crosses', built around the turn of the 19th century as bubonic plague swept across the city, killing hundreds of thousands. Bandra residents built crosses near their homes, both to seek protection from the pestilence and later in gratitude for their survival. Crosses were also built to ward off evil spirits and simply to mark property boundaries. Among Bandra's oldest streetside crosses is the wooden one that stands at the junction of Bazaar Road, Chapel Road and Waroda Road, which dates back to 1698. Chapel Road eventually leads to **Bandra Reclamation**, which has a charming promenade that runs along the Mahim Creek and has a view of the city skyline. The dominating feature in the skyline now, however, is the **Bandra-Worli Sealink** bridge.

INSIDE TRACK SPLENDID HEIGHTS

The city's highest point is not one of its towers but in fact the top of the 486-metre (1,595 ft) Jambulmal hill, inside the **Sanjay Gandhi National Park** (*see p70*). Located within a restricted section of the park (the hilltop also houses the Kanheri Hills Air Force station), Jambulmal Point makes a mockery of Mumbai's race to build taller and taller skyscrapers – it beats Mahalaxmi's 48-storey Planet Godrej, one of Mumbai's biggest, by a good 300 metres and has the added advantage of being prettier.

ANDHERI

One of the city's busiest suburbs, Andheri is packed with malls, industrial estates and high rises. While the suburb has become a breeding ground for new restaurants and nightclubs, in terms of excursions it has little to offer. One of its most obvious landmarks is **Gilbert Hill** – it looms on the right side of the road when you're travelling from South Mumbai towards Andheri – but few Mumbaikars would know its name. Composed of vertical columns of basalt, Gilbert Hill stands 60 metres (197 feet) tall. The black basalt, the result of a volcanic eruption at the end of the Mesozoic era, is estimated to be about 65 million years old. Scaling old Gilbert isn't easy, but for the devout there's an incentive – a Durga temple on top.

GOREGAON

Goregaon was a pretty tree-lined village until as late as the 1970s, before being turned into yet another noxious concrete mess. Respite remains, though, in the sprawling greenery of the **Aarey Milk Colony**, a dairy farming area with jungle-crested hills. It takes around 15 minutes to get here by autorickshaw from Goregaon station, which is about an hour's ride on the train from Churchgate. The Aarey Garden Restaurant (2685-9562, open 11am-11.30pm daily), next to the central dairy, is popular with locals for alfresco dining amid the greenery and for its BYOB policy. The milk colony is also home to **Goregaon Film City**, on the Film City Road; a major studio built in 1978 on what was rural scrubland. Officially no visitors are allowed in, but if you're really keen to enter, the gate watchmen may be persuaded with a big smile and a little largesse. You could also get inside by being cast as an extra in a Bollywood movie (*see p44* **You Too Can Be a Star**). Much like its Hollywood equivalents, Film City tends to be a little surreal, with leftovers from sets scattered about, like the staircase that leads nowhere, along with a Hindu temple and helipad.

Local Heroes

Want to get to the heart of Mumbai? Get the train.

Whether it's floods, riots or bombs, Mumbaikars have a single litmus test for the state of their city: 'Are the trains working?' On 11 July 2006, when bombs exploded in the first-class compartments of seven trains along the Western Line during the evening rush hour, Mumbai ground to a halt – but only for a few hours. Services were up and running again the same night.

Mumbaikars spend large chunks of their lives on commuter trains, known as 'locals'. They talk of 'train friends', regular co-commuters with whom they sing songs, exchange life stories and who, most importantly, will 'catch place' for them – reserve them a seat, hopefully in the sweet spots. In the morning, the best seats are on the west side, facing south for the breeze; in the evening, it's the east side.

Local trains have two classes: first class has padded seats; second class has wooden benches. They are almost equally crowded, but those who can afford it will shell out up to ten times the price of a second-class ticket for the unwritten rules: three to a bench in first, four to a bench in second; four at the door in first, six or seven in second.

The well-used ladies-only compartment is filled with women cleaning vegetables and rehashing old arguments about the rival merits of tailors. The 'general compartment' is mainly used by men, and where *bhajans* (religious songs) are sung, *prasad* ('blessed' food) is doled out and card games are played.

The compartments are scoured by vendors hawking everything from peanuts to fake moustaches. Urchins run through with brushes, sweeping the dirt on to the tracks before asking for tips.

The crush of train compartments during rush hours, between 9am and 11am and again between 6 and 9pm, defies description. Sardines have it easy. Around ten per cent of passengers during these hours aren't even in the train – you'll see them hanging out of the sides, courting death by trackside pole. Some young men even climb on to the roof, partly because the train's too crowded, partly out of sheer bravado. Inside, passengers have to start pushing their way to the door one stop before their station – any later and they'll never make it out in time. The rest of the day, though, there isn't a quicker, more efficient way of getting around Mumbai. But for the real deal, travel during peak hours. It's not exactly relaxing but you'll have bragging rights for life.

SIGHTS

BORIVALI

There's only one reason to come this far north: the **Sanjay Gandhi National Park** (Borivali, 2886-0389, open 7.30am-6.30pm Tue-Sun, admission Rs 20), one of Asia's busiest national parks. Mumbaikars come here to escape the city, get lost in the greenery with lovers, play cricket, eat vast picnics and just cool off – the temperature here is about four degrees cooler than the city's average. And at 103 square kilometres (40 square miles), it won't be crowded. The nearest station is Borivali, about an hour and 15 minutes on the train from Churchgate. From there, it's around Rs 25 in an autorickshaw to the main entrance. To the west lie the neighbourhoods of Goregaon, Malad, Kandivali, Borivali and Dahisar; and Bhandup and Mulund to the east. In recent years, the park has been encroached by numerous slum dwellings, which is not only bad for the park but also for the slum-dwellers – leopards have been known to mistake children for prey.

The park's two lakes – Vihar and Tulsi – supply Mumbai with water. The park's forest is a mix of deciduous and semi-evergreen and contains a great diversity of wildlife, including tigers, leopards, lions, pythons, cobras, spotted deer, black-naped hares, barking deer, porcupines and around 5,000 different kinds of insect. There are also crocodiles in **Tulsi Lake** (swimming, unsurprisngly, is not encouraged). The park is also home to 150 species of butterfly and the world's largest moth, the Atlas, which was discovered here. There is also a Tiger and Lion safari bus tour that departs regularly from the orientation centre around 750 metres from the main entrance (orientation centre, 2886-0362, Rs 30 for a 10 min tour, tours every 20 mins during park hours).

Also in the park are the **Kanheri Caves**, a total of 109 caves in which remarkable halls have been carved out of the rock and ornate statues and images of Buddha and the Boddhisattvas sculpted from the walls. The caves are located about 450 yards (1,345 feet) above sea level and command a panoramic view of the forest surroundings and the Arabian Sea in the distance. They date back to the Mauryan and Kushan Empires of the first century BC, although the carving continued well into the ninth century AD. Outside Cave No.3 are two 18-metre (60-foot) statues of Buddha that date back to the sixth century AD. Inscriptions found in the caves refer to the area as Krishnagiri, Krishnasila, Kanhasila or Kanhagiri. Archaeologists believe that the caves began to be permanent residences for Buddhist monks in the first century AD.

Village Life

Exploring Bandra's neighbourhoods.

Two generations ago, Bandra was made up of villages, expansive bungalows, farmland and the occasional two-storey apartment 'tower'. As late as 1960, large parts of it were wooded, and even in the '70s school children could knock on the front doors of unknown houses and come out with cake and biscuits. Today, it's a concrete jungle, but there are still pockets where the village feel has survived.

The area surrounding **Mount Mary Church** (*see p67*) is one of Bandra's oldest neighbourhoods. Walk through the compound to the Mount Mary steps at the back and down to the foot of the hill. From there, go down Chapel Road to **Ranwar Village**, where local-style Christian family cottages and new high-rises stand around the village square. The areas around Waroda Road and Veronica Road are filled with little lanes that are a joy to explore.

Further north, past the cluster of restaurants, gyms and boutiques, is **Pali Village**, which takes its name from the Portuguese port of Pallem. Here, the labyrinth of villas is punctuated by modest apartment buildings, often housing different generations of the same family. It's reached via the lane behind Toto's Garage Pub (*see p119*).

Running parallel to the Carter Road seafront is Sherly Rajan Road, which gets its name from the adjacent villages of **Sherli** and **Rajan**. While educational complexes and swanky buildings now dominate the area, local communities continue to survive. The street still retains its quiet suburban charm thanks to its out-of-the-way location and the fact that it's an inconvenient thoroughfare.

At the northern end of Carter Road is **Chuim**, near the Koli settlements at Khar Danda (and technically out of Bandra's postcode). Perhaps the quietest of the villages, Chuim is no more than a one-lane village, with alleyways branching out in labyrinthine patterns from the main street.

Day Trips

Easy escapes from the hustle and bustle.

As you'll see through this book, Mumbai's attractions are many, and you're unlikely to get bored here. But as one of the world's most chaotic cities, you are likely to get a little flustered. So, after you've had your fill of city buzz, do as locals do and get out of town. Head to the ancient caves of Elephanta Island, cool off at the hill station of Matheran or go and explore the crumbling, romantic Vasai Fort. Or, if historical and spiritual relics don't tempt, unwind with a glass of shiraz at one of India's prime vineyards in Nashik.

ELEPHANTA ISLAND

Around the seventh century AD, a prince of the Chalukya Dynasty – a political dynasty that ruled large parts of the western and southern regions of India – is said to have constructed the breathtaking cave temples at Gharapuri, a small island about 11 kilometres north-east of the Gateway of India now called Elephanta (admission Rs 250 foreigners, Rs 10 Indians, closed Mon). A trip there and back takes at least four hours, but it's more than worth it. There's even a bar near the caves if you get thirsty.

Indian temples had always been built by erecting base pillars and then laying plinths on top to support the roof, but in Maharashtra the brittle volcanic stone plinths kept breaking. At Gharapuri, the ancients decided that the only way to get round the problem was to find a large chunk of stone and chisel away anything that didn't look like a temple.

When the island was rediscovered (and renamed) in the 16th century by the Portuguese, they saw an elephant waiting for them as they approached the island. It turned out to be made of basalt, the first clue that the island was home to something remarkable. Intrigued, they decided to take it home with them, but ended up dropping it into the sea. Many years later the British recovered it and carried it back to the mainland, where it now sits at the Byculla Zoo, or Veermata Jijabai Bhosale Udyan; *see p60.*

The triple-bayed entrance to the cave doesn't look that impressive but, once inside, everyone from André Malraux to Auguste Rodin has been struck dumb by the sheer spectacle of Sadashiva ('Eternal Shiva'), a full-relief bust about six metres high, showing three faces of Lord Shiva.

The central image is one of serene contemplation; the left half-face is the face of Aghora Bhairava, the vengeful, angry Shiva; the right one is Uma, or Vamadeva, the feminine side of this complex god. Some have suggested that a fourth face remains buried in the rock.

The temple sprawls across about 5,580 square metres (60,000sq ft), with ornate pillars and exquisitely carved sculptures, many of which have been badly damaged. Demonstrating the kind of barbarism that they repeated in Goa, the Portuguese used the caves as a firing range. They must have been not only blind to beauty but hard of hearing, too; the echoes would have been deafening. It's possible to wander up to the top of the natural rock mass to see one of the old cannons. There are also a couple of villages on the island but nothing of much interest to visitors. A word of warning: don't be tempted to eat anywhere near the monkeys who populate the island; they're a rapacious bunch and have been known to pounce aggressively on visitors with food. Some locals will encourage you to take photographs of them; they will expect a tip.

Getting there

Boats to Elephanta depart every half-hour from the Gateway of India from 9am until 2.30pm and cost Rs 100-Rs 120. The journey takes about an hour. The last ferry leaves Elephanta for the Gateway around 5pm. There's nowhere to stay overnight on the island, so don't miss it.

JUHU BEACH

For those with kids in tow, Juhu beach, Mumbai's very own Coney Island, is hard to beat. Unless an ear infection is top of your take-home list swimming isn't advised, but that doesn't mean there aren't plenty of activities, including parasailing, to enjoy. It's packed at the weekends.

Getting there

For details of how to get there, *see p141*.

MATHERAN

Matheran is a hill station 109 kilometres (68 miles) from Mumbai – a small township established by British colonists to escape the city's humid summers. It's still a favourite day and weekend getaway for Mumbaikars for precisely the same reason. Once a quiet, wooded place filled with bungalows, these days it's a haven for commercial tourism, filled with restaurants and ice-cream parlours. But much of its charm has been preserved, due partly to its traditional community of cobblers, who still produce leather shoes, but largely thanks to a wise decision to ban motor vehicles from its broad streets; horses are a common way of getting around here, and you'll see them tied up Wild West-style outside restaurants. The British also built a narrow-gauge train from Neral – the so-called toy train – that curved its way up and down the hill until it was wiped out by terrible flooding in July 2005. The track has since been repaired (see below). The main thing to do in Matheran is to go walking into the woods along its red laterite paths and take in the spectacular views of forested hills and valleys from viewpoints like Panorama Point, Echo Point and Monkey Point – all of which live up to their names. There's a Rs 25 fee to enter the hill station.

Getting there

The nearest station is Neral, 88 kilometres (55 miles) from Chhatrapati Shivaji Terminus and 21 kilometres (13 miles) from Matheran. Return tickets cost Rs 125 for second class and Rs 400 for first class. The old narrow-gauge train up is a fun way to go and costs Rs 25. You can also hike it or take a taxi. If you opt for the latter, negotiate the price – around Rs 75-Rs 100 per head is reasonable.

VASAI FORT

At its peak in the 17th century, Vasai was known as Bassein, a jewel in the Portuguese crown. It boasted impressive public buildings, private mansions, soaring churches and an imposing seafacing fort. In 1557, it was the birthplace of India's only Catholic saint, Gonsalo Garcia, who sailed to Japan as a missionary. He was later accused of plotting to overthrow the Emperor Taiko-sama and crucified on a hill in Nagasaki. The Vatican declared him a saint in 1862. Today, the walls

Juhu Beach.

of Bassein Fort still stand, sprawled across 46 hectares (110 acres), although none of the buildings are completely intact. It's a romantic spot of collapsing arches and decrepit belfries, half-overrun with forest. Still standing is the seaward entrance, the Porto da Mar, an iron-clad gateway that resolutely thwarted attackers over the years. Today, it's scrawled with boasts of other conquests, like 'Sunil loves Sunita'. Nearby, there's a shop with snacks and drinks.

Getting there

Trains to Vasai leave from Churchgate with Virar as their final destination. The first train leaves at 4.15am and takes an hour and a half to reach Vasai Road, the fifth stop after Borivali. The return fare is Rs 26 for second class, or Rs 300 for first class. The fort is 30 minutes from the station by rickshaw and costs around Rs 20. The last train from Vasai Road leaves for Churchgate at 12.05am. By road, it's 76km (47 miles) from South Mumbai along the Mumbai–Ahmedabad highway via Borivali, taking two to three hours depending on traffic.

WINE TASTING IN NASHIK

Sula Wine Tasting Centre

Gate No. 35/2, Govardhan, Gangapur-Savargaon Road, Nashik (0253-223-1663).
Open 11am-11.30pm daily.
Located about 175 kilometres (110 miles) from Mumbai, Nashik has become Maharashtra's own Napa Valley: it's home to the vineyards of Sula Wines, one of India's leading brands. The vineyard was set up in 1997 on 12 hectares (30 acres) and released its first wines three years later – sauvignons and chenin blancs. Eight years later, it's expanded to 162 hectares (400 acres), growing shiraz, zinfandel and merlot varieties. Sula has opened a wine tasting centre and offers tours of the vineyard, taking visitors through the wine-making process. You can taste the wines and then drink much more of them in the impressive tasting room – an elegant 186sq m (2,000sq ft) wine bar, with a beautiful balcony overlooking the vineyards. There are also tours of the winery every hour on the hour from 11.30am to 5.30pm. It's a long way back to Mumbai – about four hours by train – but after a few glasses it'll go in a flash.

Getting there

The first train for Nashik leaves at 6.10am from Chhatrapati Shivaji Terminus – you'll have to catch this one to make it there and back in one day. Return fares for seats in the relatively comfortable AC chair car cost Rs 520. Get off at Nashik Road station and take a cab to Gangapur Road for around Rs 400-Rs 450. The last train back to CST leaves Nashik Road at 6pm. By road, Nashik is about 175km (110 miles) and takes about three hours. Check the Sula website (www.sulawines.com) for detailed directions and a road map. Organised tours of the winery are available from Tulleeho (99307-44437,www.tulleeho.com), which offers customised packages.

Juhu Beach.

Consume

Dome. *See p117.*

Hotels

Plenty of room for all budgets.

Ever since the Indian economy managed to get itself some good press and the nation became one of a billion consumers rather than one of the world's most desperately poor, it seems like everybody wants a piece of the country. Whether it's business travellers or independent explorers, the crowds are pouring in and hotels in Mumbai have mushroomed to accommodate them.

But for tourists, the results of the hospitality boom have been mixed, as prices have shot up. South Mumbai, particularly around Colaba, Marine Drive and Churchgate, is the first choice of most foreign travellers, but you won't find yourselves spoiled for choice nor will you find rooms as cheap as you might expect. The explosion of hotels has been at the top end and the boutique hotel is still almost unknown in Mumbai, with the refreshing exception of the Gordon House Hotel, which single-handedly fills the gaping hole in Mumbai's hotel offerings between high-end and moderate.

The hotel landscape is dominated by luxury five-stars, charging a minimum of around Rs14,000-Rs18,000 for a double room, with the top choice being the century-old Taj Mahal Palace (see right), perched next to the Gateway of India and the harbour. The five-stars aren't just for tourists or foreign businessmen; these hotels have always played an important role in the city's social life, providing restaurants, bars, nightclubs, shopping and private party venues for Mumbai's wealthiest. Room rates at cheaper places vary from budget (up to Rs 2,000) to moderate (Rs 6,000). We haven't listed anything that isn't scrupulously clean and decently maintained, but be prepared for hotels that are often a little rough around the edges.

INFORMATION AND BOOKING

We've included some Bandra and Khar hotels for those who want to step outside of the mainstream into the Bandra suburb, which has rapidly morphed into the city's hottest shopping and partying destination. We've also listed some hotels close to the airport in Juhu and Andheri for those on brief stopovers. With high demand for rooms across the city, it's imperative to book ahead, especially if you're visiting in the peak winter season. The simplest way is to book via the web – even the cheapest hotels have their own websites.

INSIDE TRACK COMPLIMENTARY EXTRAS

Breakfast is often included at the cheaper hotels, and many of the hotels in Juhu and Andheri offer a complimentary airport pick-up and drop-off.

PRICES AND CLASSIFICATION

We don't list official star ratings, which tend to reflect facilities rather than quality; instead we've classified hotels within each area according to the price of a double room per night, beginning with the most expensive. All of the rates we've included are for rooms with air-conditioning and attached bathrooms. Some of the cheaper hotels also offer rooms without these facilities for cheaper rates.

Some hotels sneakily quote prices exclusive of the ten per cent sales tax. Always check. We've included the tax in the rates listed here, but room prices change frequently, so please make sure you verify before you book.

FACILITIES AND ACCESSIBILITY

In this chapter, we've listed the main services offered by the hotel. Concierges can often

Gordon House Hotel.

arrange far more than listed here, including restaurant reservations, dry cleaning and minor clothes repairs. We've also listed which hotels offer rooms adapted for disabled customers, but these vary and it's always best to ring ahead to confirm the precise facilities.

COLABA

Deluxe

★ Taj Mahal Palace & Tower

Apollo Bunder (6665-3366, www.tajhotels.com). CST or Churchgate stations. **Rates** Rs14,500-Rs 31,000 double. **Credit** AmEx, DC, MC, V. **Map** p250 G5 ❶

Mumbai's most famous, oldest and most beautiful hotel, and an integral part of the city's social scene.

Bars (2). Business centre. Concierge. Disabled-adapted rooms. Gym. Internet (wireless). No smoking rooms. Parking. Pool (outdoor). Restaurants (7). Room service. Spa. TV.

▶ *See p79 Crowning glory.*

Expensive

Fariyas Hotel

25 Off Arthur Bunder Road, (2204-2911, www.fariyas.com). CST or Churchgate stations. **Rates** Rs10,000-Rs12,000 double. **Credit** AmEx, DC, MC, V. **Map** p251 G3 ❷

There's not much to distinguish this standard 1970s-built, ten-floor five-star aimed at business travellers, although it does fill a useful mid-range gap in Colaba between the Taj Mahal and the cheap hotels that feed on its scraps. Rooms are neat, standard and serviceable, although rather on the small side – as are the pool and really rather tiny gym. Despite space constraints, it's managed to pack in a perfectly decent sauna and steam room, accessed via a maze-like staircase. The position on a street off Apollo Bunder means that only the corner rooms get a slice of sea view, with north-side rooms getting a view of the Colaba skyline instead.

Bar. Business centre. Gym. Internet (wireless). Parking. Pool. Restaurant. Room service. TV.

★ Gordon House Hotel

5 Battery Street, Apollo Bunder (2287-1122,www.ghhotel.com). CST or Churchgate stations. **Rates** Rs11,000 single, Rs12,000 double. **Credit** AmEx, MC, V. **Map** p250 G5 ❸

India seems to have missed the boutique hotel boom that has hit every other major world city, and, as such, Mumbai still needs more hotels like the Gordon House, which offers a modern, stylish alternative to the standard five-stars at a competitive price. Smart, cool and beautifully designed, the courtyard atrium at its heart is a sanctuary of calming pine wood, wheatgrain tiles and soothing blues and whites under a high glass roof. Rooms on each of the three floors are themed: vibrant colours and smooth tiles on the 'Mediterranean' floor, cool blues and light woods on the 'Scandinavian' floor, and a homey, warm feel on the 'Country' floor. There's no gym on site, but a Bullworker is provided in each room, and internet access is free. This is a very popular hotel and there are just 29 rooms, so it's definitely worth booking well in advance.

Bar. Business centre. Concierge. Free parking. Internet (dial-up/wireless). Restaurants (2). Room service. TV.

Moderate

★ Ascot Hotel

38 Garden Road (6638 5566, www.ascothotel.com). CST or Churchgate stations. **Rates** Rs6,600 double. **Credit** MC, V. **Map** p251 G4 ❹

The Ascot is a little gem: not quite a boutique hotel, but easily superior to most hotels in the same price range, including all of the neighbouring hotels on Garden Road. It resides in a charming 1930s building remodelled from top to bottom inside to create a smart, contemporary hotel with ample use of light wood floors, mirrors and glass, and a soft, cream colour palette. Rooms are spacious and airy – most have flat-screen TVs, some have DVD players – and staff are friendly and efficient.

Bar. Internet (wireless). Restaurant. Room service. TV.

Garden Hotel

42 Garden Road (2284-1476/2283-1330, www.hotelgarden.co.in). CST or Churchgate stations. **Rates** Rs4,735-Rs6,121 double. **Credit** AmEx, MC, V. **Map** p251 G4 ❺

The Garden Hotel looks almost identical to its next-door neighbour, the Godwin; both are glass-and-concrete towers built in the 1970s on a street full of old Colaba buildings from the 1930s and '40s. Inside is not much better, with a breathtakingly ugly 3-metre waterfall in the lobby made of plastic climbing plants and artificial tree stumps. Still, the rooms are clean and the staff friendly; overall, a cheap and serviceable option for bedding down for the night.

Internet (shared). Room service. TV.

Hotel Godwin

41 Garden Road, Colaba (2284-1226/2287-2050). CST or Churchgate stations. **Rates** Rs5,890 - Rs6550 double. **Credit** MC, V. **Map** p251 G4 ❻

A 1970s-built concrete tower similar in external appearance to the Garden Hotel, but a superior option, with smarter decor and a large ninth-floor terrace offering sweeping views of Colaba, complete with plant pots and plaster pillars wrapped with rope lights. A front-facing room is the best choice, with large windows displaying views of the dome of the nearby Taj Mahal hotel. The suites can sleep five people, six if you request an extra mattress for the floor. The rooms are nothing to get excited about but are spacious, neat and clean, and only slightly marred by the tatty red sofas and dusty plastic chandeliers.

Room service. TV.

Sea Palace Hotel

26 PJ Ramchandani Marg, Apollo Bunder (6112-8000/2285-4404,www.seapalacehotel.net). CST or Churchgate stations. **Rates** Rs4,950-Rs7,150 double. **Credit** AmEx, MC, V. **Map** p251 G4 ❼

The best feature of the Sea Palace is its location: right on the peaceful waterfront road about ten minutes' walk from the Taj Mahal hotel, with perfect views of the harbour. It's well worth shelling out for the most expensive rooms, which have seafacing views; open the window and you can lean out and gaze at the Gateway of India. Rooms are plain and simple, and you have to go for a 'deluxe' double for decent furnishings – smart beds, lime-green walls and large, airy bathrooms. The garden at the front of the hotel is little more than a narrow strip with tables and umbrellas, but breakfast here is a very pleasant way to start the day: clean sea breezes, bobbing yachts in the harbour and the clipping of the occasional horse-drawn trap.

Parking. Room service. TV.

Cheap

Regency Inn

18 Lansdowne House, MB Marg, Apollo Bunder (2202-0292/2282-3948). CST or Churchgate stations. **Rates** Rs3,500-Rs4,500 double. **Credit** AmEx, MC, V. **Map** p250 G5 ❽

The Regency is a small, 21-room hotel on the first floor of a 19th-century colonial building of high ceilings and ancient wooden staircases. The reception and lounge areas manage to mix some of that old-world charm with modern touches – so we have a 180-year-old Belgian chandelier alongside wood-and-chrome Hunter fans, and modern chairs and tables alongside antique chests and an ornate old mirror. It works well and this could rank as a budget boutique hotel if they paid similar attention to the rooms, which are spacious but lacking in character, with brown blankets on the beds. It's clean and neat, though, and one of the better budget options in the area.

Room service. TV.

Regent Hotel

8 Best Road (2287-1854/2204-1518, www.regenthotelcolaba.com). CST or Churchgate stations. **Rates** Rs4,510 - Rs4,730 double. **Credit** AmEx, MC, V. **Map** p250 G5 ❾

The floors are marble, the walls are marble, the reception desk is marble. They like marble at the Regent – there's acres of the stuff. Add wingtip leather armchairs and prints of horses and Mughal emperors, and the decor practically hits you over the head with a (marble) hammer and screams, 'Classy, isn't it?' And it is, sort of. The paint is peeling in a few places but the rooms are spacious and the design has a genuine kitsch charm that elevates it above most city hotels in the same price range, with pastel tones, high ceilings, more of those wingtip armchairs and a faux-Edwardian feel. The location is central – just behind the Taj Mahal hotel – and the staff professional and friendly.

Internet (wireless/shared). No-smoking rooms. Room service. TV.

Profile Crowning Glory

The Taj Mahal Palace.

Taj is Hindi for 'crown', which makes the **Taj Mahal Palace** – locally known as just 'the Taj' – the crown prince of Mumbai's hotels, situated right in front of the Gateway of India and the harbour. More than a hotel, it's a tourist attraction in its own right, admired for its broad, imposing presence and architecture that blends Florentine Renaissance and Moorish styles. The Taj has served innumerable illustrious guests over the years, including Queen Elizabeth II, President Gamal Abdel Nasser of Egypt and John Lennon.

The legend of the Taj is that its creator, the renowned Parsi industrialist Jamsetji Nusserwanji Tata, ordered its construction after being refused entry to the now-defunct European-only Pyrke's Apollo Hotel, with the aim of running a grand hotel without racist entry restrictions. (His nephew JRD Tata said that he built the hotel as a reaction to an offhand remark that Bombay had no good hotels.) When it was completed in 1903, it was by far the finest hotel in the city, with the latest imported conveniences such as electric lights, electric passenger lifts and its own soda-water factory. An urban myth persists that its architect, WA Stevens, was so appalled when he saw the completed hotel that he leapt to his death from its dome; it's said that builders had misread his plans and built the hotel the wrong way round, with the rear facing the sea. In boring old reality, though, the hotel is built the way it was originally designed – Stevens actually died of natural causes.

A second wing (the Tower wing) was added in 1972. The hotel suffered during the terror attacks of 26 November 2008 when the Taj was one of the targets. It shut down for renovations and subsequently opened regaining its former grandeur.

► For listings, *see p77.*

NEED TO KNOW

The Taj has seven restaurants, including the exclusive **Wasabi**, which fans of Japanese cuisine will adore. For the review, *see p97.*

Strand Hotel

PJ Ramchandani Marg, Apollo Bunder (2288-2222/2288-0059, www.hotelstrand.com). CST or Churchgate stations. **Rates** Rs 3,300-Rs 3,850 double. **Credit** MC, V. **Map** p251 G4 ⑩

Right next door to the Sea Palace Hotel (*see p78*) is this peach harbour front hotel, which manages to hang on to some of its art deco charm in the face of 'improvements' like the gratuitous marquee stuck on to its frontage. It doesn't offer much in the way of amenities but the location and value for money make this one of the most popular cheap hotels in Colaba. Rooms are airy and clean, with high ceilings, a cream-and-brown colour scheme and simple furnishings. A few period touches have survived, like ornate designs on some of the windows and art deco balconies. Book ahead for one of the six 'deluxe' doubles (Rs4,400 a night) for a wonderful view of the harbour and the Gateway of India.

Room service. TV.

Budget

Bentley's Hotel

17 Oliver Road (2284-1474, www.bentleys hotel.com). CST or Churchgate stations. **Rates** Rs2,060-Rs2,390 (AC) double. **Credit** MC, V. **Map** p251 G4 ⑪

Nothing quite captures the faded elegance of Colaba like Bentley's, on a quiet, tree-lined street just off Colaba Causeway. Spread over three buildings built in the 1930s, the hotel is a strictly no-frills affair with plenty of period Bombay atmosphere, with antique furniture, wooden staircases and checkered black-and-white floors. Come here if you want to sample what the city used to feel like: a stay at Bentley's is a trip back to an older, less frenetic Bombay, with servants cleaning mosaic-tiled floors with floor-cloths under their bare feet, sleepy watchmen on the gate and the only noise the clatter of the cage lift door. Oliver Road looks like a suburban London street, lined with 1930s properties all in need of care and attention, but just five minutes' walk from the bustle of Colaba Causeway. The superior doubles offer views of a nearby park.

Room service. TV.

Hotel Moti

10 BEST Marg, opposite Electric House (2202-5714/2202-1654). CST or Churchgate stations. **Rates** R 3,000 double. **No credit cards**. **Map** p250 G5 ⑫

Hotel Moti sits on the ground floor of an elderly building very close to the Taj Mahal hotel and a one-minute stroll from Colaba Causeway. An excellent-value budget option for the price, it's very basic but clean and secure, with 11 spacious rooms all equipped with fridges and attached bathrooms, and a few surviving period touches, including ornate stucco work on the ceilings.

TV.

YWCA International Guest House

18 Madame Cama Road, opposite National Gallery of Modern Art (2202-5053/9161, www.ywcaic.info). CST or Churchgate stations. **Rates** Rs 3,000 double. **No credit cards.** **Map** p250 G6 ⑬

Pay a Rs 50 temporary membership fee – it doesn't matter if you're male – and you can gain access to the YWCA's International Guest House. Simply but comfortably furnished, with attached bathrooms and balconies, the YWCA rooms make a great budget option that includes buffet breakfast, lunch and dinner in the attached dining hall – and just a few minutes' walk from the Causeway. The price listed above is for air-conditioned rooms; cheaper rates are available for non-AC rooms.

CHURCHGATE

Expensive

Ambassador Hotel

Veer Nariman Road (2204-1131, www.ambassadorindia.com). Churchgate station. **Rates** Rs14,000 double. **Credit** AmEx, MC, V. **Map** p250 & p253 E8 ⑭

This survivor of the 1970s doesn't do much for the aesthetic sense – it's essentially a 14-storey tower of dull concrete, but it's famed in Mumbai for being home to the city's only revolving restaurant, the Pearl of the Orient (*see p99*), on the 12th floor, which offers some breathtaking views of the arc of Marine Drive and the Arabian Sea. Inside, a '70s Indian

Regency Inn. *See p78.*

CONSUME

vision of opulence is still maintained, with acres of marble and wood panelling, an ornate gold-painted ceiling and golden elevator doors. The Society bar and restaurant on the lobby level once set the local standard for 'luxury' kitsch against some tough competition. Rooms are standard five-star fare, functional and comfortable, although none offer inspiring views of the sea or the city.
Bar. Business centre. Concierge. Gym. Internet (shared). Restaurants (2). Room service.

Moderate

Astoria Hotel

4 Jamshedji Tata Road (6654-1234, www.astoriamumbai.com). Churchgate station. **Rates** Rs5,000-Rs6,600 double. **Credit** AmEx, MC, V. **Map** p250 & p253 F8 ⓯
Just a minute's walk from Churchgate station, the Astoria was once home to a popular jazz band and part of the lively jazz strip that dominated Churchgate in the 1950s and '60s. Now renovated, the Astoria's lobby has been given a contemporary makeover, with soft, diffused lighting, wooden floors and an elegant glass fountain. Sadly, the rooms are not nearly so smart, with the obligatory wobbly fans and plain modern furniture, but they're clean, neat and airy, with high ceilings. Bathrooms are walk-in Indian style, with showers and toilets sharing the same space.
Internet (shared). Restaurant. Room service. TV.

Ritz

5 Jamshedji Tata Road, Churchgate (2285-0500/ 2282-0141). Churchgate station. **Rates** Rs7,020 double. **Credit** MC, V. **Map** p250/3 F7 ⓰
Mumbai's Ritz isn't at all ritzy, but this 50-year-old hotel offers spacious, clean rooms with decent-sized beds and large white-tiled bathrooms. The furnishings may be staid and the mini-bar in each room consists of just a single bottle of Kingfisher beer, but it's neat and functional and the location is good – just a few minutes' walk from Churchgate station. Room 408A is a good choice: a standard room but with impressive views of Churchgate station and its own balcony. Be warned: some of the rooms do not have wall-to-wall carpets, balconies or bathtubs – you have to specify what you want when you book.
Bar. Restaurant. Room service. TV.

West End Hotel

45 New Marine Lines (2203-9121, www.westend hotelmumbai.com). Churchgate or Marine Lines stations. **Taxi** opposite Bombay Hospital. **Rates** Rs5,830 double. **Credit** AmEx, MC, V. **Map** p253 F10 ⓱
Built in 1948, the popular West End has retained its mid-20th century charm, with plenty of dark wood and original features. Scrupulously well-maintained, the spacious rooms are very simply but comfortably furnished, with bright whitewashed walls, high ceilings and black marble bathrooms with generously sized bathtubs. Rooms at the front have small balconies overlooking the crowded New Marine Lines, always buzzing with traffic to Bombay Hospital, and a nearby temple.
Bar. Free parking. Internet (wireless). Restaurant. Room service. TV.

Cheap

Chateau Windsor

86 Veer Nariman Road (2204-4455, www.chateauwindsor.com). **Rates** Rs4,950-Rs5,500 double. **Credit** AmEx, MC, V. **Map** p250/3 E8 ⓲
The brochure informs us that Chateau Windsor is a 'luxurious' and 'elegant' corporate hotel, which, frankly, is somewhat of an overstatement. It is, however, a cheap and cheerful place with a fantastic location – on a main street and just a few minutes' walk away from both Marine Drive and Churchgate station. It's popular with families, tourists, budget business travellers and even the members of the Symphony Orchestra of India. The rooms, spread across three floors of narrow, sprawling corridors, are basic but clean, with garish bedcovers and curtains, and cheap-looking 1970s furniture. Staff, though, are professional and friendly, and the hotel is equipped with a closed-circuit TV system. Your morning tea or coffee is complimentary, as is the shoe-shine service.
Internet (shared). Parking. Room service. TV.

West End Hotel.

CONSUME

INSIDE TRACK
ROOMS WITH A VIEW

Many hotels in Colaba, Churchgate, Marine Drive and Juhu are close to the Arabian Sea, but not all provide sea views. You need to specify if you want a sea view when you book – and be prepared to be charged a higher rate.

MARINE DRIVE

Deluxe

InterContinental Marine Drive

135 Marine Drive (6639-9999, www.mumbai.intercontinental.com). CST or Churchgate stations. **Rates** Rs13,000 double. **Credit** AmEx, MC, V. **Map** p250 & 253 E8 ⑳

With a prime location right on the 'Queen's Necklace', it would be a shame not to fork out the extra cash for one of its sea-facing rooms: the views are of the Arabian Sea. The view and the plush rooms put the InterCon firmly in the top rank of South Mumbai's five-stars. Rooms are spacious and smart, with wood floors, plasma TVs, Bose music systems and DVD players. You can even have the music or the TV piped through into the bathroom, which has Bvlgari toiletries and is walled off with a glass partition so you can keep watching the TV while you shower, should you desire. Or you could just go for a suite, like the massive apartment-style lodgings on the top floor, where the bathrooms all have TVs anyway. The InterContinental is also home to South Mumbai's coolest rooftop bar, the sexy and sophisticated Dome (*see p117*), and a couple of the city's most impressive hotel restaurants.

Bars (2). Business centre. Concierge. Disabled adapted rooms. Gym. Internet (wireless). No-smoking floor. Parking. Restaurants (2). Room service. TV.

Marine Plaza

29 Marine Drive (2285-1212, www.hotelmarineplaza.com). CST or Churchgate stations. **Rates** Rs12,100 double. **Credit** AmEx, MC, V. **Map** p250 & p253 E7 ㉑

The five-storey atrium of this seafront hotel just screams Indian nouveau riche: gold-topped glass elevators glide up and down walls of black-and-white marble edged with more gold. On the ground level sits a glass table supported by the tails of giant glass fish, with paintings of laughing and crying clowns on the walls. If that's a bit too much, just avert your gaze to the atrium ceiling and admire fellow guests' backstrokes in the glass-bottomed rooftop swimming pool. The rooms are not nearly as gaudy: they're modern and smart, with outstanding sea views from front-facing rooms. If the city starts to get to you, just march downstairs to the Marine Plaza's ersatz 'English' pub, Geoffrey's.

Bar. Business centre. Gym. Internet (wireless). Pool (outdoor). Restaurants (2). Room service.

★ Oberoi

Nariman Point (6632-5757, www.oberoimumbai.com). CST or Churchgate stations. **Rates** Rs31,350 double. **Credit** AmEx, MC, V. **Map** p250 D6 ㉒

The Oberoi vies with the Taj to take the top slot in the rankings of South Mumbai's luxury hotels. One of the city's first modern five-stars, it has hosted Bill Clinton, Bill Gates, Michael Jackson and numerous visiting heads of state. The hotel was also one of the targets during the 26/11 terror attacks (*see p28*) and has since been renovated. It's a luxurious establishment and each room comes with a butler-on-call, who can be summoned at any time with the press of a rather large red button. The Oberoi also offers a selection of top restaurants including Vetro (*see p99*) and Ziya (*see p98*).

Bar. Business centre. Concierge. Disabled-adapted rooms. Internet (wireless). Gym. Non-smoking floors. Parking (free). Pool (indoor). Restaurants (3). Room service. Spa.

The Trident

Nariman Point (6632-4343, www.tridenthotels.com/mumbai). CST or Churchgate stations. **Rates** Rs22,000 double. **Credit** AmEx, MC, V. **Map** p250 D6 ⑲

The Trident is the sister of the landmark Oberoi next door, and it's possible to walk through from one lobby to the other along various brass-handled staircases and designer store-fringed corridors. It may be the poor sister – rates here start marginally lower than at the Oberoi – but it is impressive. The superior rooms are comfortable, if a little staid, with city-facing views and the kind of inoffensive design, fixtures and furnishings to make Granny feel at home. Deluxe ocean-view rooms offer a much more civilised experience, with outstanding views of the Arabian Sea.

Bar. Business centre. Concierge. Disabled-adapted rooms. Gym. Internet (wireless). No-smoking floors. Parking. Pool (outdoor). Restaurants (3). Room service. TV.

Cheap

Sea Green Hotel

145 Marine Drive (6633-6525/2282-2294, www.seagreenhotel.com). CST or Churchgate stations. **Rates** Rs4,140 double. **Credit** AmEx, MC, V. **Map** p250 & 253 E8 ㉓

This green-and-white art deco hotel was originally built in 1940 as quarters for British soldiers before being converted into a hotel in the '50s. The threadbare red carpets look as if they haven't changed since then, but the Sea Green is spotlessly clean and

CONSUME

does manage to conjure up period charm, with high ceilings, some original features and the sleepy atmosphere of an older Bombay. Each room has a balcony and is reasonably spacious, although the mattresses are a little hard. Shell out a few hundred rupees more for a corner suite with an attached sitting room arrayed with 1970s furniture, where the views of the Arabian Sea are just as good as the lower floors of the plush InterContinental a few minutes up the road.
Room service. TV.
► *If the Sea Green is full, go next door to its sister, the Sea Green South Hotel.*

Sea Green South Hotel
145A Marine Drive (6633-6535/2282-1613, www.seagreensouth.com). CST or Churchgate stations. **Rates** Rs4,140 double. **Credit** AmEx, MC, V. **Map** p250 & p253 E8 ㉔
The neighbour of the Sea Green Hotel shares the same building and is identical in every respect, right down to the room rates, but run under different management. The 1940s feel is even more pronounced thanks to the gorgeous wood-panelled cage lift.
Room service. TV.

WORLI & PAREL

Deluxe

Four Seasons
Dr E Moses Road, Worli (2481-8000, www.fourseasons.com/mumbai). Mahalaxmi station. **Rates** Rs16,720-Rs18,920 double.
Credit AmEx, MC, V.
With its gleaming exterior rising out of a slum, the Four Seasons is the bricks-and-mortar embodiment of the new Mumbai. It also has the only chef in India licensed to cut the poisonous puffer fish fugu working in its Chinese restaurant. The hotel also offers pan-Asian cuisine at San Qi and boasts Mumbai's highest rooftop bar: Aer.
Bars (2). Business centre. Concierge. Disabled-adapted rooms. Gym. Internet (wireless). No-smoking rooms. Parking. Pool. Restaurants (2). Room service. Spa. TV.

ITC Grand Central
Dr Babasaheb Ambedkar Road, Parel (2410-1010, www.itcwelcomgroup.in). Lower Parel station. **Rates** Rs11,000-Rs17,600 double.
Credit AmEx, DC, MC, V.
This Parel hotel is hard to miss – the British Colonial-inspired building stands on the side of one of Mumbai's arterial roads in the middle of wholesale shops and offices. The hotel is equipped with 242 guest rooms, including rooms for solitary women travellers. The hotel is also great for little ones, owing to its Very Important Kids Programme, where children receive personalised attention and have rooms stocked with toys.
Bar. Business centre. Gym. Internet. No smoking rooms. Parking. Pool. Restaurants (5). Room service. Spa. TV.

BANDRA & KHAR

Deluxe

★ Taj Lands End
Bandstand, Bandra (W) (6668-1234, www.tajhotels.com). Bandra station.
Rates R 22,500-Rs25,000 double.
Credit AmEx, DC, MC, V.
Without doubt Bandra's most luxurious hotel, the 18-storey Taj Lands End stands close to a 16th-century fort where Portuguese cannons once kept watch over maritime trade routes. It's not uncommon to spot Bollywood stars strolling in for dinner (Shah Rukh Khan lives just down the road), though don't-expect to be rubbing shoulders with them: the restaurants are equipped with private dining rooms for the benefit of the glitterati. The hotel is so large and self-contained that it's virtually a miniature village, with enough designer shops and restaurants to serve Bandra's elite and keep guests – mostly business travellers – distracted. The vast, plant-festooned central atrium leads through to a large outdoor swimming pool and sprawling landscaped lawns, with fine views of the sea and the nearby fort. Rooms are bright and spacious and thanks to some cunning design, all offer views of the sea through broad windows.
Bar. Business centre. Concierge. Gym. Internet (wireless). Parking. Pool (outdoor). Room service. Restaurants (3). Spa. (Photo p86).

Moderate

Executive Enclave
331 Dr Ambedkar Road, Pali Hill, Bandra (W) (6696-9000/2649-0227, www.executiveenclave.com). Khar station.
Rates Rs5,000 double. **Credit** AmEx, MC, V. **Map** p249 C2 ㉕

INSIDE TRACK BUDGET BEDS

Travellers looking for something cheaper can find themselves hitting characterless mid-range business hotels built in the 1970s that are not worth the money. A better option is to seek out cheaper hotels built in the 1930s and '40s, which have the virtue of period character and manage to convey some of the sleepy charm of an older Bombay. That's usually not by design but by default – the managements simply haven't got around to changing anything in the last 70 years.

CONSUME

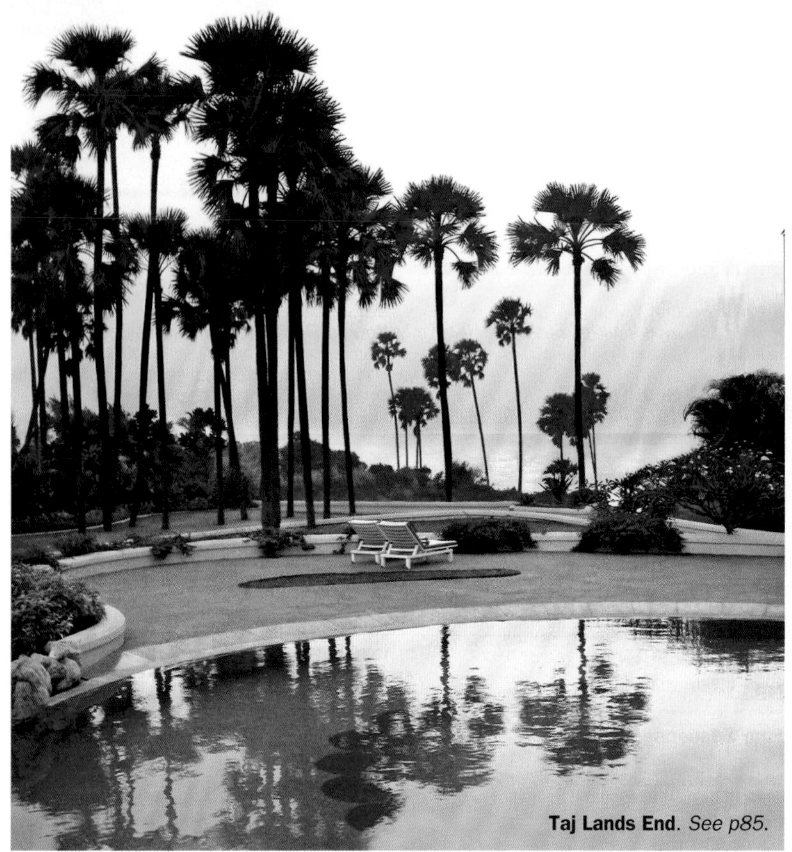
Taj Lands End. *See p85.*

One of the few mid-range options in Bandra, Executive Enclave is a small, 54-room hotel a short walk from half a dozen pubs and bars to the south and a whole range of small restaurants and cafés and the seafront promenade to the west. The rooms are spacious and clean, and while the multicoloured plastic-panel aesthetic may not be to everybody's liking, the rooms are simply furnished and predominantly free of unattractive accoutrements.
Internet (WiFi). Restaurant. Room service. TV.

Hotel Metro Palace

355 Hill Road, Bandra (W) (6774-4555, www.uniquehotelsindia.com). Bandra station. **Taxi** opposite Globus shopping centre. **Rates** Rs 6,050 double. **Credit** AmEx, MC, V. **Map** p249 D5 ㉖
The Metro Palace offers a decent no-frills deal for a stay in the heart of lively Bandra. Rooms are clean and of reasonable size, but very plainly furnished, with a typical effort at a decorative touch being a large poster of some kittens in a basket. Some of the rooms are wood-panelled and most have balconies.
Bar. Room service. Restaurant. TV.

Ramee Guestline Hotel

757 SV Road, Khar (W) (2648-5421/22, www.ramee-group.com). Khar station. **Rates** Rs8,800-Rs11,000 double. **Credit** MC, V. **Map** p249 D2 ㉗
The Ramee manages to pack quite a lot into a small space – as well as a hotel there's an 'Irish' pub, a Chinese restaurant, a hall-for-hire and a discotheque. There clearly wasn't a lot of room left over for the hotel lobby, or indeed the rooms, which are 'compact'. Still, this is one of Bandra-Khar's better options for the price, and despite space constraints the Ramee has managed to squeeze in comfortable beds and some smart design. The hotel also has a good central location.
Bar. Internet (shared). Parking. Restaurant. Room service. TV.

Cheap

Hotel Jewel Palace

Fifth Road, Khar (W) (2604-5488/2604-8662). Khar Station. **Rates** Rs2,970 double. **Credit** MC, V. **Map** p249 D2 ㉘

Nobody is going to go home from the Jewel Palace singing paeans about its wonderfulness, but if you're staying in the 'burbs, it's hard to beat for both location and price. At seven storeys, it towers over the bustling Khar market, where fruit and veg vendors haggle with local aunties. South Mumbai is easily accessible from Khar railway station, which is a two-minute walk, and all of Bandra's nightlife and eating options are a short rickshaw ride away. The rooms are cramped – with a double bed taking up most of the floor space – but they're clean and the room service fellows are cheerful.
Bar. Restaurant. Room service. TV.

VAKOLA & VILE PARLE

Deluxe

★ Grand Hyatt

Off Western Express Highway, Santa Cruz (E) (6676-1234,http://mumbai.grand.hyatt.com). Santa Cruz station. **Rates** Rs12,500-Rs21,000 double. **Credit** AmEx, MC, V.

The Grand Hyatt may have the internationally inoffensive and anonymous façade of glass and concrete, but its grey-blue walls are actually an apt reflection of the city in which it is located. It blends right in like yet another unfinished concrete shell. On the inside, it gives you everything you would expect from a business hotel about a kilometre away from Bandra-Kurla Complex, the city's shiny new glass-and-steel CBD: open-plan lobby with the restaurant and bar just barely set back from the public area; 547 clean, clinical rooms in cream and white; and efficient staff who smile a lot. Set in an as yet undeveloped wasteland, the huge complex houses five restaurants, one of the city's most popular bars, China House (*see p119*), and a shopping arcade with a nice deli. Fortunately, the designers took their culturally barren location into account and the Hyatt features the city's best collection of art outside of a gallery. If you do actually venture out of this four-hectare township, Bandra is just 15 minutes away.
Bars (2). Business centre. Concierge. Disabled-adapted rooms. Gym. Internet. No smoking rooms. Parking (free). Pool (outdoor). Restaurants (5). Room service. Spa. TV/DVD on demand.

Orchid Hotel

Near the Domestic Airport, Nehru Road, Vile Parle (E) (2616-4040,www.orchidhotel.com). Vile Parle station. **Rates** R 11,000 - Rs13,200 double. **Credit** AmEx, MC, V.

This pleasant 245-room hotel is an ISO-certified eco-friendly hotel. It won't knock you out with sharp design, but the environmentally conscious theme throughout is arguably more impressive, with furniture made with wood from sustainable forests, all-recycled paper products, smart water-saving bathrooms and energy-saving air-conditioning, among other innovations. The seven-storey atrium has an attractive 21m (70 ft) 'waterfall' that is actually a circle of plastic wires carrying individual water droplets. An open-air rooftop restaurant and bar offer relaxed dining, and there's a medium-size, non-chlorinated rooftop swimming pool. Hotels telling guests to reuse their towels is hardly news, but here the environmental concern runs deep – Mumbai is under intense environmental pressure and five-star hotels are notorious producers of waste and consumers of energy. Fortunately, the Orchid's example is something of which neighbouring hotels have started to take notice.
Bar. Business centre. Concierge. Disabled-adapted rooms. Gym. Internet (wireless). No-smoking floors. Parking. Pool (outdoor). Restaurants (3). Room service. TV.

JUHU

Deluxe

JW Marriott

Juhu Tara Road (6693-3000,www.marriott.com). Vile Parle station. **Rates** Rs12,150-Rs20,000 double. **Credit** AmEx, MC, V.

The JW Marriott is nothing less than a mini-city of five-star luxury, set back from the mad scramble that is Juhu Tara Road behind high walls (and the city's toughest hotel security) with no fewer than six restaurants, a bar, a club and one of the city's best spas. There are sea views in 90% of the rooms, which are tastefully and sumptuously decorated, with attractive jute headboards, marble bathrooms prettily stencilled with flower designs and elegant shutters opening from the entranceway into the executive rooms. The Ocean Suite, although not the largest nor the most expensive, is arguably the most attractive of the suites, with floor-to-ceiling windows offering fabulous views of the palm-tree-fringed beach that are not available in the more expensive Lotus Suite. You can even admire the view from the bath and shower, which is stocked with Bvlgari toiletries. Beach access is closed because of security concerns but the outside area offers three swimming pools, including a children's pool with a water slide and a large main pool with stone chairs for aquatic lounging.
Bars (2). Business centre. Concierge. Disabled-adapted rooms. Gym. Internet (wireless). No-smoking rooms. Parking. Pools (outdoor). Restaurants (6). Room service. Spa. TV.

> **INSIDE TRACK SECURITY**
>
> Post 26/11, security has been tightened across the city. Being frisked is standard in most five-star hotels, as is baggage screening and car checking.

INSIDE TRACK ROOMS WITH A VIEW

On January 20, 1896, the American novelist Samuel Langhorne Clemens, popularly known as Mark Twain, was on a lecturing tour of the British Empire. After checking into the Watson's Hotel (the city's poshest hotel, now Esplanade Mansion, *see p52*) he described Mumbai as 'A bewitching place, a bewildering place, an enchanting place – the Arabian Nights come again?'

Expensive

Hotel Sea Princess

Juhu Beach (2661-1111,www.seaprincess.com). Santa Cruz station. **Rates** Rs11,000 double. **Credit** AmEx, DC, MC, V.

This 20-year-old hotel is a traditional Juhu standby. It recently acquired a new wing for conferences and a swanky new bar, but the design and decor of the hotel don't seem to have changed much since the mid-1980s, except for the addition of wall-mounted flat-screen TVs to go with loud-patterned bedspreads and carpets, staid furniture and Pre-Raphaelite prints on the walls. The rooms feel a little cluttered, but the excellent sea views – Juhu Beach is just behind the hotel – help take the edge off. The outside pool area is pleasant, and there's beach access as well as a separate children's pool.

Bar. Concierge. Disabled-adapted rooms. Gym. Internet (wireless). No-smoking floor. Pools, (outdoor). Restaurant. Room service. TV.

Sun 'n' Sand

39 Juhu Beach (6693-8888/2620-1811, www.sunnsandhotel.com). Vile Parle station. **Rates** Rs8,800-Rs10,450 double. **Credit** AmEx, MC, V.

Muscle-bound Bollywood superhunk Hrithik Roshan wanders through the lobby after a photo-shoot on Juhu Beach and no one raises an eyebrow – it's just another day at the Sun 'n' Sand, suburban Mumbai's first five-star hotel (it was the first to get a pool) and a favoured destination for ad shoots thanks to its easy access to the beach and high service standards. Now over 40 years old, the Sun 'n' Sand retains an aura of 1960s Bombay with pastel shades, an easy-listening lobby soundtrack, and furniture and decor that must have been cutting-edge circa 1964 – although recent renovations in some parts do it no justice. Still a favourite with foreign film crews and old-school Bollywood producers, the rooms at Sun 'n' Sand are spick-and-span with sparkling marble bathrooms and broad windows with excellent sea views. Room rates include airport pick-up and drop-off and complimentary cocktails.

Bar. Business centre. Free parking. Gym. Internet (wireless). No-smoking rooms. Pool (outdoor). Restaurants (2). Room service. Spa. TV.

Moderate

Hotel Four Seasons

St Joseph's Church Road (6163-3971, www.hotelfourseasons.net). Vile Parle station. **Taxi** opposite Juhu Church. **Rates** Rs3,500 double. **Credit** MC, V.

Okay, it isn't fancy (and no, it's not that Four Seasons). The fans are wobbly, the rooms are plain, cramped and have no views, and the plastic climbing plants in the lobby look like they need watering. But it is clean, the cheapest decent hotel in Juhu, and former patrons include the Nobel Peace Prize-winner Shirin Ebadi, who stayed here during the 2004 World Social Forum. If it's good enough for her, it might be good enough for you. Convenient for both airports.

Restaurant. Room service. TV.

King's International

5 Juhu Tara Road (2618-4382, www.kingsinternational.com). Vile Parle station. **Taxi** near Prithvi Theatre. **Rates** Rs4,500 double. **Credit** MC, V.

The lift door sticks occasionally and needs a gentle kick to get it to shut, but don't worry, the shambling old commissionaire in a peaked cap will do that for you. This small, 30-year-old hotel won't win any awards but it is perfectly clean and decent, with surprisingly good-sized, comfortable rooms provided with fridges and TVs, and friendly service. Room service includes dishes from the excellent Temple Flower restaurant nearby. The rates include a complimentary airport drop-off. A popular coffee shop/bar/pizzeria, Alfredo's, functions out of the same building.

Free parking. Room service. TV.

ANDHERI

Deluxe

Hyatt Regency

Sahar Airport Road, (6696-1234, www.mumbai.regency.hyatt.com). Andheri station. **Rates** Rs8,250-Rs15,950 double. **Credit** AmEx, DC, MC, V.

Cocooned behind a sweeping wall of glass are the plush confines of the Hyatt Regency: acres of dark grey marble, dark wood and frosted glass. Even standard rooms are smart here: spacious and airy, with step-down showers and glass basins, and with a design laid out according to the principles of *vastu shashtra* – the Indian feng shui. That's why there's a tiny bamboo plant greeting you as soon as you step into your room, and why the mirror in the bedroom is positioned off to one side and not directly in

front of the bed – that would be bad *vastu*. The gardens include a large pool and tennis courts – a rarity here in Mumbai.
Bar. Concierge. Gym. Internet (wireless). Parking. Pool (outdoor). Restaurants (2). Room service. Spa. TV.

ITC The Maratha

Sahar Airport Road (2830-3030, www.itcwelcomegroup.in). Andheri station. **Rates** Rs11,500-16,000 double. **Credit** AmEx, MC, V.
From the white *jali*-style lattice screens that cover the walls of the hotel's tall atrium of Agra red stone, to the ayurvedic shampoos in the bathrooms, the Maratha stands out from other new five-stars with a design that works to remind you that you are actually in India. Airy rooms are adorned with modern and traditional Indian art, including fine examples of local Warli tribal painting made with rice paste and straw. The restaurants cover Indian cuisines from north to south, with a nod to the British era in a club-like bar littered with overstuffed wingtip leather armchairs. The happy marriage of five-star luxury and Indian style is tastefully restrained until you get to the outside pool, where the designers have let rip with six stone lion fountains and a giant iron and stone gazebo.
Bar. Business centre. Concierge. Gym. Internet (wireless). No-smoking rooms. Parking. Pool (outdoor). Restaurants (5). Spa. Room service. TV.

Leela Kempinski

Sahar Airport Road (6691-1234, www.theleela.com). Andheri station. **Rates** Rs19,800 double. **Credit** AmEx, MC, V.
The Leela feels a little past its prime compared to its newer five-star neighbours on the airport road. Its multi-level lobby is a sprawling field of cream marble and brass fittings, with an elderly shopping arcade and a small gallery of works by contemporary Indian artists. The centrepiece is a sunken lobby with a step waterfall rushing down to a gold-domed gazebo. Rooms are smart, spacious and tastefully decorated, each with a plasma TV.
Bar. Concierge. Gym. Internet (broadband). Restaurants (4). Room service. Spa. TV.

Le Royal Meridien

Sahar Airport Road (2838-0000, www.leroyalmeridien-mumbai.com). Andheri station. **Rates** Rs12,000-Rs21,450 double. **Credit** AmEx, MC, V.
Some nice design touches raise Le Royal Meridien above the five-star herd, most strikingly the Crystal Lounge: a long oval room in silver, white and beige with a series of glass doors opening off to other parts of the hotel under a gigantic chandelier. It's like walking into a Fabergé egg. In the Chinese restaurant next door, tables are set with specially commissioned dinner plates scrawled with the verse of Indian poet Harivanshrai Bachchan – translated into Chinese. Rooms are smart and contemporary, with wooden floors and spacious bathrooms complete with fun touches such as rubber ducks. The only thing that lets the hotel down is that the view through the broad windows is of the neighbouring wasteland.
Bars (2). Business centre. Concierge. Disabled-adapted rooms. Free parking. Internet (wireless). Gym. No-smoking floors. Pool (outdoor). Restaurants (3). Room service. Spa. TV.

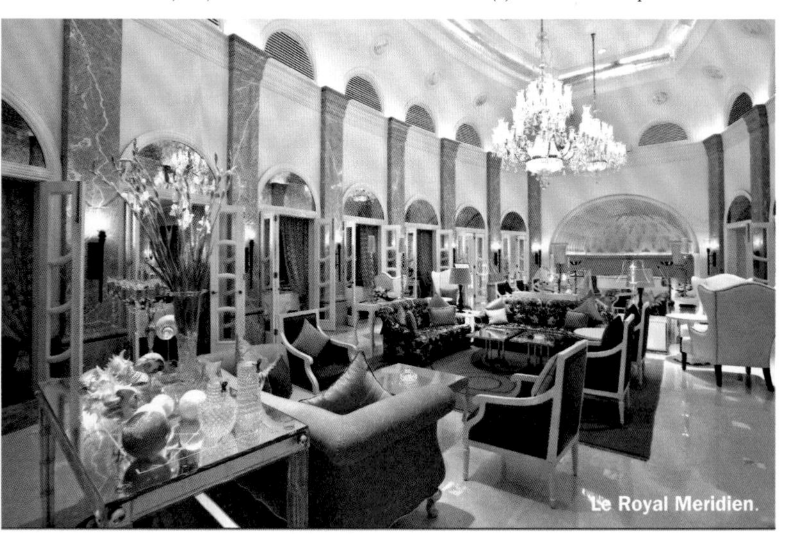
Le Royal Meridien.

CONSUME

Restaurants & Cafés

India on a plate.

Mumbaikars tend to eat out a lot. Busy lifestyles that leave little time for cooking, matchbox-size houses that aren't fit for dinner parties, and a profusion of restaurants that serve everything from kebabs from the North-west Frontier Province to *dosas* from the southern tip of the country mean that eating out has always been an integral part of the city's culture. And it's not just the huge variety of Indian cuisine that's on offer; there's Japanese, North American, Chinese, Thai, Italian, and lots more besides. Tuck in.

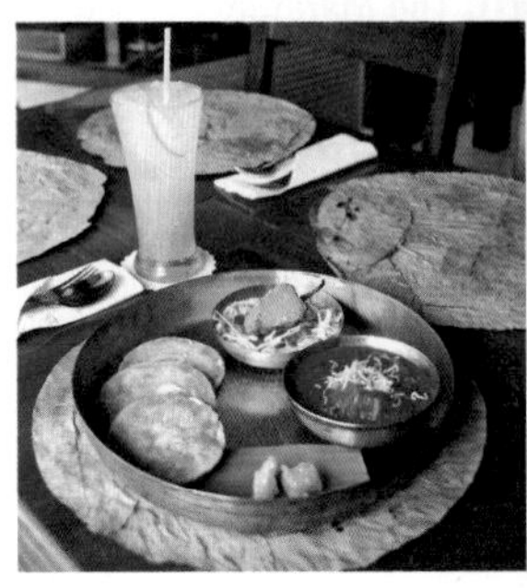

FOOD TRAIL

Indian cuisine is as diverse as the country itself and includes some entirely separate sub-cuisines like Bengali cooking. Luckily, nearly all of them are available in Mumbai, thanks to the millions of economic migrants who have come to the city from across the country over the last 200 years. The newly arrived émigrés stuck together, initially sharing familiar food in community kitchens or *khanevals*, which in time opened their doors to outsiders and became the city's first real restaurants. For a description of some of the different dishes available and where to find them, *see p94* **Vast Food Nation**.

For decades, the finest restaurants in Mumbai were confined to the insides of five-star hotels that were out of the reach of all but the city's wealthiest diners. Today, the five-star culture persists, but in recent years it has been increasingly challenged by a new breed of high-quality, stand-alone restaurants eager to grab a share of the Mumbaikar's skyrocketing disposable income. Many of these have sprung up in and around Colaba, but the biggest explosion has been in the suburb of Bandra, a 30-minute train ride north. Standards vary, but the best of the five-stars and the new stand-alones offer food that compares well with top-quality restaurants the world over – sometimes at international rates.

Chinese food is now virtually an Indian cuisine, and even the simplest restaurant offers Indianised hybrids like chicken Manchurian or chop suey *dosas* (*see p102* **Bombay Mix**). In recent years, the increasingly well-travelled Mumbaikar has begun to demand much more variety and sophistication in foreign cooking, with more and more new restaurants serving authentic Mediterranean and East Asian food, often prepared by foreign chefs. There's a lot of experimentation going on, too, with pan-Asian restaurants throwing together dishes from across the continent, often with Indian twists.

It remains to be seen how many of the glut of new restaurants (around one high-profile opening a month) will survive, but there's no doubt that there has never been a better time to eat in this city.

DOS AND DON'TS

Mumbaikars rarely make reservations, often being happy to mill around outside a restaurant until a table becomes available, but to guarantee seating and avoid wasting time, it's always best to book in advance where possible. Mumbaikars usually like to eat late; around 9pm or 10pm is the busiest period. It's easy to spot a decent restaurant – it will be packed. Food poisoning is fairly rare and hygiene not something to worry about unless you're eating from street stalls (*see p110* **Street Eats**).

The pricier eateries are liable for taxes that are usually not included in menu prices, so be aware that your final bill will mostly include a value-added tax of 12.5 per cent on food and 20 per cent on alcoholic drinks. This should be stated clearly on the menu, but you can't rely on that so it's better to ask. Most places serve alcohol, except for the cheaper restaurants, and we've listed where they do not.

We've listed a range of meal prices for each place. However, restaurants often change their menus so these prices are only guidelines. For more on the latest restaurant openings in the city, pick up a copy of *Time Out Mumbai.*

COLABA

Indian

Rs ★ Bade Miya's

Tulloch Street, off Colaba Causeway (2285-1649). CST or Churchgate stations. **Open** 7pm-3am daily. **Main courses** Rs 30-Rs 70. **No credit cards. No alcohol. Map** p250 G5 ❶ **Mughlai**

Not a restaurant, but a hugely popular streetside stall just off Colaba Causeway serving up fabulous kebabs and rolls to Colaba's post-party crowd. Bade Miya's started as a single stall a decade ago, but grew with its fame; it now consists of a couple of hard-working skewer-laden grills and rows of plastic chairs and tables. Bade's has even colonised a derelict building across the road. It's not fancy, but it is delicious. Everything's good here but the top choices are the *baida rotis* (spicy mutton, chicken or beef with egg in a grilled wrap), the spicy chicken livers, the *bhuna* mutton and *bhuna* chicken. The vegetarian seekh kebab is also excellent. On Friday and Saturday nights expect lots of traffic, alcohol-fuelled patrons and a wait for tables (though you can take your kebab rolls to go).

Baghdadi

11 Tulloch Road, off Colaba Causeway (2202-8027). CST or Churchgate stations. **Open** 7am-12.30am daily. **Main courses** Rs 50-Rs 80. **No credit cards. No alcohol. Map** p250 G5 ❷ **Mughlai**

Not so much a restaurant as a huge room with rows of six-seater benches and tables, Baghdadi is known locally as the 'poor man's Taj', after the Taj Mahal Palace hotel nearby. The portions are large, the food decent and the kitchen surprisingly clean. Even so, it's an experience best enjoyed if you leave your aesthetic sensibilities at home. The seating is a great leveller, with executives sharing tables with couriers, taxi drivers, African students and labourers. If there's space at your table you may be asked to slide a place down. Baghdadi is famous for its chicken biryani, topped with a special Baghdadi masala and buried under rice and browned onions, and the chicken masala fry, served in a sweetish red gravy. To mop it up, go for a plump, soft naan or one of the enormous rotis. Baghdadi is also one of the very few places in Mumbai where you can get a beef biryani.

Delhi Darbar

Holland House, Colaba Causeway (2202-0235/5656). CST or Churchgate stations. **Open** 11.30am-12.30am daily. **Main courses** Rs 100-Rs 150. **Credit** AmEx, MC, V. **No alcohol. Map** p250 G5 ❸ **Punjabi & Mughlai**

An old-timer (it first opened in 1973) with a huge following, Delhi Darbar is nothing much to look at: it dispenses with atmosphere in favour of cooking fumes. Doesn't matter, though, it's the food that has been bringing diners back all these years. Darbar specialises in Punjabi and Mughlai cuisine with some truly excellent kebabs, curries and biryanis.

Kailash Parbat Hindu Hotel

Sheela Mahal, 1st Pasta Lane (2287-4823). CST or Churchgate stations. **Open** 11am-11pm daily. **Main courses** Rs 65-Rs 150. **No credit cards. No alcohol. Map** p251 F4 ❹ **North Indian**

If you're looking for mouthwatering Indian snacks like *bhel puri* and *ragda pattice* (a deep-fried potato patty in a spicy chickpea gravy), few places do a better job than Kailash Parbat, a 60-year-old Colaba institution. The split-level restaurant is always packed and almost everything on the menu is worth a try. Be sure not to miss its *falooda* (a thick, creamy sweet drink), *gulab jamun* (milk powder balls in a sweet syrup) and other specialities from the Sindh province.

Konkan Café

Taj President, 90 Cuffe Parade (6665-0808). CST or Churchgate stations. **Open** 12.30-3pm, 7-11.45pm daily. **Main courses** Rs 800-Rs 1,000. **Credit** AmEx, DC, MC, V. **Map** p251 E3 ❺ **Coastal**

THE BEST RESTAURANTS

For killer kebabs
Bade Miya's (*see p91*), **Kebab Korner** (*see p103*) and **Shalimar** (*see p104*).

For fab fish
Konkan Café (*see above*), **Mahesh Lunch Home** (*see p101*) and **New Martin Lunch Home** (*see p93*).

For curries
Delhi Darbar (*see left*), **Peshawri** (*see p112*) and **Kebabs & Kurries** (*see p107*).

For vegetarian cuisine
Friends Union Joshi Club (*see p106*), **Govinda's** (*see p104*) and **Swati Snacks** (*see p106*).

For lazy weekend brunches
Indigo (*see p95*), **Olive** (*see p109*) and **Samovar** (*see p93*).

For regional delicacies
Jimmy Boy (*see p101*), **Oh! Calcutta** (*see p106*) and **Rice Boat** (*see p111*).

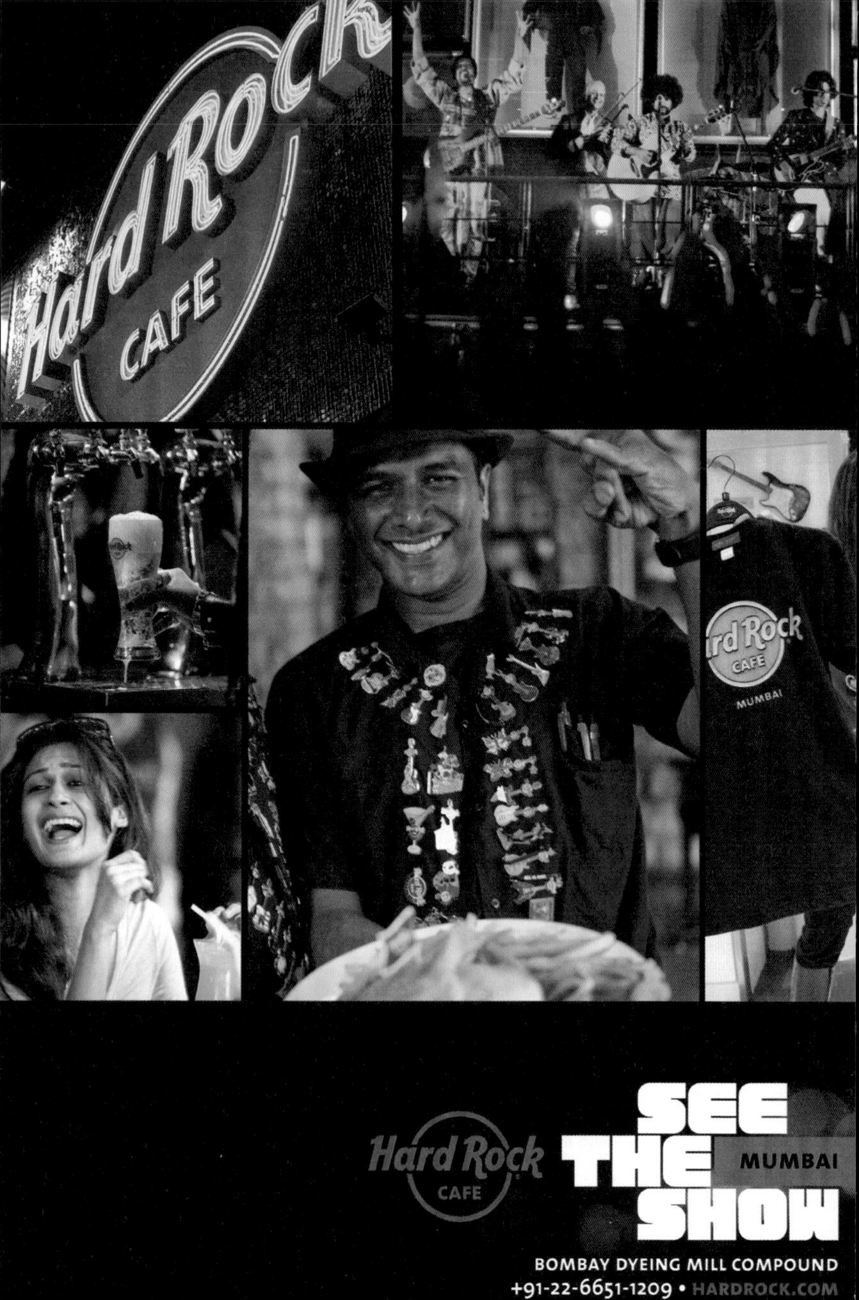

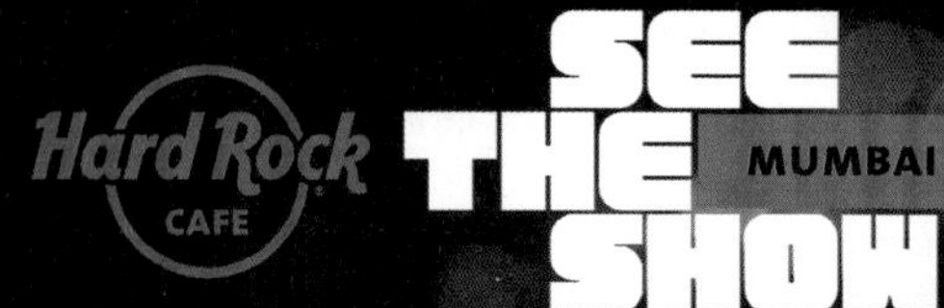

Hard Rock CAFE
Hard Rock CAFE MUMBAI
Hard Rock CAFE
SEE THE SHOW
MUMBAI
BOMBAY DYEING MILL COMPOUND
+91-22-6651-1209 • HARDROCK.COM

This is a beautifully planned and striking restaurant with decor that mirrors that of village homes along India's Konkan coast. Chef Ananda Solomon is a proponent of 'slow food' – so he sticks to authentic seasonings and methods of preparation, including hand-grinding. Although the focus is definitely on seafood (including Mangalorean-style *gassi*, steamed fish in turmeric paste and Malwani shrimp curry – all fabulous), he also serves some exquisite lamb chops in East Indian masala, mustard seeds and curry leaves.

INSIDE TRACK TIPPING

Tipping is a standard practice – generally between five and ten per cent. Service charges are usually included in the bill, so make sure you're not tipping twice. It's better to tip in cash; some establishments can't be relied upon to divide tips made by credit card to staff.

Koyla

Gulf Hotel, Arthur Bunder Road (6636-4727). CST or Churchgate stations. **Open** 7.30-12.30pm Tue-Sun. **Main courses** Rs 200-Rs 400. **Credit** MC, V. **No alcohol**. **Map** p251 G4 ❻ North Indian

When the government's slum demolition drive in ran into political flak, Koyla was torn down to defuse accusations that only illegal structures belonging to the city's poorest were being targeted. Like many of the slums, it was back in business shortly after. Koyla's best feature is its location – on the roof of a hotel overlooking the harbour and the rooftops of Colaba, with its tables under white *shamianas* (canopies). A big hit with college kids, Koyla serves up decent North-west Frontier dishes cooked over charcoal. There's no alcohol; flavoured tobacco is the substance of choice here, smoked in ornate hookahs.

Masala Kraft

Taj Mahal Palace, Apollo Bunder (6665-3366). CST or Churchgate stations. **Open** 12.30-2.45pm, 7-11.45pm daily. **Main courses** Rs 450-Rs 1,350. **Credit** AmEx, DC, MC, V. **Map** p250 G5 ❼ Modern Indian

Contemporary Indian cuisine delivered with a Western twist, like cooking in olive oil – unheard of in traditional Indian cooking. It works fabulously: try the tandoori pink salmon dipped in sugarcane vinegar, or the paneer in a white sauce (another Western import) with black peppers. The combination is reflected in the decor – imposing dark wooden pillars conjure up a regal Indian vibe, contrasted with light pine furniture.

Paradise

Sindh Chambers, Colaba Causeway (6635-2714). CST or Churchgate stations. **Open** 11am-11pm Tue-Sun. **Main courses** Rs 150. **No credit cards**. **No alcohol**. **Map** p251 F4 ❽ Parsi

This small, unassuming eaterie has been serving snacks and Parsi food for the last 53 years. The best days to go are Wednesdays and Sundays, when owner Mehroo Kadkhodai cooks her famous mutton *dhansak* (lentil and vegetable curry).

New Martin Lunch Home

Glamour House, Strand Cinema Road (2202-9606). CST or Churchgate stations. **Taxi** Strand Cinema. **Open** 11.30am-3pm, 6.30-10pm Mon-Sat. **Main courses** Rs 35-Rs 60. **No credit cards**. **No alcohol**. **Map** p251 F4 ❾ Goan

Delicious Goan food, served simply – don't expect more from Martin's than five tables with benches and tube-lighting. But it's clean and the food is fresh and tasty. Most of the dishes are shades of red, yet the masalas are quite different. The top order here is the Goan sausage: sour, spicy and swimming in tasty fat, which you can mop up with *pao* (bread). There's also great vindaloo, prawn curry, and the classic fried fish curry and rice.

Samovar

Jehangir Art Gallery, MG Road, Kala Ghoda (2284-8000). CST or Churchgate stations. **Open** 11am-7pm daily. **Main courses** Rs 75-Rs 200. **No credit cards**. **Map** p250 G6 ❿ North Indian

A sweet little restaurant within Jehangir Art Gallery, Samovar is popular with artists, students and long-time loyalists. It's a pleasant place to while away the afternoon drinking beer, eating prawn curry and rice, and staring at the museum garden.

International

All Stir Fry

Gordon House Hotel, 5 Battery Street, Apollo Bunder (2287-1122). CST or Churchgate stations. **Open** noon-3.30pm, 7pm-midnight daily. **Main courses** Rs 400. **Credit** AmEx, MC, V. **Map** p250 G5 ⓫ Asian

The selling point of this trendy restaurant has always been its all-you-can-eat wok that allows patrons to custom-make stir-fries to their tastes. Head to the noodle bar and fill your bowl with raw materials: noodles, vegetables and seafood/meats. Then proceed to the chefs, who will do the rest with your preference of sauces and condiments.

Basilico

Sentinel House, Arthur Bunder Road (6634-5670). CST or Churchgate stations. **Open** 9am-1am daily. **Main courses** Rs 350-Rs 500. **Credit** MC, V. **No alcohol**. **Map** p251 G4 ⓬ European

This stylish wood-and-glass eaterie just off Colaba Causeway specialises in European cuisine with a

CONSUME

Vast Food Nation

Sample the flavours of Mumbai.

MAHARASHTRIAN
The austere and healthy cuisine of the state of Maharashtra, of which Mumbai is the capital, is fairly mild, avoiding strong spices in favour of the more delicate flavours of sesame, turmeric and coriander.
Try these: *poha* (a light snack of beaten rice flakes, spices and peanuts); *sabudana vada* (chewy tapioca fritters); *kothimbir vada* (deep-fried squares of coriander and chickpea paste); *vada pav* (deep-fried potato with spices, served in bread).
Get it at: Jumbo King (*see p110*; Panshikar Aahar (*see p104*); Swati Snacks (*see p106*).

COASTAL
A broad term covering the cuisines of India's west coast, from southern Maharashtra right down to Kerala, all sharing a holy trinity of coconut, rice and fish. Malvani cooking from southern Maharashtra uses coconut milk and the sour-fruity kokum fruit in simple, delicious curries. Goans add Portuguese colonial influences of vinegar, pork and *pav* (bread). Further down, Mangaloreans grind a thick base of spices and grated coconut for their seafood and chicken curries. And deep in the south, Kerala-cooking makes use of banana flowers and stems.
Try these: Goan pork sausages; Mangalorean prawn *gassi* (a kind of curry); *neer dosa* (steamed rice bread); classic Goan fish curry-rice.
Get it at: Konkan Café (*see p91*); New Martin Lunch Home (*see p93*); Rice Boat (*see p111*); Sindhudurg (*see p108*); Sushegad Gomantak (*see p108*); Trishna (*see p101*).

PARSI
Parsi food is very rich (recipes routinely start with 'Take a dozen eggs'), heavy on the meat and slightly sweet, thanks to a Zoroastrian Persian tradition of cooking with dried fruits. It's a wonderful mélange of Middle Eastern cooking styles and Indian ingredients.
Try these: *dhansak* (a thick curry of meat, lentils and vegetables); *patra ni machchi* (fish cooked in banana leaves); *akuri* (spicy scrambled eggs).
Get it at: Britannia (*see p101*); Jimmy Boy (*see p101*).

UDIPI
South Indian vegetarian cuisine, renowned for popular snacks made from fermented ground rice like *idlis* (steamed rice cakes), lentil batter dishes like *dosas* and more substantial thalis. *Udipis* are ubiquitous across Mumbai and a regular lunchtime destination for healthy and cheap food.
Try these: *appams* (thick round pancakes); *dosa* (thin, crispy, savoury pancakes); *Udipi* thalis served on banana leaves.
Get it at: Shiv Sagar (*see p99*).

MUGHLAI
Think kebabs and biryanis. Mughlai is an ultra-rich non-vegetarian Muslim cuisine but there are also simpler versions created in casual Chillia Muslim-run eateries. The best time to experience Mumbai's Muslim food is unquestionably the month of Ramzan (*see p136* Calendar), when Muslim neighbourhoods like Mohammed Ali Road become dining extravaganzas after sunset.
Try these: *khichda* (thick stew of meat, wheat and lentils); *raan* (a tender leg of lamb, split so you get at the marrow); *khiri* (grilled udders).
Get it at: Shalimar (*see p104*), the streets around Minara Masjid.

BENGALI
Pungent, with liberal use of mustard in both seed and oil form. Combine that with poppy seeds, freshwater fish and an inventive range of sweets made from cottage cheese and you have a strikingly different cuisine.
Try these: *maccher jhol* (Bengali fish curry); *chingdi malai-kari* (prawns cooked in coconut cream); smoked *hilsa* (a Bengali freshwater fish); *mocchar ghanto* (stir-fried banana flower); *bhaja mungher dhal* (roast mung beans); *mishti doi* (a fabulous yoghurt dessert).
Get it at: Howrah (*see p104*); Oh! Calcutta (*see p106*).

GUJARATI
A mix of spicy and sweet food, the Gujarati cuisine is rich in flavour but sometimes a little heavy on ghee.
Try these: *panki* (a thin rice flour pancake); *handvo* (a spicy cake); *puranpoli* (sweet bread)
Get it at: Swati Snacks (*see p106*); Soam (*see p104*).

Mediterranean slant, with some excellent sandwiches and mains, and some truly delightful coolers. There's also a deli section with fresh bread, pastries, and imported cheeses.

Busaba

4 Mandlik Road, off Colaba Causeway (2204-3769). CST or Churchgate stations. **Open** 12.30-3pm, 6.30pm-1am daily. **Credit** AmEx, MC, V. **Main courses** Rs 500. **Map** p250 G5 ⓭ **Asian**

Busaba serves memorable pan-Asian cuisine while retaining a hip vibe. If it's dinner you're here for, skip upstairs to the peaceful dining room or the romantic enclosed terrace. Burmese *khao suey,* Korean *bipimbap* and *bulgogi,* Tibetan *momos* and Thai lime-chilly fish are favourites. The melting chocolate fondant with crème anglaise is exceptionally smooth and succeeds in its rather elaborate attempt to impress.

Café Churchill

103B East West Court Building, opposite Cusrow Baug, Colaba Causeway (2284-4689). **Open** 10.30am-midnight daily. **Main courses** Rs 300. **No credit cards. No alcohol. Map** p251 G4 ⓮ **International**

An old favourite on Colaba Causeway, Churchill's is a small, friendly eaterie usually heaving with diners at both lunch and dinner, with a queue waiting outside. It specialises in 'Continental' cooking with a menu heavy on pasta dishes, decently done, and great burgers. The desserts cabinet is a must-visit, filled with terrific cheesecakes, gateaux and mousses. Tables are packed in tight and elbow room is at a premium, but the food and the atmosphere are abundant.

★ Golden Dragon

Taj Mahal Palace & Tower, Apollo Bunder (6665-3366). Churchgate station. **Open** 12.30-2.45pm, 7-11.45pm daily. **Main courses** Rs 600-Rs 800. **Credit** AmEx, MC, V. **Map** p250 G5 ⓯ **Chinese**

The provenance of Golden Dragon's food roams widely, even ocean-hopping to Singapore, but the majority of the dishes originate in China's Sichuan province. Here the Indianisation effect is the reverse of the usual – Sichuan is too spicy even for Indians, so the chillies have been taken out. The master chef is Shi Xi Lin, a native of Beijing who was awarded the title of 'best Sichuan chef in China' in 1994. The hot and sour soup is a treat.

★ Indigo

4 Mandlik Road (6636-8999/80). CST or Churchgate stations. **Taxi** behind Taj Mahal hotel. **Open** 12.30-2.45pm, 7.30-11.45pm Mon-Sat; noon-4pm, 7.30-11.45pm Sun. **Main courses** Rs 500-Rs 800. **Credit** AmEx, MC, V. **Map** p250 G5 ⓰ **European**

Indigo was revolutionary when it first opened in 1999, breaking new ground with a sophisticated European menu of the kind previously confined to five-star hotels. It's still one of the city's finest standalone restaurants, serving dishes like carpaccio, lobster bisque and goat's cheese on grilled apples, all well executed. It also does an addictive all-you-can-eat Sunday champagne brunch (Rs 2,025). The open terrace upstairs is without a doubt the nicest spot to dine here in the evenings, but book in advance as Indigo is always busy.

Indigo Deli

Chhatrapati Shivaji Maharaj Street (6655-1010). CST or Churchgate stations. **Open** 9am-11pm daily. **Main courses** Rs 225-Rs 325. **Credit** AmEx, MC, V. **Map** p250 G5 ⓱ **European**

Indigo's younger sister is not far away, a few minutes' walk from the Regal Cinema and opposite Henry Tham's restaurant. There's a deli counter with a wide range of fresh breads, imported cheeses, meats, olives and more, plus a wall full of Indian and imported wines. The main attraction, though, is the sit-down dining area, smartly decked out in dark woods. Service is painfully slow, but the results are worth it, with some superb soups, salads and sandwiches. A great spot for breakfast or a snack, Indigo Deli also serves excellent coffees and smoothies.

Ling's Pavilion

19/21 KC College Hostel Building, Lansdowne Road, off Colaba Causeway (2285-0023). CST or Churchgate stations. **Open** noon-3pm, 6-11pm Mon; noon-11pm Tue-Sun. **Main courses** Rs 200-Rs 350. **Credit** AmEx, MC, V. **Map** p250 G5 ⓲ **Chinese**

Ling's isn't a restaurant, it's an institution. This old-timer just off Colaba Causeway has been feeding South Mumbaikars their favourite Chinese dishes for the last 17 years and shows no sign of slowing down. A large part of its appeal is the decor: a miniature Chinese bridge crossing a fake stream, cute ceiling clouds, and an upper gallery roofed with Chinese tiles. But it's mostly about the food: delectable honey-glazed spare ribs (Rs 180), crab steamed with soy sauce (around Rs 1,000) and whole steamed pomfret garnished with chicken and mushroom (Rs 700). Most of the regular dishes are available for around Rs 200-Rs 350, making it one of the city's best-value restaurants, with consistently high quality.

Thai Pavilion

Taj President, Lobby Level, Cuffe Parade (6665-0808). CST or Churchgate stations. **Open** 12.30-2.45pm, 7-11.45pm daily. **Main courses** Rs 800-Rs 1,200. **Credit** AmEx, DC, MC, V. **Map** p251 E3 ⓳ **Thai**

The same Japanese design firm that designed Wink at the same hotel and China House at the Grand Hyatt has redone the finest Thai restaurant in the

city (and possibly in India). Venture beyond phad thai and green curry to try the experiments that chef Ananda Solomon has introduced. If you're lucky, he might be cooking in the open kitchen himself, amid all that glass shelving and wooden fretwork.

Wasabi

Taj Mahal Palace & Tower, Apollo Bunder (6665-3202). CST or Churchgate stations. **Open** 12.30-3pm, 7-11.45pm daily. **Main courses** Rs 2,000. **Credit** AmEx, MC, V. **Map** p250 G5 ⑳ **Japanese**

For Mumbai's fans of Japanese cuisine, Wasabi is sacred: its head chef is Masaharu Morimoto of Nobu fame; his locally recruited chefs maintain his sky-high standards (matched by similar prices). Entered via a spiral staircase from a bar on the Taj's ground floor, Wasabi reeks of exclusivity and elegance. The food is fabulous, but there's only one saké on offer, its appeal extended by using it in an array of cocktails. Reservations essential – ask for a sea view.

★ Woodside Inn

Indian Mercantile Mansion, Wodehouse Road, opposite Regal cinema (2202-5525). Churchgate & CST station. **Open** 8am-midnight daily. **Main courses** Rs 265-Rs 345. **Credit** MC, V. **Map** p250 G6 ㉑ **Mediterranean**

Thin-crust pizza, pints of beer and long, leisurely views of the strollers on Colaba Causeway. These are the primary attractions of Woodside Inn, previously a dingy vegetarian restaurant and bar, now an airy Mediterranean-focused bistro. The management has also started breakfast, with all the old staples given a Woodside twist: waffles, pancakes and eggs.

Cafés

Barista

Cecil Court, Colaba Causeway (6633-6835). CST or Churchgate stations. **Taxi** Regal Cinema. **Open** 8.30am-1.30am daily. **Credit** MC, V. **No alcohol**. **Map** p250 G5 ㉒

A highly successful Indian café chain, modelled on Starbucks, which has now spread across India, Sri Lanka and the Middle East. The snacks and cakes are passable, but the hot and cold coffees are quite good and the decor soothing. This one's usually packed with college kids, shoppers and tourists.

Other locations 34 Chowpatty Seaface (2369-0104); Maker Towers, Cuffe Parade (2215-0562); Murzban Road, next to Sterling Cinema, near Chhatrapati Shivaji Terminus; Bandstand Building, Bandstand, Bandra (W) (2643-4287).

★ Moshe's Café

7 Minoo Manor, Cuffe Parade (2216-1226). CST or Churchgate stations. **Open** 9am-12.30am daily. **Main courses** Rs 250-Rs 550. **Credit** AmEx, MC, V. **Map** p251 E3 ㉓

Hidden behind a hedge on Cuffe Parade is this smart, high-ceilinged café with a small garden dining area. Better as a lunchtime stopover than a dinner place, Moshe's offers grilled sandwiches, salads and mains with Mediterranean flavours. There's also a wide range of coffees, desserts and coolers, like a killer limeade made with ginger, fennel and cloves, plus excellent smoothies – the papaya, yoghurt and vanilla are particularly good. They also make some excellent bread and jam.

Rs Olympia Café

Rahim Mansion, Colaba Causeway, Colaba (2202-1043). CST or Churchgate stations. **Open** 7am-midnight daily. **Main courses** Rs 30-Rs 60. **No credit cards. No alcohol. Map** p250 G5 ㉔

Olympia scores high on the 1940s period charm, with old chairs and tables, and lazy fans. It's cheap and popular with backpackers, office workers and taxi drivers crowded in together. A great spot for cheap biryanis and curries, and more exotic dishes like the brain fry. Finish with a caramel custard.

★ Theobroma

Cusrow Baug, Shop No 24, Colaba Causeway (6529-2929). CST or Churchgate stations. **Open** 8.30am-12.30am daily. **Credit** MC, V. **No alcohol. Map** p251 G4 ㉕

The name means 'food of the gods', and they aren't exaggerating. The decor is strictly terrestrial, but the food is divine; top quality sourdough loaves, fluffy focaccia, chocolate brownies, Danish pastries and freshly made, five-star hotel quality sandwiches. An excellent lunch and snack spot.

Other location: 29/30, Link Square Mall, Near KFC, Bandra (W) (2646-9010).

NARIMAN POINT

Indian

Moti Mahal Delux

102 CR2 Shopping Mall, First Floor, Barrister Rajni Patel Marg (6654-6454). Churchgate station. **Taxi** INOX Cinema. **Open** noon-4pm, 7pm-midnight daily. **Main courses** Rs 250-Rs 400. **Credit** MC, V. **Map** p250 E6 ㉖ **North Indian**

INSIDE TRACK ORGANIC BREAD

Moshe's Café (*see left*) now bakes organic bread as well as 100 percent fat-free bread. Available at their cafes across the city, they go well with Moshe's home-made jams – try out the chilli flavoured jam.

INSIDE TRACK
BREAKFAST OF THE GODS

Olympia's (*see p97*) is great for breakfast, but only if you time it right. It's made at 7am and stock runs out in two hours. The next batch is prepared only at 11am.

Moti Mahal (meaning 'Pearl Palace') is part of a chain of restaurants that originated in Peshawar in the 1920s. The Mumbai version is contemporary: wooden floors, sheer white drapes and a glass-wrapped kitchen. Listen out for the twang of Delhi accents – this is where expat North Indians come for home-style food. Go for the tender *lasooni* kebabs (Rs 309) and the soft naans (Rs 59). The butter chicken (Rs 309) alone makes a trip here worthwhile. Finish off with a sweet, thick lassi.

★ Ziya

The Oberoi, opposite NCPA, Nariman Point (6632-5757). **Open** 12.30-2.30pm, 7-11.30pm daily. **Set meals** Rs 1,200 upwards. **Credit** AmEx, MC, V. **Map** p250 D6 ㉗ **Modern Indian**

Ziya stops short of 'fusion' or 'nouvelle Indian', venturing only to suggest that 'the light and imaginative dishes display a clever balance between innovation and an immense respect for the history of Indian cooking'. Chef Vineet Bhatia's food is characterised by an attempt to be different. Book a table if you're willing to have familiar assumptions about Indian food rattled – in the most pleasant way possible.

► *For more international fare, try Fenix; see right.*

CONSUME

International

Fenix

Trident Hotel, Nariman Point (6632-6205). Churchgate station. **Open** 6.30am-11.30pm daily. **Set meals** *Bollinger Brut brunch* Rs 3,200; *Bollinger Rose brunch* Rs 3,800. **Credit cards** AmEx, MC, V. Mp p251 D6. Map p250 D6 ㉘ **Fusion**

Trident's new restaurant serves European, Asian and Indian cuisines along with Japanese food, which includes sushi, sashimi and temaki hand rolls. It also offers a champagne brunch.

Japengo Café

Ground Floor, CR2 Shopping Mall, Barrister Rajni Patel Marg (6633-4040). Churchgate station. **Open** 11am-11pm daily. **Main courses** Rs 300-Rs 700. **Credit** AmEx, MC, V. **No alcohol. Map** p250 E6 ㉙ **Fusion**

At the Mumbai branch of the Dubai-based chain of Japengo Café cafés the choices span everything from pasta and fish and chips to yakitori, houmous and dim sum. While the menu is rather alarmingly diverse – covering Italy, Lebanon, Japan, China and South-east Asia – it's hard to find fault with the cooking. The decor infuses a casual spirit into the place: bamboo twigs fall down the sides of ceiling lights, seating is a mix of minimal backless stools, high-backed chairs and a sit-down lounge area, and you get to watch the chefs at work.

Vetro

The Oberoi, Lobby Level, Nariman Point (6632-5757). Churchgate station. **Open** 12.30-3pm, 7-11.30pm daily. **Main courses** Rs 750-Rs 1,800. **Credit** AmEx, MC, V. **Map** p250 D6 ㉚ **Italian**

Ziya.

One of South Mumbai's high-end Italian restaurants, with a beautiful interior design. Row upon row of coloured windows line the walls, reflecting the afternoon sunlight so that it forms criss-crossing rainbows. As soon as you enter you'll be invited for a wine-tasting session before you eat. There's a walk-in antipasti bar, including juicy stuffed olives and very good carpaccio, parma ham and salads. The starters and salads are outstanding – so good, in fact, that they leave the mains a little in the shade.

VongWong

First Floor, Express Towers, Ramnath Goenka Marg (2287-5633/34). **Open** 12.30-3.30pm, 7-11.45pm daily. **Main courses** Rs 600-Rs 1,000. **Credit** AmEx, MC, V. **Map** p250 D6 ㉛ **East Asian**

Occupying the space formerly used by the printing press of the Indian Express newspaper, VongWong is a gorgeous Chinese and Thai restaurant named for its chefs, the very talented Vong and Wong. Split into three sections, including a private dining room, VongWong is expansive in both size and menu: diners have over 300 dishes to choose from and the dim sum are particularly impressive.

CHURCHGATE & MARINE LINES

Indian

Panchvati Gaurav

Vithaldas Thackersey Marg, Marine Lines (2208-4877). Marine Lines station. **Taxi** Bombay Hospital. **Open** 11am-3pm, 7-10.30pm daily. **Thali** Rs 180 **Credit** MC, V. **No alcohol**. **Map** p253 F10 ㉜ **Gujarati**

One of the city's favourite thali places, Panchvati Gaurav specialises in Gujarati thalis. Still a regular destination for the office lunch crowd, it's unbeatable value for money and boasts excellent service. The sweet, milky Gujarati curry is light and tasty, the *farsan* (snacks) delicious with papads and pickles, and dessert included.

Samrat

Prem Court, Jamsetji Tata Road, Churchgate (2282-0942). Churchgate station. **Open** noon-11pm daily. **Thali** Lunch Rs 163, dinner Rs 197. **Credit** AmEx, MC, V. **Map** p250 & p253 F7 ㉝ **Gujarati**

Samrat is almost legendary in the city for its Gujarati thalis, attracting big crowds at lunchtimes from the offices around Churchgate and Nariman Point. The thalis are 'unlimited', with a smartly uniformed waiter on hand to make sure your *katoris* are constantly filled to the brim with four types of vegetables, two *farsan*, two sweet dishes, and mountains of *puris*, papads and rice. It's consistently fabulous – just don't plan on doing anything more strenuous than digesting for a few hours afterwards.

Rs Shiv Sagar

Nagin Mahal, 82 Veer Nariman Road, Churchgate (2282-4862). Churchgate station. **Open** 9am-12.30am daily. **Main courses** Rs 70-Rs 170. **Credit** AmEx, MC, V. **Map** p250 & p253 F8 ㉞ **South Indian**

A neat, clean but hectic Udipi joint serving lunch to the office crowd in the busy Churchgate district. Skip most of the menu and head straight for the South Indian fare – crisp *dosas* and soft *idlis* – and the tasty *pao bhajis*. It also does a good selection of street-style snacks, hygienically prepared.

International

Oriental Blossom

Marine Plaza Hotel, 29 Marine Drive, Churchgate (2285-1212). Churchgate station. **Open** 12.30-2.45pm, 7.30-11.30pm daily. **Main courses** Rs 400-Rs 1,200. **Credit** AmEx, MC, V. **Map** p250 & p253 E7 ㉟ **Cantonese**

House restaurant of the Marine Plaza Hotel, the Blossom makes a very decent Cantonese cuisine. Some dishes are heavy on the sauces but the freshness of the ingredients wins out. Book in advance.

Pearl of the Orient

Ambassador Hotel, Veer Nariman Road, Churchgate (2204-1131). Churchgate station. **Open** 12.30-2.45pm, 7.30-11.45pm daily. **Main courses** Rs 350-Rs 1,200. **Credit** AmEx, MC, V. **Map** p250 & p253 E8 ㊱ **East Asian**

Mumbai's only revolving restaurant, on the 12th floor of a 1970s-built concrete tower housing the Ambassador Hotel. It's an East Asian eaterie with an emphasis on Hunan, Sichuan and Cantonese dishes, plus some sushi and Thai food – all competently prepared by a chef with a penchant for carving roses out of beetroots. It has spectacular views of the sea, the sweep of Marine Drive and the cityscape through its floor-to-ceiling windows, with the restaurant completing a circuit every 90 minutes.

Cafés

Mocha

Nagin Mahal, Veer Nariman Road, Churchgate (6633-6070). Churchgate station. **Open** 9am-1.30am daily. **Credit** AmEx, MC, V. **Map** p250 & p253 F8 ㊲

A trendy hangout for well-heeled college kids, with a Middle Eastern vibe complete with fez-adorned waiters. The thing to do here is lounge on a bolster passing around a flavoured hookah with your mates, whilst slurping on a pricey coffee. They also serve wine and Bacardi Breezers – no beer – and a range of workmanlike Euro-dishes. The service is sluggish, so be prepared to spend a few hours here. **Other locations** near Holy Family Hospital, Hill Road, Bandra (W) (2643-3098); Juhu Beach, Juhu Tara Road (2617-5495).

★ Tea Centre

Resham Bhavan, 78 Veer Nariman Road, Churchgate (2281-9142). Churchgate station. **Open** 8am-10.30pm daily. **Main courses** Rs 300-Rs 400. **Credit** AmEx, MC, V. **Map** p250 & p253 F8 38

The Tea Centre is an eminently civilised showcase of India's finest teas, served by turbaned waiters in stiff uniforms. On offer are varieties of Assam, Darjeeling and Nilgiris, both hot and iced, plus street tea, train tea and a selection of tea 'mocktails', such as mint tea with ice-cream. It's a nice spot for a light lunch as it also offers snacks and sandwiches. We recommend settling down with its hot apple butter tea and chilli garlic potatoes.

FORT & KALA GHODA

Indian

Rs Britannia

Ram Gulam Road, Ballard Estate, near Fort (2261-5264). CST station. **Taxi** opposite New Custom House. **Open** 11.30am-4pm Mon-Sat. **Main courses** Rs 60-Rs 200. **No credit cards. No alcohol. Map** p253 J8 39 **Irani & Parsi**

Despite the dilapidated wooden interior, complete with wobbly chairs, peeling walls and dusty chandeliers, Britannia, a classic Irani restaurant of a type now slowly dying out, manages to exude a homely 1940s charm. Open only for lunch, it's famous for its fabulous berry pulao, a traditional Iranian dish of boneless mutton (Rs 240) or chicken (Rs 200) in a sweet, spicy masala and garnished with tart Iranian berries. If you still have room, follow it with a creamy caramel custard.

Jimmy Boy Café

11 Bank Street, Vikas Building, Fort (2270-0880). CST station. **Taxi** Horniman Circle. **Open** 11am-10.30pm daily. **Main courses** Rs 200-Rs 250. **Credit** MC, V. **No alcohol. Map** p250 & p253 H7 40 **Parsi**

Jimmy Boy is best known for its Parsi specialities, particularly *lagan nu bhonu* – Parsi wedding food. Try the delightful *murghi na farcha* (crumb-fried spiced chicken), *patra ni machchi* (chutney-stuffed pomfret wrapped in banana leaves), *jardaloo sali boti* (boneless mutton cooked with dried apricots and an onion and tomato gravy) and the signature Parsi dish, mutton *dhansak* (a lentil and vegetable curry). It's popular with Parsis and non-Parsis alike, so make a reservation.

Khyber

145 MG Road, Kala Ghoda (2267-3227). CST or Churchgate stations. **Open** 12.30-3.30pm, 7.30-11.30pm daily. **Main courses** Rs 250-Rs 350. **Credit** AmEx, DC, MC, V. **Map** p250 G7 41 **North Indian**

A sprawling, two-level restaurant grandly furnished in wood and stone, Khyber is an old favourite of fans of North Indian cuisine, with consistently high standards. Top choices here include its tender *raan* – a slow-cooked leg of lamb – as well as the biryani and the paneer korma.

Mahesh Lunch Home

8B Cawasji Patel Street, Fort (2287-0938). CST station. **Open** noon-4pm, 6pm-midnight daily. **Main courses** Rs 250-Rs 300. **Credit** AmEx, DC, MC, V. **Map** p250 & p253 H8 42 **Konkan & Manglorean**

Less fancy in its decor than its Mangalorean seafood sister Trishna, Mahesh nevertheless keeps up with the competition with its food – excellent Konkan coastal and Mangalorean cuisine, in particular some killer *gassi* and excellent curry-rice.

Mocambo Café & Beer Bar

23A PM Road, Fort (2287-0458). CST station. **Open** 11.30am-11.30pm daily. **Main courses** Rs 200-Rs 300. **Credit** AmEx, MC, V. **Map** p250 & p253 H8 43 **Parsi & Goan**

A spruced-up old-timer, Mocambo does Parsi food, Goan curries and some of the best pork chops in town. An ancient gent on the mezzanine plonks away on a mini-piano.

Trishna

7 Sai Baba Marg, Kala Ghoda (2270-3214). CST station. **Taxi** behind Rhythm House. **Open** noon-3.30pm, 6pm-midnight daily. **Main courses** Rs 250-Rs 700. **Credit** AmEx, DC, MC, V. **Map** p250 G7 44 **Manglorean**

A popular seafood restaurant famed for its South Indian Mangalorean dishes. The decor is ornate and the food good enough to keep the South Mumbai elite and the odd celebrity coming back. Favourites include the prawn *gassi*, the butter-pepper-garlic crab and stuffed pomfret.

International

Joss

K Dubash Marg, Kala Ghoda (6633-4233). Churchgate station. **Taxi** Rhythm House. **Open** 12.30-3.30pm, 7.30-11.30pm daily. **Main courses** Rs 320-Rs 975. **Credit** AmEx, MC, V. **Map** p250 G6 45 **Asian**

This smart, subtly lit place used to be a Thai restaurant (that what the gold-and-glass Thai temple-style wall decor is all about); it's now become one of the city's most impressive pan-Asian restaurants, with a range of Singaporean, Indonesian, Thai, Chinese, Japanese and Korean dishes. It also does a fine line in fusion experiments like aki miso-marinated tenderloin. With such a broad menu, it's a great place to come if you're feeling indecisive about what to eat. All of the dishes are good, and there's an impressive array of sushi.

Royal China

SP Corporation Building, behind Sterling Cinema, Hazarimal Somani Marg, Fort (2207-2492). CST station. **Open** noon-2.30pm, 7-11.30pm daily. **Main courses** Rs 475-Rs 900. **Credit** AmEx, DC, MC, V. **Map** p253 G10 46 **Chinese**

Royal China is arguably the city's finest Cantonese restaurant, one of the few places where Mumbaikars can eat authentic Chinese food (*see below* Bombay Mix for more on Indian chinese cuisine). Big favourites with the local crowd are dishes in sauces and with strong flavours, like the crispy aromatic duck served with paper-thin pancakes and plum sauce. Royal China is also the local pioneer of dim sum – nowhere else comes close in terms of choice or quality – with a dedicated chef who prepares up to 50 different kinds daily.

Other location 192 Turner Road, Bandra (W) (6704-9553).

Bombay Mix

Indochina on a plate.

Indian-Chinese cuisine may have been born in Kolkata's China Town, but it was a Mumbaikar who invented chicken Manchurian. Heavily doused with soy sauce and flavoured with the potent triumvirate of ginger, garlic and chillies, this hugely popular dish was rapidly adopted by restaurants across the country.

Indian-Chinese takes on many forms in Mumbai. Moderately spicy Sichuan cuisine, which was introduced to the country in Mumbai, quickly metamorphosed into the fiercely sour-pungent, heart-thumping, nose-watering version. Thrice as potent is the layered triple Szechwan, consisting of fried rice topped with meat in Szechwan sauce and garnished with crispy fried noodles and a double fried egg. If you hunt hard enough you might even find a culinary rapprochement between Indian, American and Chinese cuisines in the form of the Szechwan chop suey.

Finding a parallel between the crisp noodles of a chop-suey and*sev*, the crisp broken chickpea flour noodles used in *bhel puri*, creative restauranteurs mixed the sauce with the noodles and created Chinese *bhel*. Of course, you won't find any of these ingenious dishes on a fancy restaurant menu but they're freely available at any of the multi-cuisine restaurants that dot the city.

The city's most ubiquitous and popular fast food – South Indian cuisine – couldn't escape the Sino influence either. Szechwan *dosas* and *idli* Manchurian proliferate in quick-service Udipi restaurants. The *dosas* are prepared from a regular batter, with the normal dry potato filling and usual accompaniments; the only difference is that the inner surface of the *dosa* is smeared with a Szechwan chutney. The *idli* Manchurian, however, is slightly different: soft, fluffy *idlis* are deep fried till hard, cut into halves or quarters and served in a cornflour-thickened Manchurian sauce. It is popular enough to have made it to mid-level hotel buffets.

Inspiration has come from the west, too, and one of Mumbai's iconic snacks, the Frankie, is an adaptation of Middle Eastern *shawarma*. The pitta bread has been substituted with a soft Indian roti and the mutton, chicken and potato filling was made spicier, sourer and juicier. And yes, there is a Szechwan Frankie too.

Japanese food may have only arrived in Mumbai more recently but the sizzler, a Mumbai invention based on the teppanyaki concept, has been around for a few decades. Sautéd red meat, chicken, fish or vegetable steak is accompanied with boiled vegetables, chips and noodles or rice and served on a hot cast iron plate placed in a thick wooden tray. Steaming and noisy, the sizzler is a loud culinary spectacle to behold – and tasty too. With Japanese cuisine catching on, it's only a matter of time before the city starts biting into a sushi *dosa* and tempura-style *pakodas*.

New Yorker

25 Fulchand Niwas, Chowpatty (2367-7500). Charni Road station. **Open** noon-midnight daily. **Map** p254 B15

Tibb's Frankies

Kiosk at Aga Brothers Restaurant, 16A Cusrow Baug, Colaba Causeway (2283-0692, www.tibbsfrankies.com). CST & Churchgate station. **Open** noon-9.30pm daily. **Map** p251 F4

Yoko Sizzlers

Junction of Cowasji Patel Street and Rustom Sidhwa Marg, behind Citibank, Fort (6636-4606). CST or Churchgate stations. **Open** noon-11.30pm daily. **Map** p250 H8

CONSUME

Tote on the Turf. See p105.

Cafés

Kala Ghoda Café

10 Ropewalk Lane, Kala Ghoda (2263-3866). **Open** noon-11.30pm Tue-Sun **Main courses** Rs 100-Rs 220. **No credit cards**. **Map** p250 G7 47

With its warm minimalist aesthetic and light barn-like setting, the Kala Ghoda Café definitely looks the part of an artsy hangout. It has a conversation-friendly location, polite staff and some mouthwatering chocolate cake. Try its home-blended organic coffee, which knocks the socks off the stuff doled at the chain cafés.

MARINE DRIVE

Indian

Kebab Korner

InterContinental Marine Drive, 135 Marine Drive (6639-9999). Churchgate station. **Open** 12.30-2.45pm, 7.30-11.45pm daily. **Main courses** Rs 450-Rs 1,100. **Credit** AmEx, MC, V. **Map** p250 & p253 E8 48 **North Indian**

Kebab Korner was an institution that shut down years ago, before being recreated in 2005 with its original chefs and traditional cooking style – the kebabs here are made on a *sigri* (a kind of coal-fired grill) instead of a tandoor oven. The results are stunning – tender and subtly flavoured seekh kebabs, spicy butter chicken (Rs 680) and outrageously tasty *kali dal* (Rs 600). The biryani is also to die for, as is the house special 'Busybee' stuffed chicken kebab (Rs 725) served with burnt onions and yoghurt chutney. Add a sea view and the sumptuous wood and marble decor, and you have a Mumbai classic.

International

Koh by Kittichai

InterContinental Marine Drive, 135 Marine Drive (3987-9999). Churchgate station. **Open** 12.30-3pm, 7.30-11.45pm daily. **Main courses** Rs 695-Rs 1,100. **Credit** AmEx, MC, V. **Map** p250 & p253 E8 49 **Thai**

It's clear that chef Pongtawat 'Ian' Kittichai – a Bangkok native who has been involved in restaurants in New York and Barcelona – isn't satisfied merely cooking up the standards of the Thai menu. The dishes he's created for Koh (which means 'island' in Thai) use familiar Thai ingredients such as kaffir lime, tamarind and hot basil in new contexts: they're paired with lamb chops, sea bass and fillet mignon, creating intriguing flavours that linger in the memory long after you've returned to the tribulations of the real world.

Pizzeria

Soona Mahal, 143 Marine Drive (6730-5626). Churchgate station. **Open** noon-12.30am daily. **Main courses** Rs 260-Rs 350. **Credit** AmEx, MC, V. **Map** p250 & p253 E8 50 **Italian**

On the corner of Marine Drive and Veer Nariman Road, Pizzeria offers a fine view of the bay, passing traffic and hurrying commuters. The pizzas are thoroughly enjoyable Indian versions of old favourites, but try the local inventions like the Bombay Masala: plain cheese with spices. Perfect to while away an afternoon drinking beer and watching the world go by.

Cafés

Bachelor's Juice House

Marine Drive, opposite Chowpatty Beach (2368-2211). Churney Road station. **Open** 10.30am-2.30am daily. **No credit cards**. **No alcohol**. **Map** p254 C14 51

Easy to spot from the rows of fruit and parked cars, Bachelor's isn't a 'house' at all. It's a street stall, although a superior stall on a superior street – the bayfront Marine Drive. Bachelor's has ice-cream, milkshakes and fresh juices, all made with fresh fruit. Everything is superb, but the highlights are

> **INSIDE TRACK**
> **EAT UPSIDE DOWN**
>
> If you plan to visit the city during the winter, sample *undhiyu* – a dish from Gujarat which is a medley of seven vegetables, cooked in a garlicky spice mix. The dish is named after 'undhu', the Gujarati word for upside down. In the farms of Surat (a city in Gujarat), earthen pots of fresh vegetables are buried underground with grass and twigs piled on top and ignited, hence the meal is cooked upside down, under a fire, instead of above it. Try a version of it at **Soam** (*see below*) and **Thaker Bhojnalay** (*see p107*).

the watermelon, custard apple, mango, roast almond and green chilli ice-creams (Rs 55 for a large cup).

GIRGAUM

Indian

Govinda's

Sri Sri Radha Gopinath Mandir, 7 KM Munshi Marg, near Bharatiya Vidya Bhavan, Chowpatty (2366-5566/67). Churney Road station. **Open** 11am-10pm daily. **Main courses** Rs 95-Rs 225. **Credit** MC, V. **No alcohol. Map** p254 A15 52 **Indian**

Run by the International Society for Krishna Consciousness, Govinda's serves vegetarian food but doesn't limit itself only to North Indian fare. It does stir-fries, South Indian *dosas*, and some excellent pizzas. Best of all, everything that comes out of the kitchen is first offered to, and blessed by, the gods themselves, which, say the temple staff, tastes different 'because it has been tasted by the lord so it is almost like it has his saliva on it'.

Panshikar Aahar

Govardhandas Building, Jagganath Sankarseth Road (2386-1211). Grant Road station. **Taxi** Girgaum Church. **Open** 8am-10pm daily. **Main courses** Rs 15-Rs 30. **No credit cards. No alcohol. Map** p254 C15 53 **Maharashtrian**

Maharashtrian vegetarian food, Panshikar's speciality, is the interesting category of *upvas* (fast) dishes, food meant to be eaten on traditional Hindu fast days that prohibit the consumption of 'sown' foods, meaning anything grown in a ploughed field. This includes fruits, roots and tubers. Panshikar Aahar makes most standard Mumbai snacks in *upvas* form.

★ Soam

Sadguru Sadan, Ground floor, Babulnath Road, Chowpatty (2369-8080). Grant Road station. **Taxi** Babulnath Temple. **Open** noon-midnight daily. **Main courses** Rs 120-Rs 170. **Credit** MC, V. **No alcohol. Map** p254 A15 54 **Gujarati**

The true test of a Gujarati snack joint is its *pankhi* chutney (pancakes steamed in banana leaves), and Soam passes with flying colours. The intense heat makes it almost difficult to touch, but hold up the banana leaf and the pancake falls off in one piece – perfect. Furnished in dark wood, ochre-coloured walls, bamboo blinds and comfy seating, Soam is the favourite alternative to South Mumbai's other hugely popular (and always crowded) Gujarati snack joint, Swati Snacks (*see p106*).

CRAWFORD MARKET

Indian

Howrah

Sitaram Building, B Block, Crawford Market (2344-2690). CST station. **Open** 11am-4pm, 7-11.30pm daily. **Main courses** Rs 150-Rs 200. **Credit** AmEx, DC, MC, V. **No alcohol. Map** p252 H12 55 **Bengali**

Howrah is a restaurant specialising in Bengali cuisine. Despite being right next to one of the city's most hectic markets, Howrah's one-flight-up terrace offers a relaxed dining experience, with old-fashioned ceiling fans and smiling *dhoti*-clad waiters. Just think of a lazy afternoon in Kolkata, with an '80s Bengali pop soundtrack to make expat Kolkatans (most of the customers) feel at home. Howrah is best known for its fish dishes, especially freshwater fish like the delish *ilish*, a regional delicacy flown in from Bengal. Try a creamy cardamom gravy of *malai* curry or the complex *daab* style, in which the fish is baked in a coconut shell.

▶ *Discovered a taste for Bengali food? Also check out Oh! Calcutta on p106.*

Rajdhani

361 Sheikh Memon Street, near Crawford Market (2342-6919). CST station. **Taxi** Crawford Market. **Open** noon-4pm, 7-10.30pm daily. **Thali** Rs 190 Mon-Sat, Rs 225 Sun. **Credit** AmEx, MC, V. **No alcohol. Map** p252 & p255 G13 56 **Gujarati**

Rajdhani is an oasis of calm in a narrow, frantic side street a few metres from the bustle of the historic Crawford Market. Getting here requires some Frogger-style negotiation of the local traffic of hand pulled carts, but if you make it, you'll be treated to a superior Gujarati thali with endless refills of *palak paneer* (spinach and cottage cheese), sweet *kadi* (a gram flour-based curry), *aloo subzi* (masala potato), kidney bean curry and more. Take a glass of *chaas* (buttermilk) and finish off with some *gulab jamun*.

Rs Shalimar

Vazir Building, Bhendi Bazaar, Mohammed Ali Road (2345-6632,2346-5286). CST station.

Taxi Bhendi Bazaar Fire Station. **Open** 9am-1am daily. **Main courses** Rs 35-Rs 250. **Credit** MC, V. **No alcohol**. **Map** p255 G15 (57) **Indian**
Meat, meat, and more meat... this is Mumbai Muslim food at its most carnivorous. Shalimar makes no concessions to health fads, serving up extremely rich and spicy kebabs and other delights. The traditional dishes are great – try the *raan*, a leg of lamb from the restaurant's own livestock, split so you can get at the marrow – but avoid the optimistic but ill-conceived 'Mexican' and 'Chinese' fusion dishes. It's a little claustrophobic and usually packed, so expect a short wait for a table.

MAHALAXMI

International

Tote on the Turf

Mahalaxmi Racecourse, opposite Gate Nos. 4 & 5, KK Marg (6157-7777). Mahalaxmi station. **Open** 7pm-1.30am daily. **Main courses** Rs 585-Rs 1,285. **Credit** MC, V. **Fusion**
Chef and restaurant owner Rahul Akerkar's latest show-off is spread over 2,325 stunning square metres. Open kitchens have chefs plating dishes, artfully angling one element of highly modern chow

Theme Perks

Decor-centric dining.

Mumbai's largest suburb is also its quirkiest. In which other part of the city beside Andheri could you have your order taken by a policeman and your mojito served by waiters dressed like jailbirds? Or gobble up plates of chicken chilli sitting in an open-top rickshaw? So, if you're bored of formal eateries – or if you've got kids in tow – here are some supper suggestions.

Pratap's Wild Dining is a forest-themed restaurant, where life-sized models of apes, deer, alligators, leopards and tigers stare down at diners through dense plastic foliage. As parents pick at plates of *reshmi tikka*, the kids amuse themselves hiding daddy's beer bottle caps behind statues of tribal men in grass skirts. At **the Jail**, customers can dine in cells dedicated to Bollywood baddies such as Gabbar Singh, Bandit Queen, Don and Mogambo. Everything is covered in black-and-white stripes: the table linen, the side plates, the steel glasses and the menu.

In 2009, **21 Fahrenheit** opened in Oshiwara. Everything in the bar and lounge is made of ice: the walls, tables, seating, even the glasses and the bead curtains. Patrons cough up Rs 1,250 to rent fur-lined parkas and moon boots for the evening so they don't freeze. It might be 35° outside but in here the temperature is a steady -6° celsius. On most Fridays, the bar is moderately full of people skidding along its floors, downing vodka shots and moving to hip hop.

If that's not your idea of chilling, then head to **Firangi Dhaba**, where the open-air seating has mosaic floors, charpoys (beds), lurid Bollywood posters on the walls and sewing machines that double as tables. There's also **Chandni Chowk**, where the owners have tried to recreate the iconic Delhi market in the style of a kitschy movie set. There's a plaster barber giving a never-ending haircut to his unmoving customer, sari and bangle stores on the perimeter and a shuttered store of a hakim who promises to cure male weakness and constipation. A mechanised traffic cop directs diners from the mall's food court into the restaurant's garden benches. Go ahead, indulge your senses.

21 Fahrenheit
Meera Apartments, near Mega Mall, off New Link Road, Oshiwara, Andheri (W) (2631-0021). **Open** 2pm-midnight daily. **Mains** Rs 350. **Credit** MC, V.

Firangi Dhaba
9 Remi Bizcourt, opposite Supreme Plastic, off Veera Desai Road, Andheri (W) (2674-3232). **Open** noon-3.30pm, 7pm-12.30am daily. **Mains** Rs 112-Rs 310. **Credit** Amex, MC, V.

The Jail
The Jail Sindhudurg Bhavan, Third Floor, above Grand Imperial Banquets, Four Bungalows (2631-6100). **Open** 12.30pm-1am daily. **Credit** MC, V.

Prataap's Chandni Chowk
Mega Mall, Fourth Floor, Oshiwara, Andheri (W) (2631-5353). **Open** 11am-11pm daily. **Mains** Rs 300. **Credit** MC, V. **No alcohol**.

Prataap's Wild Dining
Om Heera Panna Shopping Arcade, Third Floor, Oshiwara, Andheri (W) (2636-2020). **Open** 12.30-3.30pm, 7.30pm-12.30am daily. **Mains** Rs 300. **Credit** MC, V.

Thali Ho!

All-you-can-eat in one plate.

Bhagat Tarachand
Mumbadevi Commercial Centre, 51-53 Zaveri Bazaar (2242-0215). **Open** 11.30am-3.30pm, 7-10.30pm daily.
Bhagat Tarachand has two thali options: deluxe or Jain (no onions, potatoes and garlic). Both are just as spicy, oily and satisfying.

Friends Union Joshi Club
381A Kalbadevi Road, opposite Kalbadevi Temple, Narottamwadi (2205-8089). **Open** 11am-3pm, 7-10pm Mon-Sat; 11am-3pm Sun.
It's been around since 1947, but the FUJC remains tricky to find. Look for a large, bright red neon sign, go through the gateway underneath it and take the staircase up to the first floor. It's worth discovering, as the Gujarati shopkeepers who eat there almost daily will tell you. It offers one of the tastiest all-you-can-eat Gujarati thalis in the city.

Golden Star Thali
Raja Ram Mohan Roy Road, opposite Charni Road Station on the east side, Charni Road (2363-1983, 2367-1952). **Open** 11.30am-3.30pm, 7-10.30pm daily.
Golden Star Thali is where bottomless stomachs meet their match in endless servings of Gujarati and Rajasthani food. Come with a large appetite.

Mani Lunch Home
Model Co-Op Hostel Society, 384 Dadbawala Sadan, Telang Road, Matunga (W) (2412-7188). **Open** 7am-10.30pm daily.
Skip breakfast. Mani's serves rotis, *parippu* (dal), *kuttukari* (vegetable yam and Bengal gram), *avial* (mixed vegetables in coarse coconut), *thoran* (dry curry) along with *sambar* and *rasam* and a tall glass of buttermilk and banana chips to start with. Then there are heaps of red rice, more vegetables, curries and *payasam*

CONSUME

over another, drizzling sauce like Pollock with a paintbrush. As with other Akerkar menus Tote's is an eyebrow-raising read and this is not somewhere to take fussy eaters. There is mushroom tiramisu, and seared foie gras with a mini duck burger, morel brioche and cranberry marmalade.

WORLI

International

★ Two One Two Bar & Grill
12A Hornby Vellard Estate, opposite Nehru Centre, next to Jewel of India (2490-1994). **Open** 11am-1.30pm daily. **Credit** AmEx, MC, V. **Main courses** Rs 500-Rs 545. **Mediterranean**
The Mediterranean menu abounds with pesto, tapenade and sage butter concoctions. There's a list of thin-crust pizzas like quattro formaggio, and prosciutto and basil, as well as pastas and a grills section that boasts beef, pork and fish.

TARDEO

Indian

Oh! Calcutta
Rosewood Hotel, Tulsiwadi Lane (2496-3145). Mumbai Central station. **Open** noon-3pm, 7pm-midnight daily. **Main courses** Rs 300-Rs 450. **Credit** AmEx, MC, V. **Bengali**
Oh to be in Cal. Oh! Calcutta provides a culinary home-from-home for misty-eyed Bengali customers. The must-try dish here is the *ilish maacher apturi* – lightly spiced boneless hilsa fish from the Ganges marinated in mustard paste and green chillies, then baked. Make sure you leave enough room after your main course: there should be a law forbidding diners from leaving without trying the *mishti doi* – a creamy yoghurt.

★ Swati Snacks
248 Karai Estate (6580-8406, 2352-4994). Grant Road station. **Taxi** opposite Bhatia Hospital. **Open** 11am-11pm daily. **Main courses** Rs 50-Rs 100. **Credit** MC, V. **No alcohol. Map** p254 B18 58 **Gujarati**
Back in the 1960s, Swati Snacks was little more than a shack on the street serving Gujarati food. Now, it's a swanky, shiny spacecraft of glass and stainless steel. The menu is packed with gorgeous Gujarati staples and some Mumbai street fare like *dahi batata puri* and *idlis*. Everything on the menu is outstanding, in particular the delectable *panki chatni* (rice pancakes steamed in banana leaves) and the *dal dhokli* – a thick lentil curry with a cinnamon flavouring, filled with soft squares of chapati. There's also a good selection of fresh juices. Be warned, lunchtimes here are packed; no reservations are taken and 40-minute waits are not uncommon. Try their delicious sugarcane and ginger juice mix while you wait.

paladapradhaman, the South Indian version of *kheer* (rice pudding).

Panchvati Gaurav
Infiniti Mall, New Link Road, Lokhandwala, Andheri (W) (2634-7575). **Open** noon-4pm, 7-11pm daily.
Panchvati Gaurav's big shiny plates offers a set meal that makes it one of the most indulgent in the city.

Rama Nayak Boarding
LBS Market Building, First Floor, outside Matunga Central station (2414-2422). **Open** 10.30am-2.30pm, 7-10pm Tue-Sun.
Over 60 years after A Rama Nayak founded Mumbai's first Udipi, Rama continues to serve delicately spiced, healthy Gowd Saraswat Brahmin vegetarian food.

Swadshakti
Ayushakti Ayurved Health Centre, Bhadran Nagar Cross Road 2, off SV Road, opposite Milap Cinema, Malad (W) (2806-5757). **Open** 8.30am-10pm daily.
Swadshakti's ayurvedic thali excludes meat, tomatoes, brinjal, ladies' fingers, tamarind, curd and other fermented substances. Instead you'll find a number of rice-based dishes like noodles, *khichdis* (a mash of dal and rice), freshly ground *dosas* and pancakes topped with fruit that will make you feel like you've erased the accumulated sins of years of bad eating.

Thaker Bhojanalay
Dadyseth Agiary Lane, off Kalbadevi Road (2208-8035). **Open** 11am-3pm, 7-10pm Mon-Sat; 11am-3pm Sun.
Proprietor Gautam Purohit could have been a fashion designer but he chose to take on the family business. Give thanks to that decision with every bite of his fantastic, creamy dal. Perhaps the best way to round off *farsan* (savouries), four vegetables, *kadhis*, ghee-smeared rotis and *dal dhokli*.

PAREL & LOWER PAREL

Indian

Kebabs & Kurries
ITC Grand Central, Babasaheb Ambedkar Road, Parel (2410-1010). Lower Parel station. **Open** 12.30-2.45pm, 7.30-11.45pm daily. **Main courses** Rs 450-Rs 1,500. **Credit** AmEx, MC, V. **Indian**
A sprawling five-star hotel restaurant of light stone and dark wood, serving a range of Indian cuisines, all cooked perfectly. Choose from Punjabi, Mughlai, Hyderabadi, Malayali and more, with extensive vegetarian options. Try the rich and tender *murgh aloo qaliya* – chicken and potato in a spicy sauce – and skip the rice for the soft, napkin-sized *roomali rotis*.

International

Asia 7
Palladium, Level 3, High Street Phoenix, Senapati Bapat Marg, Lower Parel (4347-3901). Lower Parel station. **Open** noon-3.30pm, 7.30pm-midnight Mon-Thur & noon-midnight Fri-Sun. **Main courses** Rs 375-Rs 800. **Credit** MC, V. **Asian**
Asia 7 is so named for the seven countries its menu borrows from. That's Vietnam, Thailand, Korea, Burma, China, Japan and Indonesia.
▶ *Feast at the Palladium and head to the Comedy Store; see p166.*

Tasting Room
Good Earth, Raghuvanshi Mills Compound, next to High Street Phoenix, Senapati Bapat Marg, Lower Parel (2495-1954). Lower Parel station. **Open** 11am-11pm daily. **Main courses** Rs 150-Rs 180. **Credit** MC, V. **Fusion**
Located inside the very posh furniture and lifestyle accessory store Good Earth (*see p130*), the Tasting Room has an expansive wine menu teamed with salads, omelets and sandwiches.
▶ *Done with the food? Check out the home accessories at Good Earth; see p130.*

DADAR & MAHIM

Indian

Diva Maharashtracha
Next to Goa Portuguesa restaurant, near Hinduja Hospital, Kataria Road, Mahim (2445-4433, 2444-0202). Mahim station. **Open** noon-3pm, 7pm-12.30am daily. **Main courses** Rs 250-Rs 350. **Credit** MC, V. **Maharashtrian**
Here you will find a sort of 'best of' of the state's regional specialities and there's plenty to choose from such as the zesty tomato *saar* – a soup of tomato with a dash of coconut milk. The pungency of *bharali wangi*, or stuffed brinjals with crushed peanuts and a coconut-based spice mix, is balanced by the sweetish *ambat god varan*. Dig into the Kolhapuri *pandhara rasa*, delicate pieces of

Global Fusion.

marinated mutton in a coconut milk-based curry before you dive into Diva's large selection of Maharashtrian desserts.

Rs Kakori House

10 A Shiv Sagar Co-op Society, near Paradise Cinema, Lady Jamsetji Road, Mahim (W) (6522-9211). **Open** noon-midnight daily. **Main courses** Rs 160. **Credit** MC, V. Lucknowi

Kakori kebabs are supposed to be so soft that they can be enjoyed even by toothless meat aficionados, like the Lucknowi nawab for whom they were allegedly invented. The meat, which is tenderised with raw papaya and flavoured with garam masala before being cooked on a skewer in a tandoor, is so tender the waiters have to take special care while serving the kebabs so they stay intact.

Pritam da Dhaba

Hotel Midtown Pritam, Station Road, Dadar (E) (2414-5555). Dadar station. **Taxi** Pritam Dadar. **Open** noon-midnight daily. **Main courses** Rs 140-Rs 160. **Credit** AmEx, MC, V. North Indian

Your *dal makhani* is served in a copper bowl by a waiter clad in a *pathani* suit. You recline on a charpoy under open skies as you dine to the thump of bhangra. And isn't that a tiger lurking over there, lured by the aroma of your chicken tikka? Don't worry, it's just painted on the walls, along with a pastoral Punjab. Pritam da Dhaba's misty-eyed vision of the Punjabi heartland may be rose-tinted, but it's fun and the food is gorgeous. Skip the aircon section and make sure to go for dinner, because tables in the open-air courtyard are only operational after 7.30pm.

INSIDE TRACK MINERAL WATER

Ask for mineral water over tap water, and bear in mind that unfortunately most places don't allow you to bring your own.

Sindhudurg

Sita, RK Vaidya Road, Dadar (W) (2430-1610). Dadar station. **Taxi** behind Shiv Sena Bhavan. **Open** 11.30am-3.30pm, 7-11.30pm daily. **Main courses** Rs 200-Rs 250. **Credit** MC, V. **No alcohol**. Malvani

Hearty and healthy and a little bit out of the ordinary, this multi-storey, wood-panelled restaurant is an excellent place to sample dishes from the simple but delicious Malvani-style cuisine, in relative comfort. The basics to order are the prawn, fish and shellfish curries, but the fish biryani, prawn pulao and chicken curry are also good. Ask for seasonal specialities like fried fish roe (*gaboli*) or for the special flatbreads: *jowari* or *nachni bakhri*.

Rs Sushegad Gomantak

Shop No. A11, Shiv Sagar Society, opposite Paradise Cinema, Mahim (2444-5555). Mahim station. **Taxi** Paradise Cinema **Open** 11am-4pm, 7pm-midnight daily. **Main courses** Rs 50. **No credit cards**. **No alcohol**. Goan

Sushegad serves 'Gomantak' or Hindu Goan cooking as opposed to Catholic Goan cuisine. It's just as preoccupied with fish and rice but with unique masalas on offer as well. Sushegad breaks out of the *pomfret-rawas-surmai* trinity of fishes that most restaurants offer, serving less famous but no less tasty fish like *mori* (shark), *bhingi* (a kind of herring), *tarlya* (sardines), *dhodiyare* (mullet) and *verlya* (similar to whitebait).

International

Tamnak Thai

274 Veer Savarkar Marg, Shivaji Park, Dadar (W) (2447-4646). Dadar station. **Open** noon-3.30pm, 7pm-12.30am daily. **Main courses** Rs 200-Rs 450. **Credit** MC, V. Thai

Tamnak Thai seems to be one of the city's best-kept secrets, despite thousands of motorists passing it every day on their way to and from South Mumbai. That makes Tamnak Thai perfect for a quiet dinner, with sweet waiters and a great wine list.

BANDRA & KHAR

Indian

Rs ★ Highway Gomantak

44/2178 Gandhinagar, Western Express Highway, Bandra (E) (2640-9692). Bandra station. **Open** 11am-3.30pm, 7-10pm Mon-Wed, Fri-Sun. **Main courses** Rs 110—Rs 250. **Credit** MC, V. **Goan**

It's hardly the poshest address for a an often-recommended eaterie but patrons swear by Highway Gomantak's simple yet tasty fish thalis. This tiny eatery on the service road along the highway is unassuming, reasonable and serves up some mean seafood. Snack on crisp, fried prawns or have an early dinner of Goan fish curry.

Papa Pancho da Dhaba

Gasper Enclave, St John Street, Pali Naka, Bandra (W) (2651-8732). Bandra station. **Taxi** Pali Naka. **Open** noon-12.30am daily. **Main courses** Rs 200-Rs 300. **Credit** MC, V. **No alcohol**. **Map** p249 B4 59 **North Indian**

The decor is resolutely rustic: the holes in the plaster-work are fake, the sky is painted on the ceiling, and the parrots are plastic. It's a city-dweller's idea of rural charm, turned into kitsch. Modelled on Punjabi roadside inns called *dhabas*, Papa Pancho serves classic, tasty Punjabi nosh like butter chicken, *dal makhani* and the inevitable chicken tikka. By the way, the restaurant's name is a bit naughty – pancho sounds to Indian ears a little like *behenchod*, which is a grievous insult relating to a gentleman's not altogether appropriate affection for his sister.

International

★ Global Fusion

Link Square Mall, Third Floor, 33rd Road, Linking Road, Bandra (W) (2646-9001). Bandra station. **Open** noon-4pm, 7pm-1am daily. **Set meals** *Lunch* Mon-Sat Rs 650 per person; Sun Rs 804 per person. *Dinner* for women Mon-Thu Rs 650; Fri-Sun Rs 804 per head. *Dinner* for men Rs 990 per head. **Credit** MC, V. **Map** p249 D3 60 **Fusion**

There are 20 kinds of sushi and sashimi that Global Fusion serves up to its customers. Here's what makes all this particularly euphoria-inducing: it's cheap. For your money, you get the unlimited sushi and you can also wolf down a range of delicious Chinese starters, soups as well as a buffet spread of (admittedly forgettable) main courses and desserts.

Lemon Grass

Carlton Court, Turner Road-Pali Road Junction, Bandra (W) (2642-9193). **Open** noon-midnight daily. **Main courses** Rs 200-Rs 500. **Credit** MC, V. **Map** p249 B4 61 **Asian**

Lemon Grass is a cosy café in Bandra that offers food that is pan-Asian and decent Thai for those not too hung up on originality.

★ Mia Cucina

Gasper Enclave, St John Street, Pali Naka, Bandra (W) (6710-4000). Bandra station. **Taxi** Pali Naka. **Open** noon-midnight daily. **Main courses** Rs 225-Rs 400. **Credit** MC, V. **No alcohol**. **Map** p249 B4 62 **Italian**

Everything about Mia Cucina is impressive, not least the chef, Sanjay Kotian, who makes a point of going from table to table to recommend dishes and enquire about the quality of food. Dispense with the menu and ask him for suggestions. If you aren't the adventurous type, the old favourites are reliable – the Caesar salad (Rs 125) is as perfect as it gets and the quattro formaggio (Rs 300) is appropriately stinky. The spinach and goat's cheese (Rs 275) risotto is good too.

Olive Bar & Kitchen

4 Union Park, Pali Hill Tourist Hotel, Khar (W) (2605-8228). Khar station. **Taxi** near Café Coffee Day. **Open** 8pm-1.30am Mon-Sat; 12.30-3.30pm, 8pm-1.30am Sun. **Main courses** Rs 300-Rs 700. **Credit** AmEx, DC, MC, V. **Map** p249 A1 63 **Italian**

Pali Village Café. *See p110.*

A super restaurant-cum-bar serving Italian cuisine for an endless stream of Bandra models and hipsters. The salads, pastas and risottos can be a case of hit and miss, so too with the funky cocktails – but nobody is really there for the food anyway. Nights are lively, Sunday brunches are lazy – especially in the coolly lit outside dining area. Calling ahead for directions and a booking is recommended.

Cafés

Café Coffee Day

1 Bandstand Apts, 212/A BJ Road, Bandstand, Bandra (W) (3290-6436). Bandra station.
Open 9am-1.30am daily. **No credit cards**. **No alcohol**.

The coffee is bearable at best, the snacks are best avoided but the view is to die for. Located along the Bandra Bandstand promenade, a narrow street and a walking track are all that separate the café from the Arabian Sea and its sunsets. The street itself has a carnival-like atmosphere in the evening, when families, joggers and couples come out for some fresh air and streetfood. You could also move to the slightly pricier but better Barista next door; *see p97*.

Rs Candies

St John Road, near Pali Hill, Bandra (W) (2642-4124/2324). **Open** 8.30am-10.30pm Tue-Sun. **Main courses** Rs 70-Rs 150. **No credit cards**. **No alcohol**. **Map** p249 B4 64 **Fusion**

Candies is a snack shop serving sandwiches, salads, samosas, rolls and even sushi, but more than the food it's the atmosphere that makes it one of Bandra's favourite cafés. Spread over five levels, it's a sprawling space that seems to go on and on, with mosaic tiles, metal-framed furniture and a decidedly Mediterranean feel. Popular with pretty Bandra girls and their equally pretty boys, Candies is one of the most loved cafés in the suburbs. For something more substantial, pick up one of their meal combos.

Pali Village Café

Next to Janata Bar & Restaurant, Pali Naka, Bandra (W) (2605-0401). Bandra station. **Open** 10am-1.30am daily. **Main courses** Rs 300-Rs 350. **Credit** MC, V. **Map** p249 B3 65 **Italian**

Despite being on one of the noisiest, busiest and dustiest intersections in all of Bandra, the café manages to shut out the chaos outside. The place may look like a rather stylish ghost of the past, but its casual-dining menu is set firmly in the present. It's classic Italian fare – choose from pizzas, pastas and risottos.

Salt Water Café

Rose Minar Annexe, opposite Barista, near Lilavati Hospital, Chapel Road, Bandra (W) (2643-4441). Bandra station. **Open** 9am-11.50pm daily. **Main courses** Rs 350-Rs 500. **Credit** DC, MC, V. **Map** p249 B6 66 **Mediterranean**

Street Eats

Great food on the go.

Mumbai's street food is a cuisine in itself, built on Maharashtrian-Gujarati roots, with the added influence of every émigré community. Food stalls are everywhere, serving kids on their way to school, office workers on lunch breaks and commuters. The signature street snack is the *vada pav*, a fried potato fritter in a soft roll with dry chilli-garlic chutney. Another is *bhel puri*, a dry snack of puffed rice, peanuts, chickpea noodles, onions and chutney. Then there's *pav bhaji*, spicy puréed vegetables eaten with buttered bread, and *pani puri* – crispy shells filled with chickpea dumplings, mung sprouts and spiced water. Pop it in, crunch, and it all explodes in your mouth. *Bhutta* is roast corn-on-the-cob dusted with chilli and lime. It's all cheap – Rs 5-Rs 30.

You'll find street stalls everywhere, but these aren't always the cleanest places to eat; foreign visitors who aren't used to them risk getting sick. Exercise common sense: stick to the most popular stalls, like those around Churchgate station and CST or at Chowpatty Beach. Ensure the cook observes basic hygiene and that the food is piping hot. Alternatively, you can find excellent versions of street cuisine at Swati Snacks (*see p106*), and *vada-paos* are now sold in fast-food chain Jumbo King. Here are some recommended stalls:

Jai Santoshi Ma Bhel Puri Bhandar
20 Bharati Bhavan, corner of Princess Street & Kalbadevi Roada area. Marine Lines station. **Map** p252 F12

Jumbo King
308 Devji Kanji Street, Princess Street, Marine Lines. Marine Lines station.
Open 9am-10pm daily. **Map** p252 E12

Vithal Bhelwallah
5 *AK Naik Marg, near Sterling Cinema, Fort (6631-7211). CST station.* **Open** 11am-11pm daily. **Map** p253 H10

CONSUME

55 East. See p112.

To hear Salt Water Café owner Riyaz Amlani tell it, his new restaurant in Bandra takes the Hegelian dialectic out of the philosophy text books and serves it up steaming on your plate. The result is a board of offerings that includes such intriguing dishes as truffle risotto with spiced chocolate oil, smoked duck carbonara and candied orange peel, and baked lamb chops with prune chutney. the menu is anything but traditional: Molecular gastronomy makes its appearance in some dishes, which include foams of camembert and asparagus.

JUHU & VERSOVA

Indian

Rice Boat

Aram Nagar 2, JP Road, Versova, Andheri (W) (2633-6688, 2632-6688). Andheri station. **Open** noon-3.30pm, 7pm-midnight daily. **Main courses** Rs 150-Rs 250. **Credit** AmEx, MC, V. **Keralan**

Duck under the shiny temple bell on a chain by the entrance and pretend you're in Kerala. Rice Boat offers a tour of Keralan cuisine, with dishes unique to the state's Syrian-Christian community, such as *kozhi varuthathu* (tender chunks of chicken roasted on bamboo skewers) as well as more familiar Keralite dishes like Travancore *konju vechathu* – a prawn curry with coconut and garam masala. A real must-try is the *aatirachi peralan* – tender mutton and raw banana. Book a table in the upstairs room with a coconut thatch ceiling – Kerala houseboat-style.

International

Aurus

Nichani Kutir, Juhu Tara Road, near Nike showroom, Juhu (6710-6666). Santa Cruz station. **Open** 7.30pm-12.30am daily. **Main courses** Rs 500-Rs 800. **Credit** AmEx, MC, V. **American**

Aurus's outdoor deck is among the most pleasant places in the city to listen to the waves and watch the moon chart its course across the inky sky. Pretty Moroccan lamps sit on tables set with nouvelle American cuisine. The short menu is fairly exciting, featuring lemon-grass-rubbed prawns with wasabi foam and creole baby potatoes with blue-cheese dip, Moroccan lamb slices with mozzarella, and jalapeno chicken with Camembert dip. The vegetarian mains draw heavily from the Mediterranean, with several pasta offerings. Reservations are recommended if you want to sit outside.

Penne

14 Silver Beach, opposite Spinach Supermarket, AB Nair Road, Juhu (2625-5706). Vile Parle station. **Open** noon-12.30am daily. **Main courses** Rs 350-Rs 500. **Credit** MC, V. **Italian**

Located on a quiet backlane, Penne is a good place for a date, with its open courtyard seating, tables for two and understated elegance. The food is innovative and, for the most part, quite exciting.

Temple Flower

Kings International Hotel, 5 Juhu Tara Road, Juhu (6692-2222). Vile Parle station. **Taxi** Prithvi Theatre. **Open** 11.30am-3.30pm, 7.30pm-12.30am daily. **Main courses** Rs 150-Rs 250. **Credit** AmEx, MC, V. **East Asian**

Pan-asian food is big in Mumbai and while the menu here roams freely across borders Temple Flower's heart lies in Thailand and Indonesia. The basics are done simply but supremely well – try the richly flavoured Thai yellow curry with prawns. Although modestly sized, it's a good-looking place, with slate floors and lots of dark, chocolatey wood.

Cafés

Bombay Baking Company

JW Marriott, Juhu Tara Road, Juhu (6693-3399). Vile Parle station. **Taxi** Marriott. **Open** 7am-10pm. **Credit** AmEx, MC, V. **No alcohol.**

BBC, as it is known by locals, is a favourite with Bollywood stars meeting producers, scriptwriters and each other. A cute café just off from the Marriott's cavernous lobby, it has a little bookstore and does good sandwiches, salads and coffees.

Prithvi Theatre Café

Prithvi Theatre, Janki Kutir, Juhu Church Road, Juhu (2617-4118). Vile Parle station. **Open** 11am-midnight daily. **No credit cards. No alcohol.** **Indian**

This cosy alfresco café in Prithvi Theatre is the happy refuge of many a fledgling actor and director. Recently reopened under new management, Prithvi Café hasn't lost an ounce of its character. While its famous, and extremely popular (non-alcoholic) Irish Coffee has been retained, the café has introduced famous dishes from restaurants and eateries across the city on its menu, making a great place to do a little culinary tour of the city in one place. Try the kebabs, the fresh fruit ice-cream and the baked snacks.

► *Catch a play at Prithvi Theatre; see p167.*

AROUND THE AIRPORTS

Indian

Peshawri

ITC The Maratha, Sahar Airport Road, Andheri (E) (2830-3030). Andheri station. **Open** 7.30-11.45pm daily. **Main courses** Rs 400-Rs 600. **Credit** AmEx, MC, V. **Indian**

The single best import into Mumbai from the North-west Frontier Province, Peshawri at the ITC Maratha makes the sort of food that connoisseurs across the world fawn over. Food here is prepared authentically (and visibly in a glass-encased kitchen) in tandoors and gigantic bubbling vats. Kebabs are tender and juicy, rotis soft and crisp and the world-famous *dal Bukhara* (now also sold in a ready-to-eat format in branded cans) is cooked just as it should be: overnight, with lots of cream and the subtlest of seasoning. Book in advance.

International

55 East

Grand Hyatt Mumbai, off Western Express Highway, Santa Cruz (E) (6676-1149). Santa Cruz station. **Open** 6-10.30am, 12.30-3pm, 7pm-midnight daily. **Main courses** *Breakfast* Rs 790 per head, *lunch* and *dinner* Rs 1,450 (without drinks), *Sunday brunch* Rs 2,250 (with drinks). **Credit** DC, MC, V. **Fusion**

The restaurant's nomenclature anchors it proudly in the post code of Santa Cruz (East), 55 East has evidently circumnavigated the globe to assemble the bountiful range of food it serves up. Going east to west across the planet, there's Thai, Japanese, a smattering of Latin American flavours, an assortment of Continental standards, Lebanese mezze and a range of unusual subcontinental dishes. As such you can't fail to find something you want to eat here.

Celini

Grand Hyatt, Kalina, Santa Cruz (E) (6676-1234). Santa Cruz station. **Open** 12.30-3pm, 7.30pm-midnight daily. **Main courses** Rs 650-Rs 1,000. **Credit** AmEx, DC, MC, V. **Italian**

This is where you go for the perfect pizza: thin and crisp, with toppings of Italian cheese, fresh vegetables and quality meats. Celini's open kitchen and wood-and-glass interiors make it contemporary and casual, with a kitchen philosophy that's focused on home-style cooking. Don't miss the truly gorgeous pannacotta.

China House

Grand Hyatt, Kalina, Santa Cruz (E) (6676-1234). Santa Cruz station. **Open** 12.30-3pm, 7.30pm-12.30am daily. **Main courses** Rs 300-Rs 650. **Credit** AmEx, DC, MC, V. **Chinese**

China House looks like a cross between an old Beijing tea house and a hypermodern Shanghai office tower. The decor is a mix of dark wood and shiny glass. Diners sit around five open kitchens (preparing appetisers, noodles and dumplings, Peking Duck, wok dishes and desserts) or in one of four private rooms. Though the menu has a predisposition to Sichuan specialities, none of the dishes have the tongue-numbing spiciness most Indians chuck in. Instead, the food has strong, clear flavours, using spice to accentuate the taste of the ingredients rather than overwhelm them. *Photo p107.*

Pan-Asian

ITC The Maratha, Sahar Airport Road, Andheri (E) (2830-3030). Andheri station. **Open** 12.30-2.45pm, 7.30-11.45pm daily. **Main courses** Rs 500-Rs 1,400. **Credit** AmEx, MC, V. **Asian**

A sprawling, gorgeous restaurant and possibly the big daddy of Mumbai's many pan-Asian restaurants, Pan-Asian has no fewer than five separate kitchens dedicated to different cuisines: Mongolian, Chinese, Japanese, Thai and Korean. It's also unique in offering tables with built-in grills for authentic Korean barbecues. The Cantonese roasted chicken here is particularly good.

Stax

Hyatt Regency, Sahar Airport Road, Andheri (E) (6696-1234). Andheri station. **Open** 7-11.30pm daily. **Main courses** Rs 700-Rs 1,000. **Credit** AmEx, MC, V. **Italian**

Stax deftly combines modern steel-and-glass design and touches straight out of an Italian trattoria, with a live kitchen and a soundtrack of 1960s and '70s Italian hits. The food is top quality, with a stunning signature dish of seabass and leek fondue in Sicilian sauce and a gorgeous rack of lamb encrusted with pistachios in a bitter chocolate sauce.

Pubs & Bars

Dodgy dives, languid lounges and trendy taverns.

British Bombay was founded in an orgy of drunkenness and debauchery, with officials of the East India Company often dying young thanks to their intemperate habits. According to MD David's *History of Bombay 1661-1708*, Englishmen in Mumbai 'led a life which was shameful and loose with drinks, duels, frauds, luxury, immodesty and prostitution'. Nowadays, there's a touch more decorum – in some cases, really just a touch – with boozers of all descriptions catering to every sort of Mumbaikar.

HIGH SPIRITS

In the 18th century, the East India Company tried to restrain the number of punch houses by reducing the number of licences, a situation echoed in today's Mumbai, where bars are a soft target for conservative outrage. But the tradition of debauchery continues: from cheap 'country liquor' bars and working-class 'permit rooms' (*see p114* **Licence to swill**) to lively white-collar and college-kid hangouts like Toto's; and fancy cocktail bars like Busaba for when you want to splash out.

Spirits are the drink of choice in dives, while beer (sold in 330ml bottles called pints or in 650ml bottles) continues to reign supreme in the posher bars. The most famous may be the ubiquitous Kingfisher, but there's a lot more choice (and arguably tastier beers) such as Haywards 2000, Golden Eagle and Royal Challenge. There's even a home-grown stout called Haywards Black. As major international brands eye India's loaded middle class, foreign brews and spirits have come pouring in and the choice of drinks is wider than ever before. Cocktails have become hugely popular in recent years, especially fruity twists on traditional mixes, and the venerable whisky-soda is in grave danger of being overtaken in popularity by the vodka-Sprite.

But a class distinction persists in the city's drinking culture: at most of the bars listed in this guide, you're unlikely to find yourself sharing a table with a postman or a grocer. The boundaries of Mumbai's social circles may not be spelt out in words but they are clearly circumscribed in action and rarely do different demographic groups meet. Not only does this make it difficult for locals to meet people they aren't already connected to in some obvious or arcane way, but it also restricts the citizenry's perception of their fellow Mumbaikars as well, for to hang out in Mumbai bars is to play a massive game of six degrees of separation. Then there's the gender thing: working-class bars are exclusively male. Women from the upper-middle and elite classes frequent more expensive bars where it is considered acceptable, but for the mainstream, women who drink alcohol – especially without male company – are almost automatically considered to be made of low moral fibre. Many 'permit rooms' don't even have a loo for women and some deny them entry altogether (citing women's safety as the reason). On the whole, though, nobody seems to care very much.

DOS AND DON'TS

In country liquor bars or working-class haunts, female drinkers – especially foreigners – are likely to be the target of uncomfortable stares or unwelcome attention, so with a few clearly stated exceptions we've avoided listing them.

INSIDE TRACK SUNDOWNER SPOT

If you want to nurse your drink and get a great view of Mumbai while at it, drop in at **Dome** (*see p117*) before 6.30pm for the glorious pink-orange sunset.

We've divided bars and clubs on one criterion, whether there is a dancefloor or not – *see p160* **Nightlife** for club listings.

By law, bars are required to close by 1.30am, unless they have special permission or, more frequently, have paid bribes to the local police. Bars inside five-star hotels are allowed to stay open until 3am – part of the reason they remain so popular. Expect to pay the equivalent of Western prices at five-star hotel bars and most cocktail bars. All liquor is subject to 20 per cent tax. Most bars have table service; it's rare to have to fetch drinks from the bar. Tipping is at your discretion, usually around ten per cent.

COLABA

Busaba

4 Mandlik Road, off Colaba Causeway, (2204-3779/69). CST or Churchgate stations. **Taxi** behind Taj Mahal Hotel. **Open** 12.30-3pm, 6.30pm-1.30am daily. **Credit** AmEx, MC, V. **Map** p250 G5 ❶

Neighbouring Indigo may be where South Mumbai's la-di-da types go when they want to spend the GDP of a small African nation on an evening out, but we'd opt for Busaba instead. It does better (and, it has to be said, slightly cheaper) cocktails and attracts a cooler crowd.

★ Café Mondegar

Colaba Causeway, near Regal Cinema (2202-0591). CST or Churchgate stations. **Open** 7am-midnight daily. **Credit** MC, V. **Map** p250 G5 ❷

It's always ten degrees hotter inside Mondy's than out. It must be all the bodies they cram in: four to each table and as many tables wedged in as possible. The ear-splitting chatter from college students, foreign travellers and office workers competes with a chunky jukebox at the back, where Pink Floyd and the Doors seem to be on permanent rotation. Mondy's is as popular with Mumbaikars as it is with tourists, and the cute wall murals in the style of Goan caricaturist Mario Miranda make it a local landmark. Don't be offended by the service: staff are as surly with locals.

▶ *Head to nearby Bade Miyan for some kebabs; see p91.*

★ Gokul

Nawaz Building, 10 Tulloch Road, off Colaba Causeway (2284-8504). CST or Churchgate stations. **Open** 11am-12.30am daily. **No credit cards. Map** p250 G5 ❸

Once a haven for the city's gay community, these days the crowd at Gokul is far less easy to bracket – an easygoing mix of foreign travellers, students, officegoers, habitual drunks and, sometimes, even families. It's a dim back-room haunt with four sec-

CONSUME

Licence to Swill

Permit rooms: dive bars, Indian-style.

In the hierarchy of Mumbai's drinking establishments, permit rooms fall somewhere between the pubs that cater to middle-management and the country liquor bars that attract the city's working class. According to an archaic law, the state of Maharashtra is still technically a land of prohibition, with any tippler required by law to carry a permit stating that he 'continues to require foreign liquor and country liquor for preservation and maintenance of my health'. Although this rule is largely ignored, the permit rooms that sprung up as prohibition began to wane continue to bear the name and are a safe haven for men who care little for ambience or atmosphere, concentrating instead on drinking large quantities.

Unconvinced of the need for ostentatious decor or music, permit rooms are generally little more than Formica tables and benches slapped together with maybe a television in one corner. Tables are often shared and the clientele is almost always male. Liquor is served in small (30ml), large (60ml), half nip (90ml) and nip or quarter (180ml) measures.

Mumbai's permit rooms have their own uniform aesthetics. The bars in the south are older and more beaten up. They have wooden chairs and spacious halls rather than narrow corridors and English-sounding names like Lord Irwin and Felicity. Many were Irani restaurants that found greater profits in liquor. In the suburbs, wooden chairs give way to beige and red plastic but the overall design remains the same.

Frequented largely by college students, white-collar workers and small traders at the end of the day's work, permit rooms open early in the morning and close by midnight. Most patrons pick by virtue of location and convenience, but some have now been gentrified and see large numbers of tourists, kids tanking up before hitting the clubs, spillover from nearby bars and even – gasp! – women. For a taste of the cheap, Mumbai way to drink, visit **Café Oval** in Churchgate (*see p116*) or **Janata** in Bandra (*see p118*).

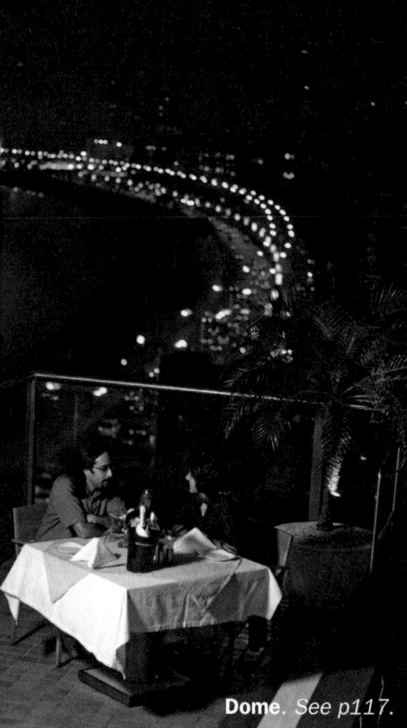
Dome. See p117.

tions, some cavernous, some pokey; the liquor is marginally cheaper in the non-air-con parts. Spirits come by the peg (30/60ml) or by the quarter bottle (180ml), the beer is always cold, and the food is down-and-dirty local Indian and Indian-Chinese.

Indus Cocktail Bar & Tandoor

Ground Floor, Hotel Diplomat, Apollo Bunder, Colaba (2202-1661). CST or Churchgate stations. **Taxi** behind Taj Mahal Hotel. **Open** noon-3pm, 6pm-midnight daily. **Credit** MC, V. **Map** p250 G5 ❹

Indus is a cute little cocktail bar that does happy hours between 6pm and 8pm and serves some delicious kebabs (with *kali dal* gratis). The clientele is a mix of tourists, couples, suits and yuppies, the drinks are competent and the bartenders friendly. It isn't particularly large but seats tend to free up on a fairly regular basis.

Indigo

4 Mandlik Road, off Colaba Causeway (6636-8999). CST or Churchgate stations. **Taxi** behind Taj Mahal Hotel. **Open** noon-3pm, 6.30pm-1am daily. **Credit** AmEx, DC, MC, V. **Map** p250 G5 ❺

South Mumbai's premier watering hole for the well-heeled, Indigo is pretty much an institution. On weekends it's packed wall-to-wall with strutting women in strapless, backless dresses and their pumped-up boys in print shirts. Nobody gets too comfortable as seats are few; the ambience is chic hotel lobby. After 11pm, the crush can get rib-cracking, so head for the upstairs lounge, or even better, the beautiful, candlelit terrace.

Leopold Café

Colaba Causeway (2202-0131). CST or Churchgate stations. **Open** 7.30am-12.30am daily. **Credit** AmEx, MC, V. **Map** p250 G5 ❻

The default drinking destination for foreign travellers, Leo's has all the atmosphere of a railway station waiting room and staff are about as friendly as the gent behind the station's enquiry counter when you ask about a much-delayed train. Yet sheer size, cheap drinks and its prominence in Gregory David Roberts' hugely popular novel, *Shantaram*, make Leo's a favourite.

► *Leo's was also one of the sites for the terrorist attacks of 26/11; see p28.*

Sports Bar Express

Regal Cinema Building, Colaba Causeway, Colaba (6639-6682). CST or Churchgate stations. **Open** noon-12.30am daily. **Credit** AmEx, MC, V. **Map** p250 G5 ❼

Sports Bar Express doesn't offer much in the way of character but it's conveniently located and inexpensive. All-American diner-ish in look and decidedly Indian in choice of sport on the plasma screen (cricket, cricket and, errr, more cricket), it's a fair option for a few drinks on a hot day. You're best advised to avoid the snacks.

Wink

Taj President, Cuffe Parade (6665-0808). Churchgate station. **Taxi** Taj President. **Open** 6.30pm-1am daily. **Credit** AmEx, MC, V. **Map** p251 E3 ❽

Restaurants in hotels are another matter but, on the whole, hotel bars in Mumbai tend to be staid, unexciting and, frankly, a waste of time. But Wink, at the President, changed all that when it opened in 2006. Intricate metal grill, angled brick walls and an island bar designed by Japanese firm SuperPotato fade into the background when you try the cocktails, mixed by some of the best bartenders in town. Electronica forms an essential part of the aural vibe but conversation thrives and the free wasabi-flavoured peas are yummy.

★ Woodside Inn

Indian Mercantile Mansion, Wodehouse Road, opposite Regal, Colaba (2202-5525,2287-5752). CST or Churchgate stations. **Open** 8am-1am daily. **Credit** AmEx, MC, V. **Map** p250 G5 ❾

One-time hole-in-the-wall dive, Woodside Inn has been refurbished and is now a cosy little tavern with framed pictures of Mumbai, smiling staff and cheap drinks. The music varies wildly from the Beatles to the Red Hot Chili Peppers, but the lack of pretension and the homely atmosphere make it a nice escape from the madness of the Causeway.

INSIDE TRACK
I SAY BOMBAY, YOU SAY MUMBAI

To find out if you are a Bombay or a Mumbai person, visit the Harbour Bar at the **Taj Mahal Palace Hotel** (*see p77*). I say Bombay, you say Mumbai, the bar's signature drink, is not one but two yummy cocktails – Bombay and Mumbai – served simultaneously. Bombay is mixed using Bombay Sapphire gin, masala-spiced sweet vermouth, and maraschino liqueur with a twist of orange. Mumbai is vodka shaken hard with cardamom-infused dry vermouth and a fat chilli-stuffed olive.

FORT

Café Universal

299 Shahid Bhagat Singh Road (2261-3985). CST or Churchgate stations. **Taxi** Ballard Estate. **Open** 9am-11pm daily. **Credit** AmEx, MC, V. **Map** p253 J9 ⑩

The 85-year-old Café Universal is an excellent example of how to renovate an old bar without losing any of its character or giving in to crass market forces. It's big and bright, with lots of natural light streaming in and the design is very art nouveau. Universal only does beer and wine but come for a laid-back lunch: an extensive food menu includes Chinese and Zoroastrian food, as well as steaks, sandwiches and soups.

Soul Fry Casa

Currimjee Building, opposite Mumbai University, MG Road (2267-1421). CST or Churchgate stations. **Taxi** Kala Ghoda. **Open** noon-3pm, 6pm-midnight daily. **Credit** AmEx, MC, V. **Map** p250 G7 ⑪

Kitschy adverts line the walls, an irony-laden colonial-era fog hangs heavy in the air and Konkani music fills the spaces in between. Munch on calamari and fried prawns and, if it's a night with live music, you can watch bands play jazz standards and vintage pop or, if you're really lucky, drunken uncles singing 'Careless Whisper'. The bar area is small but Soul Fry is pretty laid-back and staff are normally quite happy for you continue drinking in the dining area.

CHURCHGATE

Café Oval

Eros Cinema (6634-5721). Churchgate station. **Open** 9am-11pm daily. **No credit cards. Map** p250 & p253 F8 ⑫

This tiny, Irani-run bar opposite the Oval Maidan is a little sparse but has its own 1940s-style Bombay charm, walls lined with crates of beer and the waiters sliding on to the old wooden benches to chat with regulars. The decor has been given something of an update, in that the posters of superstar batsman Sachin Tendulkar have long since been replaced by ones of breathy, blond songstress Joss Stone, but little else changes here. This is a mostly male hangout but women need not feel unwelcome. After all, there's a wooden board on the wall declaring that 'Shop is open to all caste.'

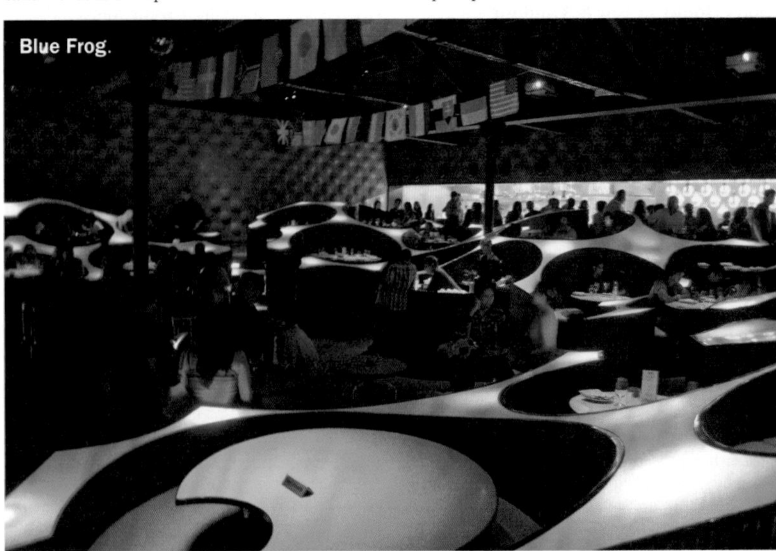
Blue Frog.

★ Dome

InterContinental Marine Drive, 135 Marine Drive (6639-9999,www.intercontinental.com). Churchgate station. **Open** 5.30pm-1.30am daily. **Credit** AmEx, DC, MC, V. **Map** p250 & p253 E8 ⑬

Undoubtedly South Mumbai's finest hotel bar. Dome is a lounge/grill occupying the InterCon's eighth-floor rooftop terrace, overlooking the fabulous arc of the seafront promenade. The walls are white, the tiled floor is white and the abundant sofas and armchairs are all wrapped in white cotton. A raised platform holds the aqua-blue swimming pool, while a corner rotunda houses a sleek aluminium-and-glass bar counter with matching stools. *Photo p115.*

Not Just Jazz by the Bay

Soona Mahal, 143 Marine Drive (2285-1876). Churchgate station. **Open** noon-3.30pm, 6pm-1.30am daily. **Credit** AmEx, MC, V. **Map** p250 & p253 E8 ⑭

Locally known simply as 'Jazz', this sole survivor of Bombay's 1950s jazz era is among the handful of live music options in the city (*see p157 music*). In general Wednesdays to Saturdays draw an older crowd for bands usually dishing out jazz, country and rock, while Sundays to Tuesdays are usually reserved for the wildly popular karaoke nights for students and young professionals seeking therapy on stage. An entry fee of Rs 100 applies.

MAHALAXMI

Ghetto

30B Bhulabhai Desai Road, near Mahalaxmi Temple, Breach Candy (2353-8418). Mahalaxmi station. **Taxi** Mahalaxmi Temple. **Open** 7pm-1.30am daily. **Credit** MC, V.

This smoky rockers' hangout has been boozing for a decade and a half, and a fanatical band of regulars is permanently fixed to its barstools. The college pub-like atmosphere is deceptive – most patrons are thirtysomething media professionals who have been coming here since their first year of university. The walls are thick with graffiti (if you don't want to feel left out ask for a felt pen at the bar) and Jim Morrison murals are illuminated by UV tubelights. Expect the obligatory 1980s rock soundtrack.

LOWER PAREL & WORLI

★ Blue Frog

Todi & Co, Mathuradas Mill Compound, Senapati Bapat Marg, Lower Parel (4033-2300, www.bluefrog.co.in). **Open** 6.30pm-1.30am daily. **Credit** AmEx, MC, V.

Often appearing in newspaper round-ups of the world's best music venues, Blue Frog is quite simply the best-looking nightspot in Mumbai. It's a swanky 560 sq m (6,000sq ft) space, designed to impress. Using circular seating 'pods', innovative lighting and an amphitheatre-like design, the architects have attempted to create an opera house-meets-warehouse hybrid. The post-industrial vibe is complemented by trendy visuals projected on the screens and bump patterns on the walls (they're apparently there to help the acoustics). It hosts local bands on weekdays and occasionally flies in international acts on the weekends, though whenever you go, it tends to be buzzing. A RS 300 entry charge applies on weekdays and Rs 500 on weekends.

Hard Rock Café

Bombay Dyeing Mills Compound, Pandurang Budhkar Marg, Worli (2438-2888, www.hardrock.com). Lower Parel station. **Taxi** Kamala Mills. **Open** noon-1.30am daily. **Credit** AmEx, MC, V.

Anywhere else in the world, it's a tourist trap. In Mumbai, it's the playground for the city's young and tasteless. Still, the Hard Rock Café is worth a visit for its sheer size and to see where all those New India rupees are going and who's spending them. It also hosts gigs on Tuesdays and Thursdays, but it's something of a misnomer – if you're expecting hard rock, you're likely to be disappointed.

Dry Days

How to get around the drinking ban.

Wine shops and bars are forbidden from selling alcohol on certain days of the year, known as dry days. These days range from the nation's Independence Day to Mahatma Gandhi's birth anniversary and even the 48 hours before an election. Even days when votes are being counted are dry, making India's tortuously long general elections a nightmare for those of us who like a tipple. By law, foreigners are exempt from the ban, but many bars just close for the day. The restriction doesn't apply to drinking at home and the dry day isn't midnight to midnight, but for the duration of a single working day. Most five-star hotel bars will serve alcohol to foreigners on production of a passport (though a non-Indian complexion will usually do).

26 January Republic Day
30 January Martyrs' Day
1 May Maharashtra Day
15 August Independence Day
August-September Ananta Chaturdashi & Gauri Visarjan (Ganesh celebrations)
2 October Gandhi Jayanti (anniversary of Gandhi's birth)
8 October End of Gandhi Week

Shiro

Ivy
Indage House, Annie Besant Road (6654-7939). Mahalaxmi station. **Taxi** Worli Naka. **Open** 11am-1am daily. **Credit** AmEx, MC, V.
Ivy is everything you wouldn't expect a wine bar to be. It has none of that trying-to-be-posh hokum with dim lighting, wood panelling and leather sofas, and it doesn't expect its patrons to wear suits, smoke cigars and talk about how badly the Dow is faring. Instead, with bright lights, blazing pink walls and an all-embracing attitude, it's a cheerful, genial wine bar that attracts a crowd as mixed as any beer bar.

Shiro
Bombay Dyeing Mills Compound, Pandurang Budhkar Marg, Worli (2438-3008). Lower Parel station. **Taxi** Kamala Mills. **Open** 7pm-1.30am daily. **Credit** AmEx, MC, V.
Located in a former mill and filled to the rafters with the city's swish set, Shiro is an East Asian-themed bar on acid. It's like drinking in Alice's Wonderland. Curtains of red-glass teardrops and a Buddhist monkette greet you as you enter. The stone walls occahouse Buddha busts and thick candles dripping wax all the way down to the floor; the beams are wood, and the drinks are stellar. It's important to remember, though, that when logic and proportion have fallen by the wayside, that shrinking feeling you experienced extends to your wallet as well.

BANDRA

Hawaiian Shack
16th Road (99873-97663). Bandra station. **Taxi** near Mini Punjab. **Open** 6pm-1.30am daily. **Credit** MC, V. **Map** p249 C3 15
What makes Hawaiian Shack Bandra's most popular pub? Is it the outstanding service? The resemblance to the inside of an old wooden ship? Or could it be that a large number of Mumbaikars still think the 1980s had the best pop music? In any other country, a bar that played so much Madonna and Boney M would probably be a gay joint, but this is India, super-camp Bollywood-obsessed India, where the two men holding hands or dancing together next to your table are probably just good friends.

Janata
Ambedkar Road, Pali Naka (W) (2600-4049). Bandra station. **Taxi** Pali Naka. **Open** 11am-1.30am daily. **Credit** MC, V. **Map** p249 B3 16
Rub shoulders with retired technocrats, broke college students, yuppies getting some beers in before hitting the clubs, Bandra boys, immigrants, policemen and everyone in between. Janata is a democratic drinking hole, its popularity, in part, explained by the superlative food, but what really works for it is the great location, friendly service and all-embracing attitude. As a now gentrified 'permit room' (*see p114*), a group of girls *sans* male escort need not feel uncomfortable.

Olive Bar & Kitchen
4 Union Park, Pali Hill Tourist Hotel, Khar (W) (2605-8228). Khar station. **Taxi** near Café Coffee Day, Carter Road. **Open** 7.30pm-1.30am daily. **Credit** AmEx, DC, MC, V.
Map p249 A1 17
One of the suburbs' swishest spots for those who want to see and be seen, packed to the gills with models, actors and Bandra's rich and shameless. The Pulitzer Prize-nominated author of *Maximum City*, Suketu Mehta, maintains that on Thursday nights the most beautiful women in Mumbai come out here to play. Pretty faces and Pilates-toned bodies certainly abound, and we're not just talking about the ladies – that goes for the chaps too (gay regulars maintain that Olive is one of the best bars in the city to pick up guys). It can be a tricky place to find, so either go with someone who knows or call ahead for directions.

Seijo & the Soul Dish
Krystal, Second Floor, Waterfield Road (2640-5555). Bandra station. **Taxi** Waterfield Road. **Open** 7.30pm-1.30am daily. **Credit** AmEx, MC, V. **Map** p249 D4 18
Aimed at professional thirtysomethings, Seijo is drenched in red-and-black hues, with Japanese pop art splashed on the walls. It does good cocktails and occasionally has live acts.

Toto's Garage

30 Lourdes Heaven, Pali Junction (2600-5494). Bandra station. **Taxi** Pali Naka. **Open** 6pm-1am daily. **Credit** AmEx, MC, V. **Map** p249 C3 ⑲

Engine parts, hubcaps and number plates emblazon the walls of Toto's Garage. One of the city's most popular watering holes with office workers and students, with an air as casual as the waiters' denim overalls. The playlist segues from the Doors (again) to Duran Duran to Rammstein without an eyebrow being raised. It's cheap too.

SANTA CRUZ

China House

Grand Hyatt, off the Western Express Highway (6676-1234). Santa Cruz station. **Taxi** Vakola Hyatt. **Open** 6pm-3am daily. **Credit** AmEx, MC, V.

Designed by the same firm that did the President's Wink, China House is located way out in the middle of nowhere but that hasn't stopped it from becoming wildly popular. Perennially afflicted by the Bollywood crowd, it's also full of pretty girls, their goofy boyfriends and just about anybody who still wants a drink in the suburbs after the 1.30am deadline. Great cocktails, sexy design, sexy people and an energetic vibe are the draws – rather than the music, which tends to be dreadful.

JUHU

Aurus

Nichani Kutir, Juhu Tara Road, between Nike & Reid and Taylor showrooms (6710-6666/67). Santa Cruz station. **Taxi** Juhu Tara Road. **Open** 8pm-1.30am daily. **Credit** AmEx, MC, V.

There is absolutely no finer place to sip a cocktail than leaning against the railings high above the sand watching the lights of airliners as they slither across the silvery waves. The crowd at Aurus is primarily the young and aspiring-to-be-famous children of Bollywood movie stars and their ilk (plus assorted hangers-on), but don't let that dissuade you. The entrance is so discreet, you'll miss it if you don't know it, so, again, go with someone in the know or call ahead for directions.

> **INSIDE TRACK FREE GIGS**
>
> Don't be put off by **Blue Frog**'s (*see p117*) entry charge. On most weekdays, the fee is a flat Rs 300 if you enter after 9pm. But get there before 9pm and you get in for free unless there's a big-ticket artist playing. You'll also be in time for the happy hours – pay for one drink and get the other free. Nurse the pints as you wait for the show to start.

Ivy.

Sea View

Behind the police station, Juhu Beach (2660-5942). Vile Parle station. **Taxi** Juhu Beach. **Open** 9am-11pm daily. **No credit cards.**

In early 2008, cries of panic went up with the news that the 70-year-old Sea View had been sold. As old-timers mourned the death of an institution, the new management surprised everyone by only changing the furniture and raising the prices a little. The antithesis of froufrou, Sea View is a series of tables and chairs lined up against a low wall, but it's what's behind the wall that counts. With spectacular views of Juhu Beach, good-value beer (and only beer) and a liberal attitude to smoking, it's the closest you get to Goa without actually getting to Goa.

► *Juhu's also the home of Prithvi Theatre; see p167.*

Vie Lounge & Deck

102 Juhu Tara Road, Juhu (2660-3003). Santa Cruz station. **Taxi** opposite Little Italy restaurant. **Open** 6pm-1am daily. **Credit** AmEx, MC, V.

Vie has a killer location on Juhu Beach and its design makes the most of it. Sloping glass planes intersect with palms, with the luminescent back-lit panels of the open-air deck glowing under the stars. As bars go, it's quite the looker. That is, once you've found it. It's set back a little from the road and can be tricky to find, so call ahead for directions.

Shops & Services

Markets and malls.

Until the last decade of the 20th century, Mumbaikars, like all Indians, wrote out long lists of requests for aunts, brothers-in-law or cousins twice removed who were planning trips abroad. Few imported consumer products were available in Indian stores, so even munching on a Kit-Kat was a status symbol. All that has now changed, with economic liberalisation and lower import duties. Mumbaikars have adapted to shopping sprees with remarkable ease, without forgetting the speciality markets and old favourites that held them in good stead for decades past.

SHOP TILL YOU DROP

Colaba is king for kitsch and trinkets, as well as a good offering of mid-range and expensive shops, but other retail hotspots have sprung up and make for an interesting portrait of the city's changing socio-economics and geography. Mumbai's glamour industry lives primarily in Bandra, where boutique stores abound with a mix of imported jeans and T-shirts, as well as home-grown designerwear. Lower Parel has become a hub of activity since its dilapidated mills were sold to private developers and converted into prime retail and residential spaces. The outsourcing boom has also made once-sleepy Malad a hot shopping destination, with the city's best-looking mall, Inorbit. With Mumbai's heat, dust and crowds, give yourself plenty of time and carry lots of water.

THE BASICS

Most stores open by 11am and close around 8pm. Visa and MasterCard are accepted almost everywhere, except at markets and street stalls, where cash is king. Some marketwallahs and street vendors might double, triple or quadruple their prices for foreigners. Friendly haggling is required and a few Hindi phrases may come in handy. And remember that bargaining in shops is considered bad form.

BOOKS

★ Crossword

Mohammed Bhai Mansion, Hughes Road, Kemp's Corner (6627-2100). Grant Road station. **Open** 11am-8.30pm Mon-Fri; 11am-9pm Sat, Sun. **Credit** AmEx, MC, V.

The flagship store of Mumbai's best-known bookstore chain also sells music and movies, toys and games, and has a great café with pastries, sandwiches and coffee. It also hosts author readings, forums and children's events. The store also has an outlet of Vividha, which retails wooden toys and baby accessories.

Other location Noor Mahal, Ground Floor, Turner Road, Bandra (W) (2640-7049).

★ Landmark

Basement, Palladium, High Street Phoenix, Senapati Bapat Marg (6457-5323). Lower Parel station. **Open** 11am-10pm daily. **Credit** AmEx, DC, MC, V.

Mumbai's biggest bookstore, with the best collection. Landmark moves beyond bestsellers to stock titles that you won't find anywhere else in the city, including a great collection of graphic novels, film books and literary fiction. It's also one of the few bookshops in town where the staff actually seem to read the books they stock.

Other location Second Floor, Infiniti Mall, New Link Road, Andheri (W) (2639-6010).

Nalanda

Taj Mahal Palace, Lobby Level, Apollo Bunder, Colaba (2202-2514). CST or Churchgate stations. **Open** 8am-midnight daily. **Credit** AmEx, DC, MC, V.

This is where to go for glossy coffee-table books on Rajasthani palaces, Benarasi textiles and the Kama Sutra. Nalanda is small but has a strong India focus, and a good collection of Indian non-fiction. It also stocks international magazines and newspapers.

New & Secondhand Bookstore

Kalbadevi Road, near Metro Cinema, Dhobi Talao (2201-3314). CST or Marine Lines stations. **Open** 10am-7.30pm Mon-Sat. **No credit cards**.

Now in its second century, New & Secondhand Bookstore is a treasure trove of collectibles, odds and ends, and out-of-prints. There is an eclectic mix of titles, which include travel guides to the Soviet Union, a history of Elephanta Island and political manifestos. It's as close to an antiquarian bookshop as it gets in Mumbai, and there's a 30% discount on the marked price.

★ Strand Book Stall

Cawasji Patel Street, off Sir PM Road, Fort (2266-1994 , www.strandbookstall.com). CST or Churchgate stations. **Open** 10am-8pm Mon-Sat; 10am-7pm Sun. **Credit** AmEx, DC, MC, V.

The favourite of journalists and novelists, this city institution is tiny and stuffed with piles and piles of assorted books. While the space is not very conducive to browsing, it does have a range of lesser-known writers and the staff let you linger as long as you like. Most importantly, it offers an average discount of 20% on every purchase.

DEPARTMENT STORES

Asiatic

Veer Nariman Road, Churchgate (2283-4541/28). Churchgate station. **Open** 10am-8.30pm Mon-Sat. **Credit** MC, V.

Lifestyle

High Street Phoenix, 462 Senapati Bapat Marg, Lower Parel (6517-2086). Lower Parel or Mahalaxmi stations. **Open** 10.30am-9.30pm daily. **Credit** AmEx, MC, V.

Pantaloons

Courtyard, High Street Phoenix, Senapati Bapat Marg, Lower Parel (3003-4800). Lower Parel or Mahalaxmi stations. **Open** 11am-10pm daily. **Credit** MC, V.

Westside

Army & Navy Building, Kala Ghoda (6636-0499/0500). CST or Churchgate stations. **Open** 10.30am-9pm daily. **Credit** AmEx, MC, V.

INSIDE TRACK LITERARY RETREAT

Bookshops make a great quiet break from Mumbai's chaos and most encourage customers to sit and read instore. **Crossword** also organises regular Sunday events for children.

ELECTRONICS

Croma

JM Marg, Vasundhara Chambers, opposite Utpal Sanghvi School, Juhu (6710-3333). **Taxi** near Chandan Cinema. **Open** 11am-8.30pm daily. **Credit** AmEx, MC, V.

You could spend days wandering around the aisles of Croma; the shop stocks everything you could ever want in electronics.

Vijay Sales

29 New Queens Road, next to Charni Road Station, Opera House (2363-9210). **Open** 10.30am-8.30pm daily. **Credit** MC, V.

Vijay Sales is a one-stop shop for gadgets, with stock ranging from refrigerators and television sets to iPods and mobile phones.

Other locations 225 Pandurang Bhuvan, Lady Jamsetjee Road, Shivaji Park (2430-9660); 108 Lady Jamsetjee Road, Mahim (2445-7959); 3 Bhatia Building, Zarina Society, SV Road, Bandra (W) (2642-2119).

FASHION

Indo-western designers

Attic

Flat No.1, Ground Floor, Bir Sagar 396/20, at the end of 17th Road, Santa Cruz (W) (3216-9292). Santa Cruz station. **Open** 11am-8.30pm daily. **Credit** MC, V.

Attic has a classy eclectic blend of clothes, home furnishings and silver jewellery by Indian designers. There are lovely linen pants, paisley shorts and summery skirts for women.

Amara

Hughes Road, Kemp's Corner (2387-9687/2530). Grant Road station. **Open** 10.30am-8pm daily. **Credit** AmEx, MC, V.

A large, ambitious project located on prime South Mumbai property, selling wares by a range of exclusive designers. It doesn't stop at retail therapy, though; you can also get a deep-tissue massage and some inspired fusion food at the attached Rudra spa-cum-salon and Ambiir restaurant.

Ananya

Burani Mahal, 59 Nepean Sea Road, behind Kotak Mahindra Bank (6571-4888). **Taxi** opposite Priyadarshani Park. **Open** 11am-8pm Mon-Sat. **Credit** MC, V.

A fashionista favourite, Ananya was originally started up in London by sisters Ansuya and Nandita Mahtani. Showcasing a range of high-profile Indian designers as well as its in-house label, it has some of the country's most colourful and quirky looks.

Other location Shop 3, Pluto Building, Turner Road, Bandra (W) (6593-0262).

THE
CARBON
NEUTRAL
COMPANY

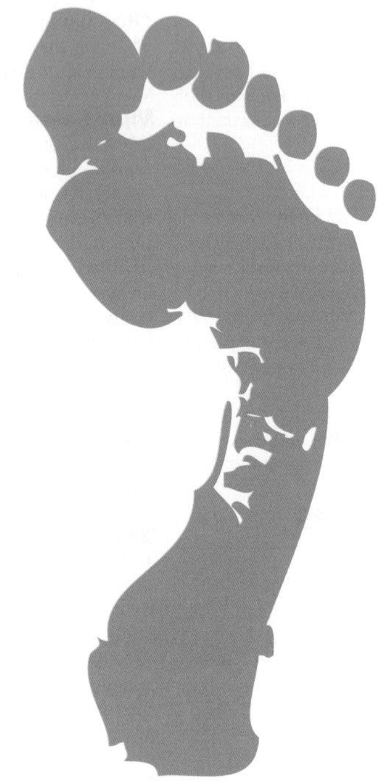

Aza
21 Siffy Apartments, Altamount Road, off Pedder Road (2351-7616). Grant Road station. **Open** 10am-8pm daily. **Credit** AmEx, MC, V.
Leafy green Altamount Road is better known for its profusion of consulates and wealthy residents (think old, old money) than its fashion quotient, but that's changed with the arrival of Aza. This big store stocks a large range of up-and-coming designers from across the country. The staff are courteous, the fitting rooms spacious and alterations are done while you wait.

Aza for Men
Cornelian, Shop No.4, 104 August Kranti Marg, Kemp's Corner (2382-1161). **Open** 10am-8pm daily. **Credit** AmEx, MC, V.
Twenty designers, a mix of established and young, showcase everything from *sherwanis* to shirts and accessories to go with them. You may have to get your trousers somewhere else, though, as it stocks just a handful.

Bombay Electric
Reay House, BEST Marg, Colaba (2287-6276). CST or Churchgate stations. **Open** 10am-9pm daily. **Credit** AmEx, DC, MC, V.
Taking its name from the street it shares with South Mumbai's electricity board, Bombay Electric has an eclectic collection of Indian and international clothes for men, women and children.

Courtyard
Minoo Desai Marg, behind Radio Club, Apollo Bunder, Colaba. CST or Churchgate stations. **Open** 11am-8pm daily. **Credit** AmEx, MC, V.
This chic enclave houses a mix of designer and boutique stores that sell everything from bridalwear and gold jewellery to Aigner handbags and bar accessories. Some top designers also have stand-alone stores here, including Suneet Verma and Narendra Kumar Ahmed.

Cypress
Windward Apartments, 21st Road, Khar (W) (2646-1747). Khar station. **Open** 11.30am-8.30pm Mon-Sat. **Credit** MC, V.
At 130sq m (1,400sq ft), Cypress houses collections from a mix of top Mumbai and Delhi designers, including Sabina Singh.

Ensemble
Great Western Building, 130/132 Colaba Causeway, Colaba (2284-3227/5167). Churchgate/CST stations. **Open** 10am-7pm Mon-Sat. **Credit** AmEx, MC, V.
The pioneer of Indian clothes retailing, Ensemble was the first store to stock high-profile Indian designers in a luxurious space – at mostly unattainable prices – and its Lion's Gate location still symbolises exclusivity and quality for many Mumbaikars. Currently, Ensemble carries big-label names such as Monisha Jaisingh, Manish Malhotra and Tarun Tahiliani, who is also an owner.
Other location West Wing, Whitehall Building, 143 August Kranti Marg, near Shalimar Hotel, Kemp's Corner (2367-2416).

First Time
483 Asha Apartments, 17th Road, Khar (W) (2604-4495). Khar station. **Open** 11am-7.30pm Mon-Sat. **Credit** DC, MC, V.
First Time stocks clothes by different designers including Divya Anand. With simple silhouettes, Anand festoons her clothes with the gorgeous brocade, pita work, zardosi, cord work and appliqué for which she is recognised.

Kimaya
3 Delstar Building, below Kemp's Corner flyover, Kemp's Corner (2386-2432,99675-97778). **Open** 10.30am-8pm daily. **Credit** AmEx, MC, V.
Juhu's film crowd loves Kimaya because it saves them a trip to South Mumbai to buy all their favourite Indian designers. South Mumbai has now cottoned on, too, and has its own branch.
Other location 2 Asha Colony, Juhu Tara Road (98920-10003).

Melange
33 Raj Mahal, Altamount Road (2385-0288). Grant Road station. **Open** 10am-7pm Mon-Sat. **Credit** AmEx, MC, V.
This pretty store is tucked away on Altamount Road, but has a dedicated crowd of buyers who prefer the more sober and grown-up, but no less stylish, offerings compared to what you'll find at most other boutique stores.

Mogra
High Street Phoenix, 462 Senapati Bapat Marg, Lower Parel (2496-0808). Lower Parel station. **Open** 11am-9pm daily. **Credit** AmEx, MC, V.
Glitz and glam is the rule at Mogra, which houses almost 100 young designers of both clothes and accessories in a brand new, massive space.

Oak Tree
18 Cusrow Baug, Colaba Causeway, Colaba (2281-9031). CST or Churchgate stations. **Open** 11am-8pm Mon-Sat. **Credit** AmEx, MC, V.
A small Colaba boutique packed with funky shoes, belts, bags, jewellery and Indo-western clothes.

OMO
204 Sagar Fortune, Second Floor, Waterfield Road, Bandra (W) (6698-1804). Bandra station. **Open** 11am-8pm daily. **Credit** AmEx, MC, V.
Way before folk became funky, OMO, or On My Own, was doing it, and it's still doing it better than most. OMO's also got the most die-hard loyalists we've seen of any store in Bandra.

INSIDE TRACK HANSIBA

In 2009, when the US Secretary of State Hillary Clinton visited Mumbai, she made a quick stop at SEWA's **Hansiba** (*see p132*), a cause she supports. Rumour has it she spent over £600.

Taxxi & Vitamin K
Shop 3 & 4, Kusum Kunj, Linking Road, opposite Citibank, Khar (W) (6525-9382). **Open** 11am-8.30pm Mon-Sat. **Credit** AmEx, MC, V.
Before they were store owners or even designers, Taxxi's owners were dissatisfied shopaholics. Which is why their clothes hit the high notes in both design and practicality. When their bright, fun collections started selling out from other stores they decided to team up with accessory designer Karishma Shanbagh of Vitamin K. It's mostly cotton, not just casual and will certainly get you noticed.

You
2 Cornelian, Kemp's Corner, 104 August Kranti Marg (2382-6972/73). Grant Road station. **Open** 10.30am-7pm Mon-Sat. **Credit** AmEx, MC, V.
Kitsch is cool at You, which stocks summer dresses, T-shirts and a changing assortment of accessories, including sequinned clutches, pretty beads and paisley *chappals*.

Indian designers

★ Abu Jani-Sandeep Khosla
Om Chambers, 2 Kemp's Corner (2367-3401/3505). Grant Road station. **Taxi** Kemp's Corner. **Open** 10.30am-6.30pm Mon-Sat. **Credit** AmEx, MC, V.
India's most exclusive designer duo, Abu Jani and Sandeep Khosla, have dressed innumerable stars and celebrities, and created an Oscar ceremony dress for Dame Judi Dench.

Azeem Khan
Shop No. 1, Usha Sadan Building, Colaba (2215-1028/0372). CST or Churchgate stations. **Taxi** Colaba Post Office. **Open** 10.30am-7pm Mon-Sat. **Credit** AmEx.
Hillary Clinton and Naomi Campbell have used Azeem Khan's styles to add some glitter to their looks. His penchant for shimmer is not surprising: he is the third generation of the SU Zariwala family, Mumbai's celebrated embroiderers.

Manish Arora
The Courtyard, Minoo Desai Marg, Apollo Bunder, Colaba (6638-5464). CST or Churchgate stations. **Open** 11am-7.30pm daily. **Credit** AmEx, MC, V.
Designer Manish Arora bears a signature style: gaudy colours that magically work, Indian pop culture references, over-the-top embellishments and a distinctly Mumbai feel.

Ritu Kumar
Block 9, Phoenix Mills Annexe, 462 Senapati Bapat Marg, Lower Parel (6666-9901). Lower Parel station. **Open** 10am-8pm daily. **Credit** AmEx, DC, MC, V.
The empress of traditional craft and colour, Kumar's creations are the kind you'll see in countless Bollywood wedding sequences.

Rohit Bal
The Courtyard, Minoo Desai Marg, Apollo Bunder, Colaba (6638-5478/79). CST or Churchgate stations. **Open** 11am-7pm daily. **Credit** AmEx, MC, V.
Best known for dressing India's most high-profile grooms, Bal's prêt line includes excellent shirts and Nehru-style tunics. His work in linen is classy too.

Satya Paul
Delstar Building, below Kemp's Corner Flyover, Kemp's Corner (2380-5239). Grant Road station. **Open** 11am-8pm daily. **Credit** MC, V.
Satya Paul is always doing something new with his trademark printed saris and hip ties.

Tarun Tahiliani
Villar Ville, Ground Floor, 16 Ramchandani Marg, Apollo Bunder, Colaba (2287-0895,2285-4603). CST or Churchgate stations. **Open** 11am-7pm Mon-Sat. **Credit** AmEx, MC, V.
India's reigning king of design, Tarun Tahiliani has been around for years and has mastered the art of sexily draping women in yards of fabric – and getting them to pay a large sum for it.

Casualwear

Chemistry
210 Govindham, Waterfield Road, Bandra (W) (2640-6601). Bandra station. **Open** 11am-8.45pm daily. **Credit** AmEx, MC, V.
Chemistry's got the formula right with good basics. Perfect for office shirts, fun t-shirts and denim.

★ Cotton World Corporation
201 Ram Nimi Building, Mandlik Road, Colaba (2285-0060). CST or Churchgate stations. **Taxi** behind Taj Mahal Hotel. **Open** 10.30am-8pm daily. **Credit** AmEx, MC, V.
Mumbai's answer to the Gap, CWC has a host of basics like T-shirts, trousers, capris, shorts and shirts that are perfect for the warm, humid climate. Shame there aren't more stores like this.
Other locations Phoenix Mills, Lower Parel (2491-8801); Vipul Apartments, Tagore Road, Santa Cruz (W) (2605-1602).

★ FabIndia
137 MG Road, Kala Ghoda (2262-6539). CST or Churchgate stations. **Open** 10am-9pm daily. **Credit** AmEx, MC, V.
One of Mumbai's most popular stores, selling stylish, high-quality Indian casualwear – from *kurtas* to *salwar kameez* – with a wide range in cotton and silk; and it's all made by rural artisans. There's also a home furnishing section.
Other location Navroze, Pali Hill, Bandra (W) (2646-5286).
▶ *When visiting FabIndia at Kala Ghoda, relax your tired feet by having coffee at Moshe's Café, which has an outlet inside the store; see p97.*

Kasab
B3 Matru Ashish, First Floor, 39 Nepean Sea Road (2362-0209,6664-8051). Grant Road station. **Open** 10am-7pm Mon-Sat. **Credit** MC, V.
This 30-year-old store has some serious value-for-money clothing. Expect *kurtas* with Rajasthani mirrorwork, tops with traditional prints cut in very modern styles and gorgeous Maheshwari cotton stoles and *dupattas*.

Reeth
Shop No. 2, Tulsi I, opposite Lo-Price Supermarket, Seven Bungalows, Andheri (W) (2639-2428). **Open** 11am-7pm Mon-Sat. **Credit** MC, V.
Reeth brims with ikkat weaves and *kalamkari* fabrics. The store is famous for its range of embroidered *salwars* and stretch *churidars*.

Soma
A/2 Amarchand Mansion, First Floor, 16 Madam Cama Road, next to YWCA, Colaba (2282-6050). **Open** 10am-8pm Mon-Sat; 10am-6pm Sun. **Credit** MC, V.
Soma is full of flirty, billowy, ultra-feminine clothes that make you want to stroll in a park swinging a parasol with the wind blowing in your hair. Floral prints in delicate pastels adorn cotton tops, *kurtas*, trousers, skirts and even underwear.

Men's chain stores

Color Plus
Unit No. 135 A & B, Atria Mall, Dr Annie Besant Road, Worli (6514-8201). Mahalaxmi station. **Open** 10.30am-9pm daily. **Credit** AmEx, MC, V.
Excellent quality trousers and khakis; this is a chain of stores that says 'export quality', which probably explains the dropped 'u' in colour.

Millionaire
132 Damodar Mahal, August Kranti Marg (2382-5555,2388-6018). Grant Road station. **Taxi** opposite Shalimar Hotel. **Open** 11am-9.30pm daily. **Credit** MC, V.
Looking for an Indian *sherwani* suit that won't break the bank? Come here for ready-to-wear versions of this classic Indian formalwear.

Provogue
Shop No. 9, Ground Floor, Cusrow Baug, Colaba (2284-0048). CST or Churchgate stations. **Taxi** Cusrow Baug. **Open** 10.30am-9.30pm daily. **Credit** MC, V.
Provogue started out as a party and loungewear brand for men, but the shop now has clothes and accessories for every occasion. These manage to look good even on regular people, not just the Bollywood stars who plug its products.

Fabindia.

Raymond
59A Bhulabhai Desai Road, Breach Candy (2351-1644). Grant Road station. **Open** 11am-8pm daily. **Credit** AmEx, MC, V.
Raymond is one of India's best-known tailors for good reason: staff are able to tailor-make a suit in just a few days, and for a fraction of the price you'd expect to pay in Europe or the United States – and the quality of the work is outstanding.

Tuscan Verve
1 Lotia Palace, Linking Road, Khar (2648-0385). Khar station. **Taxi** Khar Citibank. **Open** 10.30am-9pm daily. **Credit** AmEx, MC, V.
Tuscan Verve shirts are as colourful, loud and funky as it gets; don't bother unless you have the chutzpah to carry them off.

Zodiac
Taj Mahal Hotel, Apollo Bunder, Colaba (6591-7138). CST or Churchgate stations. **Open** 10am-midnight Mon-Sat; 10am-7pm Sun. **Credit** AmEx, MC, V.
Crisp shirts, great patterns and prints, cool ties, and prices that will make you want to buy them all.
Other locations Linking Road, opposite Shopper's Stop, Bandra (6591-7121); Grand Hyatt Mumbai, Santa Cruz (E) (6591-7130).

Jewellery

Amrapali
Shop Nos. 39 & 62, Oberoi Shopping Arcade, Nariman Point (2281-0978/81). CST or Churchgate stations. **Taxi** Oberoi Hotel. **Open** 10.45am-7pm daily. **Credit** AmEx, MC, V.
This Jaipur institution creates fine gold and silver jewellery, combining Indian tradition and craftsmanship with contemporary design and aesthetics. Naomi Campbell, Jennifer Lopez and the Prince of Morocco seem to like it.

Curio Cottage
19 Mahakavi Bhushan Marg, Colaba (2202-2607). CST or Churchgate stations. **Taxi** Regal Cinema. **Open** 10.30am-8pm Mon-Sat. **Credit** AmEx, MC, V.
A favourite with both locals and visitors, Curio Cottage sells semi-precious jewellery that fills the pages of fashion magazines as well as tiny trinkets your friends back home will love.

Orra
58/60 Zariwala Mansion, Hughes Road (2368-0606). Grant Road station. **Open** 11am-7.30pm daily. **Credit** AmEx, MC, V.
This chain of stores is a reliable place to buy gold, diamond and platinum jewellery, as well as Indian mythology-inspired pendants.
Other location 2 AN Chambers, Turner Road, Bandra (2643-3423,3291-6064).

Sia
37 Maskati Corner, 110/112 Altamount Road (2381-2628). Grant Road station. **Open** 10am-8pm Mon-Sat; 10am-6pm Sun. **Credit** MC, V.
Sia sells stunning replicas of the kind of ornate, heavy Indian jewellery that you see on display at lavish weddings.

TBZ – The Original
Zaveri Bazaar, Bhuleshwar (2343-5001). Charni Road station. **Open** 10.30am-7.30pm Mon-Sat. **Credit** AmEx, MC, V.
One of the city's oldest goldsmiths, Tribhovandas Bhimji Zaveri is known for its solid gold jewellery. It's also famous for not having copyrighted its name and as such dozens of inferior imitators have the tried to cash in on its success by using the same name. Rest assured that this is the real deal.

FOOD & DRINK

Bakeries

Kyani & Co
Jer Mahal, Dhobi Talao (2201-1492). Marine Lines or CST stations. **Taxi** Metro Cinema. **Open** 6.20am-9pm daily. **No credit cards**.
The baked delights on offer at Kyani & Co have a sort of period charm to them – custard puffs, sweet buttered buns and other treats of the sort dreamed of by Billy Bunter. Don't miss the chicken patties and the cardamom-flavoured *mava* cakes, which are beloved of Parsis.

Paris Bakery
278 Cowasji Hormusji Street, Marine Lines (2208-6619). Marine Lines station. **Taxi** near Our Lady of Dolours Church. **Open** 8.30am-2pm, and 4.30-9pm Mon-Sat; 8am-1pm Sun. **No credit cards**.
On a tiny street-side stall along a narrow potholed lane up from Our Lady of Dolours sits Paris, a well-loved local institution. Mumbaikars flock from far and wide for the bakery's impressive range of edible goodies. Try the delicious cashew macaroons and garlic-butter breadsticks among many other treats. *Photo p128.*

Theobroma
Cusrow Baug, Shop 24, Colaba Causeway, Colaba (6529-2929). CST or Churchgate stations. **Taxi** Cusrow Baug. **Open** 8am-midnight Mon-Sat; 11am-11pm Sun. **Credit** MC, V.
The name means 'food of the gods', and as far as we're concerned it's not too much of an exaggeration; top-quality sourdough loaves, fluffy focaccia, chocolate brownies, Danish pastries, fresh sandwiches and, randomly, possibly the only chip butty in Mumbai.

Beverages

Philips Tea & Coffee
Shop No. 8, Usha Sadan, Colaba Causeway, Colaba (2207-4793). CST or Churchgate stations. **Taxi** near Colaba Post Office. **Open** 9am-8pm daily. **No credit cards**.
Cheap, super quality, fresh Indian teas and coffee beans are available at this sleepy store.
► *Don't want to brew your own tea? Visit Tea Centre at Churchgate; see p99.*

Shah Wines
Sitaram Building, Ground Floor, Fort (2342-7997 , www.shahwines.com). CST or Churchgate stations. **Taxi** Crawford Market. **Open** 10am-8.30pm Mon-Sat. **Credit** MC, V.
One of the city's biggest wine shops, Shah Wines sells Indian and imported wines, spirits and beers.

Indian sweets

Brijwasi
Narayan Building, near 1st Pasta Lane, Colaba Causeway, Colaba (2282-0963 , www.brijwasi.in). CST or Churchgate stations. **Open** 10am-8pm daily. **No credit cards**.
A top choice for a glittering array of silver-wrapped *mithai* (sweets) in all their glory – try the *kaju anjeer* (cashew and fig) rolls and ghee-soaked *ladoos* (sweet balls). There's also a range of delicious fresh milk sweets and Bengali treats like *sandesh* – dry on the outside, sweet and juicy on the inside.
Other location Raj Mahal, near Ambassador Hotel, Veer Nariman Road, Churchgate (2282-2368).

Camy Wafer
5-6 Oxford House, near Colaba Market, Colaba Causeway, Colaba (2282-8430 , www.camywafer.com). CST or Churchgate stations. **Open** 9am-9pm daily. **No credit cards**.
More *mithai* than you can shake a candy cane at, all superb quality. Camy also has a great selection of savoury snacks, including *chivda* – dry snacks of puffed rice, raisins, nuts and spices.
Other locations Second Taj Building, August Kranti Marg, Gowalia Tank (2389-2288); Shop Nos. 1 & 2, Crystal Building, Junction of 16th Road, Khar Danda Road (2604-1178).

Mishty Bela
Krishnaraj Building, Walkeshwar Road, Malabar Hill (2361-6690). Grant Road station. **Taxi** near White House. **Open** 9am-8pm daily. **No credit cards**.
A wide range of traditional Indian *mithai*, including sugar-free, all-natural fruit *mithai* made from almonds, raisins, walnuts, figs and more. Don't miss the tiny *rasmalai* – sweet, milky and juicy.

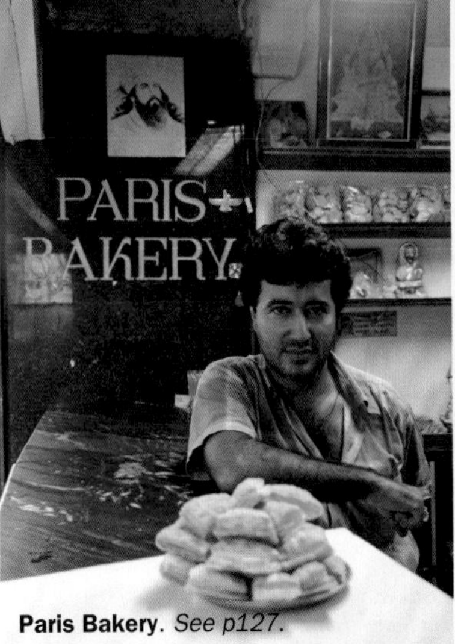

Paris Bakery. *See p127.*

GIFTS

Bombay Store
Western India House, Sir Pherozeshah Mehta Road (2288-5048/5049). CST station. **Taxi** PM Road. **Open** 10.30am-7.30pm Mon-Sat; 10.30am-6.30pm Sun. **Credit** AmEx, MC, V.
Perfect if you want to get a taste of everything, – like the modernistic stone Ganesha statues small enough to sit on the palm of your hand. The Bombay Store brings together artefacts, home accessories, clothes, jewellery, stationery and various trinkets that proudly bear a 'Made in India' stamp.

Cheemo
High Street Phoenix, 462 Senapati Bapat Marg, Lower Parel (2493-0495). Lower Parel station. **Taxi** Phoenix. **Open** 11am-8.30pm Mon-Sat. **Credit** AmEx, MC, V.
Handbags galore – from bejewelled, embroidered and studded clutches that will turn heads back home to 'Prada-inspired' purses.
Other location Mangal Darshan, Waterfield Road, Bandra (W) (2643-2493).

★ **Hidesign**
High Street Phoenix, 462 Senapati Bapat Marg, Lower Parel (2496-4309). Lower Parel station. **Open** 10.30am-8.15pm daily. **Credit** AmEx, DC, MC, V.
All manner of leather goods – from cool satchels to belts and jackets – made in Pondicherry and exported to fine stores across the world.

Ravissant
New India Building, Madame Cama Road, Colaba (2287-3405/6). CST or Churchgate stations. **Open** 9.30am-8pm Mon-Sat. **Credit** AmEx, MC, V.

One of India's oldest fine brands, Ravissant is best known for its silver items handcrafted in Holland, Germany and Switzerland. If you're looking for a one-of-a-kind metre-high Ganesh statue or an actual swing set for your bedroom (both in silver), this is the place to visit.
Other location 131 August Kranti Marg, Kemp's Corner (2363-7003,2368-4934).

Shawlart

3 Jai Tirath Mansion, Barrack Road, behind Metro Adlabs Cinema (2203-1128). CST or Marine Lines stations. **Open** 10am-6pm Mon-Sat. **Credit** AmEx, MC, V.
This speciality store for shawls, scarves and stoles is happy to send a trunk full of wares based on your requirements and tastes, so you can shop from your hotel room. Or pop in for a look. There's lots of variety in embellishments, weaves and embroideries.

★ Tribal Route

18 Aram Nagar 2, behind Rice Boat, JP Road (Machlimar), Versova, Andheri (W) (99670-58847). Andheri station. **Open** 11.30am-8.30pm daily. **Credit** AmEx, MC, V.
Nihar Mehta's curio cottage in Andheri stocks a range of furniture, handicrafts, jewellery and knick-knacks. He also sells organic T-shirts and accessories made out of recycled products.
➤ *For more socially-conscious gifts; see* **Spend to Save** *p132.*

HAIRDRESSERS

b:blunt

Block No. 1, Ground Floor, 29 Hughes Road (6598-0301). Grant Road station. **Open** 11am-7pm Tue-Sun. **Credit** MC, V.
Adhuna Bhabani, the woman behind b:blunt, also sets the biggest hair trends in Bollywood. This salon houses a Kerastase centre.

Hakim's Aalim

Union Park, Khar (W) (2646-0044). Khar station. **Taxi** Olive restaurant. **Open** 11am-9pm daily. **Credit** MC, V.
This shiny salon looks more like a sports bar: it's spread over 232sq m (2,500sq ft), with plasma screens and a resident DJ. But don't let the fluff distract you – it's quality.

INSIDE TRACK
MEMORABLE MACAROONS

Clients travel from as far as Jogeshwari and Chembur for a taste of **Paris Bakery**'s (*see p127*) garlic toast and cashew macaroons. Stock runs out fast so arrive early, and leave the calorie counter at home.

Mad-o-wot

Hemkund Society, Ground Floor, Plot No. 450, 14th Road, Bandra (W) (6698-2614). Bandra station. **Open** 10am-8pm daily. **Credit** MC, V.
Sapna Bhavnani's salon is one of the most eclectic in the city with kitsch interiors and fun haircuts.

Nalini of Nalini & Yasmin

Sagar Fortune, Second Floor, Waterfield Road, Bandra (W) (6698-2614). Bandra station. **Open** 10am-8pm daily. **Credit** MC, V.
Nalini and Yasmin are pioneers in every sense of the word and have been around long before hairstyling was considered a 'cool' thing to do in Mumbai. They have now split (amicably) but Nalini remains at their old venue.

Raih: Hair Reinvented

Arunodaya Building, 20 Nepean Sea Road (2363-5599). Grant Road station. **Taxi** opposite Contemporary Arts & Crafts. **Open** 11.15am-6.45pm daily. **Credit** MC, V.
One of the city's swankiest hair salons. Raih boasts a client book stuffed full with Mumbai's rich and pretty, including industrialist wives, celebrity regulars, sportspeople and fashion editors.

HOME

★ Anokhi

Rasik Niwas, Metro Motors Lane, off Hughes Road (2368-5308/5761). Grant Road station. **Open** 10.30am-7.30pm Mon-Sat. **Credit** AmEx, MC, V.
Rajasthani prints abound here on bed and table linens, easy-to-wash curtains and seat covers.
Other location Govinda Building, Waterfield Road, Bandra (W) (2640-8263).

★ Contemporary Arts & Crafts

19 NG House, Nepean Sea Road (2363-1979). Grant Road station. **Taxi** St Stephen's Church. **Open** 10am-8pm daily. **Credit** AmEx, MC, V.
CAC makes knick-knacks and essentials for the home, ranging from brocade cushions to Christmas lights, candlestands and lampshades. Cool designs with Indian influences.

Dhoop

First Floor, 101 Khar Sheetal Apartments, Dr Ambedkar Road, Union Park, Khar (2649-8646). Khar station. **Taxi** near Carter Road. **Open** 11am-8.30pm Mon-Sat. **Credit** MC, V.
Dhoop's focus is on handicrafts made from natural materials, but this isn't your average jute bag shop – instead think coconut shells, bamboo, banana, sugarcane, water hyacinth and many more intriguing materials. Hardly a run-of-the-mill souvenir shop, it's a great place to stock up on unique, exotic presents for the folks back home.

FabIndia
137 MG Road, Kala Ghoda (2262-6539). CST or Churchgate stations. **Open** 10am-8pm daily. **Credit** AmEx, DC, MC, V.
Indian textiles and artistry at their best in a range of cool home furnishings and accessories, all at good prices. It has great Burma teak furniture too.

Good Earth
Raghuvanshi Mills, Lower Parel (6572-0345/42). Lower Parel or Mahalaxmi stations. **Open** 11am-8pm daily. **Credit** AmEx, MC, V.
This large, pretty store sells everything from dining tables to chandeliers, spa products to coffee cups. None of it is overtly ethnic, but it is lovely.

India Weaves
Near Cymroza Art Gallery, Bhulabhai Desai Road (2368-6366). Grant Road station. **Open** 10am-8pm Mon-Sat. **Credit** MC, V.
For that majestic look and feel that comes from luxurious Indian silks and rich tissues, head to India Weaves where staff can help you create just that.

Yamini
Wodehouse Road, Colaba (2291-0309). CST or Churchgate stations. **Open** 10.30am-7.30pm daily. **Credit** AmEx, MC, V.
Yamini is the best place to go for affordable, Indian-inspired linens, textiles, bags, home accessories and delightful lamps.

Bungalow 8
E-F Block, Wankhede Stadium North Stand, D Road, Churchgate (2281-9880). Churchgate station. **Open** 11am-7pm Mon-Sat. **Credit** MC, V.
Maithili Ahluwalia's store is situated under the stands of Wankhede cricket stadium. Her choice of dinnerware, home accessories, clothes and jewellery is as eclectic as her choice of location.

GOURMET FOOD

Godrej Nature's Basket
Tirupati Apartments, near VFS Office, Bhulabhai Desai Road, Breach Candy (2352-6775). Grant Road station. **Open** 9am-10pm daily. **Credit** MC, V.
A great place to stock up on fruits, vegetables, wine, organic food and imported products.

> **INSIDE TRACK MALL PARKING**
>
> Most malls charge an hourly parking fee. Despite this, parking tends to get full at malls during weekends as families flock there. So either get there in good time or get a cab.

MALLS

Atria
Annie Besant Road, opposite Poonam Chambers, Worli (2481-3333). Mahalaxmi station. **Taxi** opposite Poonam Chambers. **Open** *Shops* 9.30am-9pm; *restaurants* 9.30am-1am daily.
The all-glass structure near the Planetarium has enough shopping and entertainment on its five levels to keep you busy for a whole day, including a 4D cinema. There's a good mix for both big spenders and mall-rats, and a food court on the top level.

CR2
Opposite Bajaj Bhavan, Nariman Point (6524-6470). Churchgate station. **Taxi** INOX. **Open** *Shops* 10am-8pm; *restaurants* 10am-midnight daily.
Fashion brands including Versace JC, restaurants like the tatty American chain Ruby Tuesday on the ground floor and South Mumbai's most popular multiplex on the top floor make this mall a popular evening and weekend hangout. The delicious kebabs at Moti Mahal have earned the place a cult following, but don't drive down the spiral car park exit right after a meal.

High Street Phoenix
462 Senapati Bapat Marg, Lower Parel (2496-4307). **Open** *Shops* 9.30am-10pm; *bowling* 10am-12.30am; *restaurants* until 1.30am daily.
The zenith or nadir of Mumbai consumerism, depending on your political leanings, this massive mall was formerly a mill. There's very little you don't get here but it's best known for accessible local designerwear, luxury stores, nightclubs and home-grown restaurant chains. There's also a multiplex.

Oberoi Mall
Oberoi Garden City, off Western Express Highway, International Business Park, Goregaon (E) (2842-4050). **Open** 11am-10pm daily.
Oberoi Mail is cool, clean and cream with glossy escalators, shiny steel railings, glass fences running smoothly through all 65,000 sq m (700,000 square ft), up to the 100m (330-ft) ceiling through which steady sunlight pours in to make artificial lighting redundant. Brands include Central, Esprit, Samsaara and Chemistry. There's also a multiplex and a sizeable food court.

Orchid City Centre
Opposite BEST Bus Depot, Mumbai Central (6610-4300). Mumbai Central station. **Open** 11am-10pm daily.
Going just by noise levels alone, this mall in the heart of Central Mumbai is mighty popular. You can buy vegetables, clothes, accessories, books, music, electronics, furniture, luggage and then some. The multi-cuisine food court swings from burgers to thalis.

Curio City

Superb city scape souvenirs.

Memorabilia seekers can find the city emblazoned on T-shirts, coasters, cups and cushions. Sweeping black-and-white shots of wide, empty city streets (Rs 6,500) by legendary 19th-century photographer Raja Deen Dayal are popular items at **Phillips Antiques** (Indian Mercantile Mansion, Madame Cama Road, opposite Regal Cinema, Colaba, 2202-0564, www.phillipsantiques.com), as are nostalgia-laced photographs of Mumbai in the 1930s and '40s. The 151-year-old store's collection includes reproductions of old maps of Mumbai and India, old illustrated advertising posters and photographs of princely India (Rs 2,000-Rs 5,000).

But why just look at Old Mumbai, when you can drink and sleep with it? **Contemporary Arts & Crafts** (19 NG House, Nepean Sea Road, Kemp's Corner, 2363-1979) sells cushion covers (Rs 930-Rs 950) and coasters (Rs 410) with sepia-tinted images of Cuffe Parade and Crawford Market. Meanwhile, **Loose Ends** (Beas Co-operative Society, 31st Road, Bandra W, 2645-3777) reproduces the city on cups, bags and paperweights (Rs 250-Rs 500). It also sells taxi- and auto-shaped cushion covers and coasters with local train station signs (Rs 50-Rs 1,500). Another store, **Tappu Ki Dukaan** (27-A, Kermani Building, Sir PM Road, opposite Citibank, Fort, 2204-3716), stocks plenty of Mumbai kitsch including Bus Kya BEST bags (Rs 550) and 'You Know You Are Indian Because' air-tight tins (Rs 225). The newest entrant on the scene is **Play Clan** (Libra Tower, Ground Floor, Hill Road, Bandra W, 2640-1675). This tiny store sports Bollywood wall murals and sells a range of stationery, cushion covers and mugs of Colaba, Crawford Market and Bandra.

If you don't mind your postcards and posters dog-eared, head to **Mini Market** (33 Mutton Street) at Chor Bazaar. The clutter inside this tiny shop hides mountains of Old Mumbai postcards (Rs 30), photographs of Parsi families (Rs 50), colourful, carved wooden busts found at the entrance of traditional Gujarati houses in Thakurdwar (Rs 5,000), old Bollywood film posters (Rs 300-Rs 2,000) and even first-day-first-show film tickets (Rs 100-Rs 500).

Phillips Antiques.

CONSUME

MARKETS

Nowhere is Mumbai's mercantile instinct more evident than in its wide range of specialised markets that sell everything from pickles to zebra-striped fabric. Credit cards are very definitely not accepted, and don't expect a money-back guarantee, but for a retail experience that really represents India, markets are a must. Here's a selection of the city's most colourful and quirky trading zones.

Antiques at Chor Bazaar

Mutton Street, opposite Null Bazaar. CST or Marine Lines stations. **Open** 10.30am-7pm Mon-Thur, Sat, Sun.

From ancient 78 RPM records by Gauhar Jaan to elaborately carved cupboards, from ships' wheels to 1950s Bollywood posters and old cameras, Chor Bazaar ('Thieves' Market') has it all. Thought to have its origins as a market where stolen goods were fenced, today it's a warren of respectable stores peddling antiques and assorted bric-a-brac. Though the shops are shut on Fridays, an informal flea market thrives in the afternoons, after 3pm.

Clothes at Fashion Street

Mahatma Gandhi Road, along Azad Maidan. CST station. **Open** 10.30am-7pm daily.

Wondering why shopping in Mumbai isn't as inexpensive as you expected? Head to Fashion Street, the unofficial name for a stretch of Mahatma Gandhi

Spend to Save

Shopping needn't always induce guilt. Here's how to shop with a conscience.

Akanksha

8-B Poonam Apartments, Shiv Sagar Estate, Annie Besant Road (2370-0253). Mahalaxmi station. **Open** 10.30am-7.30pm Tue-Sun. **No credit cards.**

This non-profit organisation, which educates underprivileged kids, sells trendy, alluring merchandise featuring delightful motifs created by children enrolled in its programmes. The range includes pebble paperweights, pen holders, handmade notebooks and hand-painted trays, canvas shoes, benches and stools.

Comet Media Foundation

Topiwala Municipal School, Lamington Road (2382-6674). Grant Road station. **Open** 10am-6pm Mon-Sat. **No credit cards.**

Comet Media is a non-profit organisation which aims to bring social change through education. Its toys are made from wood, bamboo and cotton – the pull-along wooden turtle, caterpillars, and finger and glove puppets make for lovely gifts.

Creative Handicrafts

Shop No. 1, Bandra Homeland Co-op Housing Society, Hill Road, Bandra (W) (6572-7015). Bandra station. **Open** 11am-8pm Mon-Sat. **Credit** MC, V.

This tiny store on Hill Road is part of an initiative that imparts vocational training to women who live in Mumbai's slum communities. Apart from cotton *kurtas*, Creative Handicrafts also has a range of personal and home accessories, including embroidered cushion covers, pouches and handbags.

Hansiba

14 First Floor, LD Rupareliya Marg, off Nepean Sea Road and ahead of Hyderabad Estate, opposite Jeewan Manek Building (2369-4851). Grant Road station. **Open** 11am-8pm Mon-Sat. **Credit** AmEx, MC, V.

Hansiba is the retail venture of the Self Employed Women's Association, one of India's most-admired women's collectives. Its members sew and embroider clothes and cushions as well as make bags, earrings, quilts and various knick-knacks.

Soul Fuel

Shop No. 12, 288 Perry Cross Road, Bandra (W) (6528-0465). Bandra station. **Open** 11am-8.30pm Mon-Sat. **Credit** MC, V.

Don't have time to tramp across the city? Head to Soul Fuel, where most of the space in the store is dedicated to products made by non-governmental organisations. Mugs and cushions from the Welfare of Stray Dogs, bags from Advaitya and handicrafts from Viveka are part of the range.

Shanti Hastkala

Nippon II, 37 Juhu Tara Road, behind Hotel Kings, Juhu (call Radhika Luthra on 98201-70674). By appointment only. Andheri station. **No credit cards.**

The small store of this Gujarat-based organisation is a treasure house for bags in innumerable sizes and colours. Over 100 women from 15 villages in Magod make mobile pouches, sequinned *jholas*, bags with beads for handles, and canvas bags.

Road along Azad Maidan, where stalls sell all kinds of clothing for cheap. Some export surplus makes its way here, which means that you can occasionally pick up something that's big in London or New York, for a fraction of the price. Check for flaws and don't forget to bargain.

Everything at Crawford Market

Opposite Police Headquarters, Fort. CST station. **Open** 11am-7pm Mon-Sat.

Crawford Market, which opened its iron gates to the public in 1865, is a Mumbai institution not to be missed. As well as the four broad lanes packed with stalls selling fruit, vegetables, kitchenware, spices, dry fruits and foreign foodstuffs, you'll find bloody warehouses for poultry and mutton and even live pet stores. Watch out for the wigs at the Hair House for the Bald and Beautiful, just one of the oddities.

Fabric at Mangaldas Market

Sheikh Memon Street, near Chhatrapati Shivaji Terminus. CST station. **Open** 10am-7pm Mon-Sat.

A glorious array of colours and textures and a somewhat chaotic atmosphere make this the city's most vibrant and frantic fabric market.

Fireworks at Mohammed Ali Road

Near junction of Paltan Road & Mohammed Ali Road. CST station. **Open** 10am-8pm Mon-Sat.

Diwalis past have seen natural disaster-inspired fireworks Tsunami, Katrina and Rita hitting this market, but recently it's been back to Bollywood bombshells. During Diwali, temporary stalls stretch down the pavement for kilometres. The rest of the year, weddings and other festivals keep the five firework shops here in business.

Jewellery at Zaveri Bazaar

Bhuleshwar. **Open** 11am-7pm Mon-Sat.

India is said to consume about one-third of all the gold produced in the world – roughly 800 tons every year – and one visit here is all you need to believe it. Zaveri Bazaar offers customers highly competitive rates for an astonishing variety of gold and silver jewellery. Larger stores sell diamond jewellery as well, making this a one-stop shop for brides-to-be.

Leather at Dharavi

Sant Rolida Marg, Sion-Bandra Link Road, Sion (W). Sion station. **Open** 11am-8pm Tue-Sun.

Die-hard leather fans swear by Dharavi, where world-class leather products are produced in innumerable dingy workshops. Dharavi, which has the dubious distinction of being the largest slum in India, houses over 125 shops that retail and export leather goods to Europe and West Asia. This is where Indian fashion designers source accessories like handbags, jackets and shoes for catwalk shows. Those hot pink knee-high leather boots would find little use elsewhere.

Shoes at Linking Road

Linking Road, Bandra (W). Bandra station. **Open** 11am-9pm daily.

Hundreds of slippers, stilettos and sandals for men, women and children. A steady river of people flows along its periphery, selling everything from fruit trays to silk pouches and fluorescent yo-yos.

Snacks & pickles at Lalbaug

Chivda Galli & Achar Galli, off Dr B Ambedkar Road, Lalbaug. Chinchpokli or Lower Parel stations. **Open** 10am-7pm daily.

Ten fragrant outlets line Chivda Galli, a lively lane near Lalbaug market. The *chivdas* (savoury snacks) sold here are made out of *dagadi poha* (thick rice flakes), with chillies and raisins deep-fried and tossed together with a spice mix in a round-bottomed *kadhai*. They sell for around Rs 65-Rs 90 per kilo. Next door is Achar Galli, which sells the traditional Maharashtrian *loncha* (made with lime) as well as pickles of raw mango, chillies and berries.

Wedding cards at Girgaum

Khandilkar Road, opposite Gaiwadi, Girgaum, Churney Road (E). Churney Road station. **Open** 10am-8pm Mon-Sat.

Indian wedding can be spectacularly extravagant, so before you walk down the aisle, take a stroll down Khandilkar Road for a look at its dizzying array of thousands of ready-to-print wedding invitations. There are around 200 stores, each with hundreds of clever samples on display. Most are adorned with the elephant-headed Ganesha, who symbolises new beginnings and good luck. But stores also feature at least one wall of 'Muslim, Catholic and non-religious wedding cards'. It's a fun place to browse.

MUSIC

CDs

Planet M

Courtyard, High Street Phoenix, Senapati Bapat Marg, Lower Parel (2494-4609). Lower Parel station. **Open** 11am-10pm daily. **Credit** MC, V.

The country's largest music store chain has outlets across Mumbai and has an impressive range – you'll find music from all genres. A good place to pick up the latest releases.

Rhythm House

40 K Dubash Marg, Fort (2284-2835). CST or Churchgate stations. **Open** 10am-8.30pm Mon-Sat; 11am-8.30pm Sun. **Credit** MC, V.

One of Mumbai's oldest music stores, this city institution is the best place to find old Hindi film soundtracks. In addition to current chart hits, it also stocks a wide range of Hindustani classical and fusion/lounge music and sells tickets for gigs. Best of all, most of the red jacket-clad shop assistants actually know their music.

Musical instruments

Bhargava's Musik
4/5 Imperial Plaza, 30th Road, Bandra (W) (2641-1842). Bandra station. **Open** 10am-1pm, 2-7.30pm Mon-Sat. **Credit** MC, V.
A one-stop shop for all Hindustani and Carnatic musical instruments, including sitars, tablas, *sarods* and more. This 54-year-old shop counts renowned *santoor* player Shivkumar Sharma and flautist Hariprasad Chaurasia among its clientele.

BX Furtado & Sons
Jer Mahal, Dhobi Talao (2201-3105). CST or Marine Lines stations. **Taxi** Metro Cinema. **Open** 10am-7.30pm Mon-Sat. **Credit** MC, V.
Around since 1865, Furtado's focus is on Western musical instruments but it also sells Indian classical instruments, a large collection of music books, music software, speakers and amplifiers, and pedals and processors in two stores, BX Furtado and LM Furtado, that are around the corner from each other. BX is the only place in the city that stocks albums by local rock bands.

SHOES

Catwalk
Bhulabhai Desai Road, near Gangar opticians, Kemp's Corner (2367-8488). Grant Road station. **Open** 10am-9pm Mon-Sat; 11am-9pm Sun. **Credit** AmEx, MC, V.
Diamanté-studded stilettos, strappy wedges and other shoes for a night on the town.
Other location Infiniti Mall, New Link Road, next to Fame Adlabs, Andheri (W) (3241-5335).

Inc 5
Bhulabhai Desai Road, opposite Breach Candy Hospital (2361-8616). **Open** 10am-9.30pm Mon-Sat. **Credit** MC, V.
Inc 5 carries a mix of party shoes, labels like Guess and Tommy Hilfiger, and a small but practical range of boots, which, despite the climate, Mumbai can never get enough of.
Other location High Street Phoenix , 462 Senapati Bapat Marg, Lower Parel (2495-1352).

Metro Shoes
Metro House, Colaba Causeway (6656-0444). **Open** 10am-10pm daily. **Credit** AmEx, MC, V.
If you've always dreamed of wearing Swarovski crystals on your toes, you need look no further.

Rinaldi
67/68 Sea View Terrace, 118B Wodehouse Road, Colaba (2215-2513). **Open** 11am-7.30pm Mon-Sat. **Credit** AmEx, MC, V.
Accessories designer Rina Shah makes glam shoes that work. She also does boots with Indian embellishments and makes non-leather shoes.

TRAVELLERS' NEEDS

Dry cleaning

Akash Dry Cleaners
Shop No. 2, Ratan Manzil, 64 Wodehouse Road, Colaba (6516-1616). CST or Churchgate stations. **Open** 10am-8pm Mon-Sat. **No credit cards.**

American Express Dry Cleaners
Hill Road, Bandra (W) (2643-1743). Bandra station. **Open** 8.30am-1pm, 3.30-8pm daily. **No credit cards.**

Beauty Art
Stadium House, Veer Nariman Road, Churchgate (2282-1039). Churchgate station. **Open** 9am-2pm, 4-7pm Mon-Sat. **No credit cards.**

Opticians

For **pharmacies** *see p232.*

Colaba Opticians
A/8 Fatima Manzil, near Sassoon Dock, Colaba (2287-4244). CST or Churchgate stations. **Open** 9.30am-9pm Mon-Sat; 10am-7pm Sun. **Credit** AmEx, MC, V.

Lawrence & Mayo
Dr Dadabhai Naoroji Road, Fort (2207-6049). CST or Churchgate stations. **Open** 10am-7.30pm daily. **Credit** AmEx, MC, V.

Travel agents

Also *see p228* **Getting Around**.

Akbar Travels of India
Terminus View, 169 Dr Dadabhai Naoroji Road, Fort (2263-3434). CST station. **Taxi** Crawford Market. **Open** 10am-7pm Mon-Fri; 10am-6pm Sat. **Credit** AmEx, MC, V.

Atlas Tours & Travels
53 Haji Mahal, Mohammed Ali Road (6636-1000). CST station. **Taxi** near Noor Hospital. **Open** 10am-8pm Mon-Sat. **Credit** AmEx, MC, V.

Globe Forex & Travels
102 Modi Chambers, First Floor, French Bridge Corner, Opera House (4091-6666). Churney Road station. **Taxi** French Bridge. **Open** 9.30am-6.30pm Mon-Fri; 9.30am-4.30pm Sat. **Credit** AmEx, MC, V.

Riya Travels & Tours
Atlanta Arcade, Ground Floor, Marol Church Road, Andheri (E) (2925-8611). Andheri station. **Taxi** near Leela Kempinski Hotel. **Open** 9am-6pm Mon-Sat. **Credit** AmEx, MC, V.

Arts & Entertainment

Girgaum Chowpatty. *See p65.*

Calendar

It's easy to get into the festive spirit.

With practically every single religion on earth, except maybe Rastafarianism, represented in Mumbai's population, almost every day is a festival for someone, somewhere in the city. In the past, the vast number of religious festivals (all but three of the 17 holidays allowed to public servants are related to religion) have provided fodder for thunderous newspaper editorials blaming them for India's poor economic growth. Indians, it was claimed, were too busy celebrating their festivals to get any work done. The theory doesn't hold much water – most Indians work six-day weeks, so the time lost evens out – and got soundly kicked into irrelevance by 21st-century India's economic boom.

In Mumbai the biggest and most widely celebrated festivals are **Holi**, the festival of colour (and of *bhang*, a marijuana derivative) in March, the noisy and spectacular **Ganesh Chaturthi** around September and the firework frenzy of **Diwali** in October or November – all Hindu festivals, but marked in some form by nearly every community.

APRIL-JUNE

Easter Sunday

Holy Name Cathedral, Colaba; St Michael's Church, Mahim; Mount Mary Church, Bandra; & across the city. **Date** Apr.

Easter is the most important religious festival of the Christian liturgical year, celebrated in March or April to mark the resurrection of Jesus. Easter eggs, made of marzipan and chocolate, are sold in confectionery stores across Mumbai.

Gudi Padwa

Across the city. **Date** Apr.

Also known as Ugadi, Gudi Padwa marks the beginning of *basant* or spring. It's also celebrated as the start of the New Year for Maharashtrians. *Gudis* – poles decorated with silk, marigolds, mango leaves and coconuts, with upturned metal pots sitting on the end – are hung out of windows and displayed in traditional households.

Good Friday

Holy Name Cathedral, Colaba; St Michael's Church, Mahim; St Andrew's Church, Bandra; & across the city. **Date** Apr.

Christian prayer services across the city mark the day of Jesus's crucifixion. Some churches stage ornate tableaux of the event, using a combination of human actors and life-sized clay figures.

Ramnavami

Across the city. **Date** Apr.

Celebrating the wedding day of Rama and Sita, as well as Rama's birthday, Ramnavami sees devotees performing mock wedding ceremonies with small idols of the deities. In the evening, the brightly adorned statues are paraded through the streets.

JULY-SEPTEMBER

Bandra Fair

Mount Mary Church, Bandra. **Date** Sept.

The birthday of the Virgin Mary and the associated church feast are celebrated with a noisy fair.

Ganesh Chaturthi

Lalbaug, Girgaum Chowpatty, Dadar & across the city. **Date** Sept-Oct.

Ganesh Chaturthi marks the birthday of Lord Ganesha, the elephant-headed Hindu god of auspicious beginnings. During the ten-day festival, families install idols of the deity in their homes, while some neighbourhoods get together to erect tents (known as *pandals*) in which gigantic statues of Ganesha – some three storeys high – are enthroned

The idols are immersed in the sea or in lakes after either one and a half days, three, five, seven or ten days. While they are in residence, the idols are treated to music concerts and films late into the night – or at least as late as noise regulations permit. It's Mumbai's most popular festival, but is a relatively new addition to the festive calendar, devised only in 1901, when nationalist leader Bal Gangadhar Tilak decided to create the festival to mobilise public opinion against British colonial rule.

Janmashtami or Gokulashtami

Across the city. **Date** Aug.

The birthday of Lord Krishna, the eighth incarnation of Lord Vishnu, is celebrated with prayers, plays and fasting. Clay pots of yoghurt are strung between buildings high above the street, and bands of young men form amazing human pyramids in an effort to reach and break the vessels. Onlookers try to hamper their efforts by pouring buckets of water on them from their windows. Success brings cheers from the crowd – and cash too.

National Theatre Festival

Nehru Centre Auditorium, Annie Besant Road, Worli, (2496-4676, www.nehrucentremumbai.com). **Date** Aug.

The Nehru Centre puts together a festival of drama from all over India every August. The plays are often disappointingly amateurish but every season has a gem or two.

Navratri

Colaba, Andheri & across the city. **Date** Sept-Oct.

A popular festival with the city's Gujarati community, the 'nine nights' of Navratri are a countdown to Dussehra, the 'tenth day' on which Lord Rama killed the demon Ravana, as told in the *Ramayana*. Dance events, some attended by up to 10,000 people, are held on each night; couples holding batons in their hands dance the *dandiya raas* and the *garba*. They're a rare occasion on which teenagers of conservative households are allowed to mix with the opposite sex unsupervised by their parents. (City legend has it that some plastic surgeons offer to perform hymenoplasties after the festival, to 'revirginise' women before their weddings.)

Pateti

Across the city. **Date** Aug.

Pateti is celebrated by Parsis on the eve of their New Year, with visits to fire temples or *agiaries*. After the *jashan* (prayers), sandalwood is offered to the holy fire. Parsi homes are decorated for the festival: white powder is used to fashion intricate designs of birds, flowers and fish (an art called *rangoli*) at the entrance to homes. Families exchange gifts and tuck into dishes like *patra ni machchi* (fish wrapped in banana leaves), *sali boti* (meat with potato chips) and a sweet, milky drink called *falooda*.

Raksha Bandhan

Across the city. **Date** Aug.

Raksha Bandhan commemorates the bond between brothers and sisters. Across India, sisters tie decorative bands – called *rakhis* – on their brothers' wrists to remind them that sisters need protection; in return, brothers give their sisters cash or fancy presents. It isn't only siblings who celebrate the festival: girls can blunt the affections of ardent suitors by making them their symbolic '*rakhi* brothers'.

Ramzan

Mohammed Ali Road, Bhendi Bazaar. CST station. **Date** Aug.

Diwali.

ARTS & ENTERTAINMENT

The Muslim month of fasting starts in August/ September. Mohammed Ali Road and Bhendi Bazaar turn into giant food courts and stay open all night as the feasting begins every evening.

OCTOBER-DECEMBER

Celebrate Bandra Festival

Across Bandra. **Date** Nov.

In recent years, the once-sleepy northern suburb of Bandra has become the city's hottest neighbourhood, with new nightclubs, bars, chic restaurants and trendy boutiques popping up all the time. Every two years, the 'Celebrate Bandra' festival enlivens the area with events ranging from theatre and music to sports and even a parade.

Christmas

Holy Name Cathedral, Colaba; St Michael's Church, Mahim; Mount Mary Church, Bandra; & across the city. **Date** 24-25 Dec.

Christmas in Mumbai is much like Christmas in the West – without the variable odds on it being a white Christmas. A midnight mass on Christmas Eve (except it's actually over long before midnight thanks to noise regulations), followed by an exchange of presents and Christmas Day spent with the family. However, with temperatures reaching up to 25°C, a white Christmas is unlikely; some make up for that by showering flecks of cotton over their carefully tended fir trees, while street urchins and vendors roam Colaba Causeway working up a sweat in red Santa hats.

Diwali

Across the city. **Date** Oct-Nov.

Diwali (the 'festival of lights') celebrates Lord Rama's return to the kingdom of Ayodhya after the momentous assassination of demon Ravana, described in the *Ramayana* epic. It's an Indian Christmas, marked by fireworks, sweets and merry-making. Diwali is also the day on which Indian businessmen open new accounts books for the year, and perform *puja* ceremonies at their places of work to invoke the blessings of Lakshmi, the goddess of wealth. The nights before Diwali are spent gambling at cards, inviting luck for the rest of the year.

Durga Puja

Tejpal Road, Gowalia Tank & across the city. (2380-2679). **Date** Oct.

Every year, the goddess Durga comes down to earth and stays for five days. The first time she did this she was busy killing the demon Mahisasura. Since then, her homecoming has been an excuse for Bengalis to make merry. Held on the last five days of Navratri, this festival brings out the epicurean nature of Bengali culture. Everyone wears shiny new clothes, and singers and theatre groups from Kolkata visit Mumbai and perform at the different *pandals* (the venue for the *puja* – 'ritual prayer'). Some would argue religion is simply an excuse for Bengalis to tuck into the free, well-cooked vegetarian meals that are served to everyone at the *puja.*

Dussehra

Across the city. **Date** Oct.

Dussehra, the day on which Lord Rama killed the demon Ravana, symbolises the victory of good over evil. The slaying of the demon is recreated in colourful pageants called *Ram Leelas*, which conclude with the burning of large effigies of Ravana.

Durga Puja.

Eid-ul-Fitr/Ramzan Eid

Mohammed Ali Road & across the city.
Date Oct-Nov.
Eid-ul-Fitr, often referred to simply as Eid, is an Islamic holiday that marks the end of Ramzan (or Ramadan), the month of fasting. Muslim men attend special prayers, after which there's a swirl of visiting friends and eating festive meals.

Guru Nanak Jayanti

Four Bungalows, Andheri & across the city.
Date Nov.
Celebrating the anniversary of the birth of Guru Nanak Dev, the founder of the Sikh faith, Guru Nanak Jayanti begins with early morning processions of devotees from *gurdwaras* (Sikh temples) performing *shabads* (hymns). The celebrations also include the three-day *akhand path*, during which the Sikh holy book, the *Guru Granth Sahib*, is read from beginning to end without a break.

Prithvi Theatre Festival

Prithvi Theatre, Juhu Tara Road, Juhu (2614-9546,www.prithvitheatre.org); National Centre for the Performing Arts, Nariman Point (6622-3737,www.ncpamumbai.org). **Date** Nov.
Since 1983, the Prithvi Theatre Festival – held in a cosy auditorium in Juhu, as well as in the National Centre for the Performing Arts complex in South Mumbai – has become the high point of the Mumbai theatre season. It showcases the talents of groups from around India, and often features international acts, with an emphasis on encouraging originality in local drama groups.

Thespo

Experimental Theatre, National Centre for the Performing Arts, NCPA Marg, Nariman Point (6622-3737). **Date** Dec.
A platform for young actors to parade their talents, Thespo only invites participants under the age of 25. Apart from full-length productions, Thespo offers short performances and theatre workshops.

JANUARY-MARCH

Holi

Across the city. **Date** Mar.
One of the city's most popular festivals, celebrating the death of the demoness Holika. On the morning of Holi, the festival of colours, the whole city becomes an interactive Jackson Pollock painting as Mumbaikars spray each other with brightly coloured water – called 'playing Holi' – and consume food and drink made with marijuana called *bhang* which is sold at temples on the day of the festival.

Kala Ghoda Arts Festival

Kala Ghoda, Fort (www.kalaghodaassociation.com). CST or Churchgate stations. **Date** Feb.
Started in 1999 to promote the Kala Ghoda neighbourhood in Fort as an arts district, this ten-day festival is the city's premier showcase for painting, sculpture, film, music, dance and literary events, and another opportunity to eat lots of food.

Mahashivratri

Across the city. **Date** Feb-Mar.
When the dreaded halahala poison threatened to kill them all, gods and demons prayed to Lord Shiva to save them. On the night now known as Mahashivratri, Shiva drank the poison and held it in his throat, turning his throat blue and earning two new names in the process – Vishakantha ('The One Who Held Poison in His Throat') and Neelakantha ('The One With a Blue Throat'). That night is now celebrated every year with offerings of *bhel* leaves to Lord Shiva, and fasting. But the highlight of the festival is a night-long vigil when devotees sing *bhajans* in homes and temples to honour Lord Shiva.

Makar Sankranti

Across the city. **Date** 15 Jan.
Makar Sankranti is a harvest festival celebrating the transition of the sun from Sagittarius to Capricorn, according to Hindu astrology. Across the city, children and adults go kite flying, using strings embedded with crushed glass to try and cut each other's lines in friendly dogfights. Kites are sold at shops across Mumbai, with some of the most intense aerial battles taking place at Chowpatty Beach.

Mumbai Festival

Across the city (www.mumbaifestival.in).
Date Jan.
Founded in 2004, the Mumbai Festival aims to bring all things Mumbai under one banner, with autorickshaw races, arm-wrestling challenges, fishing-trawler pulling contests, concerts, dance performances, handicrafts and, of course, local food. As festivals go it's a brilliant introduction to the city.

Mumbai International Film Festival

Various venues (www.filmsdivision.org/ www.miffindia.in). **Date** Feb.
The Mumbai International Film Festival is a biennial competitive event that showcases films from across the world. It's also a rare platform for independent Indian films, with a programme that includes documentaries, shorts and animated films. Delegate passes are available for around Rs 100.

Pongal

Across the city. **Date** Jan.
The four-day Pongal festival is a South Indian harvest festival traditionally celebrated in the home. Pongal means 'to boil over' in Tamil, but roughly represents the idea of abundance. On the second day, Surya Pongal, the sun-god Surya is worshipped for protection and nurturing crops through the previous year.

Children

There's magic among the mayhem.

At first glance, Mumbai looks like the world's worst city for kids. It's noisy, crowded, has few parks, terrible air pollution and the pavements – where they exist – are often too uneven to walk on. But it's not that bad. With a little bit of flexibility and planning, there are plenty of possibilities for family outings in the city. In a metropolis as busy and exotic as Mumbai, there is an endless variety of things to see, smell, touch and listen to – and that's not including the obvious attractions of cinemas, parks and museums.

PARENT TRAP

You'll rarely see parents with pushchairs in Mumbai; kids are carried, perched on the petrol tanks of motorbikes or found rattling around the backs of cars. There are very few clean public toilets and almost no facilities where babies can be changed, forcing parents to look for a vacant park bench (and good luck finding that park) to change a dirty nappy.

But take a second look and you'll see that Mumbai is not quite the worst city in the world for kids. With a little imagination and persistence you can find activities to keep children amused, like a ride through the lion and tiger enclosures at Sanjay Gandhi National Park (*see p70*) or a trip to Mani Bhavan; the spectacle of festivals (*see p136* **Calendar**) also make unforgettable experiences for young travellers. Also, it doesn't hurt that the sun is often shining.

ANNUAL EVENTS FOR KIDS

January is kite-flying time while **February** is crowded with activities for kids in the Kala Ghoda Arts Festival (*see p139*). The month also sees a large flower, fruit and vegetable show hosted at the Veermata Jijabai Technical Institute grounds in Matunga by Friends of the Trees (2287-0860). **May** to **July** is holiday time and weekend camps are held across the city; see *Time Out Mumbai* for a list. **June** brings in Environment Week, with events showcasing the region's flora and fauna organised by the Bombay Natural History Society (2282-1811) and the Worldwide Fund for Nature-India (2207-8105). On the first Sunday after **8 September**, the quiet lanes of Bandra come alive with a week-long fair around the Basilica of Mount Mary, celebrating the birthday of the Virgin Mother. Also around September is Ganesh Chaturthi (*see p136*), when devotees throng Chowpatty Beach to immerse large, multicoloured idols of the elephant-headed Ganesha in the Arabian Sea. In **October** or **November**, Diwali, the Hindu festival of lights (*see p138*), turns the city into a giant fireworks display. **December** is Christmas time and parts of the city deck up with beautiful lights.

THE GREAT OUTDOORS

FREE Chowpatty Beach

Marine Drive, Girgaum. Charni Road station.

Spin on the creaking, hand-cranked merry-go-round (when was the last time you saw one of those?) and miniature Ferris wheels. Located at the northern end of Marine Drive, the beach is flanked by the Balodyan children's garden with play equipment.

FREE Hanging Gardens

BG Kher Road, Malabar Hill (2363-3561). Grant Road station. **Open** 5am-9pm daily.

Hanging Gardens has broad lawns, animal-shaped hedges and breathtaking city views. Across the street stands the Kamala Nehru Park with a slide coming out of a giant cement old woman's shoe much like the nursery rhyme that inspired it.

★Harish Mahindra Children's Park

Behind the American Consulate, Breach Candy. Grant Road station. **Open** 7am-noon, 3-8pm daily. **Admission** Rs 5.

Spread over nearly a hectare, this park has a spectacular view of the Arabian Sea. But that's not the reason to visit. There are age-specific play zones, a fountain and a mini-nature trail. Additionally, information boards are placed at child's eye level.

FREE Juhu Beach

Juhu Tara Road, Juhu. Vile Parle station.

About 18 km (11 miles) north of downtown, Juhu Beach is a veritable carnival at weekends, as families throng the beach and itinerant vendors sell colourful pinwheels, balloon monkeys and candy floss, and women apply henna tattoos. Swimming isn't advisable in these waters, though.

Mahalaxmi Racecourse

Amateur Riders' Club, Mahalaxmi Racecourse, Gate No.8, Keshavrao Khadye Marg, Mahalaxmi (6500-5204). Mahalaxmi station. **Open** 9.30am-5.30pm daily. **Classes** Rs 1,103 for 30mins. **No credit cards**.

Aimed at beginners of all ages, but especially popular with children, the Amateur Riders' Club's horse-riding course at Mahalaxmi lasts for ten days and is conducted by friendly trainers with many years of experience.

► *The racecourse is also home to Tote on the Turf; see p105.*

Maharashtra Nature Park

Sion-Bandra Link Road, Sion (W) (2407-7641). Sion station. **Open** 9am-3pm daily. **Admission** Rs 5.

A charming nature trail along Mahim Creek, following leafy paths and chasing dragonflies and frogs. This park is lush with fragrant medicinal plants, under a thick canopy of trees.

★ Mumbai Port Trust Garden

Women Graduates Union Road, Colaba. CST or Churchgate stations. **Open** 5.30am-11am, 4.30-8pm daily. **Admission** Rs 2.

A beautiful 4.5-hectare (11-acre) botanical park, with more than 450 flowering shrubs, lawns, and woods with rose gardens and seashore flora. Kids get to play Tarzan on the hanging roots of banyan trees.

Veermata Jijabai Bhonsle Udyan (Byculla Zoo)

Dr Ambedkar Road, Byculla (E) (2374-2162). Byculla station. **Open** 9am-5pm Mon-Thur, Sun. **Admission** Rs 10; Rs 5 children.

Mumbai's lacklustre zoo, dating back to 1861, can be more depressing than educational, with animals confined in small, poorly maintained enclosures. But the surrounding gardens and paths are attractive and make a good spot for picnics. There's also a children's play area with slides and swings, and old statues from the British Raj era.

► *Visit the Bhau Daji Lad museum in the same compound; see p60.*

INDOOR FUN

★ Chhatrapati Shivaji Maharaj Vastu Sangrahalaya (Prince of Wales Museum)

Mahatma Gandhi Road, Kala Ghoda, Fort (2284-4484/4159). CST or Churchgate stations. **Open** 10.15am-6pm Tue-Sun. **Admission** Rs 300; Rs 5 under-12s; free under-5s.

This museum is filled with whales, rhino, deer and birds from across the region. There's an armoury as well as a collection of Indian miniature paintings.

★ FREE Mani Bhavan

19 Laburnum Road, Gamdevi (2380-5864). Grant Road station. **Open** 9.30am-5.30pm daily.

Mahatma Gandhi lived here from 1917 to 1934, planning and co-ordinating the peaceful civil disobedience movement that led to an empire's downfall. The museum here is a perfect introduction to Gandhi for kids, with cute clay doll figures depicting scenes from the great man's life.

Monetary Museum

Amar Building, Sir Pherozeshah Mehta Road, Fort (2266-0502,2261-4043). CST or Churchgate stations. **Open** 10.45am-5.15pm Mon-Sat.

Show them the money at the first-class Monetary Museum, with superb displays of ancient coins and crisp text explaining the 'Story of Money in India'.

Nehru Planetarium

Annie Besant Road, Worli (2492-0510). Mahalaxmi or Byculla stations. **Open** 11am-5pm Tue-Sun. **Admission** Rs 40; Rs 20 under-12s.

The planetarium conducts high-standard sky shows in English starting at 3pm. There's an exhibition exploring India's intellectual and cultural achievements at the Nehru Science Centre across the street.

Nehru Science Centre

Dr E Moses Road, Worli (2493-2667/4520). Mahalaxmi or Byculla stations. **Open** 10.30am-5.30pm daily. **Admission** Rs 20.

It's not a world-class but it does have interactive exhibits for kids explaining everything from how pulleys work to how the eyes see. It also has 3D science shows and films. Call direct or check *Time Out Mumbai* for the centre's child-oriented workshops.

Orama 4D Theatre

Atria Mall, First Floor, Annie Besant Road, Worli (2481-3380). **Open** noon-9.30pm daily. **Tickets** Rs150.

Orama 4D Theatre shows short animated 3D films. The fourth dimension comes courtesy of leg ticklers, air blasts, foam and fog and wind. Two categories of seats are available: 'Fun' seats, which are stationary but offer enhanced effects, and motion-based 'Krazy' seats that make you swirl and twirl.

Film

Single-screen gems continue to flicker amid the multiplex mania.

Like Los Angeles, one of the first things people think about when it comes to Mumbai is film, and while Bollywood culture reigns supreme throughout the city, movies here aren't just an industry, they're one of the city's favourite pastimes. Over the last decade, the experience of going to the movies in Mumbai has been transformed immeasurably. Middle-class families now trek to the nearest multiplex, to watch the latest release in a hall that has excellent sound and superior projection.

HALL OF FAME

Until the late 1990s, Mumbai's hours in the flickering light were always spent in single-screen halls – spacious cinemas with an average capacity of 800 seats, with just one film showing three or four times through the day, and with the audience making its opinion known by whistling, singing along to the music or hurling things at the screen.

Until multiplexes arrived, almost every neighbourhood had at least one cinema hall – usually located close to the railway station – that screened new movies, recent releases or reissued prints of older movies. English films were the preserve of a clutch of halls in the south of the city, including the still-surviving Regal and Sterling cinemas. The intimate association between single-screen cinema halls and a single film meant that a box-office hit could ensure a cinema's success. For instance, Ramesh Sippy's 1975 action epic *Sholay* ran for over five years at Minerva in Central Mumbai. (When the movie was briefly re-released in 2004, it was at Minerva that *Sholay*'s posters first reappeared.) Sooraj Barjatya's melodrama *Hum Aapke Hain Kaun…!* helped yank the splendid Liberty cinema out of the red by ticking up just over 2,300 shows in 847 days.

The relationship between movie and cinema hall is more fragmented in the day of the multiplex. Their pricing, improved sound and seating, and location – many are inside shopping malls – make most multiplexes unaffordable to the city's underprivileged. Multiplexes charge between Rs 200 and Rs 450 per ticket. The experience of going to the cinema – once India's great unifier – has now fractured, with the middle and upper classes visiting multiplexes while the city's poor keep the single-screen cinema alive.

Apart from the weekly dose of new releases, Mumbai gets added shots of cinema from a handful of film clubs and cultural centres that bring international cinema of all hues to the city. Mumbai also hosts three international film festivals – the **Mumbai International Film Festival** (www.miffindia.in) of shorts and documentaries every second February; and in October the **Mumbai Academy of Moving Images Festival** (www.mumbaifilmfest.com), and the Asian cinema-focused **Third Eye Festival** (www.affmumbai.com).

INSIDE TRACK
MORNING MULTIPLEX

Multiplex tickets are often expensive and rates go up at the weekend. But all these theatres have morning shows, which are cheaper and usually far less crowded.

BUYING TICKETS

Multiplexes allow advance bookings by credit card via phone or website, or you can buy direct from the box office. You should book ahead for first-night shows to be sure of getting a seat. Single-screen cinema halls do not take advance bookings except at the venue, and you will need to buy direct from the box office in cash. Hindi films generally do not carry English subtitles.

SINGLE-SCREEN CINEMAS

South Mumbai

★ Eros

Khambatta Building, Churchgate (2282-2335). Churchgate station. **Tickets** Rs 60-Rs 100. **No credit cards**.

Built during Mumbai's fascination with art deco, Eros almost lives up to the romance of its name. With two wings topped by a domed baby-blue ceiling, access to its 1,000-seater hall is afforded by two grand marble staircases.

Regal

SP Mukherji Chowk, Colaba (2202-1017). CST or Churchgate stations. **Tickets** Rs 70-Rs 150. **No credit cards**.

India's first cinema hall equipped with air-conditioning and an underground car park opened in 1933 and is considered one of Mumbai's finest examples of art deco architecture. Though much of its thunder has now been stolen by the multiplexes, Regal remains the queen of South Mumbai's single-screens.

Suburbs

Chitra

Dr BR Ambedkar Road, opposite Fire Brigade, Dadar (E) (2418-2264). Dadar station. **Tickets** Rs 40-Rs 75. **No credit cards**.

Chitra suffered the same woes that beset other single-screens in the late 1980s and early '90s – falling footfalls due to the video boom and, later, competition from multiplexes. It fought back by jazzing up its façade and pitching for new movie releases rather than 1980s re-runs.

G7

SV Road, Bandra (W) (2642-6963). Bandra station. **Tickets** Rs 55-Rs 100. **No credit cards**.

Triplets Gaiety, Galaxy and Gemini morphed into a quasi-multiplex in the mid-1990s by converting the 40-seater preview theatres Gem and Glamour into fully fledged auditoria. G7 later added siblings Grace, a new preview theatre, and Gossip, which screens non-mainstream films.

MULTIPLEXES

South Mumbai

INOX

CR2 Mall, Nariman Point (www.inoxmovies.com). CST or Churchgate stations. **Tickets** Rs 89-Rs 200. **Credit** AmEx, MC, V.

Art deco for fat wallets. Designed to resemble the architectural style of its single-screen neighbours, INOX screens Hindi and English movies through the

Regal.

day, starting with morning shows at reduced rates. **Other location** Second Floor, Milan Mall, Milan Subway, Santa Cruz (W) (6659-5959).

★ Metro

Dhobi Talao, Marine Lines (3989-4040, www.adlabscinemas.com). CST or Marine Lines stations. **Tickets** Rs 180-Rs 500. **Credit** MC, V.

A one-time single-screen behemoth, this cinema has now been lovingly converted to a multiplex (*see p144* **Metromorphosis**).

PVR Phoenix

High Street Phoenix, Senapati Bapat Marg, Lower Parel (www.pvrcinemas.com). Lower Parel station. **Tickets** Rs 175-Rs 450. **Credit** MC, V.

PVR set up the first multiplex in India in New Delhi in 1997. The group took its time to come to Mumbai, finally sinking roots in the Juhu neighbourhood in 2006 and in Lower Parel in 2009.

Other locations Dynamix Mall, Juhu; Nirmal Lifestyle Mall, LBS Marg Mulund (W).

Sterling

Murzban Road, Fort (2207-5187). CST station. **Tickets** Rs 120. **No credit cards**.

One of South Mumbai's best-known single-screens has now become a multiplex. Yet location, rather than decor, remains Sterling's biggest advantage. Throw a piece of popcorn and you'll hit both CST and the delights of Colaba.

Suburbs

★ Cinemax

Infiniti Mall, Versova, Andheri (W) (www.cinemax.co.in). Andheri station. **Tickets** Rs 70-Rs 500. **Credit** MC, V.

Cinemax has been busy making sure that 'a theatre near you' is a Cinemax one, with multiplexes in Andheri (E), Sion, Goregaon and Thane. This is its

swankiest property, with the option of recliner seats for Rs 450.
Other locations Andheri-Kurla Road, Andheri (E) (2631-3355); Kalanagar, Bandra (E) (2656-1501); off Sion Circle, Sion (2404-1130); and throughout the city.

Fame Adlabs
New Link Road, Andheri (W) (www.famecinemas.com). Andheri station.
Tickets Rs 70-Rs 250. **Credit** MC, V.
Fame was the first of many multiplexes that now dot New Link Road, and is still a comfortable option.
Other locations *Fame Nakshatra, Dadar (W) (6699-1212); Fame Malad, InOrbit Mall, Goregaon-Malad Link Road, Goregaon (W) (6649-0490).*

Fun Republic
Shah Industrial Estate, Veera Desai Road, Andheri (W) (6675-5675,www.funcinemas.com). Andheri station. **Tickets** Rs 70-Rs 200. **Credit** AmEx, MC, V.
Fame's rival in Andheri shares a strip with the offices of mega-producers Yashraj Films, record label T-Series and television company Balaji.

OTHER FILM VENUES

Alliance Française
Alliance Française Auditorium, Theosophy Hall, New Marine Lines, Churchgate (2203-6187, www.afindia.org). Churchgate station.
Tickets free.
The French Consulate's cultural wing screens movies and documentaries throughout the year at its headquarters in Churchgate.

Jnanapravaha
Queens Mansion, behind Khadi Bhandar, Fort (2207-2974,www.jp-india.org). CST station.
Tickets free.
A cultural and arts education centre, Jnanapravaha screens documentaries and organises lectures throughout the year.

Max Mueller Bhavan
Kala Ghoda, Colaba (2202-2085/ http://www.goethe.de/ins/in/mum/enindex.htm). CST or Churchgate stations. **Tickets** free.
Max Mueller Bhavan waves Germany's cultural flag in Mumbai with screenings of German-language films, shorts and documentaries.

Metromorphosis

A flicker of hope for Mumbai's endangered movie theatres.

As elsewhere in the world, the emergence of the multiplex has threatened many of Mumbai's independent cinemas. So, when the single-screen **Metro cinema** (*see p143*) shut in 2004 to be converted into a fancy new multiplex, there was a collective cry of protest from older Mumbaikars, a cry especially loud since several single-screens in the city have shut in recent years.

In its early days, Metro was less a cinema hall and more a place to be seen. Built in 1938, it was American studio Metro Goldwyn Mayer's effort to showcase its own musicals. The studio built art deco Metro theatres in several cities around the world, including New York, Toronto, Sydney and Chicago. In 1939, MGM built the Mumbai theatre on land it had leased for a period of 999 years. Worldwide, Metro theatres were distinctive in form and location, and Mumbai's was no exception: located at the meeting of six roads, the Metro in Mumbai was meant to be accessible to everyone.

The institution reopened as BIG Metro in August 2006 and while prices are no longer welcoming to all, not everything has been lost in restoration. The façade stands untouched (save for a lick of paint and some repairs) and though the single king-size hall has been cut into six small screens, the rest of the layout remains unchanged; the plush interiors retain many of their original features, such as the magnificent Belgian chandeliers, iron and glass railings, and tall mirror panels.

Metro is listed as a heritage structure, which means that any plan to alter it requires the approval of the municipal council's heritage committee. When consulting the blueprints, the architects found that one of the loveliest features of the building had been lost over the years: the original lobby had three ceiling-to-floor window panels. However, World War II broke out soon after it was completed and the over-enthusiastic owners built concrete walls on either side of the building to protect it and black-out the windows. When architects had the walls knocked down, they found the glass window frames still intact. Today, the sunlit windows have been restored as the high point of the lobby.

Metro's makeover raises hopes that the rest of Mumbai's iconic cinemas will be preserved rather than bulldozed. Here's hoping.

Galleries

The financial meltdown hasn't killed the gallery scene.

Every decade has its buzzword. The 1980s saw video rental stores popping up at every corner of Mumbai, while the cyber café was the cash cow of the '90s. With Indian art crossing the million-dollar mark on the auction circuit, art is the flavour of this decade. But it's not all good news. When the economic slowdown struck in 2008, chills ran along the spine of the art world, and by 2009 it seemed the art bubble had popped. But interest in Indian art, both at home and abroad, continues to grow, Mumbai's art scene is getting back on track.

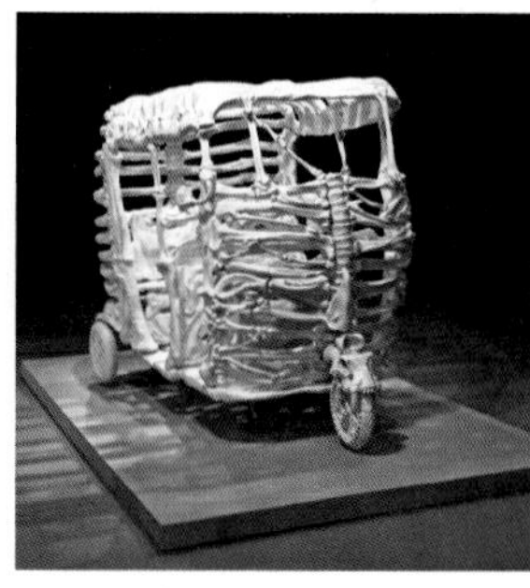

THE LOCAL SCENE

Mumbai's local art scene started with three private galleries that were established in the 1950s and a small, elite group of collectors. As of February 2008, the number of galleries has gone up to 82. In the Indian art calendar, the summer begins with April and, traditionally, the next three months are known as the slow season.

While in the 1990s Indian contemporary art was frustratingly underpriced, the noughties saw prices soar. When veteran Hindi film actress Leela Naidu bought her first SH Raza (the eminent India artist) in the 1960s, she paid a few thousand rupees. Today, a Raza of that vintage would fetch around Rs 3 million.

However, things haven't been so rosy since the latter half of 2008. Wine disappeared from openings, corporate cash dried up, purse strings were severely tightened and, much to the frustration of Indian gallerists, auction houses slashed prices. For its sale of South Asian art in March, Sotheby's scaled back on contemporary works and showcased modern paintings from the 1940s and '50s. Bodhi Art, once one of the most high-profile of Mumbai's galleries, cancelled a show of American artist Julian Schnabel's paintings. The gallery would beat a hasty retreat from the art world by September 2009. Some newer entrants into the gallery circuit, like FSCA, shut shop. Bombay Art Gallery vacated its enormous Colaba space and returned to its small, Malabar Hill home.

However, not everyone lost their nerve. Tushar Jiwarajka not only opened Volte, he also steered clear of any well-known names in his list of artists. In its tiny space, the Loft grit its teeth and showcased mostly unsaleable but thought-provoking works. Galleries that have nurtured and sustained Mumbai's art scene proved their mettle. Chemould Prescott Road opened the year with an elaborate show by LN Tallur, which required one of the pieces to be dropped into the gallery using a crane. Galerie Mirchandani + Steinruecke did not hesitate to show the digital artwork of Franco and Eva Mattes. Warehouse on Third Pasta steadfastly continued to show unconventional art despite the fact that its air-conditioning bills were frequently higher than its earnings from a show. Sakshi did not shy away from bringing international artists, known and lesser-known, to the city even though there would be fewer buyers of expensive limited-edition works by British artist Julian Opie or American photographer Gregory Crewdson.

Check *Time Out Mumbai* magazine for details of the latest art shows.

INSIDE TRACK PRIVATE VIEWS

For those who love cheap wine as much as they love art, gallery openings are held on Thursdays; you can tell there's an opening by the groups of scruffy-chic men outside, and the belligerent-looking women wearing lots of kohl. Even though these events are officially for invited audiences, Mumbai galleries love gatecrashers and no one checks for invites.

Bags packed, milk cancelled, house raised on stilts.

You've packed the suntan lotion, the snorkel set, the stay-pressed shirts. Just one more thing left to do – your bit for climate change. In some of the world's poorest countries, changing weather patterns are destroying lives.

You can help people to deal with the extreme effects of climate change. Raising houses in flood-prone regions is just one life-saving solution.

Climate change costs lives.
Give £5 and let's sort it *Here & Now*

www.oxfam.org.uk/climate-change

Oxfam is a registered charity in England and Wales (No.202918) and Scotland (SCO039042). Oxfam GB is a member of Oxfam International.

Be Humankind Oxfa

COLABA

Art Musings

1 Admiralty Building, Colaba Cross Lane, next to Sassoon Dock, Colaba (2216-3339, www.artmusings.net). CST or Churchgate stations. **Taxi** opposite Dunne's School. **Open** 11am-7pm Mon-Sat. **No credit cards.**

Renovated in 2007, this gallery shows art that is decorative and sophisticated. In the past, it's had sell-out shows by established names like Akbar Padamsee, Anjolie Ela Menon and Jitish Kallat. It's also serious about giving platforms to promising artists like Smriti Dixit and Maya Burman.

Chatterjee & Lal

First Floor, Kamal Mansion, next to Radio Club, Arthur Bunder Road, Colaba (2202-3787, www.chatterjeeandlal.com). CST or Churchgate stations. **Taxi** Radio Club. **Open** 11am-7pm Mon-Sat. **No credit cards.**

After promoting a host of young, cutting-edge artists for the past few years, Mortimer Chatterjee and Tara Lal took the plunge and opened up their own gallery in Colaba in 2007. From performance art to paintings, they're open to everything 'high art'.

Collector's Paradise

17/19 Mahakavi Bhushan Road, Apollo Bunder, Colaba (2282-4765, www.collectorsparadiseartgallery.com). CST or Churchgate stations. **Taxi** near Regal Cinema. **Open** 10.30am-6.30pm Mon-Sat. **No credit cards.**

This gallery doesn't hold regular exhibitions but it does have a fair collection of works that buyers (and oglers) are able to browse.

Galerie Mirchandani + Steinruecke

2 Sunny House, 16/18 Mereweather Road, Colaba (2202-3030, www.galeriems.com). CST or Churchgate stations. **Taxi** behind Taj Mahal Hotel. **Open** 10am-6.30pm Mon-Fri; 10am-4pm Sat. **No credit cards.**

Mother-and-daughter team Usha Mirchandani and Ranjana Steinruecke closed their Berlin gallery and came back to Mumbai to open a space to mount solos of major artists from around the world – they have hosted shows by high priestess of feminist art in America, Kiki Smith, and Saatchi Gallery's Jonathan Messe – as well as high-quality group shows.

Guild Art Gallery

First Floor, 2A Prince Chambers, Colaba (2288-0116, www.guildindia.com). CST or Churchgate stations. **Taxi** opposite Colaba Post Office. **Open** 10am-6.30pm Mon-Sat. **Credit** AmEx.

Gallery owner Shalini Sawhney displays works by contemporary Indian artists from the Progressive Artists' Group to works by the newer Bombay Boys; it also sells limited-edition prints.

Follow Your Art

Walk the gallery district.

In Mumbai, the arts village is in Colaba and Kala Ghoda, nestled between the docks and the financial district. This is the neighbourhood where the best of the city's galleries are located, and covering all of them makes for an enjoyable walk; just wear comfortable shoes.

Start with the **Museum Gallery** (*see p149*), which is generally worth a visit. Go past **Jehangir Art Gallery** (*see p149*) towards Colaba. Check to see if the **National Gallery of Modern Art** (*see p149*) has a new show and if not, head straight down to **Sakshi** (*see p149*). If there's no show on, check out its permanent collection. Come out on to Colaba Causeway and go across to **Galerie Mirchandani + Steinruecke** (*see left*), in Sunny House, which often shows interesting work. Walk down towards the Radio Club and up to **Chatterjee & Lal** (*see left*) where exhibits are always funky and intelligent. Get back on the causeway and turn left at Colaba Fire Station to reach **Project 88** (*see below*), one of the coolest spaces in the city. Come out and walk towards Sassoon Dock but keep an eye out for the sign for **Art Musings** (*see left*) on your left. The gallery generally shows paintings and has a nice seating area in which to browse past catalogues and rest your feet.

Lakeeren

6/18, Grants Building, Second Floor, Arthur Bunder Road, Colaba (6522-4179). CST or Churchgate stations. **Taxi** Radio Club. **Open** 11am-7pm Tue-Sun. **No credit cards.**

Gallery owner Arshiya Lokhandwala moved from Juhu to open a space in Colaba where she recently put up for sale 1,001 works of different Indian artists, with prices that went from Rs 25 upwards.

▶ *This gallery is situated opposite Basilico restaurant (see p93).*

Project 88

BMP Building, NA Sawant Marg, Colaba (2281-0066, www.project88.in). CST or Churchgate stations. **Taxi** near Colaba Fire Station. **Open** 11am-6.30pm Mon-Sat. **No credit cards.**

One of the most striking spaces in the city has a reputation for having exciting, original shows that aren't particularly saleable. It's also the only gallery in the city that also shows architectural projects.

Offset you
flight wit
Trees for Citie
and make you
trip mea
something fo
years to com
www.treesforcities.org/offs
Trees for Cit
Charity registration number 1

Sakshi Gallery

Tanna House, 11A Nathalal Parekh Marg, Colaba (6610-3424, www.sakshigallery.com). CST or Churchgate stations. **Taxi** opposite YMCA. **Open** 11am-7pm Mon-Sat. **No credit cards**.

In 2007, this gallery moved from mid-town and set itself up in the heart of the city's art district. Sakshi shows a range of established and upcoming artists, including traditional faves like Sudhir Patwardhan, known for his figurative paintings of Mumbai's underbelly, and new media artist Shilpa Gupta.

Volte

02/19, Kamal Mansion, First Floor, Arthur Bunder Road, Colaba (6615-6796, www.volte.in). CST or Churchgate stations. **Taxi** Colaba. **Open** 11.30am-7.30pm Tue-Sun. **No credit cards**.

The gallery houses an exhibition space for contemporary art, bookshop, studies for residencies, a café and film club. It has hosted shows by Boshudhara Mukherjee and Tara Kelton.

Warehouse on 3rd Pasta

6/7 3rd Pasta Lane, Colaba (2202-3056). CST or Churchgate stations. **Taxi** Colaba Market. **Open** 11am-7pm Tue-Sun. **No credit cards**.

Abhay Maskara began the gallery with the intention of promoting new artists and, aside from fun shows like Pandolfo's, Warehouse has showcased some bizarre, thought-provoking and intelligent exhibitions. It's hosted shows like Mathesis Dub dub dub by Avantika Bawa, Sperm Weaver by Shine Shivan, In Determination II by Monali Meher and Max Streicher's Breathe.

KALA GHODA

Art Land

Third Floor, Esplanade Mansion, MG Road, Kala Ghoda (6635-0776, www.artlandindia.com). CST or Churchgate stations. **Taxi** Army & Navy Building. **Open** 10am-7pm Mon-Sat. **No credit cards.**

Owner Sunil Chauhan opened this 74sq m (800 sq-ft) space as a platform for emerging Indian artists. Now renovated and extended, Chauhan hosts large shows and has widened the gallery's brief to include exhibitions by established artists like Prafulla Dhanukar, Padmanabh Bendre, Nayanaa Kanodia and Asit Kumar Patnaik.

Artists' Centre

First Floor, Ador House, 6 K Dubash Marg, next to Rhythm House, off MG Road, Kala Ghoda (2284-5939, www.artistscentre.org). CST or Churchgate stations. **Taxi** Rhythm House. **Open** 11am-7pm Mon-Sat. **No credit cards**.

Housed on the first floor of a heritage building, this was the first gallery to open in Mumbai's art district in 1950. It used to be the meeting point for renowned artists like KH Ara, FN Souza, MF Husain, SH Raza and S Bakre – the core of the Progressive Artists' Group that took Indian art in a new direction. It now has regular shows by young artists who haven't yet been snapped up by richer galleries.

Gallery Beyond

First Floor, 130/132 Great Western Building, Shahid Bhagat Singh Road, Fort (2283-7345, www.gallerybeyond.com). CST station. **Open** 10.30am-6.30pm Mon-Sat. **Credit** AmEx, MC, V.

Owner Vibhuraj Kapoor is committed to hosting debut solo shows by young, emerging hot properties like Prajakta Palav, Minal Damani, Anu Agarwal and Preetam Bhatty.

Jehangir Art Gallery

MG Road, Kala Ghoda, Fort (2204-8212). CST or Churchgate stations. **Taxi** Elphinstone College. **Open** 11am-7pm Mon-Sat. **Credit** MC, V.

This is the largest art gallery in Mumbai, with four exhibition halls, an art shop and a café. Opened in 1951, it's now the city's most popular contemporary art space, with hundreds of visitors each day. But Jehangir rarely offers the best of Mumbai's contemporary art. It's run by a trust that rents out the space on a first-come-first-served basis, often without careful attention to quality.

Museum Gallery

K Dubash Marg, Kala Ghoda, Fort (2284-4484). CST or Churchgate stations. **Taxi** Jehangir Art Gallery. **Open** 11am-7pm Mon-Sat. **No credit cards**.

Sharing a wall with the landmark Jehangir Art Gallery (*see above*), this 93sq m (1,000 sq-ft) gallery is also a space-for-hire, but with more discriminate taste than its neighbour; it has hosted some of the city's best solo shows.

► *The excellent Chhatrapati Shivaji Maharaj Vastu Sangrahalaya is a must-see; see* *p53.*

National Gallery of Modern Art

Cowasji Jehangir Hall, MG Road, Colaba (2288-1969, www.ngmaindia.gov.in). CST or Churchgate stations. **Taxi** opposite Regal Cinema. **Open** 11am-6pm Tue-Sun. **No credit cards**.

One of the city's most interesting art spaces. From time to time it mounts retrospectives of major Indian artists as well as shows from abroad.

NARIMAN POINT

Jehangir Nicholson Gallery of Modern Art

National Centre for the Performing Arts, Nariman Point (6622-3737). CST or Churchgate stations. **Open** 10am-6pm Mon-Sat. **No credit cards**.

Housed within the National Centre for the Performing Arts building (*see p166*), this gallery is named for legendary collector Jehangir Nicholson, who donated a significant part of his collection to the NCPA. The gallery is regularly rented out by curators and gallery owners for various exhibitions.
▶ *Visit the Piramal Gallery at the NCPA for photography shows; see p166.*

FORT & BALLARD ESTATE

Fourth Floor

Kitab Mahal, Fourth Floor, DN Road, Fort (2207-9119, www.kitabmahal.org). CST or Churchgate stations. **Taxi** near New Excelsior Cinema. **Open** 10.30am-7pm Mon-Sat. **No credit cards.**
Situated opposite Chhatrapati Shivaji Terminus, Fourth Floor is a 744sq m (8,000 sq-ft) event space with an avant-garde emphasis. Located on the top floor of a heritage building, Kitab Mahal, it's a gorgeous space that occasionally plays host to very interesting shows.
▶ *Don't miss the carvings on the Chhatrapati Shivaji Terminus; see p57.*

Gallery BMB

Queens Mansion, Ground Floor, GT Marg, Fort (6171-5757, www.gallerybmb.com). CST or Churchgate stations. **Taxi** Cathedral School. **Open** 11am-7pm, Mon-Sat. **Credit** MC, V.
A recent addition to the South Mumbai circuit is spearheaded by artist, curator and collector Bose Krishnamachari. A slick space on an attractive road road in the fort area of town, the gallery has held shows with international artists and contemporary Indian artists. After perusing the work on show check out the bookshop and café.

Matthieu Foss

Hansraj Damodar Building, Ground Floor, Goa Street, Ballard Estate (6747-7261, www.matthieufossgallery.com). CST or Churchgate stations. **Taxi** Fort Market. **Open** 11am-7pm Mon-Sat. **Credit** MC, V.
Matthieu Foss Gallery is dedicated to photography. It has hosted shows by French photographer Fabien Charuau and Anne Maniglier.

Pundole Art Gallery

369 DN Road, Flora Fountain (2284-1837, www.pundoleartgallery.in). CST or Churchgate stations. **Taxi** next to American Dry Fruit. **Open** 10.30am-6.30pm Mon-Sat. **Credit** AmEx, MC, V.
This gallery became the main building block of the Progressive Artists' Group (PAG). Run by Dadiba and Khorshed Pundole, Pundole specialises in the works of the PAG and you'll also find unique prints by these artists here. In recent times, it's been showing mid-range artists like Ebenezer Sunder Singh and Sharath Kulagatti.

BREACH CANDY

Studio Napean

Matru Ashish, 39 Nepean Sea Road (2367-3390,http://studionapean.com). Grant Road station. **Taxi** Matru Ashish. **Open** 10.30am-8pm Mon-Sat. **No credit cards.**
Kavita Singh may be better known as Bollywood star Anil Kapoor's sister-in-law but she's trying to change all that by breaking into the world of art as a gallerist. Run by her daughter Nandini, the gallery's exhibits are not bad for a casual wander.
▶ *While you're here, check out Kasab; see p125.*

WORLI

Gallery Art & Soul

1 Madhuli, Annie Besant Road, Shivsagar Estate, Worli (2496-5798, www.galleryartnsoul.com). Mahalaxmi station. **Taxi** Poonam Chambers. **Open** 11am-7pm Mon-Sat; by appointment Sun. **No credit cards.**
Tarana Khubchandani's gallery, on the ground floor of a Worli seafront high-rise, is a platform for young artists, as well as a venue for talks by artists, art historians and critics. The group shows at the gallery are generally well conceived and experimental.

Priyasri Art Gallery

4 Madhuli, Annie Besant Road, Shivsagar Estate, Worli (93235-82303). Mahalaxmi station. **Taxi** Poonam Chambers. **Open** 11am-7pm Mon-Sat. **No credit cards.**
The sea view from Priyasri is reason enough to visit the gallery, and the young artists from Baroda and Bengal that the gallery hosts are often good too.

Tao Art Gallery

Sarjan Plaza, Annie Besant Road, Worli (2491-8585, www.taoartgallery.com). Mahalaxmi station. **Taxi** Lotus. **Open** 10.30am-6.30pm Mon-Sat. **No credit cards.**
Established by collector and artist Kalpana Shah, this gallery is known for large group shows spread over its three exhibition rooms. It regularly shows the work of SH Raza, Sujata Bajaj and A Anwar.
▶ *Pop by the Akanksha Art store; see p132.*

LOWER PAREL

The Loft at Lower Parel

C/o New Mahalaxmi Silk Mills, Mathuradas Mills Compound, Tulsi Pipe Road, Lower Parel (3040-0166, www.theloft.in). Lower Parel station. **Taxi** Kamala Mills. **Open** 11am-7pm Mon-Sat; by appointment Sun. **No credit cards.**
The Loft began in 2008 as an artists' studio and a venue that has supported upcoming and experimental artists. Owner Anupa Mehta has showcased the works of Mahbubur Rahman, Inder Salim and Mayura Subhedar.

Gay & Lesbian

Mumbai's gay scene is finally coming of age.

If you're expecting San Francisco, you're going to be disappointed – gay and lesbian culture is a long way from being a so-what? part of Indian society. But things are looking up. Until recently, being gay was illegal in India, but on 2 July 2009 that changed as the Delhi High Court decriminalised homosexuality. Though opponents have taken the case to the Supreme Court, there has been much jubilation across the country. But progress is slow as Mumbai's gay culture inches out of the closet, one step at a time.

PRIDE AND PREJUDICE

Gay travellers to India are often faced with confusing contradictions. They've read the warnings about how gay couples should be discreet but men keep looking at them in the street and no, not just in the way all foreigners get stared at.

Scratch the surface and you'll find that the gay scene in Mumbai is not all that closeted. There are gay and lesbian support groups (*see p232*) in Mumbai and regular parties. Websites list treks and film screenings for the gay and lesbian community, bookshops have gay- and lesbian-themed sections and cinemas show gay and lesbian films. More so after the success of 2008's *My Brother Nikhal,* the first Bollywood film to have a gay relationship at its core. Since then queer bit-parts have been all the rage. And the media, too, regularly reports on gay issues, including Mumbai's first gay pride, **Queer Azadi March**, held on 16 August, 2009.

At the same time, don't expect things you might take for granted elsewhere. There are no fixed gay clubs (except **Voodoo** on Saturday nights; *see below*) and no restaurants flying rainbow flags. But the reasons are more Mumbai than intolerance: rents are so high that niche venues of any kind are rare. There seems to be a tacit understanding between the city and its gay and lesbian community: you can do your own thing as long as you're discreet. If that sounds repressive, it's more than most Indian cities allow.

Mumbai's dyke community is close-knit and can can be hard to crack, and for good reason. Women in India have a lot less access to public spaces than gay men or men in general, with overbearing parents and siblings and Cinderella deadlines. However, meet the right circle of friends, and you're in the gang for good.

One good way to find other women is to call the helpline **Lesbians and Bisexuals in Action** (98332-78171) or email stree.sangam@gmail.com; its aim is to reach out to the community. Organisers usually meet new members first, to ensure a protective layer for those who aren't out. Attending a **GayBombay** party is another way of meeting the few lesbians who do frequent larger spaces. **Symphony in Pink** (symphonyinpink@rediffmail.com) is an online discussion group for lesbians and bisexuals in Mumbai, and is pretty vibrant, though you may have to bear many approaches before you get to the good stuff. If you just want to pick someone up, parties and club nights are the best option; if you want a full-on gay scene, sorry – you should go to Bangkok instead. But if you want to tap into a young and lively scene, growing in size and confidence, but still small enough to be friendly, then take your chances with Mumbai.

INSIDE TRACK RAINBOW HIGH

Need a good gift with a gay Indian twist? India's first online LGBT store stocks personal and home accessories from mugs and pictures of rainbow-coloured rickshaws to T-shirts emblazoned with 'out and proud' in Gujarati. *www.azaadbazaar.com*

Out and About

Where the party's at.

Overground mainstream gay culture in Mumbai is still very much in its infancy, and **Voodoo** (*see p161*) remains the only club with a regular gay night, every Saturday. To say this place is not exclusive is a vast understatement. It's small and rather grotty, the Rs 250 entry somewhat excessive, the music variable and the loos are best avoided. Oh, and the crowd has a high percentage of hookers, male and female. And their clients. As such, we're inclined to agree, it doesn't sound that great, but unlike the mirror-and-chrome places opening all over town Voodoo has real character, and it's also relaxed and easygoing. In fact, pretty much anything goes here – which is a relief from the repressions of the moralists outside.

There are two organisations currently running regular parties for the LGBT community in Mumbai. **GayBombay** (www.gaybombay.org) is the better-established group that caters to the wider community with a taste for popular Indian music (read Bollywood). Its rates are lower and it gets slightly larger crowds at its parties, which are held at regular venues. **Salvation Star** (www.salvationstar.com) is the enthusiastic new kid on the block, catering to a more niche, trendy crowd with a taste for the latest in global music. It has a fixed venue, at a downtown club. Queer women are welcome at both venues, of course, but for occasional lesbian specific parties you need to check with the women's support groups.

Hotels in Mumbai usually don't bat an eyelid at two men or two women sharing a room. If you're a couple and don't want separate beds, just ask for a single large one and you should have no problems. Taking someone back to your room, on the otherhand, can be tricky. Most hotels don't object but a few might, so be prepared.

Irritatingly, Gay couples can also sometimes run into problems getting into bars and clubs thanks to the 'couples only' policy that many places follow. It's meant to deter boisterous straight men who might cause problems for women but if you're a group of guys you might well get given the cold shoulder, too. It's usually easier to get in if you're a (white) foreigner, but if you have problems, you might want to try explaining/convincing the bouncers that you're gay. Alternatively, and probably easier, would be to try persuading some female friends to come along.

Queer Azadi March. *See p151.*

Mind, Body & Soul

Mumbai's calming side.

Although India has a 5,000-year heritage of traditional holistic therapies, such as ayurveda, it is only in this decade that the demand for modern spas has seen a surge in cities like Mumbai. Over the past few years, wellness centres have popped up across the city, from barebones facilities like the Kerala Ayurvedic Health Spa, which offer age-old (and affordable) treatments, to swanky five-star spas that represent the last word in luxury. Yoga, too, unsurprisingly, is popular – though it has less of the designer sheen that you might find outside of India.

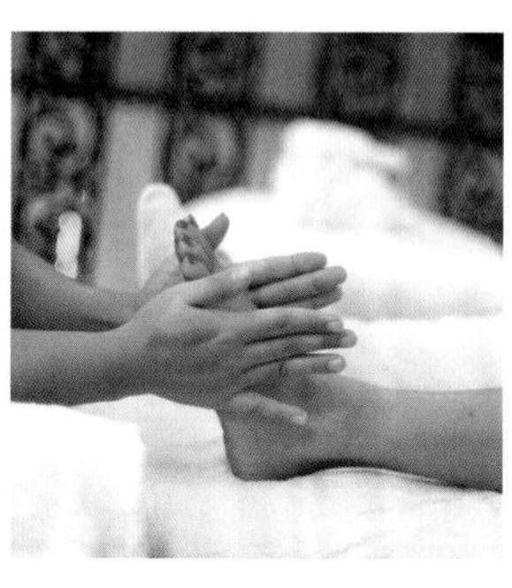

SERENE CITY

If you're looking for one discipline that will have an enduring effect on your body and mind, forget fad diets and quick fixes and stick with yoga. Mumbai might lack the new-fangled versions now popular in the West, but you can find the real thing in yoga centres across the city, as well as little-known forms (Satyananda yoga, anyone?) if you're feeling adventurous. Be warned: most yoga centres are utilitarian and spartan, so leave the Louis Vuitton yoga tote at home and experience the science in its most unadorned form.

Like yoga, ayurveda is an ancient Indian science that believes in the philosophy of rejuvenation from the inside out. Rituals like the *shiro dhara* (a full-body massage in which a steady stream of warm medicinal oil is poured on the forehead to awaken the 'third eye') are over 2,000 years old and continue to be popular across the social spectrum. Meanwhile, beauty treatments incorporate a range of organic spices, herbs, fruit, flowers and vegetables.

A novelty not to be missed is the old Indian *champi* or *tel maalish*, a vigorous scalp massage with coconut, olive or herbal oil, which improves blood circulation, cures headaches and is often credited with giving Indian women their thick, healthy locks. But as the city becomes more global, so do its offerings: you can now choose from Hawaiian, Javanese or Balinese massages by qualified masseuses in world-class spas. Spirituality is such an integral part of the Indian psyche that you won't have to look far to find offerings of interest. Newspapers are flooded with classifieds advertising everything from aromatherapy to reiki. Exercise some caution with these, but for the most part just go with the flow and don't worry too much: it isn't good for your soul (or your skin).

AYURVEDIC HEALING

Ayushakti

Bhadran Nagar, Cross Road 2, opposite Milap theatre, off SV Road, Malad (W) (2806-5757). Malad station. **Open** 10.30am-8pm Mon-Sat. **Credit** V.

Dr Pankaj Naram is famous for diagnosing patients just by taking their pulse and then prescribing a customised combination of herbs, rigorous diets and much-needed detoxification. Legend has it Naram learned the art of pulse reading from a 115-year-old Tibetan monk. Today, the centre is spread over 1,395sq m (15,000 ft) in a leafy part of Malad and has a residential complex for long-term treatments (although you'll need to book at least two years in advance). Treatment sessions start at Rs 300.

Kerala Ayurvedic Health Spa

Neelkanth, Marine Drive (2288-3210,98204-35344). Marine Lines station. **Open** 8am-8pm daily. **Credit** MC, V.

For an authentic and affordable taste of South India's natural ayurvedic treatments, visit this chain, the best-known for good reason. Sample the famous *shiro dhara* – a full-body massage carried out simultaneously by two practitioners who pour a vessel full of medicinal oil on to your forehead in a steady stream (supposedly to awaken the 'third eye'). It's an experience you'll want to sample at least once. Be warned though: you don't get to keep your undies on. The *ayushman bhava* rejuvenation therapy is also popular. The clean but no-frills set-up feels cosy and authentic, thanks in large part to the sari-clad practitioners who studiously ignore the fact that you're naked. Treatments start at Rs 1,800. **Other locations** Louis Mansion, VS Road, Prabhadevi (2430-2336); Sun 'n' Sand Hotel, 39 Juhu Beach, Juhu (6602-4043).

MASSAGE

See **Spas** for addresses and opening hours.

Balinese

The massage that originates in the only Hindu state in the Indonesian archipelago involves acupressure, stretching, reflexology and a variety of kneading and rolling movements to balance the blood, oxygen and *qi* in the body. It's a medium-intensity massage to deal with specific stress.
Oberoi Spa *Available only with spa packages. Day spa at Rs 11,500 per person or Rs 14,000 per couple. Rs 3,850 for 60mins for residents. Weekend spa package Rs 14,000 per person or Rs 16,500 per couple.*

Hawaiian Lomilomi

Lomi is the Hawaiian word for the way in which a contented cat works its claws in and out. Lomilomi works your pressure points, but unlike acupressure or reflexology, the pressure is not held for very long; the masseuse uses her forearms and elbows in smooth, gliding movements to turn you into putty.
Oberoi Spa *see above.*
Rudra *Rs 3,372 for 60mins.*

Javanese Lulur

Lulur is Javanese for the rice and turmeric scrub used during a bride's prenuptial massage, but spas also use the term loosely to describe the technique that involves thumb pressure and long palm strokes.
Rudra *Rs 4,383 for 60mins.*

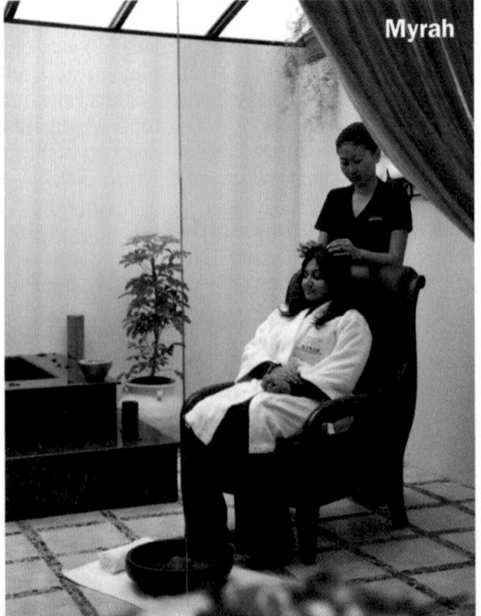
Myrah

Shiatsu

Shiatsu is an acupressure massage that follows the Japanese meridian system of energy flow in the body. *Shi* translates to fingers and *atsu* means pressure. So instead of being poked all over, pressure points in your body are merely tapped, rubbed, squeezed and pressed.
Rudra *from Rs 2,360 for 60mins.*

Thai

Thai massage practitioners don't believe in letting you lie back and blissing out. Expect to go 'ouch' as your pressure points are firmly pressed and your body stretched, folded and twisted into various yoga poses on a mat on the floor. This is somewhere between an alternative therapy and a less strenuous workout. If it makes you feel any better, you get to keep your clothes on.
Antara *Rs 2,900 for 90mins.*
Quan *Rs 3,000 for 60mins.*

SPAS

Aquamarine Day Spa

202 Patel House, Bomanji Petit Road, Kemp's Corner (2381-1118). Grant Road station. **Open** 10am-7pm daily.
Credit AmEx, MC, V.
Aquamarine was started by European beauty giant Thalgo and offers a range of treatments including lymphatic drainage massages, facials, body wraps and hot-stone therapy.

Caressaa Day Spa

19-28/29, Janki Kutir, Juhu Church Road, Juhu (6526-2640). Andheri station. **Open** 10am-10pm daily. **Credit** MC, V.
Rekha Chaudhari, co-owner of Juhu's Caressaa Day Spa, has been retailing products to top Indian spas for the past 20 years, so it isn't surprising that her latest venture is a fascinating showcase of treatments. The Dermalife spa capsule offers a combination of steam, aroma, LED lights, and a Vichy shower that allows guests to get a shower while lying down. The Alpha LED Oxylight spa capsule is a dry heat, oxygenising sauna.

Centre for Colon Therapy

92 Lady Ratan Tata Medical & Research Centre, Maharshi Karve Road, Cooperage (6585-4474, www.thecoloncentre.com). CST or Churchgate stations. **Open** 10am-6pm daily. **Credit** AmEx, MC, V.
Dedicated solely to colonic irrigation, or hydrotherapy, the Centre is small, friendly and private. It employs the latest US technology, which 'offers the most advanced methods in lower bowel evacuation'.

Press Here

Put your feet up.

In a quiet corner of the labyrinthine Atria Mall (*see p130*), a glass door swings open and a woman walks out, her eyes glazed over. Inside the darkened room, someone seems to be getting paddled. Despite initial impressions, it's clear this place is more doctor's office than debauched dungeon. It's a branch of **My Foot Reflexology**, offering relief to manic shoppers, Mumbai marathon runners and party animals alike. People come here to put their feet up in the essential-oil-scented air and have their calves thwacked, sciatic nerves kneaded and heels knuckled until they feel blissful enough to step out into the real world again.

Practitioners of foot reflexology believe that certain pressure points on the foot correspond to different organs in the body, so applying pressure to these points can improve organ function, benefit circulation, help relaxation and release toxins. Done right, fans claim, it can shake off stomach ailments, diabetes and migraines.

My Foot Reflexology started 11 years ago in Singapore, in the city's famous shopping district, Orchard Street. It has since branched out into many malls and has a section in Changi Airport's transit lounge. Since shopping and tired feet go hand-in-hand, both the firm's Mumbai branches opened last year in high-end, busy malls with heavy footfalls. More branches are planned at the city's airports. The Singapore-based company has been brought to India by Bhavna Vora, who also runs an NGO for primary education. Vora says she knew she was on to a good thing when she found out that My Foot trains differently-abled women as therapists around the world – a step in the right direction indeed.

My Foot Reflexology Nirmal Life Style
Shop No. 224/225, Second Floor, LBS Marg, Mulund (W) (2592-1600). Also at Atria Mall, Shop No. 105A/116, First Floor, Annie Besant Road, Worli (2481-3660). **Open** 10.30am-10pm daily. Rs 699 for 30mins, Rs 945 for 40mins, Rs 1,345 for 60mins, excluding taxes. Upper body and hand therapies are available too.

Cosmic

Amarchand Mansion, Madam Cama Road, Fort (2204-3737). Churchgate or CST stations. **Open** 10am-9pm daily. **Credit** MC, V.

The spa's express glow face mask is designed to reduce sun tan and imparts a glow to dull skin. The two-and-a-half-hour treatment includes a foot reflexology massage to balance energy and relieve aching joints, and a back massage with aromatic oils of lavender, ylang-ylang and champaka.

▶ *Cosmic's location makes it ideal for pampering after exploring the Fort area; see p54.*

Four Seasons Spa

Four Seasons Hotel, Dr E Moses Road, Worli (2481-8000). Mahalaxmi station. **Open** 6am-10pm daily. **Credit** AmEx, MC, V

Guests at the Four Seasons Spa can use the hotel's Vitality Lounge for as long as they like. It comprises a herb-infused steam room, which uses quartz crystals to help balance the body's energy. There's an ice fountain and cold mist menthol shower, a tropical rain hot shower that smells of leaves and a Vitality Pool – a recliner submerged in water that has sensors for making the water bubbly or calm.

★ Jiva

Taj President, 90 Cuffe Parade (6665-0808). CST or Churchgate stations. **Open** 9am-8pm daily. **Credit** AmEx, MC, V.

The Taj President's Jiva Spa is a great place to de-stress with a relaxation room, a hammam bath, sauna and a fitness zone.

Kerala Ayurvedic Health Spa

See p153 **Ayurvedic Healing**.

Lakme

Arsiwala Building, Wodehouse Road, Colaba (2218-1747,6631-5277, www.lakemeindia.com). CST or Churchgate stations. **Taxi** Wodehouse Road. **Open** 10am-7pm daily. **Credit** MC, V.

Lakme offer a range of beauty services, including waxing, threading and hot-oil scalp massages.

Other location Shop No. 1, Kailash, Waterfield Road, Bandra (2642-1410,2643-7220).

★ Myrah

11 Palm Springs Society, opposite Chandan Cinema parking lot, JVPD Scheme, Juhu (2625-3968, www.myrahspa.com). Vile Parle station. **Open** 10am-8pm Mon-Fri; 10am-9pm Sat, Sun. **Credit** AmEx, MC, V.

Myrah has an aloe herbal polish comprising 64 herbs. The Divine Rose Aroma massage uses rose-based products. Try the Hibiscus and Caviar Envelopment for dehydrated skin.

Oberoi

Oberoi Hotel, Nariman Point (6632-5757). Churchgate station. **Open** 8am-8.30pm daily. **Credit** AmEx, MC, V.

It's Asian exotica through and through at this spa run by the Thai Banyan Tree chain. The Thai masseuses with soft hands and softer voices are experts at pampering you and they have fancy, natural ingredients. Steam, sauna, jacuzzi – this place has the works. All you need to do is lose your inhibitions when faced with the mirrored walls and let their hands do the rest.

Parcos

White Hall, Kemp's Corner (2364-3685). Grant Road station. **Open** *Shop* 10.30am-7.30pm. *Studio* 10am-6pm. **Credit** AmEx, MC, V.

This Clarins-run spa is small but neat, and offers signature face and body treatments.

Quan

JW Marriott, Juhu Tara Road, Juhu (6693-3610). Santa Cruz or Vile Parle stations. **Open** 9am-9pm daily. **Credit** AmEx, MC, V.

For five-star comfort and cutting-edge design, you can't really go wrong with a visit to Quan at the JW Marriott in suburban Juhu. Quan earned itself the new spa of the year award back in 2006 at the Asia Spa Baccarat Awards, which honour innovation in the spa industry. And if you're travelling with your significant other, don't forget to luxuriate in the couples room.

► *Booking here is essential.*

Rudra

Kwality House, Kemp's Corner, Hughes Road (2387-2530/31). Grant Road station. **Taxi** Kemp's Corner. **Open** 8am-9.30pm daily. **Credit** AmEx, MC, V.

Rudra's interiors display attention to detail: the mood lighting, ornate furniture and meditative chants are all carefully chosen to provide 'soulitude'. All 13 rooms feature DVD players that play the music of your choice, and high-end showers that double up as saunas. But while the interiors are fancy, the treatments emphasise traditional Tibetan and ayurvedic techniques. Give the Himalayan herbs scrub a shot: the two-hour treatment involves a massage with aromatic herbs like turmeric, sandalwood and cinnamon and is likely to lull you into deep sleep.

Sva

Sva Spa, Gauri Kunj, Kishore Kumar Ganguly Marg, Juhu Tara Road, Juhu (2660-7326/28 /68, www.svaspasalon.com). Santa Cruz station. **Open** 11am-9pm daily. **Credit** MC, V.

Therapists at Sva Spa undergo 600 hours of training, we are told. The spa offers spa treatments, stone therapy, massages and foot reflexology.

YOGA

Ishwardas Chunnilal Yogic Health Centre – Kaivalyadhama

43 Marine Drive (2281-8417). Charni Road station. **Open** 6.30-9.30am, 3.30-6.30pm Mon-Sat. **No credit cards.**

The roomy Kaivalyadhama centre at Marine Drive is part of a 60-year-old organisation set up by Swami Kuvalayananda to promote yoga for health and healing. It costs Rs 300 for a check-up and about Rs 500 for a monthly class.

Iyengar Yogashraya

Elmac House, Senapati Bapat Marg, Lower Parel (W) (2494-8416). Lower Parel station. **Open** 7am-4pm Mon, Sat; 7am-8pm Tue-Fri. **No credit cards.**

Though the 90-year-old BKS Iyengar personally conducts classes only in Pune, the Mumbai branch of the Iyengar Institute, which opened in 2002, is a good place for beginners. It's warm and welcoming but that's not to say the *asanas* are comfortable; but props designed by the master – wooden gadgets, belts and ropes – help tremendously.

Satyananda (Bihar) Yoga Centre

Group classes at Walkeshwar 7-8am, 10-11am, 7-8pm Mon-Thur. Private classes also available on request. Call Sarvath Palanpur on 98701-11094 for details. **No credit cards.**

Practise yoga in the comfort of your hotel room under the guidance of instructors from the Satyananda Centre. Founded by Swami Satyananda Saraswati, the school integrates techniques from various traditional branches of yoga, including Raja, Bhakti, Karma, Hatha, Kundalini and Kriya. It costs around Rs 1,000 per month for two classes a week.

Yoga Institute

Prabhat Colony, Shree Yogendra Marg, Santa Cruz (E) (2611-0506). Santa Cruz station. **Open** 7am-7.30pm daily. **No credit cards.**

If you want a serious crash course in the fundamentals of yoga, try the Yoga Institute's seven-day health camp (Rs 2,200 inclusive of four meals), which includes an introduction to the philosophy of yoga and its practical applications. The centre combines traditional yogic values and techniques with Western science to spread the word about well-being. Put down the self-help book and register.

★ Yogacara

Rewa House Bungalow, Bhulabhai Desai Road (98331-98371). Grant Road station. **Open** 7.15am-9.30pm Mon-Sat. **Credit** MC, V.

In addition to yoga, pranayama and meditation classes, Yogacara offers massage therapies that complement its focus on releasing distress while strengthening the body.

Music

Everything from Indian classical to classic rock.

Mumbai is the home of Bollywood, and by extension, the home of Indian pop music, almost all of which is film songs. Bollywood music blares from every nightclub, autorickshaw, radio station and music channel; it would seem that the city listens to nothing else. Yet, listen carefully and you will find that there's a lot more. Indian classical music is popular, rock is big, too, retro rock even bigger, and India's new status as an economic powerhouse means that megastar pop acts have started playing Mumbai on their world tours.

IN TUNE

Mumbai has a thriving scene of classic rock and death metal, a burgeoning local hip hop culture, a growing interest in jazz, and the occasional regional pop and rock act. The number and variety of gigs has grown over the last couple of years, thanks to new venues.

However, it's Hindustani (North Indian) and Carnatic (South Indian) classical music that dominate Mumbai's live music scene. Most classical concerts are organised by *sabhas* or music circles, whose members pay an annual subscription fee to attend concerts arranged by the circle. Non-members can attend by paying a nominal guest fee. There are also larger concerts during the winter, the traditional classical music season, when names like Ravi Shankar and Zakir Hussain make their annual visit to the city for a series of gigs.

Your best chance to catch some Bombay jazz is at **Not Just Jazz by the Bay** (*see p117*) and bars such as **Blue Frog** and **Soul Fry Casa** (*see p113* **Pubs & Bars**). Mumbai also has one of India's biggest college rock scenes and three of the biggest Mumbai bands, Zero, Pentagram and Pin Drop Violence, play at college festivals and at rock-friendly venues such as **B69** and **Razzberry Rhinoceros**. There are also occasional larger festivals like **Independence Rock** (*see p158* **Music festivals**). You can find Indian rock CDs at the **BX Furtado** shop (*see p34*).

As for international acts, you're more likely to see veteran rock than the pop world's latest superstar. That said, Beyoncé, 50 Cent and Shakira have all dropped in recently.

There's also a small Western classical music scene, which plays at just one venue – the **National Centre for the Performing Arts** (NCPA; 2282-4567, 6654-8135, www.ncpamumbai.com) at Nariman Point. **The Symphony Orchestra of India**, currently under the direction of Kazakh violinist Marat Bisengaliev, performs seasonal concerts every February and September.

One of the city's most interesting live music experiences takes place on the first, third, seventh, tenth and 11th days of the annual **Ganesh Chaturthi festival** (*see p136*) around September, when the city streets are taken over with lines of devotees dancing to the sound of *nashik bajas* – amateur bands who beat out frenetic rhythms of Maharashtrian folk music.

BUYING TICKETS

For what's on and where to go, check *Time Out Mumbai* magazine and city's newspaper supplements to find out who's playing during your stay, or call music circles (see listings below) for information on upcoming classical performances. Guests are welcome to attend music circle concerts for a fee of Rs 50-Rs 100 payable at the venue on the night. Concerts of Hindi film classics are also worth checking out and usually take place around the birth or death anniversaries of famous singers, composers and lyricists. Again, check *Time Out* or the newspapers. Tickets cost between Rs 50 and Rs 300. Except for larger concerts or performances at the NCPA, concert organisers generally do not accept credit cards or take advance bookings.

MUSIC CIRCLES

Most of today's household names in Indian classical music made their debut at concerts organised by *sabhas* or music circles, which emerged in the late 19th century to popularise classical music. Indian classical music still lacks funding and music circles remain vital in supporting the form. Most of the venues below are small and simple, and often lack air-con.

B69
21 Bhaidas Bhuta Compound, Mogra Lane, off Old Nagardas Road, near Andheri Subway, Andheri (E). Andheri station.
Mumbaikars who are into metal flock to this Andheri East mosh pit.
► *Cross over to the West side and visit Gilbert Hill; see p68.*

Dadar Matunga Cultural Centre
122A JK Sawant Road, near Ruparel College, Matunga (2430-4150). Matunga Road station.
One of the city's oldest music circles, it puts on at least one concert a month. It also hosts two annual events dedicated to the memory of musicologist Vishnu Narayan Bhatkhande: a music festival in January and a lecture in September.

★ Fine Arts Society, Chembur
Sivaswamy Auditorium, Fine Arts Society, Fine Arts Chowk, near Chembur Flyover, RC Marg, Chembur (2522-2988). Chembur station.
One of the city's main venues for Carnatic classical music performances.

Indian Music Group
St Xavier's College Hall, St Xavier's College, 5 Mahapalika Marg (2263-4548). CST or Churchgate stations.
The Indian Music Group organises four prestigious Hindustani concerts every year.

★ Kala Bharati
Karnataka Sangha, Dr Vishveshawarayya Samarak Mandir, CHM Marg, Matunga (W) (2437-7022). Matunga Road station.
Hosts a classical music or dance performance every Sunday morning in an air-conditioned auditorium. It also organises three major festivals every year, held in August, September and December.

Sri Shanmukhananda Fine Arts & Sangeet Sabha
Shanmukhananda Hall, Plot No. 292, behind Gandhi Market, Comrade Harbans Lal Marg, Sion (E) (2407-8888). Sion station.
Carnatic music dominates this *Sabha*'s calendar and the monthly list of performers includes both established and new artists. The Shanmukhananda Hall with seating for over 3,000.

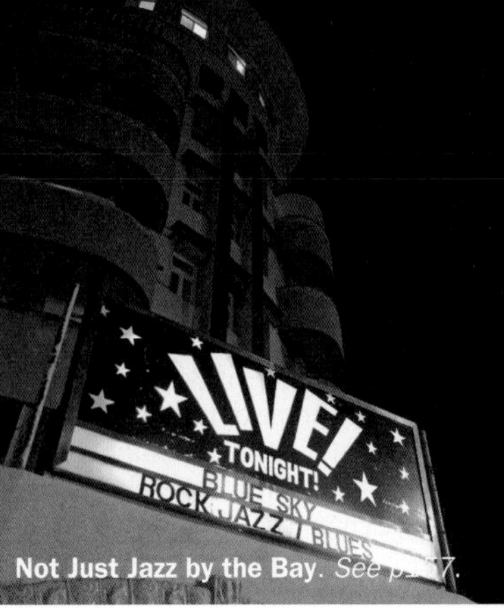

Not Just Jazz by the Bay. See p157.

Swar Sadhana Samiti
Mumbai Marathi Sahitya Sangh Mandir, Dr Bhalerao Marg, near St Mary's High School, Girgaum (2385-6303). Charni Road station.
Stages a monthly concert to showcase the work of upcoming Hindustani classical musicians.

Udayan
National Gallery of Modern Art, Cowasji Jehangir Hall, near Regal Cinema, MG Road, Colaba (2288-1969). CST or Churchgate stations.
Udayan organises classical music, dance and theatre performances on Saturdays at the National Gallery of Modern Art in Colaba. Send an email to udayan_cultural_organisation@hotmail.com.

MUSIC FESTIVALS

See also p136 **Calendar** for cultural festivals featuring music performances. Events tend to be planned in accordance to the Hindu calendar – call ahead for the exact dates.

January/February

★ Alla Rakha Khan Barsi Concert
Shanmukhananda Hall, Plot No. 292, behind Gandhi Market, Comrade Harbans Lal Marg, Sion (E) (2407-8888). Sion station.
Zakir Hussain and his brothers pay tribute to their father, the legendary tabla player, in a one-day festival at Shanmukhananda Hall.

Hridayesh Arts Vile Parle Festival
Parle Tilak Vidyalaya Ground, Hanuman Road, Vile Parle (E). Vile Parle station.
This festivalis one of the most prestigious Hindustani classical music events. Organised by Hridayesh Arts (2614-8556).

JanFest
St Xavier's College Hall, St Xavier's College, 5 Mahapalika Marg (2263-4548). CST or Churchgate stations.

ARTS & ENTERTAINMENT

College kids outnumber the oldies at this concert by students of St Xavier's College. Organised by the Indian Music Group.

One Tree Music Festival
MMRDA Grounds, Bandra-Kurla Complex, Bandra (E). Bandra station.
Two to three days of rock, blues and funk. Organised by Fountainhead (2600-4640).

Smriti Sandhya
St Andrew's Auditorium, St Andrew's College, St Dominic Road, Bandra (W) (2640-3041/ www.bimalroymemorial.org). Bandra station.
A concert of film music held in memory of one of India's greatest directors, Bimal Roy. Organised by the Bimal Roy Memorial Committee.

March/April

Alladiya Khan Festival
Balvikas Sangh Hall, Balvikas Sangh Marg, near Gandhi Maidan, Chembur (2527-2388). Chembur station.
This four-day concert pays tribute to the founder of the Agra gharana of Hindustani classical music.

May/June

Aarohi
YB Chavan Centre, near Mantralaya, General Jagannath Bhosle Marg (2285-2081). CST or Churchgate stations.
Performances by the future stars of Hindustani classical music. Organised by Pancham Nishad (2412-4750).

Megh Malhar
Nehru Centre Auditorium, Annie Besant Road, Worli (2496-4676/www.nehrucentre mumbai.com). Mahalaxmi station.
Maestros perform romantic monsoon ragas.

Rabigeetika
Mysore Association Hall, 393 Bhau Daji Road, near Maheshwari Udayan, Matunga (E) (2402-4647). Matunga station.
A concert of Rabindra Sangeet, the music written and composed by Bengali writer Rabindranath Tagore. Organised by Rabigeetika (2262-4709).

July/August

★ Independence Rock
Various venues (www.gigpad.com).
Two adrenaline-charged days of headbanging courtesy of the country's best-loved rock and metal acts, this two-decade old festival is meant to coincide with the Independence Day weekend in mid August but is actually often tends to be postponed by a few weeks.

Janmashtami Flute Concert
Brindavan Gurukul, Haridwar Marg, Versova Link Road, Andheri (W) (2646-3535/ www.brindavangurukul.org). Andheri station.
Legendary flautist Hariprasad Chaurasia and his students perform a 24-hour concert at his music school during the festival of Janmashtami (*see p137* **Festivals & Events**).

Khazana
Various venues (www.pankajudhas.com).
An annual ghazal festival organised by singer Pankaj Udhas.

September/October

Zia Mohiuddin Dagar Barsi Festival
YB Chavan Centre, near Mantralaya, General Jagannath Bhosle Marg (2285-2081). CST or Churchgate stations.
The city's only Hindustani classical festival dedicated to dhrupad, a style of singing that was the dominant form until khayal – the style rendered by most singers today – started gaining popularity.

November/December

A Festival of Festive Music
National Centre for the Performing Arts, Nariman Point. CST or Churchgate stations.
Twelve choirs from around the country perform Christmas music. Organised by the Stop Gaps Cultural Academy (2421-2120).

★Jazz Utsav
Land's End Amphitheatre. Bandstand, near Lands Ends Hotel, Bandra (W). Bandra station.
mainly offering Indian jazz, the venue is one of Mumbai's prettiest: an amphitheatre inside Bandra Fort at Land's End, against the backdrop of the Arabian Sea. Organised by Capital Jazz. Email Prakash Thadani (prakash@jazzutsav.com).

Ruhaniyat
Horniman Circle Gardens, Horniman Circle, Fort (2363-3561). CST or Churchgate stations.
A Sufi music festival. Organised by Banyan Tree Events (2826-0674).

Sangat
National Centre for the Performing Arts, Nariman Point (www.ncpamumbai.com). CST or Churchgate stations.
A chamber music festival organised by the Mehli Mehta Music Foundation (2382-3644).

★ Spiritual Morning
Gateway of India, Apollo Bunder, Colaba. CST or Churchgate stations.
Morning *ragas* at the Gateway of India. Organised by Pancham Nishad (2412-4750).

Nightlife

Clubbing under a curfew.

Mumbaikars like to think of their city as the nightlife capital of India, but the reality is slightly different – clubland is currently in a bit of a funk with a 1.30am curfew. It's not all doom and gloom, though, and Mumbaikers still sure like to party. Whether you want to join the Bollywood A-list in gleaming venues in Juhu or get down and dirty at super-dive bar, Voodoo, the city's scene offers something for pretty much everyone. Including those into the simple pleasures of clutching a beer and screeching along to Madonna.

RAISE A TOAST

It's been a downward spiral ever since the state government's conservative Deputy Chief Minister decided in 2005 that 'dance bars', uniquely Mumbai establishments in which fully clothed women danced to Bollywood songs for the enjoyment of their male patrons, were dens of vice and must be shut to protect the virtues of bar girls.

Many of these bars were part-owned by police officers, who decided that if they couldn't continue running their bars, clubs for middle- and upper middle-class clients had no business staying open until 5am either. That year, the palm-greasing of the police by club owners, which had allowed them to stay open beyond the official 1.30am deadline, came to a halt.

This made life very tough for a lot of city clubs. Clubbers rarely step out before 11pm, meaning there simply isn't time to make enough money before the 1.30am deadline kicks in. The only beneficiaries of the new regime are the clubs within luxury hotels, which are allowed to operate until 3am. But the biggest fallout of the 1.30am law has been its effect on creativity. With restricted business hours, club owners are wary of experimenting with new music, and prefer mainstream sets that are indistinguishable from venue to venue. This may be popular with the majority of clubbers, but it keeps the city from developing any newer niche scenes.

In 2006, things looked like they might improve, as independent DJs started club nights in venues across town, but by early 2007, the last of them had withered away thanks to high costs and low turnout. To add to the city's woes, the once-thumping Insomnia at the Taj Mahal Hotel turned off the music for the last time in 2007, when the management decided that high-end retail stores would be more profitable than a club.

Mumbai has found an increasing interest in live music, and artists from the city and around the country now regularly play at venues like **Blue Frog**, **Hard Rock Café** and **Soul Fry Casa** (for all, *see p113-119* **Pubs & Bars**), while lounge bars often book DJs to play house and electronica sets, too, ensuring that Mumbai may not be the best city in the country in which to go dancing, but it's still tops for good gigs and an energetic, buzzing vibe to its nightlife scene.

DOS & DON'TS

Mumbai nightclubs have notoriously complicated cover charges, depending which night of the week you go, whether you are a male-female couple, a single woman or a stag (a single male). Most cover charges range between Rs 600 and Rs 1,500 and include the cost of a few drinks. Clubs occasionally enforce no-stag policies on Friday and Saturday nights, but they're often more lax when it comes to (white) foreign men, thanks to the continuing popularity of the idea that foreigners spend more or that they add a touch of glamour – but don't count on this. Clubs are notorious for turning away black men; bouncers commonly assume that if you're black and in Mumbai you must be Nigerian and therefore involved in the drug trade. If you suspect that you're the victim of a racist entry policy, demand to see the manager and tell him you're going to call the local press – stories like that make club owners very uncomfortable.

The admission prices given in the listings are for male-female couples and stags, with the lower price applying for weekdays, and the higher price for Fridays and Saturdays. Single women can expect to pay about half that, or sometimes nothing at all.

COLABA

★Polly Esther's

First Floor, Gordon House Hotel, Battery Street, Apollo Bunder, Colaba (2287-1122). CST or Churchgate stations. **Open** 9pm-3am Tue-Sun. **Admission** Rs 1,000-Rs 1,200.

A fun, roomy club that's part of the Gordon House Hotel, decked out with flower-power decor, posters of Rocky and a young Bollywood-starlet-of-yesteryear Zeenat Aman toking on a chillum. Most nights at Polly's are dedicated to retro at its purest – Prince, the Pet Shop Boys and the Bee Gees all do heavy-duty rotation – but there's also plenty of present-day fare. Few places in this town offer as much plain, pure fun on a Saturday night. The enthusiasm and the gay abandon with which the crowd sings along are infectious. Best of all, it's free entry on weekdays.

Voodoo

Arthur Bunder Road, off Colaba Causeway, near Radio Club, Colaba (2284-1959). CST or Churchgate stations. **Taxi** Radio Club. **Open** 8pm-1.30am daily. **Admission** Rs 250.

Voodoo is the most risqué little bar in Mumbai. It's got girls aplenty and they certainly do dance, but they also sit, talk and drink with the male clientele – a motley collection of minor-league businessmen, both local and visiting. In other words, you can look and you can touch. The lights are dim, the air is heavy and the atmosphere is sweaty, going on edgy. For entertainment value, nothing beats it (but don't visit the loos alone). It's also the only club in town with a gay night, on Saturday.

► *For more on Mumbai's gay scene, see Gay & Lesbian p151.*

FORT

★ Red Light

Above Khyber restaurant, 145 Mahatma Gandhi Road, Kala Ghoda, Fort (2267-3227,6634-6248). CST or Churchgate stations. **Open** 7pm-1am daily. **Admission** Rs 1,200-Rs 1,800.

A destination for the prettiest students in South Mumbai, paying for their drinks with plentiful allowances from daddy. The music on weekends is a mishmash of Hindi commercial grind (and you really have to like crowds), but the DJs serve up some old school Snoop, Dre and Pac on Wednesdays, and there's plenty of Brit-Bolly-bhangra beats on offer for the city's bling bling crew. However, be warned: a clear head is necessary for a visit to the loos, where the mirrored corridor causes such disorientation that desperate and dazed patrons have been known to relieve themselves on the floor.

► *Khyber downstairs dishes up great North Indian food; see p101.*

LOWER PAREL & WORLI

Hype

Atria Mall, Fourth Floor, Annie Besant Road, Worli (2481-3799). Mahalaxmi station. **Open** 9pm-1.30am daily. **Admission** Rs 3,000 for a couple.

In a city where clubs are all about underground, cutting-edge music, Hype is anything but. The club's playlist consists of completely commercial English and Hindi numbers peppered with retro songs. You might think 'Like a Prayer', JLo's 'Jenny from the Block' and 'Oh, Oh Jaane Janaa' have no place on any self-respecting club's playlist but DJ Aqeel (who owns the place) couldn't care less and neither will you.

Play

High Street Phoenix, 462 Senapati Bapat Marg, Lower Parel (6661-4343). Lower Parel station. Taxi Phoenix Mills. **Open** 9pm-1.30am Wed-Sun. **Admission** Rs 1,500.

Until the last few months of 2007 it was called Ra, but in an effort to revive flagging interest the management gave this club a minor makeover and a new name: Play Superclub Mumbai. While this is patently untrue – Play is not particularly large nor terribly cutting-edge – it's certainly an excellent club to listen to Bollywood and hip hop and to watch kids wear oversize dollar sign pendants without a fleck of irony. The new name and design changes are little more than a reboot of an old franchise; the dancefloor is still exactly where it used to be, the bar hasn't moved and even the cover charge is the same. Located in between town and the 'burbs, Play attracts a mixed crowd; and with an unabashedly mainstream bent to the setlist and a liberal attitude towards the way you dress, it's the sort of place that has no hang-ups, as long as you don't.

Shiro

Bombay Dyeing Mills Compound, Pandurang Budhkar Marg, Worli (2438-3008). Mahalaxmi station. **Open** 7pm-1.30am daily. **Credit** AmEx, MC, V.

Located in a former mill, Shiro is an East Asian-themed bar on acid. It's like drinking in Alice's Wonderland. With three bars at three corners and cleverly divided drinking areas that serve to make the huge space seem cosier, it's clear an immense amount of thought has gone into Shiro. Even when it's packed, though – close to 700 people cram in on the weekend – Shiro is still pleasant enough to not break a sweat, to manage a drink without too much elbowing and to conduct a conversation without having to yell over the (pop with lite lounge beats) music.

BANDRA & KHAR

H20: The Liquid Lounge

Sheetal Bukhara, off Linking Road, Khar (W) (2649-5151/98203-49168 guestlist, www.clubh2o.in). Khar station. **Taxi** Khar Telephone Exchange. **Open** 6.30pm-1.30am daily. **Admission** Rs 500-Rs 1,000.

Four split levels, three open-air terraces each with its own bar, walls in seven hues of blue and circular water-filled windows with colourful plants dancing in the currents. H2O is like an underwater lair from a Bond film (minus the bikini babes). The music is upbeat lounge in the early evening, followed by a smattering of house, ending up with Bollywood beats – standard Mumbai fare to keep the boys and girls bouncing.

Trilogy.

JUHU

Enigma

JW Marriott Hotel, Juhu Tara Road, Juhu (6693-3000). Vile Parle station. **Open** 8.30pm-2.30am Tue-Sat. **Admission** Rs 1,000-Rs 2,500.

Enigma, the JW Marriott's superclub, has defied the competition by managing to keep pulling in the crowds almost continuously since 2003. Known as Bollywood's favourite nightclub, it tends to get filled up with paunchy movie producers, but you won't hear the girls complaining when they also get the chance to shake booty alongside regulars like movie stars Abhishek Bachchan and Fardeen Khan. The decor radiates an appropriate aura of kitsch-cool: a dramatic chandelier is suspended above a large circular bar in the centre of a space decked out with dark-hued drapes, plush sofas, flickering candles and ottomans. Show up before midnight if you don't want to encounter serpentine queues.

Rock Bottom

Hotel Ramee Guestline, AB Nair Road, Juhu (6693-5555, www.rockbottommumbai.com). Vile Parle station. **Open** 9.30pm-2.45am Tue-Sun. **Admission** Rs 600-Rs 1,500.

When Rock Bottom opened for business in late 2003, the hype was huge, with no less than living Bollywood legend Amitabh Bachchan seen regularly striding through this sleek Juhu nightclub. It isn't quite so hip any more but it remains an attractive club, with a cavernous dancefloor, vast screens over the DJ booth, a stellar sound system and a late-night licence. The crowd is largely suburban kids who don't want to travel (especially since the drink and drive laws were stringently implemented in 2007). Expect standard commercial fare as far as music is concerned.

★ Trilogy

Hotel Sea Princess, Juhu Tara Road, Juhu Beach (2646-9689, www.seaprincess.com). Santa Cruz station. **Open** 8pm-midnight Wed-Mon. **Credit** MC, V.

With its lipstick-red sheen and procession of stiletto-heeled women, the staircase at Trilogy, the new Juhu nightclub-lounge run by Keenan and Ryan Tham at the Sea Princess Hotel, feels like a Bollywood red carpet with steps. The Tham boys want Trilogy to be the city's premier place to see and be seen. Mixing nightclub with lounge, the nightspot has a striking interior that the Thams no doubt hope will rank with Blue Frog and Tote as among Mumbai's most distinctive-looking nightspots. A great place to sit in a corner and admire Mumbai's social set while sipping tasty cocktails.

Sport & Fitness

Where cricket is king

Stroll down to the Azad Maidan on a weekend afternoon and watch as dozens of cricket matches take place simultaneously, with no sign of even a token football anywhere on the ground. Such is the dominance of cricket in Mumbai that it knocks every other sport off the calendar and away from the collective consciousness. But there's more to the city's sporting spirit than cricket. Traditional Indian games such as mallakhamb, Kabaddi and Kho kho are still played in the city, and football, hockey and horseriding are all available as well – providing you know where to look.

PITCH CALL

Little wonder, when cricket bats and balls are thrust into Mumbaikars' hands as soon as they're old enough to grip them, and when the city has produced so many Test cricketers for the national side, including the great Sachin Tendulkar. Many Mumbaikars have fond memories of days spent at **Brabourne Stadium** watching visiting teams play the Board President's XI, and at **Wankhede Stadium**, watching the great Bombay cricket team crush opponent after opponent to win the inter-state Ranji Trophy 37 times since the trophy's inception in 1935.

Public parks and sports grounds are few, but do-it-yourself 'gully cricket' prevails in alleys, patches of ground and even busy streets everywhere in the city. Oval and Azad Maidans in South Mumbai, though home to cricket in the dry months, are colonised by football when the monsoon begins in June, and the maidans turn into muddy battlegrounds. Mumbai has a lively football league run by the Western India Football Association, in which sides with names like Maharashtra State Police battle Orkay Silk Mills at the Cooperage ground in South Mumbai and at other venues. Hockey, once a thriving city sport that produced numerous players for India's national side, now comes a distant third, popular in the schools and colleges of suburban Malad. Also in the suburbs, **Shivaji park** in Dadar, sees hundreds of children gather everyday to learn traditional Indian games like mallakhamb and Kabaddi.

As they have done for over a century, private sports clubs and gymkhanas like the Bombay Gymkhana remain important, although snobbish, centres for amateur and recreational sports like squash, tennis, badminton, cricket, rugby and swimming. Club memberships are expensive and waiting lists long, and these aren't accessible to visitors. But modern gyms have mushroomed in recent years, some offering short-term or day memberships.

Major events in the city's sporting calendar include the **Indian Premier League**, **Ranji Trophy** from October to January, the Royal Western India Turf Club **Derby** at the Mahalaxmi Racecourse in February and the **Mumbai Marathon** (www.thegreatestrace.com), started in 2004 and now an annual January event that attracts thousands of runners (and a surprising number of men in Gandhi costumes) for prize money of up to $30,000.

SPECTATOR SPORTS

Check the newspapers for details of sporting events during your stay, or call sports associations directly.

INSIDE TRACK
MONSOON MATCHES

One of the most popular cricket tournaments in the city is the Kanga League, which is played during the rainy season. Rumour has it that Mumbai players prepare by familiarising themselves with the wet conditions in England.

Cricket

Teeming maidans like the **Oval** (Maharshi Karve Road, Churchgate) and **Shivaji Park** (Veer Savarkar Road) have become part of cricketing folklore for being training grounds for future superstars. The 24-year-old Wankhede Stadium, the second largest in the country with a capacity of 45,000, is currently being renovated to prepare for the 2011 One-day World Cup final. The Mumbai Cricket Association's plans for the ground include improved drainage, more seats and air-conditioned stands. Until the renovation is completed, the much prettier **Brabourne Stadium** (Dinshaw Wachha Road, Churchgate, 6659-4100) will host international fixtures as well as domestic league matches.

Football

Mumbai has two major football venues, the larger of which is the **Cooperage** (Cooperage Road, Churchgate), a no-frills 12,000-capacity stadium near Colaba. There's also **St Xavier's Ground** (near Parel Flyover, Parel). Both the grounds are plain and functional, with simple facilities. Call the **Western India Football Association** on 2202-4020 for match details.

► *After a tiring football match, have a beer at the Woodside Inn; see p115.*

Hockey

Mahindra Stadium

D Road, Churchgate (W). Churchgate station.

The Bombay Hockey Association's Mahindra Stadium is the only hockey stadium in Mumbai with an AstroTurf surface. Situated right next to Wankhede Stadium, it hosts Mumbai Hockey League games and all the city's major tournaments, most famously the Bombay Gold Cup in April-May and the women's Tommy Emar Gold Cup in April. Call the **Bombay Hockey Association** on 2281-1271 for match details. Entry is free.

Horse racing

Mahalaxmi Racecourse

Keshavrao Khadye Marg, Mahalaxmi (2307-1401). Mahalaxmi station.
Admission Rs 25.

Mumbai has one of India's top horse racing venues at the Mahalaxmi Racecourse, also the headquarters of the **Royal Western India Turf Club**, equipped with the smart Gallops restaurant. The year's biggest races are the Indian Derby, the Poonawalla Breeders' Multimillion and the Indian 2000 Guineas, held every February. On these days, the racecourse becomes an Ascot-style photo-op for Bollywood stars and local celebs.

ACTIVE SPORTS

Horse riding

Amateur Riders' Club

Mahalaxmi Racecourse, Gate No. 8, Keshavrao Khadye Marg, Mahalaxmi (6527-8987). Mahalaxmi station. **Open** 9.30am-5.30pm daily. **Classes** Rs 1,103 for 30mins. **No credit cards.**

Take a half-hour horse ride at the racecourse or take a beginners or advanced riding course. But don't expect to spend all your time charging around on Seabiscuit; the courses are in-depth and you're also expected to take theory classes to familiarise yourself with riding equipment as well as the anatomy and psychology of the animal.

Swimming

★ Bodyrhythm

Advent, 12A Gen J Bhosale Marg, Churchgate (2284-8011). Churchgate station. **Taxi** next to YB Chavan Auditorium. **Open** 7am-12.30pm, 3.30-9pm daily. **Fees** Rs 13,000 annual membership; Rs 300 1 visit. **No credit cards.**

Look for the staircase at the right side of the Advent building for Bodyrhythm's 22-m pool. Nothing fancy, but those who just want to hit the water will have no complaints.

Tennis

Maharashtra State Lawn Tennis Association (MSLTA)

Maharshi Karve Road, Cooperage (2287-4806/08/09). Churchgate station. **Open** 10am-2pm for non-members. **Court charges** Rs 200 per hr; Rs 300 extra for partner. **No credit cards.**

Work on your backhand at the state-run MSLTA. You can hire a court and play against a partner supplied by the Association or bring your own willing opponent along.

Water sports

★ Aquasail Club

Boats leave from the Gateway of India, Colaba (99876-81826). CST or Churchgate stations. **Open** 9.30am Sat, Sun. **No credit cards.**

This Mandwa-based club offers sailing, windsurfing and kayaking.

H20 Water Sports Complex

Chowpatty (2367-7584/46). Charni Road station. **Open** 10am-7pm daily. **No credit cards.**

The H20 Water Sports Complex on Chowpatty Beach offers waterskiing, speedboating, kayaking, plus jetskiing, parasailing and even beach volleyball. It also conducts week-long classes in windsurfing, waterskiing and rowing.

Theatre & Dance

There's much ado about the performing arts in the city.

English-language theatre in Mumbai has come a long way since the 1980s, when it was the preserve of wealthy South Mumbai amateurs who produced classic British and American plays and musicals, sometimes with an Indian twist. Today, the English-language theatre scene is booming, finally doing justice to the myriad stories in the metropolis. That said, it's still Indian productions that dominate here; with Marathi work among the most exciting, covering a variety of themes and staged anywhere from the city's bars to its pavements.

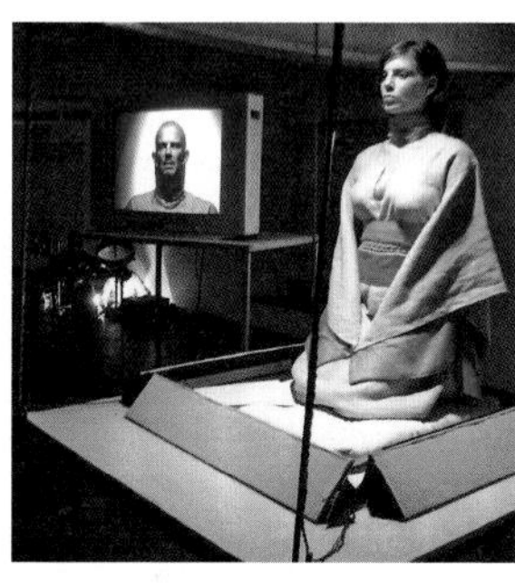

MUMBAI'S THEATRE SCENE

Now a growing citywide movement, English theatre has a cadre of writers producing original drama, such as Rage Production's One on One, a set of ten monologues by eight playwrights about contemporary India. Yet Mumbai's theatre scene is dominated by productions in Hindi, Gujarati and Marathi. Gujarati theatre and Hindi drama to a certain extent consist largely of commercial drama – mostly coarse bedroom comedies and Indian-adapted versions of Neil Simon plays. But Mumbai's most popular, exciting and innovative theatre is without doubt Marathi, which has a strong modern history of experimental drama (*see p166* **Pushing the Boundaries**). One of India's most caustic and cutting-edge playwrights was the late Marathi playwright Vijay Tendulkar, whose plays are regularly performed in Mumbai theatres.

In recent years, an increasing taste for innovation has led theatre groups to use unconventional spaces like bars, libraries and out on the street – no mean feat in a desperately crowded city. In 2005, the **Prithvi Theatre** in Juhu, one of Mumbai's most popular, had performers take to the streets at its annual festival; in March 2006, the 19th-century David Sassoon Library at Kala Ghoda hosted a production of Shakespeare's *Much Ado About Nothing*. In 2007, the art gallery Project 88 hosted a number of productions by avant-garde director Rehaan Engineer (including *The Secret Love Life of Ophelia*). Frequent theatre festivals also offer a chance to catch independent drama from around the country and the occasional visiting international company.

BUYING TICKETS

Check *Time Out Mumbai* and city newspapers for details of productions showing during your stay. It's also worth taking a look at www.mumbaitheatreguide.com – although its listings are not exhaustive – and www.bookmyshow.com, at which you can buy tickets for shows at Juhu's Prithvi Theatre. There are no one-stop ticketing agencies and tickets must usually be bought direct and in person from the box office. With the exception of the **National Centre for the Performing Arts** in Nariman Point, Mumbai's theatres do not accept credit cards. Theatre box offices are usually closed on Sundays unless there is a performance scheduled on that day. Calling the theatre in advance to enquire whether tickets are available is always a good idea. Ticket prices vary considerably depending on the production, and can cost anything between Rs 50 and Rs 500 each. The average price for a ticket for an international production is Rs 1,000.

INSIDE TRACK
SCIENCE SEMINARS

Scientifically inclined? Then head to **Prithvi** (*see p167*) in Juhu on the first Sunday of every month at 11am for a talk by the Tata Institute of Fundamental Research. But don't be put off if it sounds a little like school: topics so far have included everything from extra-solar planets to science in the kitchen.

VENUES

South Mumbai

The Comedy Store

Palladium Mall, High Street Phoenix, Senapati Bapat Marg, Lower Parel (4348-5010, http://www.thecomedystore.in/). **Tickets** www.bookmyshow.com. **Credit** MC, V.

The UK-based outfit Mumbai branch gets international comics to perform. Shows are held from Thur-Sun. The space also has a bar, diner and café.

► *Comedy not your scene? Cross the road and hop over to Blue Frog for a musical evening; see p117.*

Mumbai Marathi Sahitya Sangh

Dr Bhalerao Marg, Gaiwadi, near Charni Road station, Charni Road (2385-6303). Charni Road station. **Box office** 5-9pm Mon-Sat. **No credit cards.**

Mumbai Marathi Sahitya Sangh is a theatre devoted to experimental Marathi work. The hall suffers from poor acoustics, compensated for by some ridiculously low ticket prices – a mere Rs 30 – and high standards of performance.

National Centre for the Performing Arts

NCPA Marg, near Oberoi Hotel, Nariman Point (6622-3737,www.ncpamumbai.com). CST or Churchgate stations. **Box office** 9am-7pm Mon-Sat. **Credit** MC, V.

The National Centre for the Performing Arts is Mumbai's one claim to a world-class performance space. A complex of theatres, galleries and outdoor spaces set at the very end of the narrow strip of Nariman Point and against the backdrop of the

Pushing the Boundaries

The Marathi theatre tradition is anything but traditional.

In Marathi playwright Sachin Kundalkar's riff on power in relationships, *Fridge Madhe Thevalele Prem*, a quarrelsome couple decide to preserve the meagre remnants of their love in the fridge, then consume a daily ration and top it up once a week. But when the husband demands a second helping, the system breaks down with disastrous consequences. Offbeat, funny and shamelessly absurd, *Fridge Madhe Thevalele Prem* is nothing out of the ordinary in effervescent Marathi stagecraft, which consistently shines in terms of both originality and productivity.

That's partly thanks to the Maharashtrian community's long and distinguished heritage in the performing arts, with traditional forms like *sangeetnatak*, a kind of musical, and *tamasha*, which typically features raunchy dancing to risqué songs. Theatregoing remains a popular community recreation, with middle-class Maharashtrian families going to see plays in the way other communities go to the movies, storming theatres from Thane to Dadar every weekend. This has fostered an audience accustomed to theatrical conventions, and who are open to seeing them broken, giving rise to an energetic subculture of experimental Marathi theatre.

It's a subculture that's produced Vijay Tendulkar, regarded as the most controversial as well as greatest living Marathi playwright. Tendulkar is best known for *Sakharam Binder*, *Ghashiram Kotwal* and *Gidhade*, plays that altered the course of Marathi theatre in the 1970s with a furious critique of the Indian caste system and shocking on-stage depictions of violence and blasphemy – something Maharashtrian theatre audiences had never seen before.

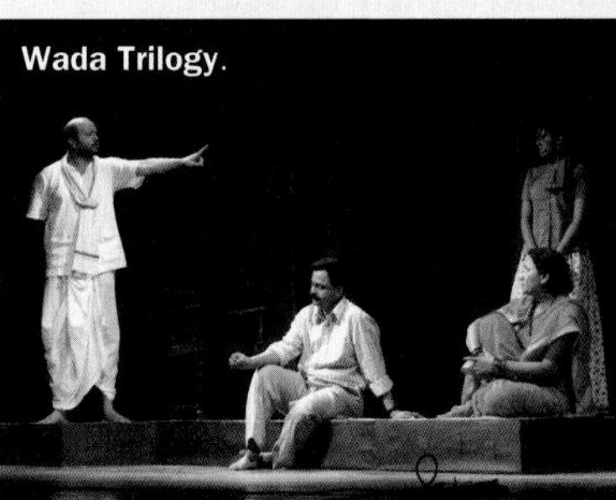
Wada Trilogy.

Tendulkar was joined by other innovators like Satish Alekar, famous for his darkly witty *Mahanirvan* and the fantastical *Begum Barve*, and Mahesh Elkunchwar, whose gritty modern plays include the *Wada Trilogy* (*pictured*), *Party* and *Vasanakand*. Following in their footsteps, a new breed of young Marathi writers continues to push the boundaries with politically driven plots and experimental dramatic forms. But after Tendulkar, it's become harder to shock Maharashtrian audiences.

Arabian Sea, the NCPA includes the Jamshed Bhabha, Experimental, Tata, Little and Godrej Dance Academy theatres. The jewel in its crown is the Jamshed Bhabha, resembling a Victorian townhouse with its double marble staircases, but the smaller Experimental Theatre remains the most popular venue for plays. Despite the name, the Experimental is indiscriminate in its line-up – romantic comedies and avant-garde drama all find a home here. Happily, all the theatres serve good sandwiches in the intervals, so it's easy to pick up a snack. The NCPA is popular: its box office opens in advance and you'll need to buy tickets in good time. Likewise, if you're going for a free show or talk, try to get there early.

Nehru Centre Auditorium

Nehru Centre, Annie Besant Road, Worli (2496-4676,www.nehrucentremumbai.com). Mahalaxmi station. **Box office** 10am-6pm Mon-Sat. **No credit cards.**

A part of the Nehru Centre complex, the auditorium hosts plays and music concerts. The highlight of its theatre calendar is a month-long festival in August of works from around the country.

Ravindra Natya Mandir

PL Deshpande Maharashtra Kala Academy, Sayani Road, Prabhadevi (2431-2956). Elphinstone Road station. **Taxi** near Siddhivinayak Temple. **Box office** 11am-10pm Mon-Sat. **No credit cards.**

Ravindra Natya Mandir and its smaller sister in the same complex, the PL Deshpande Hall, host performances from all the city's language theatres, as well as regular Bengali dance dramas and college theatre festivals.

► *While you're here, visit Siddhivinayak Temple, which is just down the lane.*

Sophia Bhabha Hall

Sophia College Campus, off Bhulabhai Desai Road (2353-8550). Grant Road station. **Box office** 10am-6pm Mon-Sat. **No credit cards.**

This large, plush auditorium is part of the palatial Sophia College campus, which was home to the Maharaja of Indore and subsequently the Maharaja of Bhavnagar between 1923 and 1940. Nowadays, the theatre is worth checking out for its decent lineups of both serious and light English drama.

Tejpal Hall

Tejpal Road, August Kranti Maidan, Gowalia Tank (2380-2679). Grant Road station. **Box office** 9am-noon, 4-7pm Wed-Sun. **No credit cards.**

Tending to mainly put on Gujarati plays, Tejpal Hall is a spacious theatre that's tucked away in a quiet corner of Gowalia Tank. Dance dramas and plays in Bengali are performed at Tejpal during the Durga Puja festival; *see p138.*

INSIDE TRACK PRITHVI TIPS

If you're watching a play at **Prithvi**, get there in good time. Patrons tend to queue up at least 15mins before the play starts and the theatre doesn't allow late entrants. Also, on Tuesdays and Wednesdays tickets are just Rs 80.

Suburbs

New Mahim Municipal School

Miya Mohammed Chotani Marg, Teesari Galli, Mahim (W) (2444-5871). Mahim station. **Box office** 7pm onwards Mon-Sat. **No credit cards.**

Awishkar, one of Mumbai's most active Marathi experimental theatre groups, operates out of this state-run school, and regularly performs plays by the country's upcoming playwrights *(see left* **Pushing the Boundaries***).*

★ Prithvi Theatre

Janki Kutir, Juhu Church Road, Juhu (2614-9546, www.prithvitheatre.org). Vile Parle station. Taxi near Juhu Market. **Box office** 10am-1pm, 2-7pm daily. **No credit cards.**

Built in 1978 to promote Hindi theatre, the Prithvi managed to snatch audiences away from the older, classier National Centre for the Performing Arts, despite being far away uptown in Juhu. An intimate 200-seater, Prithvi is partial to Hindi drama but also hosts English, Marathi and Gujarati plays. It has a casual, cosy atmosphere with a leafy outside café that attracts the occasional Juhu celeb and is famous for its (non-alcoholic) Irish coffees. In November, Prithvi hosts its popular annual theatre festival; *see p139.*

Rangsharda

Hotel Rangsharda, Bandra Reclamation, near Lilavati Hospital, Bandra (W) (2643-0544, www.hotelrangsharda.com). **Box office** 10am-6pm Mon-Sat. **No credit cards.**

Located in Hotel Rangsharda, the theatre hosts commercial plays in Hindi, Gujarati and English.

Shivaji Mandir

Shivaji Mandir, NC Kelkar Road, Dadar (W) (2438-9387). Dadar station. **Taxi** opposite Plaza Cinema. **Box office** 8.30-11am, 5-8pm daily. **No credit cards.**

A pitstop for those with a taste for ribald humour and slapstick – the mainstays of commercial Marathi theatre – Shivaji Mandir is also a venue for travelling *lavani* troupes. A Maharashtrian folk performance form, *lavani* features peppy dancing to risqué songs.

► *Try some Maharashtrian cuisine while at Dadar; see p94.*

St Andrew's Auditorium

St Dominic Road, Bandra (W) (2645-9667). Bandra station. **Box office** 10am-6pm daily. **No credit cards.**

Musicals and English comedies take centre stage at the cavernous St Andrew's Auditorium, which boasts an excellent sound system.

DANCE

There are seven classical dance forms in India, but only three – *bharatanatyam*, *kathak* and *Odissi* – are regularly performed in the city. The rest, *Manipuri*, *mohiniattam*, *kuchipudi* and *kathakali*, are taught in some of Mumbai's established dance schools but rarely seen on stage. Traditionally, dances were performed in temples as an expression of devotion, later becoming courtly entertainment under Mughal rule in the 16th and 17th centuries. Most of the dances were performed by men; it was only in the 18th century that dancing became socially acceptable for women, who today dominate.

Bharatanatyam was first performed in temples in the state of Tamil Nadu by *devdasis*, girls who devoted their lives to Lord Shiva. Its origins can be traced to the Natya Shastra, a 2,000-year-old discourse on dance and drama written by the sage Bharata. Even today, most Indian classical dances' vocabulary is based on guidelines laid out by Bharata's work.

Sculptures of women dancers and musicians discovered in caves in Orissa suggest that **Odissi** was being performed as far back as 200 BC, but it gained acceptance as a classical dance form only in the 1950s, through the efforts of celebrated male performers such as Pankajcharan Das and Kelucharan Mahapatra. *Odissi* is a subtle dance of lyrical, curving movements of the wrists and torso.

Kathak comes from North India and is a storytelling dance form (*katha* means 'story'). *Kathak* originated with the *kathakars*, dancers and musicians who travelled from village to village performing tales from the *Mahabharata* and the *Ramayana*. There are three *gharanas* or schools of *kathak* in Lucknow, Jaipur and Varanasi. Each has a different style, but the form is generally characterised by vigorous, fast-paced footwork.

While classical dance continues to rule the stage, the occasional contemporary performance also finds space in Mumbai and Western styles such as salsa, modern dance, ballroom and Latin have gained prominence. Freestyle forms – such as Bollywood – are immensely popular, too; Bollywood instructors combine the best of classical, Western, folk and trademark *jhatkas* (pelvic thrusts) to create an eclectic style. To learn the popular Bollywood moves, contact the Shiamak Davar Institute of Performing Arts (2353-7930), Terence Lewis Contemporary Dance Company (2623-8651) or Bosco & Caesar Dance Company (2639-9064/0264).

BUYING TICKETS

To find out what's on, check newspaper listings or look in *Time Out Mumbai*. Alternatively, log on to www.narthaki.com, where Indian classical and contemporary dancers and groups post updates about their tours. Ticketed events are rare; most dance performances are arranged for free by cultural organisations or for a 'guest charge', typically Rs 50-Rs 100. Guest passes can be bought from the box office on the night of a show or up to three days before a performance. Tickets are also sold at the Rhythm House music store at Kala Ghoda (*see p120* **Shops & Services**). Credit card bookings are not available except at the Godrej Dance Academy at the National Centre for the Performing Arts.

VENUES

★ Bhavan's Cultural Centre

Bhavan's Campus, Munshi Nagar, Dadabhai Road, Andheri (W) (3293-8017, 6528-0107/www.bcca.in). Andheri station. **Entry** free.

Mysore Association Hall

Near Maheshwari Udayan, 393 Bhau Daji Road, Matunga (E) (2402-4647). Matunga or King's Circle stations. **Box office** 10am-6pm daily. **No credit cards.**

★ National Centre for the Performing Arts

NCPA Marg, Nariman Point (2283-3838,www.ncpamumbai.com). CST or Churchgate stations. **Box office** 9am-7pm daily. **Credit** MC, V.

Visit the Piramal Gallery at the NCPA for photography shows.

► *There is good eating to be had around Nariman point, from modern Indian to Italian; see p97.*

Nehru Centre Auditorium

Annie Besant Road, near Shiv Sagar Estate, Worli (2496-4680, www.nehrucentremumbai.com). Mahalaxmi station. **Box office** 10am-6pm daily. **No credit cards.**

► *Hop across to the Planetarium to see stars and planets; see p141.*

Sivaswamy Auditorium

The Fine Arts Society, Fine Arts Chowk, RC Marg, Chembur (2522-2988). Chembur station. **Taxi** near Chembur Flyover. **Box office** 10am-6pm daily. **No credit cards.**

Goa

Benaulim beach. *See p219.*

wouldn't you rather
be at cidade?
CIDADE DE GOA®
Goa in a resort
www.cidadedegoa.com

Getting Started

India's smallest state packs a powerful punch.

Goa is the smallest state in the subcontinent by a considerable margin, but its pocket-sized charms still exert a powerful allure. The difference becomes apparent immediately on arrival – subcontinental bustle and jostling give way to measured languor and charming smiles, and the skies clear to a distant horizon. Just 3,700 square kilometres (1,429 square miles), with a population of 1.5 million, this is where the crowded cityscapes of urban India yield to coconut groves and rice paddies, and the blare of car horns yields to birdcalls and the insistent whisper of sea on sand.

LIE OF THE LAND

Goa's landscape is remarkably varied, ranging from the thickly forested Western Ghats mountain range on its interior border through lush river valleys, to the beaches of its roughly 120-kilometre (75-mile) coast. It has a tropical climate, with average temperatures of 25-30°C from November to April, and up to 40° with high humidity in October and May. The Goan monsoon lasts from early June to late September, with the heaviest rains in July. Between highland mining areas lie protected reserves that feature great biodiversity, including leopards, hundreds of bird species, crocodiles, wild boar, and the occasional tiger and elephant. Another resident is the gaur, the largest wild cattle species in the world, and the state's official animal.

GETTING THERE

More information on getting there and around is given in individual Goa chapters.

From Mumbai

BY AIR

Over 20 direct flights make the short hop from Mumbai to Goa each day. Jet Airways (www.jetairways.com) and Air India (1800-180-1407,www.airindia.in) offer impressive service and inflight meals, but you might find better deals from Kingfisher Airlines (1800-1800-101, www.flykingfisher.com), or low cost airlines Deccan (3900-8888, www.airdeccan.net), GoAir (1800-222-111, www.goair.in), Indigo (1800-180-3838, www.goindigo.in) and SpiceJet (1800-180-3333, www.spicejet.com). For easy booking, metasearch websites such as www.cleartrip.com and www.makemytrip.co.in crawl through various airline websites and present all available flights on a single page. One-way flights range from Rs 2,000 to Rs 5,500. Book at least a week ahead in the peak winter season.

BY BUS

Dozens of bus services make the 12- to 14-hour trip from Mumbai to Goa each day, from decrepit decades-old coaches to comfortable modern Volvo behemoths with air-conditioning and reclining seats. Go for the latter. Paulo Travels (022-2645-2624 Mumbai, 0832-243-8531/37 Panjim, www.paulotravels.com) is the biggest coach company, with daily services. Return fares range from Rs 700 to Rs 1,400.

BY TRAIN

Trains chug into Goa five times each day from Mumbai. The 11-hour trip offers magnificent views of the Ghats and the lush riverine plains of the Konkan coastline if you travel in the daytime, or you can take a sleeper overnight and be there fresh in the morning. The major stops are Tivim for North Goa, Karmali for Panjim and Margao for South Goa. You can book online (www.konkanrailway.com, www.irctc.co.in) but it can tend to be a little complicated. In peak season berths can be hard to come by, but there's a 'foreigners' quota' for one-way tickets (*see p229*). Return tickets for berths in air-conditioned carriages range from Rs 1,600 to Rs 3,500.

GOA

GETTING AROUND

BY AUTORICKSHAW

Unlike Mumbai, autorickshaws are neither plentiful nor hassle-free, so it's best to approach with caution; you have to bargain hard for a price that's outlandish anywhere else in the country. But they're good for short trips and can usually be rented by the hour or day. A half-day rental costs around Rs 250.

BY BUS

Goa has a well-connected bus network, with stops in every major village. Buses aren't particularly clean or punctual, but they are cheap; a ride from Panjim to Candolim, for example, costs just Rs 12. Non-stop Kadamba shuttle buses run between major towns, charging Rs 7-Rs 20.

THE BEST BEACHES

For idyllic lazing

Once deserted, most of Palolem is now firmly on the beaten track, but neighbouring **Agonda** is a good place to get a taste of the idyllic experience that put Goa on the global tourism map (*see p221*).

For following the hippie trail

The legendary paradise beach of the 1970s hippie scene, **Arambol** retains an edgy counter-cultural atmosphere (*see p201*).

For getting back to nature

Morjim and **Ashvem** are a half-hour drive from the tourist hub of North Goa, but a world away in atmosphere. A few protected Olive Ridley turtles come here every year to lay eggs, fending off most major construction in the process (*see p197*).

For an escape from the tourists

The last undeveloped beach in North Goa, **Keri** remains a long and almost empty stretch of sand, where you can sit blissfully alone in the shadow of casuarinas trees (*see p202*).

For watching locals at play

Miramar Beach in Panjim isn't safe for swimming but it is impressively broad, and well situated at the mouth of the Mandovi. Crowds of Indian tourists and Panjim residents head to the water to watch the sunset in a pleasant, convivial atmosphere (*see p210*).

BY MOTORCYCLE

Goa's motorcycle taxis are known as 'pilots', whose bikes are distinguished by their bright yellow front fenders, with the name of the 'home stand' painted on. Designated stands can be found near all main bus stops, and village and city markets. Around Rs 12.5 per Kilometre.

BY FERRY

Goa's rickety, slow-moving, flat-bottomed ferries offer a scenic way to cross the state's many rivers. Pedestrians ride for free and two-wheelers are charged Rs 10, cars Rs 15. Ferries on the Mandovi cross from Betim Jetty to Panjim, from Ribandar to Divar and Chorao, from Old Goa to Divar, and from Pomburpa to Chorao. They ply on the River Zuari from Agassaim to Cortalim and the River Tiracol from Keri to Tiracol.

BICYCLE RENTAL

Much of Goa's coast is flat and perfect for bikes. Bicycles can be rented for around Rs 50-Rs 100 per day; look for signs near village bus stands, or ask at the nearest petrol station. Be careful: drivers show little consideration for cyclists.

MOTORCYCLE RENTAL

Hundreds of people informally rent out motorbikes and scooters; you'll see them advertised everywhere in the coastal areas. Paulo Travels offers two-wheeler rentals available from its garage near the Mahalaxmi Temple in Panjim (0832-243-8531/8537; scooter Rs 300 per day, 100cc motorbike Rs 400 per day, Enfield Bullet Rs 450 per day.) Two-wheelers are well suited for Goa's narrow roads and parking is rarely a problem. Check the vehicle carefully before renting because you will be asked to pay for any damage.

TAXIS & CAR RENTALS

Goa's semi-regulated taxi industry can create headaches for tourists. Drivers routinely charge extortionate rates. If you intend to run around a bit, hire one for the day for around Rs 1,000. Most car rentals include a driver; drive-your-own deals offer only negligible savings. Reliable taxis and rentals are available from Joey's in Panjim (0832-222-8989, fully insured Hyundai Santro Rs 1,000 per day) and Vailankanni in Candolim (0832-248-9047/9658, Hyundai Santro Rs 800 per day, cheaper rates for long rentals). Parking is often a pain.

TOURIST INFORMATION

Directorate of Tourism

Rua de Ourem Patto, Panjim (0832-222-6515).
Open 9.30am-1.15pm, 2-5.45pm daily.

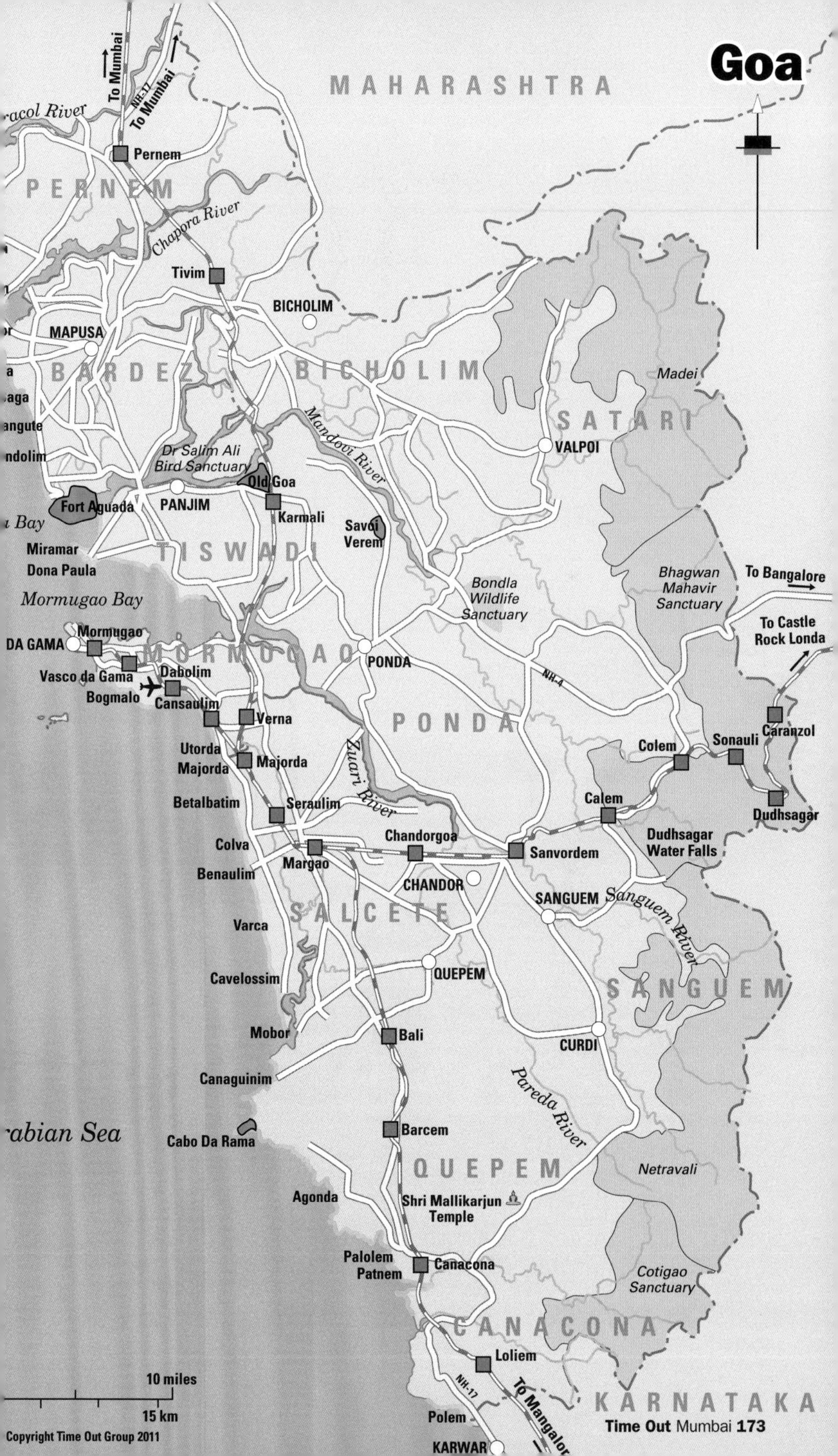
Goa
MAHARASHTRA
To Mumbai
NH-17
To Mumbai
Pernem
PERNEM
Chapora River
Tivim
BICHOLIM
MAPUSA
BARDEZ
BICHOLIM
Madei
SATARI
VALPOI
Mandovi River
Dr Salim Ali
Bird Sanctuary
Old Goa
Fort Aguada
PANJIM
Karmali
Savoi
Verem
TISWADI
Miramar
Dona Paula
Mormugao Bay
Bondla
Wildlife
Sanctuary
Bhagwan
Mahavir
Sanctuary
To Bangalore
To Castle
Rock Londa
Mormugao
DA GAMA
MORMUGAO
PONDA
NH-4
Vasco da Gama
Dabolim
Bogmalo
Cansaulim
Verna
PONDA
Caranzol
Colem
Sonauli
Utorda
Majorda
Majorda
Zuari River
Calem
Dudhsagar
Betalbatim
Seraulim
Dudhsagar
Water Falls
Chandorgoa
Colva
Margao
Sanvordem
Benaulim
CHANDOR
SANGUEM
Sanguem River
SALCETE
Varca
QUEPEM
Cavelossim
SANGUEM
Mobor
Bali
CURDI
Canaguinim
Pareda River
Arabian Sea
Cabo Da Rama
Barcem
QUEPEM
Netravali
Agonda
Shri Mallikarjun
Temple
Palolem
Patnem
Canacona
Cotigao
Sanctuary
CANACONA
Loliem
NH-17
To Mangalore
KARNATAKA
10 miles
15 km
Polem
KARWAR

Goa in Context

A history apart from the rest of the subcontinent

Goa's distinct character set it somewhat apart from the rest of the subcontinent even many centuries before the Portuguese colonial episode, which was to set the state on a different course to the rest of India for almost 500 years. It experienced other invasions too, both bellicose – in the form of various conquerors – and peace-loving in the form of the hippies that came in the 1970s. Some of the latter still remain, lending a relaxed, alternative vibe to an area that's a hit with Muscovites and Mumbaikars alike.

GOAN HISTORY

The territory had always been an entrepot for trade with the rich hinterlands of the Deccan, and a window on the outside world for Indian kingdoms. For centuries, the ports of Goa were the main points of entry for the weapons of mass destruction of the times – Arabian warhorses – into the fiercely contested neighbouring kingdoms. This trade continued for centuries, with many Arab traders settling in Goa. The territory was fitfully exchanged between subcontinental empires and then remained stable for 500 years under the Kadamba Dynasty, which ruled a kingdom that stretched far into the rest of India from its capital on the Zuari River. But the relatively tolerant atmosphere changed in 1312, when Muslim armies from the Delhi Sultanate swept into power, destroying temples built by the Kadambas. Just 30 years later, the Delhi Sultanate was itself challenged by a breakaway group from the Deccan, the Bahamanis, who unleashed another orgy of destruction. Both were finally displaced by the Hindu kings of Vijaynagar, who oversaw an interlude of prosperity and relative calm.

Successive waves of conquerors were lured by Goa's superb ports and lucrative trade. By the late 15th century, Goa had fallen under the control of the Sultanate of Bijapur, a splinter of the Bahamani Empire ruled by the Turkish-born Sultan Yusuf Adil Shah. Under his relatively enlightened rule, Goa developed once again into a rich trading post and crossroads between East and West, crowded by ships from Arabia and the Far East.

In 1497, the Portuguese explorer Vasco da Gama made a historic turn round the Horn of Africa and set off towards the Indian coast. The Portuguese kingdom had recently emerged independent from Moorish domination and da Gama was determined to wrest control of the near-priceless spice trade from the Arabs, and win souls for Christendom. On his first trip, da Gama landed to the south of Goa in Calicut. There he harvested no souls but gathered plenty of black pepper – a treasure that made his fortune back in Lisbon, and spurred all future European colonial adventures in the Indian Ocean.

Vasco da Gama actually never made it to Goa. But his successor, Afonso de Albuquerque, kept his eye on the territory on a trading voyage to Calicut, where he received word that Goan Hindus were unsatisfied with the rule of the Sultan of Bijapur. They were struggling under heavy taxes and would support a transfer of possession to these unknown foreigners should they manage to take control. Albuquerque duly seized what is now Old Goa on 1 March 1510. The Bijapuris briefly regained possession but were ejected by the Portuguese in a bloody rout nine months later.

The first colonial possession of the Portuguese was Tiswadi, a huge promontory containing two excellent natural harbours between the Mandovi and Zuari rivers. In time, the Portuguese added the territories of Bardez and Salcete, lands that are still commonly known as the 'Old Conquests'. By the middle of the 16th century, the Estado da India had developed into one of the great international trading outposts, and a magnet for foreign adventurers. A new elite of Portuguese (and

Fertility Feast

Phallic monument.

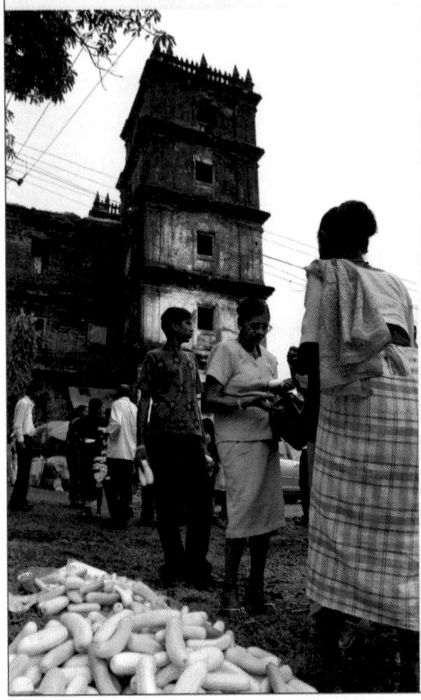

The grandest baroque structure from Goa's colonial period isn't among the churches that make up Old Goa's UNESCO-designated World Heritage precinct. Instead, the genuinely magnificent Church of St Anne is some distance away in the ancient village of Talaulim, standing alone in a landscape of laterite ruins that are covered by thick jungle, at the rim of a vast bowl of rice fields. This outsized building, described by the World Monument Fund as 'a living treasure', stands empty most of the year, with only the sun's rays to light up its lavishly detailed plaster interior. But on its feast day of 26 July, Santana de Talaulim, as the church is popularly known, draws thousands of Hindus and Christians to a fertility-oriented 'cucumber feast', where offerings of cucumbers are reputed to yield unfailing results of male offspring.

It's not easy to get to Santana de Talaulim by public transport, despite its proximity to Panjim (5km) and to National Highway 17 (3km). Take NH-17 to the junction with Goa Velha, and then stick to the sole village road that runs north on a winding path through fields and backwaters, and winds up at the foot of the church's imposing laterite stairways.

other European) administrators and soldiers were married off to the widows and daughters of the erstwhile ruling class. Franciscan, Jesuit, Dominican and Augustinian priests arrived in Goa and were each granted territories in which to begin the process of converting native Goans to Catholicism. A unique European-Indian cultural exchange began that would completely remake Goa, and eventually affect the entire subcontinent. Chillies first entered India via Goa, as did cashews, corn, potatoes, papayas and countless other imports now taken for granted, including Asia's first modern printing press, medical college, public library and lighthouse.

THE ERA OF 'GOLDEN GOA'

By the end of the 16th century, the Portuguese-controlled city that mushroomed on the bank of the Mandovi was one of the richest places in the world, a crowded metropolis bigger than London or Paris, and home to what are still the largest church and convent complexes in Asia. Portugal itself has no religious buildings on this grand scale. The territory became known as Goa Dourada, or 'Golden Goa', and was of as much importance to the Portuguese court as Lisbon itself. It raked in such vast profits that it came under constant threat from envious newcomers to the Indian Ocean trade. The Dutch levelled crippling blockades against the city twice in the early decades of the 17th century, and a series of plagues devastated the European population. And the Inquisition chased off or killed the large population of Jews who had provided the mercantile backbone to the Estado da India. Eventually, however, Portuguese interest in the colony waned, as the royal court became preoccupied with its new holdings in Brazil. The colony, too, was occasionally threatened by the Marathas to the north, and was almost conquered by Shivaji's Maratha Confederacy before the Mughals distracted them away, and so Goa remained in European hands.

From the 18th century, a native aristocracy steadily gained power and influence at the cost of a distracted ruling class in Lisbon. This cadre of converted upper-caste landlords and the offspring of Indo-Portuguese marriages

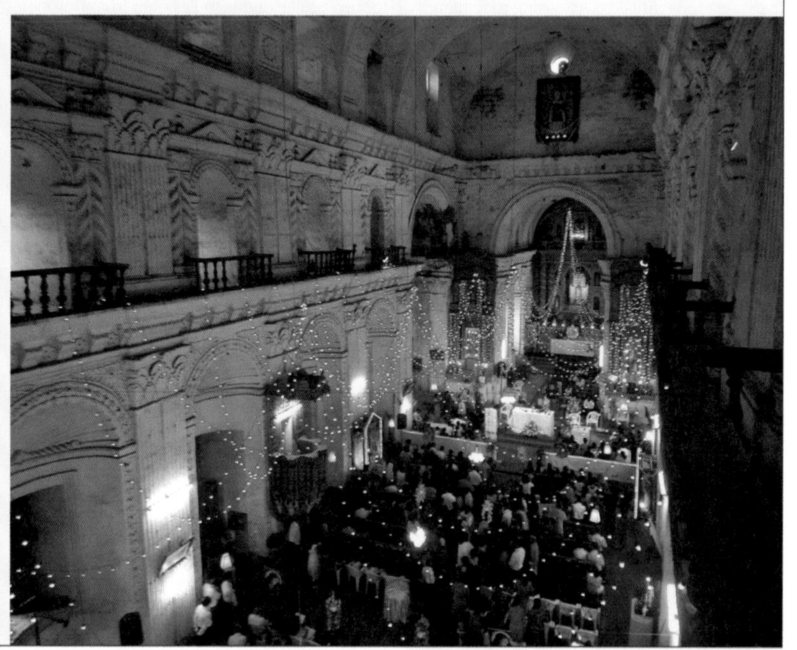

embarked on a spate of estate building that left a permanent mark on Goa's landscape, a constellation of agrarian villages organised in a largely feudal manner, with a few landlords holding sway over large numbers of subject tenants. Unlike British India, there was never any colonial emphasis on secular education, infrastructure improvement or the exploitation of natural resources. Goans began to leave their homeland to pursue opportunity elsewhere, initially to the Portuguese territories in Africa and Asia.

During the Napoleonic Wars, when British troops were stationed in Goa to deter French attacks, the aspirations of ambitious Goans shifted to the British Empire. Thousands of Goans left to work in British cantonments in India and in British East African colonies where they became administrators, clerks, cooks, musicians and ayahs or nannies. Their success further transformed their native villages – as Graham Greene noted in the late 1960s, there is a significant and affluent middle class across the territory of Goa that was entirely absent in the rest of India until very recently.

LIBERATION

At the end of World War II, the writing was on the wall for the European imperial project. India became independent in a cataclysm of sectarian violence in 1947, and the Portuguese immediately came under heavy pressure to hand Goa over to the new Indian government.

But though there were only a few dozen Portuguese officials left in the territory, the fascist dictator Salazar declared that it would remain eternally Portuguese and embarked on a violent, occasionally lavish campaign to persuade Goans that their future lay with Portugal and not the Indian republic. The majority of Goans became increasingly impatient for change, and increasingly radicalised when Portuguese police responded to minor provocations with heavy-handed tactics, including firing on unarmed crowds and mercilessly beating peaceful protesters.

Meanwhile, Salazar's own secret reports indicated that support for the Portuguese colonial regime had dwindled to less than ten percent of the population. In 1961, India's first prime minister, Jawaharlal Nehru, sent in the army and took Goa virtually unopposed on 19 December, ending the European colonial era on Indian soil. Almost immediately afterwards, Goan voters rejected a proposal to merge with the state of Maharashtra, choosing to remain a territory administered by the central government. On 30 May 1987, Goa finally became a full-fledged state of the Indian Union and Konkani became an official national language.

GOA TODAY

Goa's tourism development in the last 30 years has been anything but relaxed. The northern coastal strip from Aguada to Arambol has a vibrant, noisy, multinational resort culture, with restaurants lined along winding access roads and hundreds of beach shacks crowding the dunes. None of this existed when the first tourists started arriving in Goa in the 1970s, when backpackers and hippies trickled in on an overland route from Europe. They found idyllic, empty beaches fringed with thick coconut groves, and friendly locals familiar with Westerners. The so-called 'Goa Freaks' lived hedonistic lives on the cheap, giving the state an international reputation as a party paradise *par excellence*, with unbeatable sunsets, memorable moonlight parties and a cheap and plentiful supply of drugs and alcohol (*see p184* **Hippie and You Know It**).

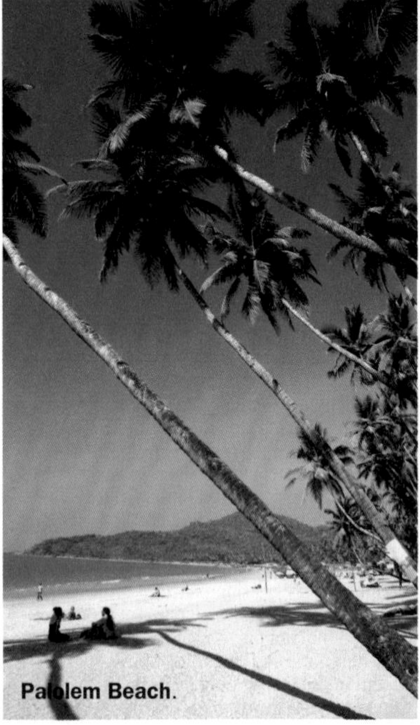
Palolem Beach.

In the mid 1980s, charter operators began to run regular flights to Dabolim from Europe despite vocal resistance from local activists who issued prescient warnings of dangerous environmental and social damage from mass tourism. The first charters patronised five-star hotels, which then made up almost all of the tourism infrastructure, but small hotels and guesthouses immediately proliferated to occupy the rest of the beachfront landscape as local entrepreneurs rushed to cash in on the emerging tourism boom. More than two million foreign and domestic tourists now visit Goa every year, a number set to rise as Indians travel more. In recent years, there's been a clear shift from budget accommodation to the boutique hotel, with some stunning and unique properties such as **Pousada Tauma** (*see p190*) offering visitors exclusive and luxurious surroundings with price-tags to match. Thousands of foreigners and an equal number of India's moneyed elite have bought property and permanently settled in Goa in the last seven years, seeking a high standard of living at prices that are a fraction of almost anywhere else.

A giant new international airport is under construction at Mopa in North Goa, which is sure to tilt the balance decisively towards greater mass tourism. Deep-pocketed foreign and Indian developers are racing to meet the projected demand. But the majority of Goans bemoan what is happening to their once-peaceful land. An impressive show of force in 2007 halted a controversial Regional Plan that would have opened huge swathes of the hinterland to real estate and other development, but recent setbacks have opened the door for India's biggest property developers nonetheless.

Mainstream Goan society also remains resolutely opposed to drug use, rave parties and trance tourists, who are seen as an immoral influence on their relatively conservative society. Responding to a series of legal judgements, raves have been banned by the Goa state government since the 2005-06 tourist season, though some underground parties still take place in and around Arambol in the north and near Palolem in the south. It's hard to predict what will happen next to the rave sub-culture that spawned the globally popular Goa Trance groove. While it is unlikely to recover its past glories, parties are certain to continue on a smaller, more discreet scale.

There is also widespread anger about illegal construction, the abuse of strict coastal land laws, and the state government's decision to allow casinos to operate in the Mandovi River opposite the state capital, Panjim. Legislation

Invasion vs Liberation

Over four decades of occupation?

2010 was a significant year for the Goans – it was the 500th anniversary of the arrival of Alfonso da Albuquerque and the military takeover of the territory by the Iberian conquistadors. The anniversary was universally acknowledged but there were no public ceremonies of any kind. This is partly because of the looming anniversary on 19 December 2011, which marks 50 years since the final nail in the coffin of the 451-year-old Portuguese Estado da India, and the military takeover of the territory by Indian troops.

In the official terminology, the latter date is referred to as Liberation. But many Goans reject that word as propaganda, and refer to the takeover as the Invasion and point out that it has had similar repercussions to the European invasion centuries past. In both cases, the concerns of the majority of Goans were ignored by the conquering forces, and local interests have been ceaselessly trampled in favour of the diktats of a faraway capital and its elites. In recent years, Goans have become increasingly vocal about what they see as a demographic tsunami from the subcontinent that is rapidly changing the essential character of their homeland, and have begun to petition for special status (such as enjoyed by Indian states like Kashmir and Meghalaya) which would bar property purchase by non-Goans.

There's very little likelihood of this happening at this stage, however, and the result of local disgruntlement has been a steady wave of migration by both Hindu and Catholic Goans to the big Indian cities, and to Australia and to Europe, assisted by the current Portuguese policy of awarding passports to anyone with a grandparent born in the old Estado da India.

forbids new permanent construction within 500 metres of the high-tide line and restricts it for another 500 metres. These laws have been blatantly flouted along the entire coastline of the state, often with the connivance of government officials. The state claims to have several hundred cases ready for 'appropriate action', a claim at which most Goans ruefully laugh. The number of illegal developments has clearly mounted far higher, and transgressors include many of the five-star hotels in the state. However, with the real estate and tourism lobbies hand-in-glove with a thoroughly corrupt political class, a serious effort to deal with illegal developments seems unlikely.

CULTURE AND COMMUNITIES

Despite 250 years of the Portuguese Inquisition, a ruthless regime which lasted from 1560 to 1812, Hindus have always been the majority population in Goa, though you might not guess it from all those whitewashed churches. Hindus now make up around 65 per cent of the population, with the same caste divisions as the rest of India. In recent years, Goa has felt a surge in right-wing Hinduism, part of a nationwide phenomenon, but it remains relatively free of religious feuding. In early 2006, Goa experienced its first religious riot when a mob vandalised Muslim businesses in Sanvordem. Public reaction was nearly unanimous in condemnation; Goa's communities tend to respect (and even worship at) each other's holy sites, even as they maintain a certain social distance from each other.

Christians in Goa have tenaciously hung on to caste affiliations, though these have been adapted into three broad categories – Brahmin, Chardo (or Kshatriya) and Sudra (*see p38* **Stuck in the Caste**). Despite the strenuous efforts of the Portuguese, strict Christian conservatism never really took root in Goa. The majority of Goan Catholics continue to cherish the indigenous influences that have helped create a mystical, goddess-centred Christianity with deep roots in pre-colonial Goan culture and beliefs.

Islam has a long history in Goa but today Muslims have a small presence, grown through migration from nearby states and Kashmir.

Konkani is the native language of Goa and remains ubiquitous despite centuries of colonial efforts to eradicate it. By law, all state-funded primary schools must teach in Konkani, and there are hundreds of Konkani books published each year. Readership is dwindling, however, as the language steadily loses relevance in the face of competition from giant national media markets for English and Hindi. Portuguese is surprisingly widespread, and there is a recent upsurge in interest in studying the language as a new post-colonial generation has become interested in their own cultural roots.

North Goa

Still feeling the hippie buzz half a decade on.

North Goa is the epicentre of the tourism scene in Goa, and has been ever since the iconic Goa Freaks settled on its then-remote beaches almost 50 years ago. In the decades since the arrival of the hippies, North Goa's clutch of pristine sands have transformed into a multicultural Indian tourism power house, with thousands of permanent resident expatriates from around the world, and almost two million visitors a year. But it's not just Russians, Israelis, Brits and Germans that want a slice – Indians want a slice, too.

INTRODUCTION

The original hippie trail of the early 1960s started off in Europe, and proceeded slowly overland through Turkey and Iran to Pakistan, and then on through Kathmandu and other parts of the Himalayas all the way down to a handful of remote beaches inset in the rocky coastline of North Goa. The beachfront stretches all the way from the **Aguada Plateau**, which drops to the Mandovi River, to the **Tiracol Fort** on the Maharashtra border – a drive you can make in about two hours. In between, there's charter tourism congestion in **Candolim**, the Indian middle class packing the sands of **Calangute**, party central for India's twentysomethings at **Baga**, and the sprawling luxury villas of India's rich and famous in **Sinquerim**. Further up the coast are the dream beaches of the '60s hippie trail, the first of which was **Anjuna**, where a remnant of septuagenarian Goa Freaks lingers on in a wildly international mix that still retains its alternative vibe. There's also the more edgy **Chapora** and **Vagator**, where cafés are jammed with tokers openly puffing on smokestack-sized chillums under the watchful gaze of well-connected locals.

North of Vagator, the beaches begin to empty out and some are relatively deserted. **Morjim**, where protected Olive Ridley sea turtles still come to lay eggs on the beach, now hosts a thriving Russian community that peaks in the tens of thousands at year-end. **Ashvem**, with its rugged rock outcrops and windswept sands, is home to Goa's best beach restaurant, **La Plage** (*see p199*). Beyond **Mandrem**'s unique marriage of swift-running freshwater and ocean surf, all roads lead to the legendary **Arambol**, where latter-day versions of the first flower children spend months living in thatched huts under coconut palms. In peak season, your day on the beach here could easily be spent with 20,000 other travellers, with Hebrew as the lingua franca and waiters and hawkers the only Indians in sight. Apart from the beaches, North Goa is also home to some of the most ambitious restaurants in India, including Burmese, Turkish, Italian and French establishments – and now there's a whole slew of Russian, Bulgarian and even Uzbek restaurants that cater to the Eastern European travellers who are now by far Goa's largest foreign contingent.

North Goa's attractions aren't just confined to the coast, they extend to hill-hugging cashew plantations that blanket much of **Pernem** (Goa's *feni*-producing heartland), the noisy riot of colours that is **Mapusa** market in the heart of Bardez district, and the hidden, curiously hybrid Hindu temples of **Ponda**.

SINQUERIM & FORT AGUADA

Goa tourism began here, at the far end of what was once a pristine 6.5 kilometre stretch of broad golden sand lined with rolling dunes and backed by hectares of coconut plantations. Long before strict coastal development laws, the hotel arm of the Indian business house Tata built a sprawling five-star hotel complex amid the crumbling ruins of an early 17th-century Portuguese fortress. The **Fort Aguada Beach Resort** threw open the floodgates to mass tourism when it started operations in 1972.

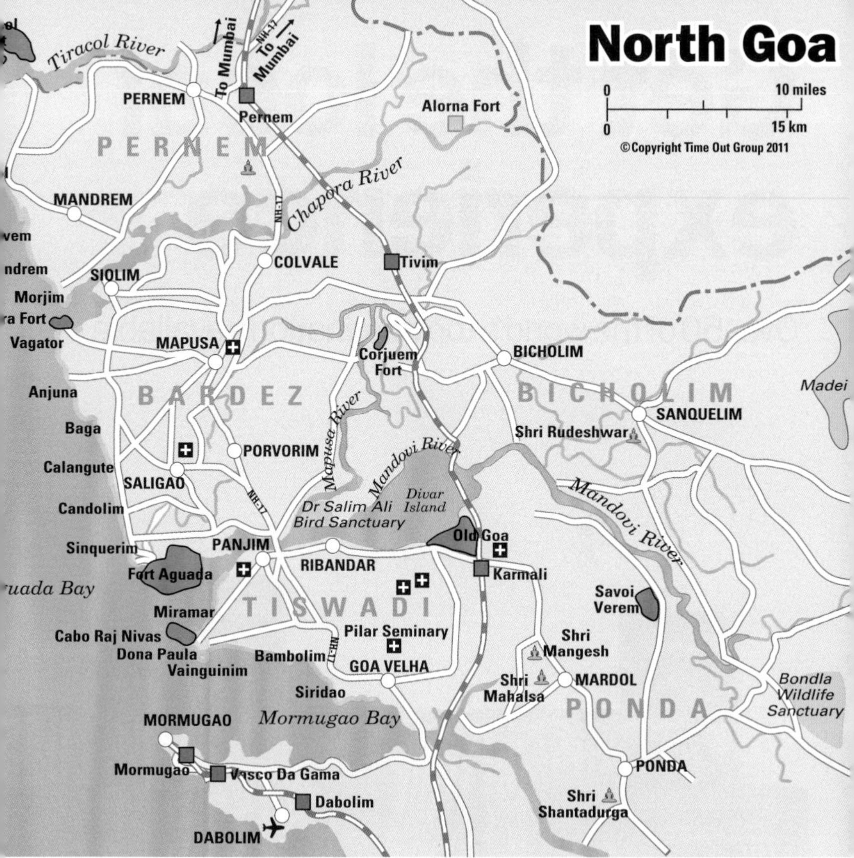

By the late '90s, the beach had become lined elbow-to-elbow with beach shacks and a warren of hotels, shopping centres, pubs, restaurants and supermarkets. The plateau atop the Sinquerim headland, near the modern, squat **Aguada Lighthouse**, offers one of the best ocean views in Goa, with the wide mouths of the Mandovi and Zuari rivers on one side, and that glorious beach on the other. Next door sits its ancestor – the first lighthouse in Asia, built by the Portuguese in 1864.

Under the lighthouse is the low-rise complex of Goa's main prison, the **Fort Aguada Jail**, once packed with anti-colonial activists in the days of the Portuguese, now home to local crooks plus a couple of dozen foreigners busted under India's very severe but selectively applied anti-drug laws. The nearby **Church of St Lawrence** (open for Sunday Mass at 8am), built in 1630, commands another spectacular view of the Mandovi River, receding to the east.

Down the hill, past a curve overlooking the quiet **Nerul River**, tourist development takes over both sides of the road. The Fort Aguada hotel complex covers almost 36 hectares (90 acres) onto the beachfront right up to its sister **Taj Holiday Village**. The Taj is now building a massive stone bulwark to protect the property from the rapid, destructive beach erosion that has followed the grounding of the *River Princess*, a huge iron-ore cargo ship, during a storm in 2001. The rusting hulk is still stuck just off the beach, as its powerful mining-company owner fights through the courts to ensure he never has to pay the huge cost of removing it. At the time of writing it looked likely that the Indian government had finally arranged for a contractor to remove the ship, which is breaking into pieces. Off the road, just beyond the gardens of the Taj complex, is the palatial entranceway to **Kingfisher Villa**, the private pleasure palace of flamboyant brewery and airline tycoon Vijay Mallya (he makes Kingfisher beer). Around New Year, these gates are jammed with eager locals and frantic paparazzi clamouring to catch a glimpse of Mallya's celeb-heavy guest list.

Aguada Lighthouse. *See p181.*

Where to eat & drink

Sinquerim and Fort Aguada are the most expensive parts of the North Goan tourism strip, so expect high prices. The **Banyan Tree** (Taj Holiday Village, 0832-664-5858, main course Rs 350, noon-2.30pm, 7.30-10.30pm daily), one of Goa's best Thai restaurants, sits beside a magnificent specimen of its namesake in the Taj Holiday Village. North of Fort Aguada, there's **Santa Lucia** (Fort Aguada Road, 0832-561-5213, main course Rs 180, 6.30-10.30pm daily), a tiny, relaxed terrace restaurant serving Italian and Swiss food.

Nightlife

Near the Taj Holiday Village is **Sweet Chilli Garden Restaurant & Lounge** (Lighthouse Road, 0832-247-9446, main course Rs 120, 11am-midnight daily), a popular open-air restaurant on several levels, with live music every night. Down the road towards Candolim is **Butter** (98221-26262, main course Rs 150, noon-midnight), a stylish lounge and live music venue that hosts busy parties every weekend.

Entertainment

Although Sinquerim Beach has been cut to a tiny sliver of its former breadth by the erosion caused by the marooned ore-carrier *River Princess*, it's still a good centre for water sports. Morgan D'Souza of **Thunder Waves** (on the beach near Fort Aguada, 98221-76986, 9am-sunset daily) offers dolphin trips (Rs 500 per head for a half-hour excursion), speedboat-driven parasailing from the beach (Rs 1,000-Rs 1,500 for 5-10mins), and jetskiing (Rs 1,000 for 15mins). The Taj Aguada has one of the best spas in India, **Jiva** (0832-664-5858, 8am-8pm daily), which offers massages from Rs 750.

Where to stay

The **Fort Aguada Beach Resort** (Fort Aguada, 0832-664-5858, www.tajhotels.com, Rs 7,000-Rs 11,000 double), the luxury tourism pioneer, is showing its age and might not live up to the hype, but it's still the playground for India's A-list, especially at New Year. The **Taj Holiday Village** (0832-664-5858, www.tajhotels.com, Rs 8,000-Rs 9,000 double) offers attractive individual villas with private balconies. Near the Taj is the **Marbella Guesthouse** (Fort Aguada Beach Road, near Jojo's Corner restaurant, 0832-247-9551, Rs 1,200-Rs 2,500 double) with six eccentrically decorated but well-appointed rooms in a pretty house under a mango tree.

Getting there

Tivim is the nearest train stop to the north beaches; the half-hour taxi ride from Tivim to Sinquerim costs Rs 350. From Dabolim Airport, it's Rs 650 and takes an hour. From Panjim, take the Mandovi Bridge towards Mapusa and turn left off the NH-17 at O Coqueiro junction. Turn left at St Alex Church and Sinquerim is 5 kilometres down the road. Taxis cost Rs 250 from Panjim.

Hippie and You Know It

Trance tourism trundles on.

In 1969, Gilbert Levey left the Haight-Ashbury district of San Francisco and took the overland trail through Afghanistan and Pakistan, first to Bombay and then Goa. He'd been a roadie for Sons of Champlain, a pioneering acid rock band, but in India he studied spirituality, and eventually adopted the saffron robes and matted hair of a Hindu sadhu, or wise man, and became Goa Gil, a pioneer of the early hippie scene at Anjuna Beach. Throughout the 1970s, Gil organised legendary parties at Anjuna – moonlight jams of non-stop music, dancing and chemical experimentation that lasted from Christmas Eve to New Year's Day for a tribe of fellow overland travellers who called themselves the Goa Freaks. Gil describes these epic parties as efforts to 'tell the story of humanity'.

In the '90s, Gil started to use snippets from industrial music, ethno-techno, acid house and psychedelic rock to help create Goa Trance, dance music with a heavy spiritual accent. Today, the genre has morphed into a global multi-million-dollar industry and is played at clubs as far away as New York, Iceland and Israel. Gil survives at the centre of the scene, DJing full-moon parties around the world in what he calls attempts 'to redefine ancient tribal ritual for the 21st century' and 'to uplift the consciousness of the participants', although a cynic might say that drugs have as much to do with that as the music. For Gil, Goa Trance is a logical continuation of what hippies were doing back in the '60s and '70s. 'The Psychedelic Revolution never really stopped,' he said. 'It just had to go halfway round the world to the end of a dirt road on a deserted beach, and there it was allowed to evolve and mutate, without government or media pressures.'

But government pressure did catch up with the revolution in Goa. Because of their association with drugs, raves are viewed with suspicion by a local government anxious to mend the state's reputation as a destination for low-rent travellers. Raves have been banned entirely since the 2005-06 tourist season, while the flow of drugs has continued uninterrupted. Still, dance parties do take place, sometimes starting at 4am on remote beaches, or in forests. Ask staff at local bars and the 'pilots' who operate motorcycle taxis to find out when and where the next party is happening.

NERUL (COCO BEACH)

Before the beach road hits Candolim, a sharp right turn on to a narrow, scenic road leads to Nerul and Coco Beach on the Mandovi River, with views of the Panjim waterfront. Nerul feels slightly schizophrenic, alternating between the ultra-luxurious villas of Indian and foreign millionaires, and small village homes of local fishermen and farmers. The beach is popular with Goan families, wealthy Indians and older Europeans. The water off Coco Beach is a little murkier than that of Candolim or Calangute but it is clean and safe to swim out to a distance of about 100 metres.

Where to eat & drink

Under the Nerul Bridge (off which Matt Damon crashed a car in the action film *The Bourne Supremacy*) is **Amigo's** (0832-240-1123, main course Rs 120, 11am-10.30pm daily), a local-run restaurant in a beautiful spot on the mangrove-fringed riverbank, with strong ties to local fisherfolk – hence the super-fresh mussels, shrimp and estuarine crabs.

CANDOLIM

Once a deserted expanse of banyan trees and soaring palm trees, Candolim is now mass tourism's ground zero in Goa. It's a maze of lanes and byways lined with hundreds of guesthouses, shops and restaurants and choked with traffic in peak season. Candolim is the heart of the British invasion, both by budget travellers and expatriates, and abounds with fish-and-chip shops and pubs festooned with Premier League memorabilia. Candolim is as close as Goa gets to mass-tourism hotspots like Cancun and the Costa del Sol, but it's still reasonably relaxed and has some excellent restaurants hidden among the neon-lit also-rans. Unlike the beaches to the north, Candolim is a one-stop vacation destination – everything you need is within walking distance.

In the interior of the village, just over a kilometre from the main road, the impressive **Our Lady of Hope Church** (open for Sunday mass 5.45pm) sits on an elevated location with a good view of the carefully tended bund (earthen dam) system that keeps the surrounding farmland protected from flooding from the

Nerul marshes. The sluices for these bunds are called *kandoli* in Konkani – hence the name Candolim. The village played a prominent role in Goan history, and was the site of a major campaign of revolt against Portuguese rule in 1787 led by disaffected Catholic priests, including the clergyman father of the adventurer-hypnotist Abbé Faria (*see p208* **All the fun of the Faria**). The revolt was put down, but locals proudly refer to the episode as just the second anti-colonial uprising in history after the American Revolution of 1776. In the north of the village stands the Casa dos Monteiros, a beautifully preserved 17th-century private home. It can be approached from the road, but unfortunately for those interested in exploring, just like the similarly impressive **Casa dos Costa-Frias** near Bosio Hospital, no visitors are allowed.

Where to eat & drink

Candolim has some of Goa's best restaurants, but the stand-out eaterie here is **Bomra's** (Souza Vaddo, 98221-06236, main course Rs 300, 7-10pm Mon-Sat, closed Apr-Sept), which serves innovative versions of Burmese and Kachin dishes, prepared by a London-trained Burmese chef. Opened in the 2006 season, Bomra's has received lots of attention and makes a credible claim to being the world's best Burmese restaurant. Another unusual eating option is **Cuckoo Zen Garden** (near Bob's Inn, Ximer, 98221-26031, www.cuckoozen.com, main course Rs 150, 7-11pm Mon-Sat, closed Apr-Sept), run by an eccentric commune of Taiwanese (with names like Soup and Elephant) who live in the shadow of Cuckoo, a Taiwanese acupuncturist and self-styled Zen master. Down the road, near Tarcar ice factory, is **Lloyd's** (94224-38230, main course Rs 120, 7pm-6am Mon-Sat), a basic space with dismal bathrooms that becomes extremely popular late at night for alcohol-soaked home-cooked dinners including Goan-style spare ribs. The beach road opposite the Tarcar ice factory leads to the Italian-run

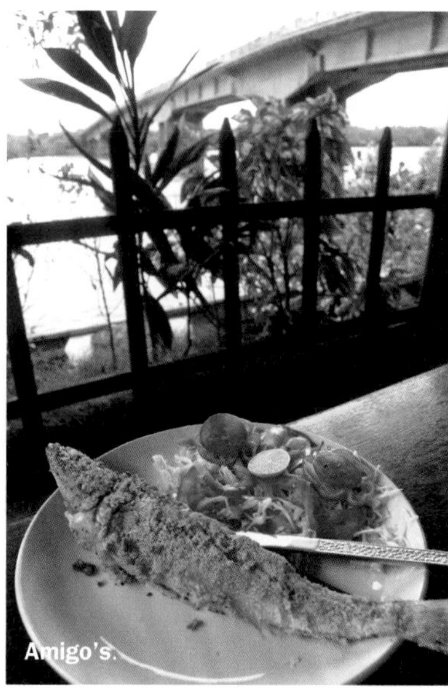
Amigo's.

La Fenice (0832-228-1182, main course Rs 150, 11am-10pm daily). At the top of a long flight of stairs are some spacious, atmospheric terraces where you can dine on tasty and authentic Italian food – the best on offer in the state. Down on the beach, the pick of Candolim's endless line of shacks is **Calamari** (0832-309-0506, main course Rs 150, 8.30am-9.30pm daily, closed May-Sept), where the hedonistic motto is 'Bathe and Binge'. It has very friendly staff, tasty Goan-style seafood, and offers patrons an outdoor shower and free towels. Right opposite is a fabulous breakfast and lunch choice, **Café Chocolatti** (Fort Aguada Road, 0832-247-9340, main course Rs 200), run by Ricardo and Nazneen Rebelo. Chocolatti specialises in superb salads, sandwiches and baked goods (with delicious biscuits and chocolates for sale in the tiny attached store).

INSIDE TRACK NOVEL MENU

At **Bomra's** restaurant, make sure to ask for the separate Glass Palace menu – it won't be offered unless you request it. It's a list of dishes chosen by the award-winning author (and part-time Goa resident) Amitav Ghosh, whose novel with the same name spans 100 years of Burmese history. More importantly, he obviously knows his food: everything on his menu is a sure-fire winner.

Nightlife

These days, nightlife in Candolim is relatively sleepy. However, an ambitious entry into the Goan market by **Shiro** (0832-645-1718, 11am-1am daily) occupies a prime stretch of beachside land, and draws a loyal crowd of well-heeled Mumbai visitors, who presumably frequent the original bar (*see p118*). Opposite St Anthony's Chapel is the **Bar** (no phone, noon-3am daily), a cosy bar with low cane seating, a couple of pool tables and a club-like feel. Try the masala *feni*.

Shopping

One of Goa's most popular shopping centres is the **Acron Arcade** (283 Fort Aguada Road, 0832-564-3671, 10am-10pm daily). Downstairs, half the building is devoted to home decor from **Yamini**, an Indian chain of stores selling beautiful handmade fabrics and furnishings. It has a variety of men's and women's clothes with an emphasis on handloom and labels from Pondicherry and Bangalore. Down the road from the Tarcar ice factory, after La Fenice and in a charming old house, is the **Literati Bookshop & Café** (98226-82566, 0832-227-7740), Goa's best bookstore/café and hangout for India's A-list writers when they're on vacation. Not far away, the Swiss-owned store **Sotohaus** (1266F Anna Vaddo, Candolim, 0832-248-9983, www.sotodecor.com) offers beautifully worked iron-and-paper lamps, tables and other furniture, many made using found objects like banana, driftwood and even shed snakeskins, all under thick layers of lacquer.

Where to stay

This is charter tourism country, so most hotels in Candolim are built to specifications dictated by travel companies – virtually everything is identical, clean and well run but there are few non-full board options available. The pick of this bunch is the lovingly decorated **Aldeia Santa Rita** (near Kingfisher Villa, 0832-247-9868, Rs 3,500-Rs 7,500 double), close to the beach. Nearby is **Whispering Palms** (off Candolim Main Road, 0832-247-9140, www.whisperingpalms.com, Rs 6,000-Rs 8,000 double), which has an excellent swimming pool and well-appointed rooms. More basic than either of these, though equally packed with British charter tourists, is the **Summerville Beach Resort** (off Candolim Main Road, 0832-247-9075, www.summervillebeachresort.com, Rs 1,500-Rs 1,800 double), which has 23 well-maintained rooms, a pleasant rooftop restaurant and a small swimming pool.

Resources

Internet

Sify I-way Bake N Byte *Laxmi Apartments, near Candolim Market (no phone).* **Open** 9am-10pm daily.

Getting there

Taxis from Tivim take around half an hour and cost Rs 400. From Dabolim Airport, it's Rs 600 and takes an hour; from Panjim, it's around Rs 200 for a 20-minute trip. When driving from Panjim, cross the Mandovi Bridge and go about three kilometres straight up the NH-17 highway towards Mapusa. Turn left at the O Coqueiro junction, and pass through Sangolda until you reach the Church of St Alex in Calangute. From there, turn left on to Candolim Road.

Feni for Your Thoughts

The story behind Goa's much-loved hooch.

The French have their champagne, the Greeks have their ouzo, but Goans have *feni* – and they don't really need anything else, thank you very much.

Every April and May, the heavy scent of fermenting cashew drifts across the countryside and traditional stills fire up to make the year's batch of this deeply loved drink – a drink as synonymous with Goa as beaches and fish-curry-rice, and decreed by state law to be made only by hand in small batches. *Feni* (pronounced fey-nee) is a clear, powerful spirit that comes in two varieties: cashew and coconut. Coconut *feni* (also known as palm *feni*) is made all year round, mostly in South Goa, but is considered by purists to be an inferior version of the 'original' cashew *feni*, which can only be made after the cashew fruit harvest in March. The fruits are crushed and the juice left to ferment, which is then heated in large copper or earthen pots over firewood and the distillate collected through a coiled pipe. The first distillate is weak and makes a drink called *urrak*; it takes two or three distillations to make proper, strong *feni*, which is around 40 per cent alcohol.

Connoisseurs insist that good *feni* can be as smooth and nuanced as the finest single malt whiskies. It's by far the state's most popular drink, available at hole-in-the-wall taverns everywhere, poured from jerry cans or unlabelled plastic bottles. Hospedaria Venite in Panjim (*see p206*) sells an excellent home-produced *feni* by the bottle for about Rs 150, but there are lots of big-name brands such as Big Boss (Rs 150 for 750ml) available from wine shops. Drink it neat, with a squeeze of lime, a pinch of salt, or with lemonade. It's also fabulous in fruit cocktails. Watch out, though – it has a kick like a gaur.

INSIDE TRACK EASY ESCAPE

Trek across the bridge to **Baga Creek** and hang left on the narrow road that becomes increasingly narrower as it heads up the headland. In a few minutes, you will feel many miles away from all the tourist mayhem, and in a kind of private forest that stretches to the modest Jesuit retreat that occupies the peak. Few tourists venture here, but ask a local for the path down to the waterline, where there's a tiny, pebble-strewn cove that's an unbeatable place to watch the sunset.

CALANGUTE & BAGA

Long before tourists washed up on Goan shores, **Calangute** was a seafront idyll for genteel Goan families from all over the state. Through the hot summer months of April and May, they retired here to simple rented accommodation and borrowed fishermen's houses to take early morning 'sea baths' and evening walks along a rudimentary boardwalk. All that is long gone: Calangute's broad sands are as golden as ever but have been swamped with Goa's most congested tourist scene, with huge crowds of Indian visitors rubbing elbows with Scandinavians and Brits, and a beach lined with tightly packed sunbeds. The interior is just as crowded, with Indian day-trippers, and the usual collection of Kashmiri rug merchants, fast-food outlets, and cheap souvenir shops.

It's hard to tell where Calangute ends and **Baga** begins. Baga is now one of the most famous party hotspots in India, with a range of bars that pack in twentysomethings from Mumbai, Bangalore and Delhi. Slightly quieter is Baga Creek, across a concrete bridge, where a long line of some of Goa's best eating options operate out of converted old houses just metres from the riverbank.

A couple of reminders of the past do remain, notably the private home **Casa dos Proenças**, just north of the main Calangute market. It was built with several unusual features, including a gorgeous seashell-screen enclosed veranda and an ingenious natural cooling system. Away from the beach, on the road towards Saligao, stands the spectacular rococo **Church of St Alex**, an 18th-century construction with a bulging dome and Indianised bell towers. Regular returnees to Calangute like to begin their vacation with a shave and a haircut in the barber shop (the sign reads 'Barberia') in the mirrored octagon in the centre of the Calangute market crossroads – a 200-year-old colonial customs post.

Where to eat & drink

Baga Creek has numerous exciting and ambitious restaurants, of which **J&A's Little Italy** (Baga Creek, 98231-39488, main course Rs 350, 6pm-midnight daily, closed Apr-Sept) is easily the poshest, serving delicious Italian food with an emphasis on superb ingredients and flawless presentation. Close by is the hillside **La Terrase** (Baga Creek, 0832-395-0832, www.laterrasse.in, main course Rs 250, 6.30-10.30pm daily, closed Apr-Sept) high up a couple of flights of steps with great views of the creek and authentic Southern French food. On the same stretch is the brilliant daytime hangout **Lila Café** (0832-227-9843, main course Rs 150, 9am-6pm Mon, Wed-Sun, closed May-Sept), whose German owners keep a devoted crowd of regulars happy with fresh German bread, mushroom pâté, water-buffalo ham and other Euro-style treats.

Heading towards the beach, there's old-timer **Britto's** (last corner on Baga Road, 0832-227-7331, main course Rs 175, 8.30am-10.30pm daily), a friendly Baga institution serving decent Goan dishes, and a fine selection of

Calangute Beach.

desserts and baked goods. A little further down the beach road towards Calangute is **Casa Portuguesa** (Beach Road, 0832-227-7024, www.casa-portuguesa-goa.com, main course Rs 250, 7-11pm, closed season May-Oct), a pleasant restaurant in a converted ancestral home specialising in authentic Portuguese food. Across the road is the lane that leads to **Tito's** (Tito's Lane, Baga, 0832-227-5028/6154, main course Rs 250, 7pm-midnight daily, closed May-Sept), the party hotspot that also serves decent pastas and steaks. Much better fare is available directly opposite at **Fiesta** (Tito's Lane, Baga, 0832-227-9894/228-1440, www.fiestagoa.com, main course Rs 300, 7-11pm Mon,Wed-Sun, closed Apr-Oct), a beautifully decorated open-air restaurant with a Caribbean feel and a German chef who makes great wood-fired pizzas and outstanding desserts. Nearby is the pick of Baga's beach shacks, **Zanzibar** (no phone, main course Rs 175, 9am-11pm daily, closed May-Sept), which serves good Indian food with an emphasis on fresh fish and shrimp. Further down the road is an unusual little nook of a restaurant, **Simply South** (98231-28567, main course Rs 200, 6-11.30pm daily), which serves outstanding meals derived from the South Indian non-vegetarian cuisines of Tamil Nadu and Kerala.

Just before the Calangute roundabout is the old Goan favourite **Infantaria** (0832-227-7421, main course Rs 100, 8.30am-10pm daily), which has been dishing up old-fashioned chops and potato croquettes to generations of day-trippers. Heading south, **I-95** (0832-227-5213, main course Rs 250, 7pm-midnight daily) has quickly made a name for itself as one of the best fine-dining destinations in Goa, with lavish ingredients and highly attentive service. The restaurant occupies the garden of an impressive art gallery and the studio of Yolanda Kammermeier, one of the state's leading artists, and a former national soccer player. All the way back in Gaurawaddo, in the part of Calangute that merges into Candolim, **Waves** (0832-227-6017, main course Rs 200, 7-10pm daily, closed May-Sept) is another restaurant that fuses art and great food, in the pleasant Kerkar Art Complex. It specialises in Hindu Goan, or 'Gomantak', specialities.

Nightlife

Being major tourist centres, Calangute and Baga are home to some of Goa's most hectic nightlife; both beaches are crammed with chilled-out shacks serving drinks until late, and the streets behind are lined with hole-in-the-wall bars. Baga's (and maybe Goa's) most famous club is **Tito's** (Tito's Lane, Baga, 0832-227-9895, www.titosgoa.com, 10pm-4am daily, Rs 800-Rs 1,000), a Baga institution that attracts hundreds of Kingfisher-fuelled boys and girls from Mumbai for Bollywood beats and dancing on three levels, with extra entertainment provided by professional dancers and – something you wouldn't get in the Ministry of Sound – the occasional magician. Just down the lane towards the beach is **Mambo's** (Tito's Lane, Baga, 0832-227-9895, 7pm-3.30am, cover charge Rs 300), a wooden beach pub run by Tito's management but with a more relaxed vibe. It usually plays a mix of hip hop and house, with some country music thrown in. Open even during the depths of the monsoon, the bar at **Cavala** (Saunta Vaddo, Baga, 0832-227-6090, 9am-midnight daily), an old Baga hotel, offers a warm welcome to a friendly (and older) crowd of locals, expats and regular returnees, with live music and retro nights most Fridays and Saturdays.

Lila Café.

GOA

INSIDE TRACK FADO FANATIC

Ask to see the owner of **Casa Portuguesa**'s signed pictures of Amália Rodrigues, the legendary Portuguese fado singer he idolises. Ask nicely and he might sing some of her powerful, deeply melancholic standards.

Cavala. *See p189.*

Where to stay

Pousada Tauma (Porba Vaddo, Calangute, 0832-227-9061, www.pousada-tauma.com, Rs 14,000-Rs 20,000 double), is a lush complex of villas set around an inviting pool with an enchanting restaurant beneath a laterite colonnade and a top-notch ayurvedic spa. **Villa Goesa** (Cobra Vaddo, 0832-227-7535, www.vilagoesa.com, Rs 1,700-Rs 2,700 double) is particularly close to the beach and set in well-maintained gardens. The nearby **Chalston Beach Resort** (Cobra Vaddo, 0832-227-6080, Rs 1,200-Rs 1,800 double) is a clean, reasonably priced option popular with Scandinavians. Its beach shack is one of the best on this stretch. On the road in the thick of Baga's action is **Cavala** (Baga Main Road, 0832-227-7587, www.cavala.com, Rs 1,200-Rs 1,700 double), not far from the beach and with attractive, great-value rooms.

Resources

Post office

Calangute Post Office *near St Alex Church (0832-227-6030).* **Open** 9am-5pm Mon-Fri.

Internet

Sify I-way *Shop No. 1, Sunshine Complex, Baga Road (no phone).* **Open** 9am-9pm daily.

Getting there

Taxis from Tivim cost around Rs 400 for the half-hour trip. From Dabolim Airport, it's Rs 750 and takes around an hour and 15 minutes. From Candolim, turn right at St Anthony's Chapel for Calangute; for Baga, take another right at the main traffic circle just before Calangute Beach.

ANJUNA

Anjuna is where the first tie-dyed '60s refugees came in search of freedom, sunshine and cheap drugs. Some never left: you can still find Eight-fingered Eddie (now in his eighties) playing ball on the beach he 'discovered' 40 years ago, and the spirit of the Goa Freaks lives on in the hundreds of raised chillums that hail each sunset on the beachfront. But Anjuna is also home to writers and artists who simply like the vibe, and even has a very well-regarded private school, the British-operated Little Yellow School House-catering almost entirely to expat children.

Long before the Goa Freaks skipped on to its beaches, Anjuna was a cosmopolitan trade outpost controlled by the Arabs (hence the name, derived from *hanjuman*, meaning 'trading post') in the tenth century. But most Muslim (and Hindu) traces were wiped out by the Portuguese zeal to Christianise the region as fast and as bloodily as possible. The sprawling **Church of St Michael the Archangel** (open for Mass 7am Sun) dates back to that violent era.

Anjuna's famous **flea market** (South Anjuna, 8am-sunset Wed) is a relic from the early hippie days in the 1960s and '70s when hashish was legal and sold just like today's vendors hawk cheap T-shirts. The market's original avatar was small-scale, sometimes relied on barter rather than cash, and was mostly used by foreigners looking to raise the money to stay on or get home. Now tens of thousands converge on the flea market every Wednesday from October to April in a convoy of scooters, motorbikes and trucks that throws up huge clouds of dust. The market sprawls over a plateau by the beach with hundreds of stalls selling everything from tie-dye bikinis to chillums and sitars to cushion covers.

Boutique Beds

Small is beautiful.

For years, visitors to Goa had to choose between beach huts and informal guesthouses with plenty of character but often little comfort, or sprawling five-stars where the reverse was true. But in recent years, Goa's hotel market has been energised by the rise of boutique hotels and luxury villas for rent – small and stylish properties offering an exclusive experience much more suited to Goa's naturally laid-back vibe. Since 2000, this new option has become extremely popular, routinely charging more than the five-stars during the peak season around Christmas and New Year's Eve.

The grandfather of the trend is the **Nilaya Hermitage** (Arpora, 0832-227-6794, www.nilayahermitage.com, Rs 12,000-Rs 25,000 double), an ethereal fortress of domes on an Arpora hilltop, with an eagle's-eye view of the jungle landscape below. The atmosphere is otherworldly – Arabian Nights meets New Age – with twelve exceptional rooms themed according to the 'cosmic elements', with names like 'sun', 'earth' and 'fire'. Under its largest dome is a 'music room' decked out with white cotton mattresses and a superb sound system – a veritable temple of chill-out. Nilaya has attracted numerous famous guests, including designer Giorgio Armani, supermodel Kate Moss and Hollywood star Richard Gere.

Pousada Tauma (Porba Vaddo, 0832-227-9061, www.pousadatauma.com, Rs 12,000-Rs 26,500 double) is a secluded dell of lush greenery and beautiful cottages around an attractive pool. It also has one of Goa's most enchanting restaurants.

Getting away from it all is guaranteed at **Elsewhere** (Mandrem, 98200-37387, www.aseascape.com, Rs 6,100-Rs 24,000 per day, closed June-mid Oct), the ancestral home of Mumbai fashion photographer Denzil Sequeira and a stunning beach house-for-hire. It's set on an isolated strip of beach in Ashvem, with a veranda overlooking the surf, shuttered windows and discreet staff on hand to cater to every whim. Overlooking a creek to the rear, Sequeira has set up a few tents – the word doesn't really do them justice – each with hot and cold running water, a private jetty and a four-poster bed (Rs 2,300-Rs 5,700 per night).

Quite close to each other on the chaotic beach strip of Candolim are two exquisite beachfront options with extensive private gardens, and an air of exclusivity that's impossible to beat in the crowded surroundings. **Aashyana Lakhanpal** is the creation of an Indian business magnate and art collector, who has filled his own villa and attached cottages with superb paintings and sculpture by India's best known contemporary artists. (Candolim, 0832-248-9225, www.ashyanalak hanpal.com, cottages from Rs. 49,000 per week). **Rockheart** has more subtle charms, a tasteful, tiny bungalow set very close to the beach that offers extraordinary privacy and direct access to the best swimming area for miles around. (Candolim, 98193-27284, www.rockheartgoa.com, from Rs. 80,000 per week.)

Far inland, around 90 minutes' drive from Panjim, is **Wildernest** (Swapnagandha, Chorla Ghat, off highway to Belgaum, 0831-520-7954, www.wildernest-goa.com, Rs 2,500-Rs 5,500 double), a unique complex of wood-and-glass cottages located 800 metres above sea level in the Western Ghats. Run by nature-lovers, Wildernest offers secluded and highly comfortable cottages hidden away in the woods, with floor-to-ceiling glass walls that make you feel like you're camping out. Splash around the infinity pool, gaze out over the Vazra Waterfall and the entire Mandovi River valley, and then strap on your boots for a leisurely hike in the woods.

Pousada Tauma.

Anjuna flea market. See p190.

In the late '90s and early 2000s, Anjuna became famous all over again for its moonlight parties and raves – legendary open-air happenings that drew thousands of wildly dressed revellers. That scene is on hold while the Goa government wrings its hands over a coherent policy towards rave tourists. But it seems unlikely that the rave scene will ever return to Anjuna in quite the same way again.

Where to eat & drink

All roads lead to **Curlies** (South Anjuna Beach, 98221-68628, main course Rs 100, 6am-4am daily), a low-slung beach shack in South Anjuna, where a tightly knit staff of Anjuna villagers watches over a veritable United Nations of beach bums. Sunset on the steps feels like an ancient ritual, with dozens of bleary-eyed patrons watching children and dogs caper in the surf a few metres away. Up the beach is **Café Looda** (0832-562-9323, main course Rs 200, 8.30am-11.30pm daily, closed May-Oct), perched on the rocks overlooking the beach, at its best after the flea market slows down on Wednesdays. A bit further up the beach is the excellent **Shore Bar** (Anjuna Beach, 98223-83795, 7am-11pm daily), a stylish beach shack for grown-ups, run by a chef who trained with the Roux brothers in England. Try the home-made seafood soup. Quite near all three, behind a small chapel, is the Anjuna landmark **Xavier's** (Praia de San Miguel, 0832 227-3402, main course Rs 150, 9am-11pm daily), once a small, basic shack and now a multi-cuisine establishment with three kitchens whipping up Indian, Chinese and Continental dishes. Another local landmark is **Basilico** (D'mello Vaddo, 0832-227-3721, main course Rs 150, 11am-midnight daily), which serves excellent home-made pesto and wood-fired pizzas. On the outskirts of the village is **Bean Me Up** (Soranto Vaddo, 0832-227-3977, www.travelingoa.com/beanmeup, main course Rs 120, 9.30am-10.30pm daily), a world-class American-run vegetarian restaurant with super home-made tofu and salads. On the main Anjuna village road, the **Blue Tao Organic Restaurant & Café** (before Starco turn-off, 0832-309-0829, main course Rs 100, 9.30am-10.30pm daily) is a welcoming family restaurant selling home-made cakes and ice-creams, herbal teas & fresh juices, and tasty, healthy breakfasts. At the far north end of Anjuna Beach, near the Paradiso nightclub, is **Zoories** (no phone, main course Rs 150, 11am-11pm daily), with a stunning setting high on a cliff overlooking a rocky cove and a menu ranging from houmous and tahini to fajitas and enchiladas. A few minutes' drive away from the beach is the outstanding **Yoga Magic** (Grand Chinvar Vaddo, next to Bobby Bar, 0832-562-3796, 93705-65717, www.yogamagic.net, main course Rs 400, 11.30am-1.30pm, 7-9pm daily, closed Apr), a popular eco-friendly getaway offering super 'Indian fusion' vegetarian meals to non-resident guests. Dinner bookings are required.

Nightlife

Both **Curlies** and **Café Looda** (*see left*) turn into lively beachside nightspots after sunset, with Curlies going heavy on the trance and ambient sounds. The **Shore Bar** (Anjuna Beach, 98223-83795), a few minutes' walk up the beach north of Café Looda, hosts regular trance nights from 6pm to 11pm. Goa's most stylish club is **Club Cubana** (82 Xim Waddo, Arpora Hill, 98235-39000, www.cubana.net, 9.30pm-5am daily, closed May-Oct, cover charge Rs 1,000-Rs 1,500), perched on an Arpora hilltop, a short drive from Anjuna. Cubana sprawls across a maze of levels and staircases, with terraces offering starry night views across Goa for its decently mixed crowd of European tourists and weekend-break visitors from Mumbai. Trance is firmly rejected here in favour of hip hop, house and R&B. Towels are provided for patrons who fancy jumping into the swimming pool, and the drinks are unlimited once you pay the cover charge (it can hit Rs 1,500 each for couples and single men around Christmas and New Year). Less fancy but even bigger is **Paradiso** (Anjuna, 93261-00013, 10pm-5am daily, cover charge Rs 300-Rs 600), a huge club built on a series of psychedelically painted terraces overlooking the sea. Paradiso attracts some of India's best DJs and even the likes of Goa Gil (*see p184)* **Hippie and You Know It**). When it's packed, the energy level is hard to beat, pumped up by non-stop trance beats and the rhythm of the waves. **Underground Kingdom** (Grand Peddem, Anjuna, no phone, 10pm-6am daily, entry Rs 200) has got around the rave ban by burying itself in a large World War II-style concrete bunker in the middle of a forest, where DJs drop trance beats that echo insanely off the walls. Patrons can give their eardrums a break outside at relaxed open-air bars and canopies with soft cushions. The famous **Saturday Night Bazaar** – a popular weekly night market at Arpora – features an amazing array of foods and artisanal crafts from around the world. It seems back for good after more than a year of ongoing legal limbo for the Swiss impresario, Ingo Grill, who organises the event each year. Make sure to visit if it's on while you're in Goa. There's nothing quite like this energetic, wildly international mix of art, design, great food and live music anywhere else in the world.

INSIDE TRACK
LATE-NIGHT LOWDOWN

The people at **Curlies** are all well-connected locals – Curlie himself has been the *sarpanch* (a bit like the mayor) of the village – and they know everything there is to know about the local party scene. As it's open pretty much 24/7 the best way to find out what's happening in this part of Goa is to walk up to the bar and ask.

Curlies.

Temples across the Ponda

Serene sanctuaries.

Very soon after their military conquest of Goa, which was undertaken with the tacit support of regional Hindu strongmen, the Portuguese conquistadors set out to destroy every single 'heathen' temple they could find, with one particularly zealous officer, Diogo Rodrigues, tearing down over 280 temples across 58 villages in one single year, 1567. By the turn of the 17th century, there were none left standing.

However, many of the revered deities housed within them were spirited away by loyal devotees, who stole across the rivers towards Ponda, a redoubt in the hinterland that didn't come under Portuguese rule until the 18th century, by which time much of their religious fervour had waned, and a certain modus vivendi with the Hindu community had been achieved. There, nestled in thickly forested valleys, new temples went up to house the idols, with the result that Ponda is still home to some of Goa's most important Hindu sites.

The most famous of all is the **Shri Mangesh Temple** (Priol, north-west of Ponda on NH-4, open 7am-6.30pm daily, free; pictured). The resident *shivalingam* (a clay phallus representing Lord Shiva) was brought across the Zuari River from Curtorim and is housed in a temple that's embellished with baroque flourishes adapted from Goa's churches, and an impressive octagonal tower that can be seen from a considerable distance.

A few kilometres away is the Shri Mahalsa Temple (Mardol, north-west of Ponda off NH-4, 7am-6pm daily, free). At the end of a marble courtyard, there's a beautiful water tank fed by a freshwater spring, lined with coconut palms and traditional ghats used for ritual bathing (and often for doing the locals' laundry).

Built by the Marathas in 1738, right on the edge of unbroken jungle south-west of Ponda, it's Goa's largest and perhaps most important Hindu temple, devoted to **Shri Shantadurga**, the goddess of peace (an avatar of Durga, Lord Shiva's consort). She is widely venerated by Catholics and other non-Hindus and the temple's design bears influences of Goan church architecture.

But if you can only visit one temple in Goa, it should be **Tambdi Surla** 11 kilometres north of Molem in Sanguem Taluka, 30 minutes from Ponda along NH-4, take the left to Sancordem and follow signs, open 6am-4pm daily, free), a 12th-century survivor that escaped the Portuguese because of its remote location. Hewn from massive slabs of basalt, carried across the mountains from the Deccan region beyond, it's a stunning and mysterious relic of the Kadamba era, the home-grown dynasty that ruled Goa until the 14th century.

Chapora Fort.

Where to stay

Anjuna is fast catching up with other beachfront villages' acommodation options. The most atmospheric of all is **Granpa's Inn** (Gaun Vaddo, 0832-227-3270, Rs 850-Rs 1,750 double), the converted ancestral home of the Faria family. It has a great atmosphere, lovely gardens and terrace, and a pool. A similar, though more downmarket version is **Palacete Rodrigues** (Mazal Vaddo, 0832-227-3358, Rs 1,000-Rs 1,200 double), a converted 200-year-old house with the feel of a family home. Back in the present century, **Laguna Anjuna** (Soranto Vaddo, 0832-227-4305, www.lagunaanjuna.com, Rs 2,500-Rs 7,500 double) is one of Anjuna's best hotels, a stylish, if slightly tired-looking, set of cottages set around an attractive pool. In the far north of Anjuna is **Lotus Inn** (Zor Vaddo, 0832-227-4015, www.lotusinn.com, Rs 1,000-Rs 4,500 double), a family-friendly modern hotel with a pool and a popular restaurant serving a mix of German and Indian food. Something different is offered by **Yoga Magic** (Grand Chinvar Vaddo, by Bobby Bar, 0832-562-3796, 93705-65717, www.yogamagic.net), an environmentally friendly, tented yoga camp (tents Rs 1,200 per person) that also offers a luxurious room (Rs 5,000 per night) in the main house.

Resources

Post office

Anjuna Post Office *near Football Grounds (0832-227-3221).* **Open** 9am-5pm Mon-Fri.

Internet

Sify I-way *next to Tembi Café, Mazal Vaddo (no phone).* **Open** 9am-9pm daily.

Getting there

The taxi from Tivim takes 25 minutes and costs Rs 350. From Dabolim Airport, taxis take an hour and 15 minutes and charge Rs 750. From Panjim, take the NH-17 toward Mapusa and turn left near the Green Park Hotel. Follow the narrow road; Anjuna is signposted.

VAGATOR AND CHAPORA

As Anjuna steadily turns more mainstream and family-friendly, some of the hard core of trance music pilgrims, dropouts and committed stoners have shifted further north to the beaches and headland in the shadow of the rugged **Chapora Fort**. The Portuguese rebuilt this bastion at the turn of the 18th century on the ruins of a much older fort built by Bijapuri Sultan Adil Shah (the name Chapora comes from *Shah-pura*, or 'Place of the Shah'). In the early 18th century, the son of the great Mughal Emperor Aurangzeb holed up here while scheming to topple his father in a pact with the enemy Marathas. The fortress is crumbling to bits and overrun with vegetation, but the views are magnificent, with the Arabian Sea on one side and the gorgeous harbour at the mouth of the Chapora River on the other. All this makes Chapora Fort one of the best sunset spots in Goa, often attracting hundreds of Indian tourists from neighbouring states.

Chapora.

In recent years, the winding palm-lined lanes of Chapora and the beaches of 'little' and 'big' Vagator have become home to a hard-edged sub-culture of Russians, Israelis, Italians and other Europeans. Many visitors stay for months, renting tiny no-frills rooms in the same local houses each year, watched over by Goan vigilantes well connected with the local police. The atmosphere can be a little off-putting, with hundreds of foreigners jammed into pocket-sized tavernas and chai shops, openly smoking chillums under the watchful presence of slightly menacing fix-it men and local minders. Big Vagator is a good swimming spot, dramatically situated under the ramparts of the fort. It is a lovely beach that gets crowded in season (especially with Indian day-trippers). **Ozran** (aka **Little Vagator**), to the south, is where party folk congregate at beach shacks and the popular Nine Bar.

Where to eat & drink

There's a high turnover of restaurants in this area, but there are a few long-stayers like **Le Bluebird** (Ozran, 0832-227-3695, main course Rs 250, 9am-2pm, 7-11pm daily, closed May-Oct), a remarkably good French restaurant with an excellent (and pricey) wine list. There's also the local institution, **Primrose Café** (Coutinho Vaddo, 0832-227-3210, main course Rs 100, 9am-midnight daily), which fills up after 10pm. Another good option is the **Alcove** (no phone, main course Rs 200, 9am-9pm daily), a Goan restaurant on the cliff above Ozran. By far the best option in the area is **Thalassa** (Little Vagator Beach, 4pm-midnight daily, 98500-33537, www.myspace.com/thalassagoa) where the friendly Greek owner, Mariketty, has magically recreated an Aegean Sea atmosphere as well as superb Meditteranean food.

Nightlife

Evenings kick off at **Nine Bar** (above Little Vagator Beach, no phone, 6-10pm daily), a mini-version of Paradiso, with a cliff-top sea view and a packed house of the Indian and European party crowd warming up to some intense trance (what else?). That finishes early, and since the clampdown on raves, open moonlight party venues like Disco Valley and Spaghetti Valley have fallen silent; instead, many opt for the **Primrose Café** (see p196), entry Rs 100-Rs 200), a grungy indoor trance club with a heavy stoner contingent. The **Hill Top** (Vagator, 98221-51690, closed Apr-Oct) is an isolated hotel with a sprawling garden filled with fluorescent-painted palm trees and is large enough for a few thousand revellers. It still manages the occasional rave; give it a call to see if any are planned.

Where to stay

Chapora and Vagator have a few professionally run guesthouses, including the bright **Bethany Inn** (538/6 Vagator Road, near Chinatown Restaurant, 0832-227-3731/3163 www.bethanyinn.com, Rs 1,000-Rs 1,200 double), where each room has a private balcony and minibar. There are two other options run by the same management: **Julie Jolly** (near Ozran, 0832-227-3357, Rs 1,000 double), and the slightly more upscale **Jolly Jolly Roma** (Vagator Beach Road, 0832-227-3001, Rs 1,000-Rs 1,500 double). To the right of the road leading to Disco Valley is **Leoney's Resort** (0832-227-3634, www.leoneyresort.com, Rs 1,500-Rs 2,600 double), with Indo-Portuguese villas and cottages set around a pool. Leoney's doesn't take advance bookings for high season. Inland, ten minutes' drive away, is the atmospheric **Siolim House** (Wadi, 0832-227-2138, www.siolimhouse.com, Rs 3,000-Rs 5,000 double), a converted 200-year-old Indo-Portuguese mansion with a beautiful courtyard, huge rooms and a swimming pool. Check the website for 'silent auctions' that can get you a cheaper deal on a room.

Getting there

Taxis from Tivim charge Rs 500 for a 30-minute trip to Chapora. From Dabolim Airport, it's around Rs 800 and takes an hour. To get there from Anjuna, turn left at the crossroads just outside the village.

MORJIM & ASHVEM

Across the long Siolim Bridge into Pernem district, the landscape shifts into deep countryside. This part of Goa was annexed by the Portuguese much later than the lands to the south, after the regional chieftain Deshprabhu family accepted a royal title, Viscondes de Pernem, and allowed their holdings to be assimilated into the Estado da India. There is a separate character to this part of the 'New Conquests', overwhelmingly Hindu rather than culturally mixed, and far less developed than the Bardez district south of the river.

Until the bridge was built in 2002, mass tourism had never made it past the long queues for the ferries across the Chapora River. A few travellers reached the strip of beach starting at **Morjim** and stretching north into **Ashvem**, but now that it's just a brisk 20-minute drive more development is on the way. The only thing holding back the hordes is the breeding habits of the migratory Olive Ridley turtle. It's not that it's a large nesting site (Orissa on India's east coast has far more) but this species is officially endangered and ecologically conscious local officials have limited development in the area. In recent years,

Culture Capital

Goan talent is finally being represented on home turf.

Few people connect the dots to realize just how impactful Goa's small territory has been on modern and contemporary subcontinental culture. It has produced a disproportionately high number of the greatest artists and musicians of twentieth-century India. The first Indian editor of the national newspaper, the *Times of India*, was a Goan, Frank Moraes, and his son, Dom Moraes was India's acknowledged greatest poet in the English language.

Goans played an outsized role in the creation of the Bollywood sound. The legendary Lata Mangeshkar and Asha Bhonsle, the most recorded singers in history (according to Guinness World Records) are Goan sisters who have provided the soundtrack to innumerable Hindi movies. Two Goans – Vasudeo Gaitonde and his mentor, Francis Newton Souza, together created and fostered the Progressive Artists Movement in post-World War II Mumbai, which is by far the most significant historical factor in the development and growth of modern Indian art. Today, their paintings sell for vast sums of money – both have set auction records, selling work for millions of dollars.

But, almost all of the achievements took place outside Goa, in the diaspora in Mumbai, Delhi, and beyond to London and New York. And despite this legacy – peerless in the subcontinent – there were few signs of cultural life in Goa itself until very recently. Today, there are a few small museums, art-galleries and cultural centres that are beginning to showcase Goan talent in Goa itself. These include the museum of modern Goan art at the **Xavier Centre of Historical Research** (Porvorim, 832-241-7772, 9.30am-5pm Mon-Fri, Entry Rs.100), the charming little **Architectural Museum** created by the award-winning architect, Gerard da Cunha (Salvador do Mundo, 832-241-0711, 10am-7.30pm, Entry Rs.100 (includes 50Rs coupon for purchases at shop), and the kid-friendly and unique **Ethnographic Museum** in South Goa, Goa Chitra (*see p219*) Pulwaddo, Benaulim Entry: Rs 50, open 9am-6pm Tue-Sun, www.goachitra.com, 0832-657-9877, 0832-277-2910, 09850466165).

the influx of mainly Russian travellers has inhibited turtle hatchings to just twice a year, but the government plans to turn the beach into a nature sanctuary, putting paid to plans to develop the village and the beachfront. Even now, this stretch of very broad sands feels empty, with casuarinas and palm groves standing untouched, and traditional fishing boats lining the northern and southern ends of the beach.

Where to eat & drink

The Morjim/Ashvem culinary landscape is dominated by five very different eateries. **Glavfish** (Vithaldas Vaddo, 98812-87433, main course Rs 300, 8am-midnight daily) is an all-Russian hangout where patrons lounge on simple stone slabs and rough wooden benches. Just 100 metres away but radically different in atmosphere is the restaurant at **Montego Bay**

Goan Grub

The origins of Goan cuisine.

'Please Sir, Mr God of Death
Don't make it my turn today, not today,
There's fish curry for dinner.'
- Bakibab Borkar, Goan poet

The most essential food fact about Goa is that a common colloquial way of asking 'How are you?' in Konkani is '*Nisteak kitem aslem*?' which translates as: 'What fish did you have today?' As this would indicate, seafood is a Goan obsession, and every local household – no matter how humble or aristocratic – consumes seafood at least once a day, and often thrice. Goan cuisine is far removed from familiar North Indian staples like butter chicken and biryani, but today's local cuisine would be almost unrecognisable to a 16th-century Goan. That's because the cuisine was transformed by the arrival of the Portuguese, who brought with them a cornucopia of culinary treasures harvested from farther-flung adventures in South East Asia, Africa and South America: chillies, tomatoes, potatoes and corn, fruit like guavas, pineapples and chikoos, and cashews.

As Portuguese influence took hold so did their diet, edging out the traditional cuisine of Saraswat and other dishes from the Konkan region. The ubiquitous vindaloo (which tastes nothing like the British copy) is a corruption of *vinho e alhos*, a garlicky Portuguese wine-vinegar marinade. *Chouriço*, those chubby links of spiced pork, are a piquant Goan version of the Iberian sausage. *Sorpotel* started off as *Sarabulho*, a Portuguese stew of pork meat and offal. Indigenous touches added to the mix as a new Goan cuisine evolved over the years – turmeric, cumin, cinnamon and cloves found their way into Portuguese *asados* or roasts and coconut and semolina showed up in *bolos* (cakes).

Today the staple dish remains fish-curry-rice, the exact ingredients of which vary widely from region to region, village to village, and even house to house. For most of the year, Goans tuck into prized *estuarine* shrimp and tiger prawns, mussels, langoustines, lobsters, pomfrets, kingfish and river perch – and shark in the hot-and-sour *ambotik* curry. In the monsoon, deep-sea fishing is banned to allow stocks to replenish, and Goans take to eating the *muddasho* (ladyfish), a slender fish with a buttery taste. Other speciality Goan curries include the mild *caldine*, a children's favourite often made with eggs or vegetables, and the complex, vinegary *xacuti* usually made with chicken, goat meat or beef.

The original Saraswat cuisine did survive as what is now known as '*Gomantak*' cooking, and is increasingly better-known. A representative meal could consist of thick-grained, nutty, red-veined parboiled rice taken with a fish or shellfish curry, with a shelping of fried seafood on the side. It's accompanied by mildly spiced seasonal vegetables, perhaps flavoured with *kokum*, dark palm sugar (jaggery) or tamarind, with lashings of coconut ubiquitous in every form. Mud vessels and wood fires give traditional Goan food its characteristic smoky aroma, nicely captured in a steaming bowl of *canjee* (rice gruel) with dried salt fish and a wicked piece of mango pickle on the side.

In Goa, always leave room for dessert. Along with *bebinca*, a layered cake made with dozens of egg yolks, comes *bolo sans rival*, a cake made with the left-over whites. Many sweet dishes are heavy on the coconut, including the *batika* cake and steamed coconut-jaggery festival favourite *pattoyos*, which come wrapped in a segment of banana leaf.

Beach Village (Vithaldas Vaddo, 98221-50847, main course Rs 150, 8am-10pm daily), a Goan family favourite serving excellent food, staffed by friendly and helpful locals. Nearby is **Mojito** (no phone, main course Rs 150, 8am-midnight daily), from the same crew that runs Palolem's iconic Café del Mar, a thatched-roof complex of huts that draws a good mix of visitors and locals. Further down the road is the expensive, upmarket **Ku** (93261-23570, main course Rs 400, 8am-midnight), a little Balinese-style hotel/restaurant run by a European couple with kids. Right opposite is the all white-on-white Miami Beach-style bling of **Club Fresh**, with its all-day DJ and Thai menu, considered by many to be the plushest beach restaurant in Goa (Gawdevaddo, 0832-651-4971, main course Rs 500, 8.30am-10.30pm daily). But the pick of the bunch is in a stand of mature coconut palms down the beach in Ashvem. **La Plage** (98221-21712, main course Rs 250, 8.30am-10pm daily) is the best beachside restaurant in Goa, with an outstanding menu including superb carpaccio, zesty ceviche, and much more. Highly recommended.

INSIDE TRACK MORJIM TURTLES

Ask a local to point out the Olive Ridley turtle nesting sites at **Morjim Beach**. There are several each year, which are discreetly protected from beachgoers by cane barriers and watchful volunteers. If you're lucky, they will tell you when a hatching is expected, and you can join a stream of wildlife enthusiasts in observing the miraculous pop-pop-popping out of the sand of scores of tiny hatchling turtles, as they make their way in a row down to the waterline.

Where to stay

This stretch of beach offers little outside the informal options of huts and ultra-basic rented rooms. The warmest welcome is found at **Montego Bay Beach Village** (Vithaldas Vaddo, 98221-50847), which centres around a charming two-bedroom beach house (Rs 2,500-Rs 6,000), but also offers well-appointed tents with attached bathrooms (Rs 2,000-Rs 5,500) and air-conditioned rooms (Rs 2,500-Rs 6,000) with breakfast included. The friendly owner, Alwyn Fernandes, is a mine of information on Morjim. Well up the beach towards Ashvem is **Papa Jolly's** (New Vaddo, 0832-224-4114, www.papajollysgoa.com, Rs 2,500-Rs 10,000 double), run by a resident Punjabi owner who lived for decades in Austria. You're unlikely to have your peace disturbed – children are not welcome.

Resources

Internet

Sify I-way *C-Shell Café, Mendonsa Vaddo (no phone).* **Open** 9am-10pm daily.

La Plage.

INSIDE TRACK
BEACH BAR HEAVEN

The most impressive of all the Russian beach shacks is Shanti (Ashvem, 98226-42624, 10am-midnight daily), a multi-level space with live music, an impressive menu, right on one of the best patches of beach in the entire state. The man behind its success is Alexander Sukhochev, an energetic entrepreneur and novelist, whose best-selling *The Goa Syndrome* is partly responsible for the Goa hype that continues to grow in Russia (*see p201* **Russian Revolution**).

Getting there

Taxis from Tivim station charge Rs 500 for a 40-minute ride to Morjim and Ashvem. From Dabolim Airport, taxis cost Rs 850 and take around an hour and a half. From Panjim, take the NH-17 past Mapusa and turn left at Vrindavan Hospital for Siolim. Cross Siolim Bridge and follow the signs for Morjim. Taxis from Panjim charge around Rs 650 and take about an hour.

MANDREM

Mandrem still offers the secluded beach experience that first brought travellers to Goa, with friendly locals, communal games of football on the beach in the evenings and total quiet by late evening. Many of the kilometres of broad sand sweeping north towards Arambol are bound by a narrow river running parallel to the ocean, and there's little development here, with a local economy that runs on fishing, toddy-tapping (*see p215* **Toddy and Soul**) and a calm, low-key tourist industry. In the centre of the village is the Ravalnatha Temple, which contains some centuries-old paintings and carvings including an unusual depiction of Garuda, a divine eagle, here shown with a man's arms.

Where to eat & drink

There are few decent eateries in Mandrem, but **Kimaya World Foods** (House 444, Junaswada, 0832-224-7604, 8am-8pm daily), in the centre of Mandrem village, has all the ingredients for a perfect picnic on the beach. Run by the engaging Tanishq Mahajan, Kimaya is a one-stop emporium for home-made products from an emerging local cottage industry in organic food. Grab bunches of peppery rocket, fresh multigrain bread, home-made tofu, pesto, brownies and peanut butter, and head for the beach.

Where to stay

One of Goa's most beautiful beachfront properties is the secluded **Elsewhere** (*see p191* **Boutique Beds**), the converted ancestral home of Mumbai photographer Denzil Sequeira, which also features luxury tents and three newly built guesthouses that mimic the original. Pleasant, but overrun with cats, is **Villa River Cat** (438/1 Junaswada, 0832-224-

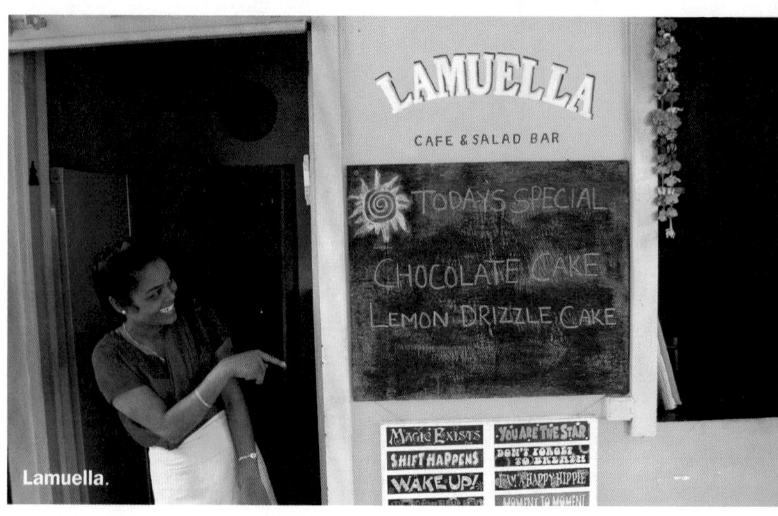

Lamuella.

Russian Revolution

From Russia with luggage.

All through the Cold War and right up to the fall of the Berlin Wall, India and the former Soviet Union kept close diplomatic relations, and warm cultural ties, so both populations maintained a certain affection for each other. But travel was relatively restricted – Aeroflot flew to Delhi and Mumbai, carrying a few privileged bureaucrats who spent all their time filling up vast suitcases with cheap clothes and leather goods to sell on the black market on their return. They never showed up in Goa, where the international tourism scene was dominated for decades by the British and German contingents.

However, all that started to change in 2001, when the very first charter plane from Russia landed at Dabolim airport with around 200 passengers. The next year, the number of flights from Russia shot up to 54, and by 2007, the number of charter travelers from the former Soviet Union were challenging the dominance of the Western European nations. From 2009, there have been over 350 flights arriving from Russia each peak season – scores of which are from places you've probably never heard of like Samara, Ufa, and Rostov-on-Don. Also, more than 100 flights a year connect Siberia to Goa, ferrying tens of thousands of Russians to the Konkan coast of India. Many of these tourists have never left Russia before.

They congregate in huge numbers all along the North Goa coastline, especially in the strip running from Morjim to Ashvem, and Mandrem which has acquired a Slavic flavour with dozens of restaurants serving Russian, Bulgarian, Uzbek and other regional fare. Another hotspot for Russians is the Saturday Night Bazaar in **Arpora** (*see p193*) where you could rub shoulders with upward of 10,000 visitors on any given evening.

7928, www.villarivercat.com, Rs 2,200-Rs 3,200 double), a highly individualistic riverside hotel run by fervent animal-lover Rinoo Sehgal. It features 16 intensely decorated rooms, many with balconies and hammocks overlooking the shore, and a great little vantage point overlooking the beach.

Getting there

Taxis from Tivim take around 45 minutes and charge Rs 600. From Dabolim Airport, taxis cost Rs 850 and take just under two hours. From Siolim Bridge, go straight on the 'new road' and look for signs to Mandrem after eight or nine miles. Taxis from Panjim charge about Rs 600 and take around an hour.

ARAMBOL

Arambol was once the Holy Grail of the later hippie years, the dream beach for travellers seeking the precise location of the middle of nowhere. Arambol is the largest coastal village in Pernem district, with a wide beach clustered with shacks that hosts several thousand visitors a day in high season from November to March. It's become part of the well-beaten track that so many once came here to avoid, with endless lines of travellers hiking up the coastal path to the 'lakeside' beach – an arc of soft sand between the sea and an increasingly polluted lake behind. The lake is bound by thick jungle where naked hippies still occasionally sleep under the stars like their 1960s ancestors.

Where to eat & drink

Relax Inn (Socoilo Vaddo, 98223-87618, main course Rs 120, 8am-11pm daily), run by five Goan brothers, is a friendly shack at the northern end of the beach, serving excellent Italian dishes. Great for seafood is **Fellini's** (Arambol Beach, no phone, main course Rs 200, 11am-11pm daily), a popular Italian restaurant with outstanding home-made gnocchi and wood-fired pizzas. Decent Tibetan and other East Asian food is available at **Rice Bowl** (Socoilo Vaddo, 98507-27329, main course Rs 250, 8am-11pm daily), a Nepali-run restaurant which serves home-made noodles, dumplings and tempura. The new **Café Pacha** (93267-8123/22/21, 11am-midnight daily) has brought a bit of Baga nightlife to Arambol, and hosts ambitious parties every weekend in season.

Where to stay

Arambol's beach huts are basic compared to the sophisticated set-ups available at Palolem. The Naik family rents out over 100 small huts with basic amenities (some have attached toilets, some do not) scattered across the cliffs on the northern end of the beach, with fabulous sea

Keri Beach.

views. Call or ask at the Naik-run **Relax Inn** (Socoilo Vaddo, 98223-87618, huts Rs 500-Rs 750) for details. Modern, airy rooms are available at the Israeli-run **Lamuella Guesthouse** (Arambol Beach Road, 0832-561-4563, Rs 750 double), the smartest (and most expensive) guesthouse in Arambol.

Shopping

Down the beach in Khalcha Vaddo is **Arambol Hammocks** (House 564, no phone, www.arambol.com), a cottage industry set-up selling excellent hand-made hammocks (from Rs 1,000) including extra-wide 'flying carpets'.

Resources

Post office

Arambol Post Office *near Mount Carmel Church (0832-229-7665).* **Open** 9am-5pm Mon-Fri.

Internet

Famafa Hotel *Khalcha Vaddo (0832-229-2516).* **Open** 9am-11pm daily.

Getting there

Taxis from Tivim take an hour and charge Rs 600. From Dabolim Airport taxis cost Rs 850 and take just under two hours. On the 'new road' after Siolim Bridge, look for signs for the Arambol turn-off after 16 kilometres.

TIRACOL

From Arambol, the coastal road climbs to the top of a rugged plateau, then descends through jungle back towards the shoreline and the pristine Tiracol River. Just before the tiny ferry point is **Keri**, a long sliver of shining sand untouched by development. You can spend hours here without seeing another soul, except at weekends when picnickers wander over from neighbouring Maharashtra. High on the headland **Tiracol Fort** stands sentinel over Goa's northern border. Now a heritage hotel, the fort courtyard contains a small, beautiful chapel that is still used by Tiracol villagers three times a week for Mass. You can get there via the free ferry across the Tiracol (every half-hour from 6.30am to 9.30pm). Built by the Marathas in the 18th century and then snatched by the Portuguese, Tiracol Fort became the base

INSIDE TRACK MARKET BARGAINING

The **Mapusa market** (*see p180*) is the best place to stock up on cashew nuts, superbly spiced Goa sausages, and the fiery cashew aguardiente, *feni*. Don't forget to bargain – start off at at least 50 per cent of whatever price you've been offered, and settle for around 75 per cent.

for a disastrous anti-colonial insurrection in 1825, which ended in a bloody rout for the rebels. A plaque in the fort commemorates a later act of anti-colonial resistance in the Gandhian tradition of *satyagraha*, or 'truth-led struggle', by unarmed Goan freedom fighters in 1954. They took the fort and raised an Indian flag, but were later captured after Portuguese troops opened fire, killing two.

INSIDE TRACK BEACH BOATS

As well as backwater trips up the Tiracol River, the **Fort Tiracol Heritage Hotel** offers transport to the beaches of Mandrem and Morjim by boat. It might sound like an overly glamorous way to arrive at a hippie beach but it's a lot more fun than the winding local roads.

Where to stay

In 2004, the **Fort Tiracol Heritage Hotel** (Tiracol, 0832-622-7631, Rs 4,500-Rs 7,000 double) was given a touch of glamour by new management – the owners of the Nilaya Hermitage, the pioneering boutique hotel in **Arpora** (*see p189* **Boutique beds**). It offers seven well-appointed rooms with a lovely self-contained air of privacy, including two suites, each with a turreted balcony and a superb cliff-top view of the Goan coast. It also has an impressive promenade lined with charpoys and tables for alfresco dining, and an excellent restaurant that welcomes day-trippers.

MAPUSA

A half-hour drive inland from the beaches is Mapusa, the commercial, administrative and transport hub of North Goa. Mapusa is a dusty smudge of urban India amid rich, sprawling agricultural lands, and hosts a raucous market spilling across several acres close to the city's main road. Much of Mapusa can be safely avoided, although the Friday market is lively and features an array of local produce trucked in from across the state. A little over kilometres east of the city is **Tivim**, the nearest stop on the Konkan Railway for North Goa's beaches. On the eastern edge of the city is the 'Milagres' ('Miracles') church, **Our Lady of Miracles** (open for Mass 7.30am daily), built on an ancient sacred site where a Hindu temple once stood and now worshipped at by Goans of all religions.

Where to eat & drink

The **Golden Oven** (opposite Mapusa Market, 0832-226-4210, 8am-8.30pm Mon-Sat) is an attractive bakery-café serving freshlymade baked goods – try the delicious beef patties (Rs 19) or the Goa sausage pizza (Rs 24).

Tiracol Fort.

Where to stay

The tourism strip's myriad options are a short drive away. But if you absolutely have to stay in Mapusa, the **GTDC Mapusa Residency** (opposite Kadamba bus stand, 0832-226-2794, Rs 550-Rs 750 double) offers just about adequate en suite rooms, and has a convenient tourist information kiosk in the lobby.

Shopping

Goa's most interesting bookshop lurks in an undistinguished building on the slope of Mapusa Hill. The **Other India Bookshop** (near Mapusa clinic, 0832-226-3306, www.otherindiabookstore.com, 9am-5pm Mon-Fri, 9am-1pm Sat) has over 1,000 books on Goa and Goan history, organic farming, environmentalism, and what seems like every anti-globalisation text ever written.

Getting there

From Panjim, take the NH-17 straight to Mapusa. Taxis usually charge around Rs 200 and take 20 minutes. From Tivim by taxi, it takes around 20 minutes and costs Rs 300. From Dabolim Airport, it's Rs 650 for the one-hour trip.

Resources

Hospital

Vrindavan Hospital *off NH-17 Highway (0832-225-0022).* **Open** 24hrs.

Internet

Sify I-way *Angod, near market, opposite the mosque.* **Open** 9am-9pm Mon-Sat.

Police

Mapusa Police Station *near Municipal Gardens.* **Emergency number** 100.

Post office

Mapusa Post Office *next to Mapusa Police Station (0832-226-2881).* **Open** 9.30am-1pm, 2-5.30pm Mon-Sat.

Tourist information

Goa Tourism Development Corporation Information Office *Mapusa Residency Hotel lobby, opposite Kadamba bus stand, Mapusa (0832-226-2390).*
Open 9.30am-5.30pm Mon-Fri.

GOA

Shalom, Namaste

Israel's love affair with Goa.

Take a walk on Vagator or Arambol Beach during peak season, and you find yourself in a parallel Hebrew-speaking universe that could easily fit into the beachscapes of Tel Aviv and Haifa. More than 25,000 Israelis visit Goa during the winter months each year, and large stretches of the North Goan coastline have developed to cater almost exclusively to them.

This long-running cultural intermingling has historical antecedents. The Konkan coastline has ancient links to the Mediterranean, and the commercial activity of Jewish traders in the area has been recorded for more than 2,000 years. For example, the Chapel of Jesus of Nazareth at Siridao is no less than a converted synagogue, the sole survivor from the Portuguese occupation when several others were reportedly destroyed along with hundreds of Hindu temples.

Even decades after the Portuguese takeover in 1510, Goa hosted tens of thousands of European Jews (including many forced converts to Christianity, aka *Marranos*) as they fled the Inquisition. Among these newcomers was the great Garcia da Orta, whose pioneering work on the medicinal plants of India introduced a wholly new pharmacology to the West. Da Orta died before the Inquisition was imported into Goa in 1560, but his bones were burned at the stake nonetheless, as Goa quickly drained of its Jewish population. His sister was burned alive, and the terrors raged on for two and a half centuries.

In the 1990s, the Jewish presence picked up again, as Israel and India renewed diplomatic relations. And now, in what has become a national rite of passage for Israelis after they've finished military service – backpacking around the world, particularly to India and South America – many end up in Goa. And a lot of them stay on here, as part of the counter cultural world that survives in Goa. It's a New Age phenomenon with deep roots; today's adventurers are completing an ancient circle that has always linked the Konkan coast with the shoreline of the Levant.

Panjim & Old Goa

Goa's capital is full of crumbling colonial charm.

Despite a real estate boom that has set prices soaring and apartment complexes sprouting on its outskirts, Panjim retains an old-fashioned character that feels decidedly different from any other state capital in India. Investment here hasn't been flashy, the architecture remains low-rise and colonial, with plenty of green spaces set in-between, and the riverfront setting ensures the town has a pleasant and breezy atmosphere that would feel positively Caribbean, were it not for the creaky old Portuguese feel.

INTRODUCING PANJIM

Panjim began to emerge around the late 18th century and by the 1820s had become the bustling administrative centre of the Portuguese Estado da India. Beautiful buildings from this period still crowd many of the old neighbourhoods and give the city much of its character. In recent years many of these architectural jewels have been restored and brightly repainted in characteristically Goan tones (white was reserved for the churches).

The city is best explored on foot. Wander along the Mandovi riverfront, take a stroll under the overhanging street arcades of **18th June Road** (named for the day in 1946 when Indian socialist Ram Manohar Lohia called for the Portuguese to be chucked out) and amble through the old quarter of **Fontainhas** – a Latinate labyrinth of sun-kissed ochre and magenta buildings, pocket-sized balconies and tiny plazas, and trees laden with ripening breadfruit and guavas.

The original colonial capital, now known simply as **Old Goa**, is an area of empty avenues and ancient churches. It's a few kilometres away, linked to modern Panjim by a centuries-old causeway that stretches through backwaters and traditional salt pans, and passes through some of the state's earliest colonial architecture at **Ribandar**.

CITY CENTRE

Panjim's commercial centre is dominated by the baroque **Church of Our Lady of the Immaculate Conception** (*see p207*), near the Municipal Garden. An impressively large church sitting atop criss-crossing whitewashed stairways, it has become an instantly recognisable symbol of the city, and looms over the road leading to the **Altinho Hill**, with the Garcia da Orta Garden on one side. Along the Dada Vaidya Road that hugs the Altinho Hill is the **Mahalaxmi Temple**, the first new Hindu temple to be allowed in Portuguese territory after the Inquisition was finally abandoned in the early 19th century after pressure from the British. During the time of the holy terrors, the idol of the goddess Mahalaxmi now kept here was trucked around in the hinterlands in a bullock-cart by devotees anxious to save it from desecration. Just down the road is the attractive Boca de Vaca Spring, where fresh water flows year-round from a cow's head spigot.

Panjim's old Latin Quarter and heritage district is Fontainhas, where strict development laws now preserve hidden gems after senseless

INSIDE TRACK SUPERLATIVE SUNSETS

Skip the 'sunset cruise' up the Mandovi, a kind of Bollywood-flavoured Bateaux Mouche experience complete with flashing lights and ear-splitting music. A much better way to enjoy sunset on the water is on the entirely free ferry that crosses the river from near the Mandovi Hotel to Betim and back all through the day and most of the night. Less noisy, much better people-watching, and you just might see one of the rare estuarine dolphins, which never go anywhere near the noisy party boats.

INSIDE TRACK PANSAIMOL

Visit the **Goa State Archaeological Museum** to see reproductions of the entire Pansaimol shelf (*see p207*) along with all of the most interesting carvings.

demolitions in the 1970s and '80s. A beautifully restored colonial mansion now houses the **Fundaçao Oriente** (Filipe Neri Road, 0832-223-0728), a European NGO founded on a pile of casino lucre from Macao, which works to maintain Goa's colonial-era cultural legacy. Nearby is the neatly maintained heritage inn complex run by the Sukhijia family, which includes **Panjim Pousada**, a restored traditional Hindu home; **Panjim Inn**, a quirky old Goan double-storey house; and the more upmarket **Panjim People's**, formerly a high school. Further down the road is the landmark restaurant, **Ernesto's**, where two scions of an old Panjim family run a gourmet, but very relaxed restaurant.

A short walk along the river leads to two iconic Panjim eating establishments: **Horseshoe**, where chef Vasco Silveira turns out superb Luso-Indian food, and the more modest **Avanti**, serving delicious home-style Goan food with an accent on pork and seafood.

Nearby is the landmark **San Sebastian Chapel**, which houses the large wooden crucifix that once towered over the bloody deliberations at the old Palace of the Inquisition in Old Goa. The collection of altars and paintings here is one of the best in Goa, gathered by refugees who fled the plagues that decimated Old Goa throughout the 17th century. The **Afonso Guesthouse** near here has a rooftop terrace where you can sip coffee and get a bird's-eye view of the neighbourhood. Literally in the middle of the crowded block, accessible only by narrow pathways, is the charming, family-style **Viva Panjim** restaurant.

On the other side of the concrete walkway that crosses the **Ourem River**, a short walk brings you to the ugly concrete high-rise locality called Patto and the **Goa State Archaeological Museum** (*see p207*). A leisurely amble through Fontainhas towards the Mandovi riverfront brings you to the delightful **31st January Road** (named for the date on which the Portuguese republican revolution erupted in 1910), which is lined on both sides with colonial-era buildings, many adorned with public shrines. In the evenings, these icons of Mary and ornate crosses are often visited by groups of hymn-singing supplicants, a village tradition that has survived the shift to the city. At the end of the street is the seashell-encrusted entrance to **Hospedaria Venite**, a popular backpacker hotel and restaurant, whose owner, Luis, is always happy to talk about the neighbourhood and Goa's history.

A couple of minutes' walk towards the waterfront, on one side of the **Secretariat**, is a low, crumbling double-storey building still owned by the Mhamai Kamat family, a Hindu clan that (well in the past) made its fortune trading opium, African slaves and socks (yes, socks) throughout the Portuguese colonies. Its 250-year-old ancestral home still houses around

Viva Panjim.

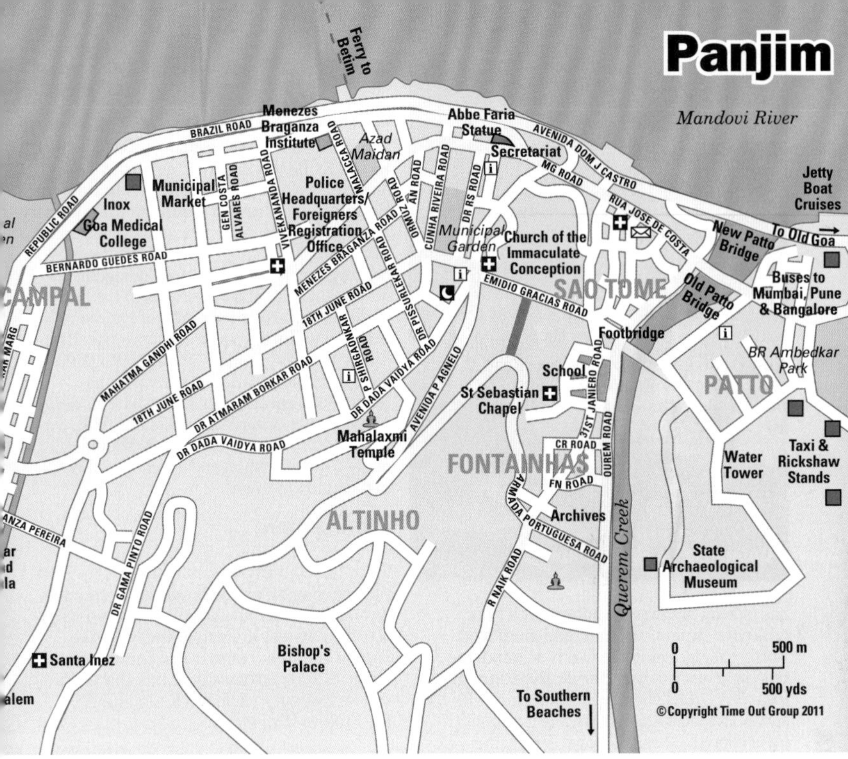

30 people, and is strictly private, but you can still through open wooden doors to the colonnaded inner courtyard distinctive of Konkani Hindu architecture. Right opposite is a statue of **Abbé Faria**, a charismatic 18th-century Goan abbot, political radical and hypnotist (*see p209* **Hypnotic Figure**).

FREE Church of Our Lady of Immaculate Conception

Church Square, Emidio Gracia Road, near Municipal Garden.

A symbol of Portuguese ambition and power when it was built in 1541, with gilded and ornate interiors. The church was then expanded repeatedly, most recently in 1871 to accommodate a huge bell that once hung at the Tower of St Augustine in Old Goa. The church hosts one of the most popular Goan feasts in December, the Feast of Our Lady of the Immaculate Conception, when the nearby square is lit with thousands of candles.

FREE Goa State Archaeological Museum

Near the State Bank of India building, Patto.

Open 9.30am-1.15pm, 2-5.30pm Mon-Fri.

A rather ramshackle museum with a random collection of exhibits, but a few intriguing pieces as well, like the huge table used by the Grand Inquisitor in Old Goa, and an unusual antique lottery machine imported from Lisbon by the colonial administration for weekly state lottery draws.

Where to eat & drink

There's a smörgåsbord of eateries in Panjim offering excellent Goan cooking with an emphasis on super-fresh seafood. In Fontainhas there's **Hotel Avanti** (Rua de Ourem, 0832-242-7179, main course Rs 100, closed Sun), one of Panjim's most typical and popular old-fashioned eateries, run by a hard-working couple who possess an expert home-style touch. Nearby is the great-value **Horseshoe** (Rua de Ourem, Fontainhas, 0832-243-1788, main course Rs 250-Rs 250, closed Sun) where chef Vasco Silveira crafts outstanding Luso-Indian dishes with flavours from his years in Portugal and in the Angolan army. **Viva Panjim** (off 31st January Road, Fontainhas, 0832-242-2405, main course Rs 120) is a backpacker favourite with excellent Goan fare and a sweet courtyard for alfresco dining. Further into the Latin Quarter is **Ernesto's** (Mala, 98230-15921, main course Rs 250), where a man-mountain of a chef (naturally called 'Little Vasco') serves up spirited variations of his grandmother's cooking. The charming, 50-year-old **Hospedaria Venite** (31st January Road, 0832-242-5537, main course Rs 150, closed Sun)

Corina Bar & Restaurant.

has old oak shipwreck timbers for a floor, tables-for-two on balconies and great food. Further down, set in the Old Bus Stand, the unglamorous **Corina Bar & Restaurant** (near PWD, 0832-664-3915, main course Rs 100) serves excellent Goan curries to a fervently loyal clientele. Near the town centre, the popular **Ritz Classic Family Restaurant** (18th June Road, 0832-564-4796, main course Rs 150) is always packed with Panjimites attracted by its super-fresh seafood at great prices. For pastries and snacks, visit the nearby **Mr Baker** (Jesuit House, opposite Municipal Garden, 0832-222-4622, closed Sun), a landmark Panjim bakery since 1922. Try the cashew drops, fantastically addictive little nut meringues invented by the owner, Delia Vaz.

Shopping

In Fontainhas, **Velha Goa** (4/191 Rua de Ourem, 0832-242-6628, www.costavin.com) sells azulejos, hand-painted tiles made in the Iberian tradition, and has a nearby studio where you can watch the artisans at work. Not far away, **Sosa's** (E245, Rua de Ourem, 0832-222-8063) offers clothes by top Indian designers, including funky retro designs by Goa's Savio Jon, all at reasonable prices. Over at Azad Maidan, **UK Traders** (0832-242-7172) sells super Goa-grown cashew nuts for around Rs 300 per kilo.

Where to stay

The **Directorate of Tourism** (Rua de Ourem, Patto, 0832-222-6515) has a list of private homes open to paying guests. The Fontainhas heritage district offers several attractive places to stay, including the family-run **Afonso Guesthouse** (San Sebastian Chapel Square, 0832-222-2359, Rs 600-Rs 700 double) with an attractive terrace. Nearby are the **Panjim Inn**, **Panjim People's** and **Panjim Pousada** (31st January Road, 0832-222-6523, www.panjiminn.com, Rs 2,000-Rs 5,500 double), three atmospheric heritage hotels with the same management, nestled together at a crossroads in the heart of the district. Near the centre of Panjim is **Manvin's Hotel** (Souza Towers, opposite Municipal Garden, 0832-222-4412, Rs 1,000 double), an unremarkable hotel with basic rooms but pleasant river views. The modern **Nova Goa** (Borkar Road, 0832-222-6231, www.hotelnovagoa.com, Rs 2,500 double) offers a good location and excellent value in the centre of town.

Getting there

From Dabolim airport, pre-paid taxis for a ride into Panjim can be hired from a counter just outside the arrivals hall for around Rs 500. The nearest Konkan Railway stop to Panjim is Karmali (also called Carambolim) about 13 kilometres away. Taxis charge Rs 200-Rs 250, autorickshaws Rs 150-Rs 200 for a ride to Panjim.

THE WATERFRONT

The Mandovi riverfront road that links the district of **Sao Tome** to the rest of Panjim, and then to **Campal** and **Miramar** is named after Dayanand Bandodkar, Goa's charismatic first Chief Minister after local government was established in 1963. A pleasant riverfront walkway runs along almost the entire length from the quayside where innumerable brightly lit tourist cruisers are berthed. Near here the waterfront is dominated by the Idalcao Palace, now known as the **Old Secretariat** (*see p210*), an imposing 400-year-old mansion. Further down D Bandodkar Marg is the Mandovi Hotel, once the city's premier hotel and still good-value accommodation. Nearby is the somewhat down-at-heel **Central Library** (the oldest public library in Asia) and the Menezes-Braganza Institute, occupying one corner of a massive structure that also houses a dozen government offices and the Panjim police headquarters. Just outside is **Azad Maidan**, a cheerful open space teeming with schoolboys playing cricket through the afternoon. It holds a pavilion of Corinthian columns, salvaged from Old Goa, which shade a memorial to **Tristao Braganza Cunha**, an important Goan anti-colonial freedom fighter. Further up on D Bandodkar Marg is the vibrant **Municipal Market** (*see p210*), still holding on to its traditional patch in the face of efforts to shift vendors to a new building. Slightly further on, the recently renovated Goa Medical College Heritage District includes some of the cinema infrastructure that's used for the annual International Film Festival of India.

The pretty, aristocratic locality of Campal houses a set of the grandest houses in the city. They're all out of bounds for visitors, but an upper floor of one has been converted by Goan designer **Wendell Rodricks** (*see p211*) into an airy boutique selling elegant couture and all kinds of accessories from furniture to skin cream. Across the road stands a statue of Francis Luis Gomes, an eloquent orator who was the lone Goan representative in the Portuguese parliament, and argued passionately for pan-Indian nationalism 50 years before the freedom movement began in the rest of the country.

The statue overlooks the entrance to the **Campal Children's Park**, a beautifully situated public garden that spreads right up to the bank of the river under the shade of hundreds of casuarina trees. It's a great place to people-watch in the evenings, with Goan families from across the social spectrum happily wandering the curving pathways and hoisting ecstatic youngsters on to swings and slides, and now features a pleasant little vegetarian café. A similar riverfront garden is located a bit further down the road in the grounds of the **Kala Academy** (D Bandodkar Marg, Campal, 0832-242-0451, open 9am-9pm

Hypnotic Figure

Goa's highly-influential master of suggestion.

On the Panjim waterfront right next to the sprawling Secretariat building stands a 60-year-old bronze statue of **Jose Custodio Faria** standing with his arms outstretched over a hypnotised woman. It's a distinctive piece of public art that celebrates a highly unusual man. Faria was an abbot, revolutionary schemer and pioneering 18th-century hypnotist, and one of the first Indians to become truly famous in Europe.

He was born in Candolim in 1746 to aristocratic, ambitious parents who soon separated. His mother became a nun, and eventually rose to the still exalted position of Mother Superior at the massive Santa Monica convent in Old Goa that is still the largest in Asia. His father became a priest, and the young Faria eventually followed his father into the Church. Realising that the young man's prodigious intellect and charisma would be stifled in the colonies, Faria's father took him to Europe, where he was enrolled in Rome's elite Propaganda Fide college. Within a few years, his brilliance in theological studies brought him renown. He was invited by the Pope to deliver a Pentecost sermon at the Sistine Chapel, and soon after to preside over Mass at the royal Portuguese court at the Queluz Palace near Lisbon. On this occasion, Faria was bedazalled at the sight of the queen and her courtiers, and became tongue-tied. He later recounted that a whispered phrase in Konkani from his father – '*Hi sogli bhaji, kathor re bhaji*' ('They're all vegetables, just cut the vegetables') – unfroze him. It was this early lesson in the power of suggestion that set Faria on the path to ground-breaking ideas about hypnotism.

Many of the historical details are sketchy, but Faria and his father were later accused of plotting to expel the Portuguese from Goa and were forced to flee the court, turning up in 1787 in revolutionary France. There Faria commanded a battalion against the anti-Royalist National Convention, which was crushed by the young Napoleon Bonaparte, before he was locked up in the Bastille. During his time in jail, Faria supposedly invented the modern version of the game of draughts, further developed his scientific study of hypnotism and became so notorious that Alexandre Dumas even included a fictional version of him as the 'mad abbé' in *The Count of Monte Cristo*.

Faria emerged from prison at the start of the 19th century to engage in a series of acrimonious public debates with Anton Mesmer about the nature of hypnosis. The Frenchman believed that hypnosis was the result of an exceptional 'animal magnetism' exuded by the hypnotist. But Faria declared that the hypnotist merely implanted suggestions in the mind of the subject, and that hypnosis was a kind of pact in which the subject's own imagination was paramount. This idea was later proved essentially correct, and is now known as 'post-hypnotic suggestion'. But although Faria provided a crucial insight that underpins modern psychoanalysis, it is his rival Mesmer who remains celebrated in the West with the word 'mesmerise'.

daily), where you can buy a cup of coffee for Rs 5, and relax on lawns and benches overlooking the river. The complex was designed by Charles Correa, the internationally renowned Goan architect. It's a couple of kilometres on to **Miramar Beach**. The beach is broadest right off Miramar Circle where middle-class Panjimites gather every evening for sunsets, walks in the fresh breeze and streetside snacks. Unfortunately, the water isn't clean enough for swimming, but the beach is long and pretty, with sweeping views of the mouth of the Mandovi River and the Aguada headland.

A few kilometres further down the riverfront highway is Dona Paula, home to the huge **National Institute of Oceanography** at Dona Paula Circle (0832-245-0450, public science seminars every Thursday), a world-class research institute and the leading scientific authority on the biology of the Indian Ocean. Nearby is the tiny British Cemetery left over from a brief occupation during the Napoleonic Wars, and restored after a chance visit by Margaret Thatcher a couple of decades ago. Further up, the road leads to the **Cabo Raj Nivas** – the mansion of the state Governor. The complex includes a magnificently situated chapel on a promontory between the Zuari and Mandovi rivers. Visitors can only enter for Sunday services (from 8am) and Midnight Mass on Christmas Eve. The effort is worth it for the location, the beautiful chapel and a rousing choir considered the best in Goa.

Idalcao Palace/Old Secretariat

Panjim Waterfront.

Idalcao Palace is a mansion built as a summer palace in the early 16th century by the Bijapuri ruler Yusuf Adil Shah. It stood virtually isolated on the island for centuries until Panjim began to grow around it under the rule of the Portuguese, who used it as the seat of the Viceroys of the Portuguese East Indies for over a century. The grand arch over the main entrance used to carry the Viceroy's ornate crest; it now displays India's national symbol, the Ashoka Chakra.

FREE Menezes-Braganza Institute

Malacca Road, opposite Azad Maidan.
Open 9.30am-1pm, 2-5.45pm Mon-Fri.

INSIDE TRACK
BRILLIANT BRUNCH

Head to **Farm Products** before 10.30am for some of the most delicious home-made potato-chops, croquettes and other Goan delicacies which get polished off long before lunchtime.

Before 1961, the Institute was named after Vasco da Gama and the entranceway still holds a mesmerising floor-to-ceiling mural of hand-painted tiles commemorating the colonisation of the Indies, adorned with stanzas from the epic *Os Lusiades* written by the Portuguese national poet, Luís Vaz de Camões.

Where to eat & drink

At Azad Maidan, **Delhi Darbar** (0832-222-2544, main course Rs 250-Rs 300) is the best of Panjim's tandoori restaurants, with good service. Also on the Maidan is **Farm Products** (0832-222-5287), a cute three-seater snack shop run by octogenarian Goan freedom fighter Alvaro Pereira, who serves a clientele of old Panjim characters. Along the waterfront road, Miramar's **Mum's Kitchen** (98221-75559, main course Rs 250) serves a fascinating menu of dishes from Goa's various culinary traditions, which it calls 'our move to save Goa's cuisine'.

Nightlife

For Indian tourists in Panjim the evening river cruises departing from the Santa Monica pier are a must-do. Boats leave all evening, starting from 5pm, and chug up to the mouth of the Mandovi with an enthusiastically performed song-and-dance routine to entertain passengers en route (Rs 100 per person). Night cruises depart from 8.30pm. Contact the **Goa Tourism Development Corporation** (0832-222-3396, www.goa-tourism.com) for further details. Panjim's only proper nightclub is **O-Zone** (Goa Marriott Resort, Miramar, 0832-246-3333, www.goamarriottresort.com, open from 7pm daily, Rs 500 cover charge Sat), a bit on the small side but coolly lit and decked out in white. Open throughout the year, it's popular with Panjim's posh kids but usually comes into its own when there's nothing else to do – in the tourist off-season, from May to September. The newest nightspot in the area is **Ice Cube** (Miramar, 98221-02991, open from 7pm daily), which features live music almost every evening, including a range of international jazz acts. More and better live jazz becomes available a few times a year at an impromptu venue run out of a stately house in Campal by the genial Armando Gonsalves. Check www.heritagejazz.com for listings.

Shopping

Municipal Market

D Bandodkar Marg, Panjim Waterfront.
Open dawn-dusk daily.

Lively and crowded, Goa's municipal market is packed with Goa-grown produce like Alphonso,

Basilica of Bom Jesus. *See p212.*

Mankurade, Ilario and Monserrate mangoes and dozens of bananas, from delicate fingerlings to enormous green plantains. Early mornings here are the best time to visit, with fisherwomen in full voice and baskets spilling over with white river prawns, estuarine fish and baby sharks.

Wendell Rodricks Design Space

Campal, near Francis Luis Gomes garden (0832-2238-177/2420-604/www.wendellrodricks.com). **Open** 10am-6.30pm Mon-Sat. **Credit** AmEx, MC, V.
Elegant couture by Goa's most celebrated designer and favourite of the Bollywood set.

Entertainment

Check out the latest Bollywood offerings at the **INOX Cinema** (behind Goa Medical College building, Campal, 0832-242-0999), a modern multiplex built for the first International Film Festival of India to be held in Goa, in 2004.

Where to stay

The **Mandovi Hotel** (D Bandodkar Marg, 0832-242-6270, www.hotelmandovigoa.com, Rs 3,000 double) on the riverfront road was once Panjim's most exclusive hotel. These days it's an art deco oldie in need of renovation, but still provides good service and value. It's been supplanted by the **Goa Marriott** (Mandovi Waterfront, Miramar, 0832-246-3333, www.goamarriottresort.com, Rs 6,000 double), easily the most luxurious hotel in Panjim and a kind of clubhouse for Goa's moneyed elite, with an unbeatable location on the waterfront. Also contending for the top spot is the excellent **Cidade de Goa** (Vainguinim Beach, 0832-245-4545, www.cidadedegoa.com, Rs 4,000 double), with its own private beach. A little cheaper is **Prainha** (Dona Paula 0832-245-3881, www.prainha.com, Rs 2,000-Rs 3,000 double), a cantilevered hotel with a secluded private beach and a lovely outdoor pool.

OLD GOA

Old Goa was the original capital of the Portuguese colony, a European-style metropolis whose grand architecture reflected its tremendous power, wealth and prestige. Known as Goa Dourada or 'Golden Goa', it made a fortune in spices and slaves. In the western part of the city lay a huge barracks, the first European-style hospital in Asia, a foundry and a vast arsenal. In the east was its sprawling marketplace and a waterfront slave market, which sent African slaves across Asia. Dominating the centre were churches, cathedrals, monasteries and convents built by the Franciscans, Dominicans, Augustinians and other religious orders. Plague outbreaks in the 17th century forced residents to flee. Today, only the soaring architecture remains.

On the crest of the city's tallest hill sits the **Chapel of Our Lady of the Mount**, one of the earliest Portuguese buildings in Goa, commissioned by Afonso de Albuquerque after he took control of the city in 1510. It's built on the site of a fierce battle between Bijapuri troops and the Portuguese. The chapel has been restored and hosts a classical music festival (*see p213*) every March. Come here at sunrise to enjoy a magical view of slanting sunlight slowly illuminating the churches' whitewashed façades in the distance below. Perched on the slope of **Holy Hill** is the fortress-like **Convent of Santa Monica**, the largest convent in Asia. Access is restricted, but if you ask nicely, you might be allowed into the private chapel at the rear, which is covered with stunning 17th-century frescoes. One wing open to the public houses the **Museum of Christian Art** (0832-

INSIDE TRACK
THE QUEST FOR KETAVAN

Underneath the **St Augustine Tower** (*see p212*) you'll find an archaeologists' enclosure. Enquire here about the search for Ketavan, the Georgian queen who was martyred in Shiraz in the 16th century, and whose body was spirited away to Goa. The Indians have been trying to locate her body in the ruins for years, ever since the former Soviet state achieved independence and asked for its Queen back.

GOA

Monte Music Festival.

228-5299) – a collection of intricate chalices and other ritual objects, along with a few important Christian paintings.

Opposite the Convent of Santa Monica a turret of laterite stone, now known as the **St Augustine Tower**, is all that's left of a grand church complex of the Augustinian mission. Over the centuries the eight chapels, plus the covent and library that were here collapsed, with the last sections crumbling in 1942.

Nearby is the **Royal Chapel of St Anthony**, another mid-16th-century church (dedicated to the patron saint of Portugal) that fell into decrepitude until it was restored in 1960. The simple painted idol of St Anthony kept here was treated as a full captain in the Portuguese army and each year was taken for a ceremonial ride through Old Goa to collect his officer's wages from the colony's Treasurer.

Just behind is the beautifully detailed **Chapel of Our Lady of the Rosary**, one of the first buildings built by the Portuguese in Goa, on the site of a pitched battle that Afonso de Albuquerque considered the turning point in his campaign for a foothold in the subcontinent. Down the hill along Rua Das Naus de Ormuz is the World Heritage Site precinct of the **Basilica of Bom Jesus**, Goa's most famous church and resting place of the body of St Francis Xavier. Each decade, his body is removed and put on public display at the impressive **Sé Cathedral** (7am-6pm daily) across the central square from the Basilica of Bom Jesus. This huge Dominican-built church remains the largest in Asia, despite one of its towers collapsing after being struck by lightning in the 18th century. Its typically Corinthian interior includes a barrel-vaulted ceiling and two long side aisles, and a masterpiece of a gilded altar.

Across the road towards the riverfront from the Se Cathedral sits another baroque architectural jewel, the **Convent and Church of St Cajetan**. Further on, at the riverfront, new arrivals to the colonies first set eyes on the fabled Goa Dourada through the granite-faced **Arch of the Viceroys**.

Arch of the Viceroys

Near the riverfront.

This dilapidated stone gateway is the Portuguese equivalent of the Gateway of India built by the British in Mumbai – but this one came first, by 200 years. It was built by Vasco da Gama's great-grandson, Francisco da Gama, who became Viceroy of Goa at the end of the 16th century and promptly erected this tribute to his ancestor. It was the main entrance to the city and the symbolic spot where Portuguese supreme commanders of the Indies handed responsibility to their successors.

Basilica of Bom Jesus

Rua das Naus de Ormuz, opposite Sé Cathedral, Old Goa. **Open** 7am-6pm daily.

Goa's best-known church and the one whose façade and layout shows no local influences – it has a clearly Italianate look. The last of the Medicis, Cosimo II, the Grand Duke of Tuscany, financed the opulent altar that now holds the body of St Francis Xavier. It was sculpted by the Florentine artist Giovanni Batista Foggini. He took ten years to carve the three tiers of marble and jasper with intricate scenes from Xavier's life. Inside, in a silver casket, lies the 'incorruptible' body, whose face can be seen through a glass window. The body has become an object of mass pilgrimage for its Exposition held once every decade – the last one was in 2004.

Chapel of Our Lady of the Rosary

Near St Augustine Tower.

Built by Hindu and Muslim workmen inherited from the Bijapuri kingdom, the church developed a unique hybrid style of Eastern detail combined with a Western layout. The chapel's style was later

INSIDE TRACK MUSEUM OF CHRISTIAN ART

At the **Museum of Christian Art** (*see p211*), ask for Natasha Fernandes, the wonderfully pleasant and incredibly well-informed curator. She can guide you around the museum and make up for the unfortunate paucity of information resources on the objects – she'll also point you to the best sites in Old Goa that fall outside the usual tours.

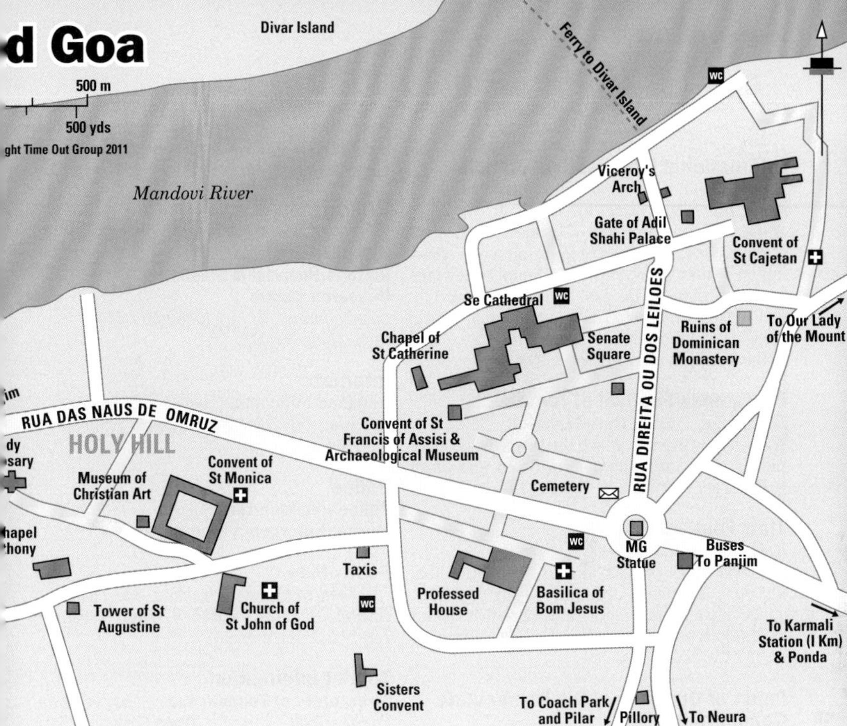

widely copied across the new territory, a crucible for the fusion architecture now called Luso-Indian.

Convent & Church of St Cajetan

Rua Direita, near the Arch of the Viceroys.
Built by a team of Italian friars dispatched to India by Pope Urban III, this is the last domed church in Goa, supposedly modelled on St Peter's in Rome. At its centre lies a mystery, a large slab of stone that covers a well that supposedly belongs to a Hindu temple that once stood on this spot. The story of the temple and the reason for the well's prominence here are lost to history. The church altar is an exuberant work of art, with angels and cherubs rising to a spectacular gilded crown. In the crypt below, sealed caskets hold the remains of senior Portuguese officials who never made it home.

Where to eat & drink

Star Bar (Near Goa Institute of Management, Ribandar, no phone, main course Rs 100) has bad service and indifferent decor, but its mussels and fish are legendary; Goans will drive across the state for them.

Getting there

Old Goa is about 9.5 kilometres from Panjim on a scenic road alongside the Mandovi River. Taxis routinely charge an exorbitant Rs 300 one-way, autorickshaws Rs 200. Buses leave from the Kadamba bus stand (Patto, opposite Ambedkar Garden) every half-hour. One-way fare to Old Goa is Rs 20.

Festivals

Carnival

Panjim Waterfront. **Date** Feb.
It might not be as risqué as its Brazilian counterpart but this Latin-flavoured street party in the heart of Goa is worth hanging around for. An afternoon parade of colourful floats along the waterfront, which is then followed by a charming fancy-dress ball on the city streets behind.

Monte Music Festival

Chapel of Our Lady of the Mount, Old Goa.
Date Mar.
One of Goa's best annual events, a festival of Indian and Western classical music. Concerts take full advantage of the stunning setting: both inside the church and in a small amphitheatre nearby. Call Fundaçao Oriente on 0832-243-6108 for details.

Shigmo

Panjim Waterfront. **Date** Mar.
Shigmo is the spring festival celebrated as Holi in other parts of India. Goa's Hindu hinterland takes

centre stage on the capital's streets with vibrant, noisy, colourful displays and floats.

International Film Festival of India

Kala Academy/INOX Cinema, Campal, Panjim (www.iffigoa.org). **Date** Nov.
A pleasant Indian version of Cannes. The festival encompasses two weeks of non-stop movie viewing on Panjim's waterfront, and public viewings across the state. In the past, IFFI has been accompanied by open-air screenings on Miramar Beach, displays of public art and a parade of floats to add to the festive atmosphere.

Fontainhas Festival of the Arts

Fontainhas, Panjim. **Date** November.
A week-long event in which the heritage houses of India's only Latin Quarter turn into temporary galleries showcasing Goa's best artists.

Tiatr Festival

Kala Academy. **Date** Nov.
Crowded, super-popular annual competition that functions as a kind of Olympics of Tiatr, the folksy, vaudevillian Konkani musical theatre that retains tremendous popularity in Goa. Call Kala Academy (0832-242-0451) for details.

Feast of Our Lady of the Immaculate Conception

Panjim Church Square. **Date** 8 Dec.
The largest of Panjim's traditional street fairs. Stalls crowd the roads in front of the church selling everything from peanuts to plastic buckets to candles as big as your arm.

Resources

Hospital

Vintage Hospital & Medical Research Centre
Caculo Enclave, St Inez (0832-564-4401, www.vintage3.com).

Internet

Reliance Infocomm *Campal, near Kala Academy (0832-243-8176).* **Open** 10am-8pm Mon-Sat.

Police

Police Headquarters *opposite Azad Maidan, Panjim.* **Emergency number** 100.

Post office

Old Tobacco Exchange building, Sao Tome, Panjim. (0832-222-3704/06). **Open** 9.30am-1pm, 2-5.30pm Mon-Sat.

Tourist information

Directorate of Tourism *Rua de Ourem, Patto, Panjm (0832-222-6515).* **Open** 9.30am-1.15pm, 2pm-5.45 pm.

Club Portugal

Life in Lusophone Goa.

Colonial-era Panjim lingers on under the high ceilings and slow-spinning fans of the **Clube Vasco da Gama** (*1st Floor, D-Souza Towers, Panjim Market, 0832-242-3768*) near the Municipal Garden. Established in 1909, Clube Vasco was a social club reserved for the Portuguese-speaking elite until Liberation in 1961. After that, they faced resentment and suspicion from Indian nationalists, and many emigrated first to Portugal and Brazil, and later to the UK, Canada and Australia.

Those who stayed behind self-consciously stepped into the shadows: they largely stopped speaking Portuguese in public, and bent over backwards to prove that they were as Indian as everyone else.

But a solid 50 years later, many such families still reside in the houses their ancestors built in the city's sleepy neighbourhoods of Campal, Fontainhas and Sao Tome. And Clube Vasco remains at the centre of social life. Members still congregate there every day, to while away idle afternoons enjoying the steady breeze through the French windows overlooking the nicely renovated Jardim de Garcia da Orta (named after a pioneering botanist), prop up the bar with glasses of *feni*, the local cashew liquor (*see p187*), and to listen to live music or sing karaoke in the evenings. Tourists are made more than welcome. The afternoons are particularly atmospheric: the clock ticks slowly, the roast tongue sandwiches on distinctive Goan bread go down well with the *feni*, and the next thing you know, the sun is going down.

In a newly self-confident India, Portuguese-speaking Panjimites feel a lot less reticent about expressing their hybrid identity. It'll only take a little prodding to hear stories of life in Goa before the Indian 'invasion', when goods were imported tax-free from Europe, Panjim's roadways and marketplaces were clean, and law enforcement had an efficient, fascist bite.

South Goa

South Goa showcases the original charms of India's sunshine state.

It's bigger, less developed, more rustic, and has by far the best of Goa's beaches: 24 kilometres of shining, uninterrupted white sands that stretch from **Cansaulim** to **Mobor**. And then there are the spectacular ruins of the **Cabo de Rama Fort**, as well – certainly, South Goa's seaside charms are plenty. But the interior, too, has lots to offer, with astounding Mesolithic carvings at **Pansaimol**, resident tigers and leopards in the jungle of **Cotigao Wildlife Sanctuary**, and the lush agricultural bounty of the hinterland of **Quepem**.

INTRODUCTION

Rich farmlands and billions of dollars in annual mining income have so far kept South Goa from racing to replicate North Goa's neon lights and crowded party strip, which means it has been relatively untouched by mass-market or charter tourism. It's also the home turf of fading generations of Luso-Indian grandees – the aristocracy whose mansions still line the streets of **Margao**, where Portuguese is still widely spoken. These days, the south's idyllic character is coming under threat from a rash of proposed development. Construction companies and real-estate entrepreneurs have snapped up stretches of land all the way down to the Karnataka border, and though it will probably take years to become as hectic as the north, larger-scale development looks inevitable as several five-star hotel projects have been cleared for construction. Until that happens, much of the south offers a glimpse of an older Goa, where farmers work the same fields and orchards that their families have tended for centuries. Splendid rococo and baroque churches gleam whitewashed on slow-moving backwaters. Centuries-old colonial-era houses are still meticulously maintained, and locals retain the gracious culture and beautiful manners that still count in Goa.

BOGMALO

Right in the path of approaching jet-liners, the hidden cove-like beach of Bogmalo is becoming increasingly popular with visitors who want no-frills sun-and-sand holidays without the crowds of the north strip. Locals also come here to party when other beaches get too crowded, and there's a long line of restaurants and bars trailing up Bogmalo Beach. It's relaxed and uncluttered, with a few family-run hotels and the somewhat dated and dilapidated five-star **Bogmalo Beach Resort**. The beach road ends at **Joet's Bar & Restaurant**, a local institution that started out as a beach shack run by a fisherman serving his day's catch. Now it's a friendly bar and restaurant run by his son, with a clean, good-value guesthouse at the back and the neat **Coconut Creek Hotel** a few hundred metres across the road. If you have just one day in Goa and can't stray far from the airport, Bogmalo would be your beach.

Where to eat & drink

★ Joet's Bar & Restaurant

Bogmalo Beach (0832-253-8036). **Open** 8am-midnight daily. **Main course** Rs 250. **Credit** MC, V.

Clean and bright, with a non-stop rock 'n' roll soundtrack, this is one of Goa's best beachfront hangouts and a favourite with locals, who will drive across the state to while away an evening here.

Entertainment

A 15-minute drive north from Bogmalo, on Vasco's Baina Beach, **H20** (Baina Beach, 0832-394-6052, closed after sunset), offers a range of water sports including parasailing (Rs 900), kayaking (Rs 150 for 30mins), jet skiing (Rs 250 for 5mins), glass-bottomed boat rides (Rs 150 for a 30min tour) and speedboat rides (Rs 450 for a six-seater for 5-10mins).

> **INSIDE TRACK**
> **KID-FRIENDLY BEACHES**
>
> If you're travelling with children, **Utorda** is the best beach bet in South Goa. It has clean sands and waters, and the main part of the beach is comfortably flat and not subject to the dangerous riptides that claim dozens of lives in Goa each year. Best of all, there are always trained lifeguards on watch all through the season.

Where to stay

Coconut Creek

Bimut Ward, near Sts Cosme & Damian Church, Bogmalo (0832-253-8090). **Rates** Rs 3,950 double. **Credit** AmEx, MC, V.

You'll need to reserve a fair way in advance as getting a room here can be tough in peak season. It's heavily booked up by repeat customers and the loyalty is well deserved: Coconut Creek's staff go the extra mile with warm, friendly service (including, much to the delight of Mumbaikars used to the city's 1.30am curfew, keeping the bar open 'until the last guest leaves').

Getting there

A taxi from Dabolim Airport to Bogmalo takes about ten minutes and costs around Rs 200. From Margao station, it's a 40-minute taxi ride for around Rs 400.

CANSAULIM TO BETALBATIM

South of Bogmalo, the beach turns to rocky cliffside for a few kilometres before descending on to a 24-kilometre (15-mile) stretch of white-sand beach from **Cansaulim** to **Betalbatim** and beyond through **Utorda** and **Majorda**. Much like North Goa, the entire beach is lined with palm-thatched restaurant-bar beach shacks, backed by thick coconut palms yielding to hectares of well-tended paddy fields. The **Park Hyatt** in Cansaulim is arguably the state's most luxurious hotel, but unfortunately it is loomed over by a hideous, colossal agrochemical plant. **Zeebop by the Sea**, a restaurant in Utorda, is a pretty shack with tables on the sand and perfect sunset views.

Another couple of kilometres down the surf's edge and you're in Betalbatim, another popular hangout for Goans. One big reason is **Martin's Corner**, a kitschy and hugely popular Goan restaurant five minutes' walk from the waterline. If you feel like a change of scene, take a five- to seven-minute ride inland to Casa **Walfrido Antao** (next to the turning for Nanu Resorts), a whimsically ornate Indo-Portuguese home with windows made of oyster shells, unfortunately closed to visitors but worth admiring from the outside.

Where to eat & drink

Martin's Corner

Betalbatim (0832-288-0061). **Open** 11am-3pm, 6.30pm-midnight daily. **Main course** Rs 300. **Credit** MC, V.

GOA

A beloved South Goa institution, with a devoted Indian clientele that includes the cricketer Sachin Tendulkar (his favourite dish is the king crab, as every waiter is sure to remind you). Dine under arches of red laterite and bamboo thatch under the gaze of caricatures of Goan folk. Serving mostly Goan seafood, the truth be told, Martin's cooking is not outstanding, but it is decent and the setting and atmosphere are lovely – and frankly, there's very little else worthwhile around for miles.

★ Zeebop by the Sea

Opposite Kenilworth Beach Resort, Utorda Beach (0832-275-5333). **Open** *Oct-Apr* 10am-10pm daily. **Main course** Rs 270. **Credit** MC, V.

One of the best beach shacks in Goa, on an empty, atmospheric stretch of white-sand beach. It's by far the most popular beach restaurant for a cross-section of middle-class Goan families, who pile in on weekends and stay late into the night for the live bar's music.

Where to stay

Despite the presence of a monstrous agrochemical plant nearby, the **Park Hyatt Goa Resort and Spa** in Cansaulim (Arossim Beach, Cansaulim, 0832-272-1234, www.goa.park.hyatt.com, Rs 9,000 double) has won a clutch of awards for its magnificently landscaped grounds and offers every imaginable facility, including optional private gardens and the largest swimming pool in India. Further south in Utorda, the **Casa Ligorio** (near Kenilworth Beach Resort, Utorda, 0832-275-5405, www.casaligorio.com, Rs 3,000 double) isn't attractive to look at but offers decent value, with nine well-appointed rooms, each with its own balcony, set in pleasant gardens. In Majorda the best option is the **Alila Diwa** (Adao Vaddo, 0832-274-6800, www.alilahotels.com/diwagoa, Rs 10,000-Rs 15,000 doubles), a new hotel with outstanding service and a large swimming pool. There is also the **Kenilworth Beach Resort** (Majorda Beach, 0832-275-4180, www.kenilworthhotels.com, Rs 7,500 double), a sprawling five-star just metres from the beach, with a modern spa specialising in ayurvedic massages and treatments. Unusual facilities make the difference at the **Majorda Beach Resort** (Majorda Beach, 0832-275-4871, www.majordabeachresort.com, Rs 7,500 double), which include separate gymnasiums for men and women, indoor and outdoor pools and squash and tennis courts. An ambitious new entry is **Vivenda dos Palhacos** (Costa Vaddo, Majorda, 0832-322-1119, Rs 6,000-Rs 10,000 double), a converted villa run by the Hayward siblings, British expatriates with a long family connection to India.

Entertainment

The **Go Kart Race Track** (Belloy-Nuvem, just off NH-17, 98225-89313, open from 4pm Mon-Sat, all day Sun) is widely considered India's finest go-karting track – 375 metres of asphalt with fabulous views of the coastline and the Arabian Sea. Spin around at speeds of up to 65 kph (40mph) in four-stroke, six-horsepower karts. Ten laps cost Rs 120.

Getting there

Taxis from Dabolim Airport or Margao station to Cansaulim, Utorda or Majorda both take around 20 minutes and cost Rs 400.

COLVA

Like Calangute, its spiritual doppelganger in the north, poor old Colva gets a bad rap. Part of the reason is that, just like Calangute, it was once a favoured getaway for the landed local elite during the summer months, and has now been taken over by tourists from neighbouring states, who paddle in the surf in their saris and generally behave like the first-time beachgoers they are. But Colva has an outstandingly broad expanse of sand and plenty of room for everyone. Unlike Calangute and Baga, there are no deckchairs hogging the sand at high-tide mark, and relatively few vendors hawking rugs and massages. Also, it's still a working beach: dozens of fishing boats depart each day from here before dawn. On the downside the dunes have been levelled for no good reason, and the area near Colva bus stand is always strewn with unsightly garbage.

INSIDE TRACK
EARLY MORNING CATCH

It's worth getting up early at least once and heading down to the beach to see the catch come in on the traditional fishing boats. The sight of silvery shoals of fish being unloaded in the morning light is unforgettable, but beware if you're reasonably fit, or just fit-looking – you might be thrust right into the action and asked to haul a rope or throw a shoulder into the pulling-up of the boats on to the beach.

Where to eat & drink

Amici Gelato

Near Colva Police Station, before turn-off to Benaulim (98221-23173). **Open** 10am-midnight daily. **Ice-cream** cone Rs 100.

Kentuckee

Shop No. 28, Colva Beach (0832-278-8107). **Open** 24 hrs. **Main course** Rs 200. **Credit** MC, V.

The best of an undistinguished scrum of beachfront restaurants and shacks. One of the original Colva institutions, Kentuckee has a decades-old reputation for good seafood.

Where to stay

A great location sets the excellent-value **Longuinho's** (Colva beachfront, 0832-278-8068, www.longuinhos.net, Rs 1,500-Rs 1,700 double) apart from the pack, on a prime spot of beach with lawns leading right up to the sand. The **Star Beach Resort** (near football ground, 0832-278-8166, www.starbeachresortgoa.com, Rs 1,200-Rs 1,500 double) is a newly built hotel offering good-value rooms, many with pleasant views of nearby rice fields, and the best pool in the area. **La Ben** (Colva Beach Road, 0832-278-8040, www.laben.net, Rs 1,000 double) offers clean rooms in a modern building, with an open-air rooftop restaurant. **Soul Vacation** (Colva beachfront, 0832-278-8144, www.soulvacation.in, Rs 5,000-Rs 6,500 double) is a slightly cramped but ambitious 'concept hotel' located close to the beach, with an attached restaurant, **Shalom**, that's rapidly becoming a popular nightspot with young, moneyed visitors to South Goa.

Nightlife

The **Boomerang** (4th Ward, Colva Beach, 0832-278-8071, open until the last person leaves) has a circular bar right on the beach and attracts a crowd of locals and older Brits with regular live music and karaoke. **Gatsby's**

Longuinho's.

(Colva Beach Road, 0832-278-9745, open 9pm-2am, entry Rs 250 including two drinks) is Colva's only 'nightclub'; a tiny, dark disco with mirrored walls playing house and hip hop for Euro-tourists.

Resources

Internet

Hello Mae *Colva Beach Road (0832-278-0108).* **Open** 7.30am-11pm daily.

Getting around

Taxis from Dabolim Airport take around 45 minutes to Colva and charge Rs 500. From Margao, it's a 15-minute ride for around Rs 150.

BENAULIM

According to the *Skanda Purana*, an ancient Hindu text, Goa was created by Lord Parashurama, an avatar of Lord Vishnu. He stood atop the mountains of the Western Ghats and shot an arrow far into the sea, and commanded the waters to retreat to where it landed. That spot is 'Bannali', or 'where the arrow landed' – now named Benaulim. Just 15 years ago, this beach was deserted, used mainly by resident fishermen whose decorated wooden boats still line the sand. But tourism is steadily taking over as Benaulim's main trade as travellers branch out from the behemoth **Taj Exotica** resort to a range of new hotels. Just beyond Benaulim village, the 'monte' (hill) is crested by the **Church of St John the Baptist** (open for mass 8am daily). Built at the turn of the 16th century, it's one of the prettiest examples of classic neo-Roman church architecture in Goa. Benaulim, like other coastal villages in South Goa, displays much enthusiasm for *dhirio*, old-fashioned bull-fighting, which is now banned but continues nevertheless. One of Goa's most interesting and unmissable attractions is **Goa Chitra** (Pulwaddo, www.goachitra.com, 0832-657-9877, 0832-277-2910, open 9am-6pm Tue-Sun, entry Rs 50), a fascinating ethnographic museum dedicated to the ancestral heritage of Goa that houses thousands of antique farm implements, all beautifully displayed in the context of a working farm.

Where to eat & drink

As you'd imagine for a working fishing village, Benaulim's many shacks and restaurants all specialise in super-fresh seafood from the catch of the day. First among equals is **Johncy's Beach Shack** (Benaulim Beach, 0832-277-1390, main course Rs 220, open 7am-1am daily), which features excellent tandoori specialities. **Fiplee's Bar & Restaurant** (off Benaulim Beach Road, near Maria Hall, 0832-277-0123, main course Rs 150, open noon-3pm, 7pm-2am daily) is more of an entertainment magnet than a restaurant. Very popular with locals, it features an air-conditioned pub, a multi-cuisine menu, a cybercafé and 'leisure' zone with snooker tables and dartboards. **Joecon's Garden** (near Taj Exotica, 0832-277-0099, main course Rs 200, open 11am-midnight daily) is another favourite.

Where to stay

Camilson's Beach Resort (Sernabatim Beach Road, Colva, 0832-277-1582, Rs 2,500 double) has a great location just off the beach and offers clean double rooms with private terraces and a well-maintained garden. The super-cheap **Succorina Guesthouse** (1711

INSIDE TRACK FAST TRACK

Taxi drivers tend to insist on the nausea-inducing scenic route going south from Margao because it's longer and earns them higher fares; bear in mind that there is also a modern highway, which is quicker.

Vas Vaddo, Benaulim, 0832-277-0365, Rs 400 double) is low-budget, offering peace, friendly service and small rooms with sea views. A few minutes' walk from the beachfront are the secluded, family-run **Palm Grove Cottages** (Tamdi Mati, 149 Vas Vaddo, Benaulim, 0832-277-0059, www.palmgrovegoa.com, Rs 1,200 double) with spacious, airy rooms overlooking the greenery and a good restaurant. Set on over 20 hectares (50 acres) of headland, with access to the prettiest part of the beach, is the sprawling **Taj Exotica** resort (Cal Vaddo, Benaulim, 0832-277-1234, www.tajhotels.com, Rs 12,000-Rs 18,000 double), offering private villas and luxurious facilities.

Nightlife

Benaulim is quiet in the evenings but **Pedro's** (Benaulim Beach, near Beach Road, 0832-277-0563) has live music every Tuesday and Saturday evening. Nearby, **Coco's Beach Shack** (Benaulim Beach, 20 metres north of Beach Road, 98224-88079) has live music every Friday and Monday evening. **Joecon's Garden** (near Taj Exotica, 0832-277-0099) has live music every night.

Shopping

A lovely old mansion has been turned into **Manthan** (near Benaulim church, 0832-277-1659, 9.30am-8pm daily), a many-roomed lifestyle boutique that sells everything from carpets to paintings.

Resources

Internet

New Horizon *1595 Beach Road (0832-277-1218/19).* **Open** 9am-11pm daily.

Getting there

From Dabolim Airport, taxi rides to Benaulim take 50 minutes and cost Rs 500. From Margao it's a 20-minute trip for Rs 250.

VARCA, CAVELOSSIM & MOBOR

The beachfront runs straight down to **Mobor**, trailing through giant five-star complexes around **Varca** and the charter-tourist destination of **Cavelossim**. The beaches are beautiful but the fishing villages here have never been particularly prosperous, and there's little to do outside the five-star hotels. Beyond Mobor, the beach tapers off at the junction with the Sal River estuary where another cluster of five-stars has sprouted up along with a mess of charmless fast-food outlets, imitation pubs and even an air-conditioned mini-mall.

Where to eat & drink

Outside the five-stars and beach shacks, **Fisherman's Wharf** (near Leela Hotel, Cavelossim, 93261-29810, main course Rs 200, open 11am-midnight daily) is a smart restaurant with tables overlooking the calm Sal

Benaulim Beach. *See p219.*

River and a pretty wooden interior. Better still, take the free ferry across the river to Betul and the charming **Hotel River Sal** (near Cutbona jetty, Betul, 0832-309-6313, main course Rs 150, open 7am-midnight daily), which specialises in fresh seafood straight from the next-door trawler jetty. Instead of the ferry, simply wave from the beach next to the Leela hotel – staff will happily send a boat over for you.

Where to stay

Once part of the Marriott chain, the ostentatious **Ramada Caravela Goa Resort** (Varca Beach Road, Varca, 0832-274-5200, www.caravelabeachresort.com, Rs 9,000-Rs 15,000 double) looms over its surroundings with an in-house casino and a nine-hole golf course. A favourite with charter tourists is **Dona Sylvia** (opposite shopping mall, Mobor, 0832-287-1321, www.donasylvia.com, Rs 8,000-Rs 12,000 double), with spacious cottages in large, manicured gardens. The **Holiday Inn Resort** (next to Leela hotel, Mobor, 0832-287-1303, www.holidayinngoa.com, Rs 8,000-Rs 10,500 double) is an undistinguished five-star but located very close to the beach. Arguably ahead of even the Park Hyatt for over-the-top luxury is The **Leela** (Mobor Beach, 0832-287-1234, www.ghmhotels.com, Rs 12,000-Rs 20,000 double), a massive hotel complex built despite strong opposition from local environmental activists. It has seven restaurants, a spa, tennis courts and a 12-hole golf course.

Entertainment

Dolphin rides & deep-sea fishing

Boat rides to view the dolphins that frolic in Goan waters (the silvery Indo-Pacific humpbacked dolphin is the most common) are available through most hotels. Expect to pay around Rs 400 per person for an hour and a half on the water in the early morning, leaving around 7am. **Betty's Place** (near Leela Beach, Mobor, 0832-287-1456, www.bettysgoa.com) offers dolphin boat rides departing at 8am and 10am (Rs 300 per person for around two hours) and deep-sea fishing (Rs 500 per person for four hours).

Cycle tours

The British expat-run **Cycle Goa** (Shop 7, Mobor Beach Resort, Cavelossim, 0832-287-1369, 98223-80031, 9am-1pm, 2-6pm daily) conducts a variety of rides, including pretty half-day village tours (Rs 750) and day-long rides pitched at different fitness levels, including a beautiful ride up to the Cabo de Rama Fort (Rs 1,800). It also does a two-week cycling tour of Goa covering around 25 miles a day. It supplies bikes, lunches and a back-up vehicle in case it all gets too much.

INSIDE TRACK CHITRA BUFFET

As well as being the curator of **Goa Chitra**, the poetically named Victor Hugo Gomes is also a huge fan of music and food. Call or email in advance to find out if your visit coincides with one of his irregular jazz shows or buffet lunches. The music is always great in the setting of the museum, but it's the food that's especially memorable – spectacular spreads featuring at least a dozen dishes, all sustainably grown, locally sourced and impeccably prepared.

Getting there

Taxis from Dabolim Airport to Varca and Cavelossim take around an hour and a quarter and cost Rs 800. From Margao, it's a 30-minute ride, costing Rs 500, which takes you along the coast past Benaulim, then off a turn through Varca and Carmona.

AGONDA

South of Mobor, a winding coastal road see-saws through valleys cut with rice terraces and coconut and areca nut palm groves. On the way, the road forks right to the forbidding Cabo de Rama fort, which overlooks the sea from a dramatic headland. Leaving the cape, the road to Palolem cuts through cashew plantations and rice fields until another right turn leading to Agonda. This road is not officially marked, but look for signs advertising beach shacks. Agonda remains one of Goa's best beaches, a small stretch of tranquillity that has escaped major tourist development thanks to strong and organised local opposition. It's perfect for lazy beach days, and from October to April there are a few temporary shacks here offering food and drinks.

Cabo de Rama Fort

Off the Palolem Road.

The Cabo de Rama had already been a prized fortress for centuries when the Portuguese seized it in 1763. According to Hindu mythology, Lord Rama, the hero of the epic *Ramayana*, rested at this fort after being exiled from Ayodhya. A decrepit gateway leads to a copse of fruit trees alive with wide-eyed Hanuman langur monkeys. On one side are the remains of the battlements, still mounted with a rusting cannon, which afford spectacular views up and

GOA

down the coastline. Walk past the monkeys and tangled vegetation, and you emerge on a small plateau that offers more superb views.

PALOLEM

The old coastal road is the most enchanting way to arrive in Palolem; turn a corner near the summit of the hill for an unmatched view of the beach's graceful arc far below. Palolem is the dream beach of picture-postcards – a beautiful bay lined with rippling golden sand and fringed by soaring coconut palms, with thick jungle rising from the southern end into the foothills of the Western Ghats. Once a distant point well off the beaten track, today Palolem has become the beach of choice for party-minded young backpackers and independent travellers, and heaves with visitors from October to April, peaking with at least 20,000 visitors during Christmas and New Year. More than 50 shacks line the bay like beads on a necklace, many of them run by expat foreigners – it's now easy to find wood-fired pizzas, home-made houmous, and artery-clogging English breakfasts. A leisurely 15-minute amble down the rocky coastline is Patnem, an escape from the crowds of Palolem.

Where to eat & drink

The restaurant scene in Palolem shifts wildly from season to season and even month to month, as itinerant entrepreneurs and chefs pick up and leave whenever they feel like it. One reliable institution is **Smuggler's Inn** (Palolem Beach Road, 98229-86093, main course Rs 300, 9am-10pm daily), a Brit-run eaterie with friendly local staff offering decent Euro-fare including roasts, mountains of mashed potatoes and old-fashioned bangers. Another is **Magic View** (Colomb Cove, no phone, main course Rs 150, 10am-10pm daily) on a slope with a great view of the ocean, featuring excellent Italian home cooking including very tasty pizzas. **Home** (Patnem Beach, 0832-264-3916, main course Rs 140, 8.30am-5pm daily) is an enthusiastically run guesthouse and café offering real Lavazza coffee, bountiful fresh salads and very good homemade desserts. **Dropadi Beach Restaurant & Bar** (Palolem Beach Road, 98226-85138, main course Rs 200, 8am-10pm, Aug-Apr,) is a popular place for everything from lasagne to tandoori chicken, and is always the most crowded in the area.

Palolem Beach.

Where to stay

The most interesting place to stay in Palolem is **Bhakti Kutir** (south end of Palolem Beach, take the fork right, near the mosque, and look for a sign, 0832-264-3469, www.bhaktikutir.com, Rs 1,200-Rs 2,500 double). Run by an idealistic Goan-German couple, the hotel has a strict environment-friendly philosophy, with non-AC cabanas entirely fashioned from local materials like rice straw, bamboo and mud. Most rooms have Indian-style squat toilets. Cleanse yourself with wheatgrass juice drinks and mud baths at their ayurvedic healing centre, and enjoy equally rejuvenating meals at the attached restaurant, which is one of the best health-food eateries in Goa. Of the beach huts, **Ciaran's Camp** (Palolem Beach, 0832-264-3477, www.ciarans10.com, Rs 2,000-Rs 2,500 double) is the most established and attractive, with a smart lawn and well-designed cottages with walk-in showers. The sea-facing cottages command higher prices, at Rs 2,000 to Rs 2,500 a night. A 12-minute hike from the beach is **Oceanic** (Temba Vaddo, Palolem, 0832-264-3059, www.hotel-oceanic.com, Rs 1,500-Rs 2,000 double), run by a British expat couple to a good standard, with spacious and clean rooms equipped with mosquito nets. Unlike many other places in Palolem, it's child-friendly, with a good restaurant and the only swimming pool in the area. Slightly off the beaten track, a

Going Wild

Nature reserves that are worth the trip.

In April 2006, an adult 50-kilo (110-pound) male leopard wandered into the heart of residential Miramar in Panjim, causing panic until he was brought down by a tranquilliser dart. While that case was a bit unusual, it illustrates the fact that Goa's settlement zones are all in close proximity to nature preserves and sanctuaries (which cover a fifth of Goa's land area). Some of these are large tracts of unspoiled jungle, filled with a wide variety of wildlife. In 2007, local wildlife experts found that Goa had registered the presence of resident tigers for the first time in many years, and villages that border with Maharashtra and Karnataka are frequently plagued by stray elephants that feast on sugarcane and other crops. Leopards are actually quite common; every year around half a dozen have to be rescued from wells or are trapped by rangers after eating dogs near human settlements.

Although the state's sanctuaries are open to visitors, most lack basic tourist facilities such as trained guides, visitor centres or even bathrooms. Of all Goa's reserves, the **Cotigao Wildlife Sanctuary** is perhaps the most accessible and rewarding, and is only 20 minutes from Palolem by road (along the NH-17 to Karwar, entry fees Rs 5 per person, plus Rs 100 car, Rs 50 motorbike, Rs 50 camera charge). Stretching across 40 square kilometres (33 square miles) of mixed deciduous forest, Cotigao is home to large numbers of gaur (the world's largest species of wild cattle, and Goa's state animal), langur and macaque monkeys, wild boar, porcupines, leopards, jackals and even a few sloth bears. Less wild, but a great option for families with kids, is **Bondla** (Ponda, Off NH-4, Rs 5, 9.30am-5.30pm, closed Thursdays), which is Goa's smallest sanctuary at just 7.7 square kilometres, but contains a wildlife rescue centre that serves as the state's zoo. The animals are looked after well, and there are some excellent specimens to view – a pair of tigers, several sleek leopards with glinting eyes, a large herd of hulking gaur, and even a magnificent King Cobra – the deadliest snake in the world.

Bondla.

INSIDE TRACK FANTASTIC FRESCO

Just a kilometre down the main road out of Margao in the direction of Gogol, is the modest Chapel of St Joaquim, known widely as the **Borda chapel**. It might not look like much, but visit in daylight hours and the parish priest will show you the painted ceiling in one wing. It was rendered in the genuine *fresco buono* medieval technique by Goan artist (and NY-based theologian) Dr Jose Pereira and is arguably the most important and ambitious *fresco buono* artwork of the 20th century.

couple of minutes' walk from the beach across a bamboo footbridge is **Ordosounsar** (north end of Palolem Beach, 98224-88769, Rs 400-Rs 800 cottages), a collection of 12 huts that feels nicely isolated from the rest of Palolem.

Nightlife

Rave parties do happen in and around Palolem – its remoteness makes it easier to evade late-night music bans. Details of when and where are circulated by word of mouth at the innumerable shacks along Palolem Beach. Otherwise, Palolem's nightlife is dedicated to shameless chilling out. Daytime beach parties sometimes happen outside **Café Del Mar** (Palolem Beach, 98232-76520), the most popular of Palolem's beach shacks and a sprawling, deeply relaxed wood-and-bamboo den serving hookah pipes, cocktails and snacks to a pounding soundtrack. Further down the beach is the **Cuba Beach Café** (Palolem Beach, 98221-83775), another popular lounge-vibe shack on a wooden platform on the sand, with sofas and chairs and a house guitar.

Resources

Internet

Bliss Travels *near main gate, Palolem Beach. (0832-264-3912).* **Open** 9am-11pm daily. **Rates** Rs 50 per hour.

Getting there

The nearest major train stop for Palolem is Margao. From Margao station you can then take a taxi to Palolem for about Rs 800. The trip takes about an hour. From Dabolim Airport taxis charge Rs 1,000 for the one hour and 45 minute-journey. From Panjim, the cab is around Rs 1,200 and takes an hour and a half.

Margao

Margao is a small city with a big opinion of itself. In the early 20th century, it was a town of opulent mansions that styled itself as a centre for scholars and the arts, and its grandee families prided themselves on their sophistication and refinement. After the 1961 liberation of Goa by Indian troops, many of the old Portuguese guard left for Portugal and Brazil and their huge estates were redistributed to tenant farmers. Residents still like to talk of Margao as Goa's second city after Panjim, but today much of its character has been written over by modern concrete sprawl, its narrow streets are choked with traffic and for most people it is only the dusty little town they have to pass through to get to or from the railway station (maybe stopping for a drink on the way).

A walk around the **Largo de Igreja**, the old church square surrounding the **Church of the Holy Spirit** (closed after 11.30am daily) in the centre of town, yields a glimmer of Margao's former glory, lined as it is with ornate colonial-era buildings. The baroque church has definitely seen better days, but the façade is still impressive. Down from the church square, the road skirts some old grandee palacios, not open to visitors but worth a look from outside, particularly the so-called **House of Seven Gables**, a mansion that lost four of its famous pitched roofs after generations of neglect. There's not much else to see in Margao other than the pretty **Chapel of Our Lady of Mercy** on the Monte Hill.

Where to eat & drink

The Margao branch of **Café Tato** (behind Collectorate, 0832-273-6014, main course Rs 30, open 7am-10pm Mon-Sat) serves fabulous vegetarian thalis and *puri bhaji*. **Banjara** (De Souza Chambers, behind Grace Church, 0832-271-4837, main course Rs 175, 11am-3pm, 6-11pm daily) is regarded by many as being the best North Indian restaurant in the south, serving particularly good tandoori breads. A short drive away in neighbouring Raia is **Fernando's Nostalgia** (0832-277-7098, main course Rs 250, 11am-midnight daily), a labour of love of the late Fernando da Costa, who passionately pursued the preservation of old-style, painstakingly prepared Goan food. The result brings people from far and wide – it's the best restaurant in South Goa. Near the old commercial centre, the 60-year-old **Longuinho's** (0832-273-9908, main course Rs 200, 8.15am-10.30pm daily) serves a selection of old-fashioned Goan dishes (try the beef roulade).

Wake and Bake

The legacy of the Portuguese loaf.

The semi-affectionate nickname given to Goans in much of the rest of India is 'Makapao'. It means, roughly, 'I want bread', a humorous reference to the community's preference for European-style leavened bread over the chapatis, rotis and naans that are eaten across the subcontinent. 'Pao' is, in fact, the Portuguese word for bread, which is probably the most successful European cultural import across Asia, as demonstrated by the fact that the same word shows up in a bewildering range of languages from Marathi to Japanese, almost always referring to identical little round Iberian-style loaves.

In Goa, the cult of bread and baking is taken extremely seriously, and every Goan of every community considers it his birthright to have 'pao' delivered at least twice a day. There are ancient coal-fired ovens in every little village and hamlet, and at least one in each neighbourhood. These are often family-run by the original licencees from the colonial era, a community of traditional bakers called 'poders' who still make bread by hand, in several varieties each day. Streams of bicycle-salesmen honking distinctive bulb-horns fan out from the bakeries at dawn and dusk each day, bringing bread to virtually every home in Goa at the state-set price of just Rs. 2.50 per loaf.

Baking was also the means to prosperity for many Goans who followed the British Raj from Rangoon to Karachi across the subcontinent. Many of them learned more advanced baking techniques and returned to Goa to set up upmarket cake shops, which similarly dot the entire landscape of the state, and often specialize in intricate hand-made patisserie.

Paramount among these is the astonishing **Jila bakery**, found down a winding road in the South Goa village of Ambora, where a zen atmosphere of exactitude pervades the workspaces of the baking Antao brothers. Jila is a miraculously intact time capsule of exquisitely refined techniques. Antonio, Reginald and Joao Brito Antao do not use mixers or any electric equipment of any kind, and every recipe they use is many decades old. It's entirely artisanal: every item that they make is carefully sourced, mixed, kneaded and baked entirely by hand in an ancient coal-fired oven. The results are mindblowing; éclairs the equal of any in Paris, stunning apple strudels, and biscuits of all kinds, and prices so low as to be trivial.

Jila Bakery
Ambora, Loutolim (0832-277-7224).
Open Mon-Sat 7am-7.30pm, Sun 7-11am by appointment only.

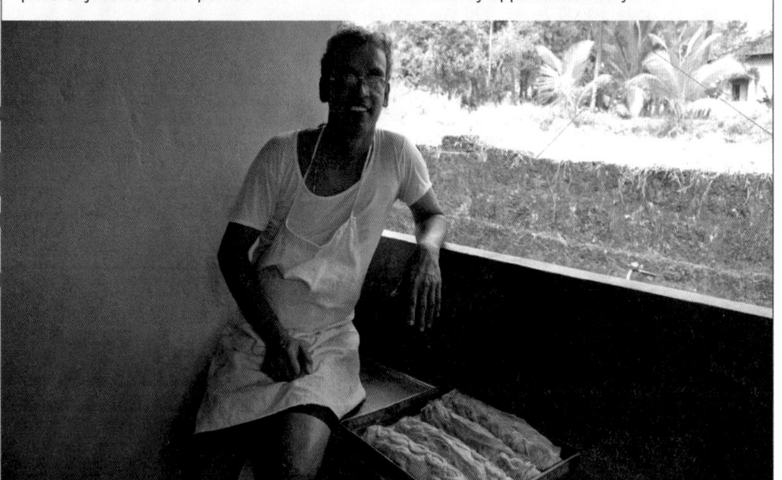

Where to stay

★ Casa dos Colacos
Bernardo da Costa Road, Margao (0832-272-6860, www.casadoscolacos.com).
Rates Rs 2,500 double.
Until Philip and Lorna Colaco opened this lovely boutique bed and breakfast, there wasn't a single decent place to stay in Margao. But thanks to this dynamic retired couple, there's now a suitably atmospheric location in the heritage part of Old Margao to use as a base to explore the city's unbeatable colonial-era architecture. The Colacos are outstandingly helpful, and can arrange daily itineraries with a difference.

Pansaimol

Goa's 30,000-year-old gallery.

In 1993, a group of Goan farmers led a team from the Archaeological Survey of India to a football field-sized shelf of laterite near a bend in the Kushavati River at Pansaimol. Scraping away some of the silt, the villagers revealed ancient carvings of bison and deer, some with shafts of spears sticking from their sides. The astonished archaeologists went on to uncover over 100 carvings spread across 600 square metres, many of them depictions of hunts. They most likely date back to the Upper Paleolithic or Mesolithic eras between 20,000 and 30,000 years ago. Alongside the animals are elegant line etchings of human figures, including an energetic 'dancing woman', and several strange triskelions – concentric rings that archaeologists speculate may have been used as rudimentary clocks.

The site is hidden in the rural interior of South Goa about an hour's drive from Margao (around Rs 1,000-Rs 1,200 in a taxi). Take the NH-17 south from Margao to the Tilamol crossroads, from where you head towards Rivona. From Rivona, head south through the tiny village of Colomb (also the last stop for toilets, food and drink) until you see a round red and green Archaeological Survey of India sign that points to the site along a winding dirt track.

Entertainment

Crocodile spotting

Crocodile Station (61 Thana, Cortalim, 98221-27936, 0832-255-0334, Rs 750 per person) runs lazy rides up the ancient Cumbarajua Canal to view the two dozen or so crocodiles lazing around on the mud flats and canal banks. Crocodiles aren't the shyest of creatures, and the tour company promises your money back if you don't see one – it says hasn't needed to pay a penny back yet.

Getting there

Margao station on the Konkan Railway line running from Mumbai to Kerala is the main station for South Goa. Buses run regularly to the station from Panjim (Rs 30, one hour) and Calangute (Rs 50, one hour 30mins). Or you can take a taxi from Panjim to Margao (around Rs 800, 50 minutes) or from Calangute (around Rs 1,000, one hour). Taxis from Dabolim Airport charge around Rs 500 for a 40-minute trip.

Resources

Hospital

Apollo Victor Hospital *near Carmelite Monastery, Aquem, Margao (0832-272-8888).* **Open** 24hrs.

Internet

Cyberocks *Shop 5, Reliance Residency, Colmarod, Navelim (0832-270-2407).* **Open** 9am-9pm daily.
Phoenix *Apna Bazaar, behind Collector's Office (0832-271-2430).* **Open** 8.45am-9pm Mon-Sat.

Police

Police Station *near Municipal Gardens.* **Emergency number** 100.

Post Office

Margao General Post Office *Municipal Gardens (0832-271-5791).* **Open** 9.30am-1pm, 2-5.30pm Mon-Sat.

Tourist Information

Goa Tourism Development Corporation Information Office *Margao Residency lobby, behind Municipality Building, opposite Municipal Gardens (0832-271-5528).* **Open** 9.30am-5.30pm Mon-Fri.

Directory

Anjuna Beach. *See p190.*

Getting Around

ARRIVING & LEAVING

By air

Chhatrapati Shivaji International Airport
www.csia.in
International Terminal (2A & 2C)
2681-3000.
Mumbai's international airport, recently sold to a private consortium and currently being upgraded, is located off the Western Express Highway about 21 km (13 miles) north of Mumbai Central and 29km (18 miles) from Colaba by road. For transiting to the domestic terminal, there is a free bus that runs between the international and the domestic terminals every 15 minutes.
Domestic Terminal (1A & 1B)
2626-4000/01.
The domestic terminal at Santa Cruz is about 5km south of the international terminal and has recently got a makeover. The state-run Air India (formerly Indian Airlines) and Kingfisher Airlines fly out of terminal 1A while Jet Airways and the low-budget carriers operate out of swanky terminal 1B. Both are connected by the newly-commissioned terminal 1C. The domestic airport is well connected to destinations across India. The Brihanmumbai Electric Supply & Transport (BEST) runs the BRTS-2 bus from the domestic terminal to Churchgate through the day.

Taxis from the airports

Most five-star hotels offer pick-ups from the airport. If yours doesn't, you can take a pre-paid taxi from a counter at the exit of the arrivals lounge in terminal 2B and 2C), which saves you the trouble of haggling later. Regular taxis and blue air-conditioned taxis called 'cool cabs' are also available from the taxi stand outside. Ignore the shouts from touts and take a place in the queue. Drivers routinely overcharge, demand inflated 'luggage charges' and offer sob stories about having to spend three days in line waiting for a fare. Ask for the tariff card to check the correct fare (*see p229* **Taxis**).

International airlines

Terminals are in brackets.

Air France-KLM (2C)
2202 4818/www.airfrance.com/in
Air India (2C)
2279-6666/www.airindia.com
Alitalia (2A)
5663-0800/0810/www.alitalia.com
British Airways (2A)
98925-77470/
www.britishairways.com/india
Cathay Pacific (2A)
6657-2345/www.cathaypacific.com
Delta Air Lines (2A)
2283-9712/www.delta.com
El Al Israel Airlines (2C)
2215-4701/www.elal.co.il
Emirates (2C)
2879-7979/www.emirates.com/in
Lufthansa (2A)
6630-1940/www.lufthansa.com.in
Qantas (2A)
2200-7440/www.qantas.com
Singapore Airlines (2C)
2202-2747/www.singaporeair.com
South African Airways (2C)
2282-3450/www.flysaa.com
Virgin Atlantic (2A)
4130-3030/*www.virgin-atlantic.com*

Domestic airlines

Terminals are in brackets.

Air India (1A)
1800-180-1407/
www.indianairlines.in
Deccan (1B)
98925-77008/www.airdeccan.net
Go Air (1B)
1800-222-111/www.goair.in
Indigo (1B)
1800-180-3838/www.goindigo.in
Jet Airways (1B)
3989-3333/www.jetairways.com
Kingfisher (1A)
1800-209
3030/www.flykingfisher.com
Spicejet (1B)
98718-03333/www.spicejet.com

By road

There are three points at which to enter Mumbai by road. The Western Express Highway runs in from the north-west through Borivali to the airports and the western suburbs. If you're coming in on the highway from Pune, you'll come off the bridge from Navi Mumbai into Chembur and then on to the city's central suburbs. For cars, a toll of Rs 25 is levied to take the bridge. The Eastern Express Highway enters from the north through Thane. Two tolls of Rs 10 and Rs 20 are levied on this road if you're in a car.

By train

Mumbai is well connected to most parts of India through the country's extensive railway network. The Western Railway's (2600-2977, www.wr.indianrail.gov.in) termini in the city are Mumbai Central, Dadar, Bandra and Vasai. The Central Railway's (2262-1450, www.centralrailwayonline.com) are Chhatrapati Shivaji Terminus, Dadar and Kurla's Lokmanya Tilak Terminus.

MAPS

General maps of the city and road maps are available at the Maharashtra Tourism Development Corporation office in Nariman Point (*see p234* **Tourist information**). Other city maps are available at bookstores and at stalls at major railway stations. The most detailed map is published by Eicher, priced Rs 250.

For maps, *see p248-255*.

PUBLIC TRANSPORT

Mumbai's tourist and business districts are located at its southern tip in Colaba, Fort and Nariman Point. Taxis and buses are a good way to get around this part of the city, although much of Colaba and Fort can be covered on foot. To travel north into the suburbs, especially if you're headed past Dadar, the local train service is far quicker than battling Mumbai's notoriously slow and noisy traffic in a cab. A train from Churchgate to Bandra takes 30 minutes; the same journey from Churchgate by car in rush hour will take at least an hour and a half.

Buses

Mumbai's public bus system is run by the Brihanmumbai Electric Supply & Transport, whose red double- and single-decker buses are marked with big 'BEST' signs on the side. They're efficient across city districts. BEST runs 3, 500 buses on 350 routes, carrying 4.5 million passengers every day. A short trip costs Rs 5.

Local trains

Mumbai's suburban train network has three lines – Western, Central and Harbour. The Western Line starts from Churchgate and ends at Dahanu Road, which is outside the city limits of Greater Mumbai. The Central and Harbour lines start at Chhatrapati Shivaji Terminus. The Central Line has two branches, which extend to Khopoli on the mainland in the south-east and Kasara to the north-east. The Harbour Line also has two branches. One runs to Panvel in the north-east, going via Navi Mumbai and Belapur, while the other runs to Andheri in the north, running along the Western Line from Mahim onwards. Mumbai's trains are reliable, efficient and frequent – you'll rarely wait more than ten minutes for a train.

The service carries six million commuters a day and the general compartments are densely packed in rush hours (9-11am, 6-9pm) and can be a highly uncomfortable, sweaty experience. First-class compartments have padded seats and are less crowded because fewer people can afford the fares. There are separate coaches for women, marked 'Ladies 24 hours', which are usually less crowded and highly recommended for women travellers. These coaches are located at the north end of the train and in the middle, next to the general first-class compartment. For a map of the suburban railway network, *see p256*.

Tickets

Travel in the general compartment is cheap, at just Rs 6 from Churchgate to Bandra, for example, jumping to Rs 52 for first-class travel. Tickets are sold only at railway station counters. Return tickets are valid for return travel up to the following day. You can save a lot of time by buying a booklet of travel coupons instead of tickets for individual journeys. Just punch coupons to the value of your ticket in a red machine near the ticket counter before you travel. These machines are often broken, in which case you must apply a rubber stamp, available at the coupon booklet window, on your coupon. Fares for different destinations are displayed on a chart at each station. If you're staying for a while, you could buy a monthly or three-month pass for travel in either class, which allows unlimited travel between the stations you choose for great savings. A single route pass allows travel only on either the Central, Western or Harbour line, or you can buy a 'two-route' or a 'three-route' pass that allows for universal travel.

Autorickshaws

Autorickshaws (often locally called 'ricks' or 'autos') are three-wheeled taxis that operate in the suburbs north from Bandra in the west and Sion in Central Mumbai. They are not allowed to ply in South Mumbai. Many rickshaws are mobile art installations, with colourful upholstery, movie-star images adorning the cabins and blaring Hindi film music. The fare is calculated on the basis of the imperial system of measurement, the metric system and waiting time: the minimum is Rs11 for one mile. Each additional 500metres adds Rs 6.50 to the fare. To figure out your total fare at your destination, multiply the number on the meter by ten, and subtract one. So if the meter shows 01.00, the fare is RS 9; if it reads 03.40, the fare is Rs 33. Between midnight and 5am, there's a 25% night charge.

Taxis

Mumbai's distinctive black-and-yellow Padmini taxis are elderly, but built like tanks. In the 1990s, they were converted from petrol engines to compressed natural gas as an environmental measure. They charge Rs 16 for the first mile and Rs 10 for every additional 500 metres. As with rickshaws, there's a 25% night charge for travel between midnight and 5am. Although many cabbies are honest, some will hike their prices dramatically for foreign tourists. Ask for the tariff card ('*card dikhao*') to check. Private operators also run taxi services, referred to as 'call cabs', but these cannot be hailed on the street. Call cabs offer new, air-conditioned vehicles, printed receipts and uniformed drivers, and must be booked at least a few hours in advance.

Gold Cabs *3244-3333.*
Meru Cabs *4422-4422.*

LONG-DISTANCE

Coaches

An array of luxury coach companies have made long-distance bus travel comfortable, though Indian buses still lack toilet facilities. Be forewarned that 'video coaches' will blare Bollywood films almost non-stop until you get to your destination, so take earplugs. It's also worth packing warm clothes, as the air conditioning can sometimes be glacial.

Gohil Travels
64/66 Gohil Sadan, SJ Marg, Lower Parel (W) (2496-1211/1113, www.gohiltravels.com). Lower Parel station. **Credit** AmEx, MC, V.

Neeta Travels
19 Saraswati Niwas, Rokadia Lane, SVP Road, Borivali (W) (2890-2666, 2888-3335). Borivali station. **No credit cards.**

Swarmeet Travels
41 Ganga Niwas, Ranade Road, Dadar (W) (98697-05166). Dadar station. **No credit cards.**

Travel Today
104 Sapna, SK Bole Road, Agar Bazaar, Dadar (W) (2430-3686, 2437-0801). Dadar station. **No credit cards.**

Trains

Trains are a slow but comfortable way to travel long distances. Seats or berths on popular routes like Mumbai-Goa are often booked weeks in advance in peak season (November-March). For foreign travellers there is a 'foreign tourist quota' of seats that can be bought on the day before or on the day of travel from the Chhatrapati Shivaji Terminus first-floor booking hall (counter 52). It's open from 8am to 8pm Mon-Sat and 11am to 2pm Sun. A passport is required as proof of foreign nationality. US dollars, British pounds and euros are accepted, but if you pay in rupees you may be asked to show a foreign exchange receipt or an ATM slip. Tickets can also be reserved and bought online from www.indianrail.gov.in or www.irctc.co.in, which offer e-ticketing on certain routes. If you're doing a lot of travelling, you can buy an Indrail pass (from counter 52), which offers unlimited rail travel across India for up to 90 days. It's an easy way to see a lot in one trip, but although reservations can be made in advance , it's advisable reconfirming your seat when you get to the station.

Driving

In some cities driving is a great way to get around, but despite the fact that many Mumbaikars seem welded to their vehicles, driving here isn't recommended. Nor is it in any way relaxing. Indians drive on the left (usually) but driving in Mumbai can be a nerve-racking experience; traffic is heavy and many roads are badly maintained. With few decent pavements, and encroachments on the ones that do exist, pedestrians are forced to walk on the road, and often wander in front of traffic without looking, apparently in the expectation that any approaching motorist will be equipped with good brakes. Motorists make ample use of the horn to inform everybody of their presence, jostling aggressively for position with routine disregard for lanes, traffic signals or other vehicles to the sides or behind. Do not expect other motorists to check what's behind them before pulling out.

To drive you will need a valid driving licence and international driving permit, both issued in your home country. Carry them with you whenever you drive. Drink-driving is an offence: drivers found with over 0.03% alcohol in their blood can be prosecuted. Unlike most rules, this is one the traffic police have started taking seriously after a spate of incidents where drunk drivers mowed down pedestrians or homeless people sleeping on the streets. Since June 2007, over 3, 000 motorists have been fined or imprisoned for drink-driving. It is also an offence to drive without wearing a seatbelt or while using a mobile phone. Traffic is intense during rush hours, usually 9.30am to noon and 5.30pm to 9.30pm.

Car hire

Mumbai doesn't have any agencies that rent out self-drive cars; only chauffer-driven vehicles are available. A typical rental fee is about Rs 1, 300 for eight hours or 80km (50 miles), inclusive of driver, fuel and insurance, with surcharges for every additional hour/km. Make sure to check carefully for terms and conditions, and any regional limits on where you can take the vehicle.

Car Care
42 Kedia Apartments, 29F Dongersi Road, Malabar Hill (98210-12685, 2367-7724). Grant Road station. **Open** 24hrs daily. **No credit cards**.

Hertz
Mahakali Caves Road, next to BMC school, Andheri (E) (4422-2222). **Open** 24hrs daily. **Credit** AmEx, DC, MC, V.

Royal Cars
7/27 Grant Building, Arthur Bunder Road, Colaba (2283-2928/1844). CST or Churchgate stations. **Open** 24hrs daily. **No credit cards**.

Walking

Getting around parts of Mumbai on foot can be difficult – many roads do not have pavements, and where they exist they are often broken or obstructed by hawkers. But walking is a really good way to enjoy some of the heritage parts of the city such as Colaba and Fort, where pavements are generally in better condition. Bandra is also best seen on foot, though the suburb's pavements aren't always even or well-paved. **Fort Walks** by Sharada Dwivedi and Rahul Mehrotra contains a list of picturesque walks through the Fort district (*see p238* **Books**).

TOURS

By bus

Neelambari (2202-6713; Rs 50 upwards) is an open-top, double-decker bus that offers one-hour evening rides through Fort's heritage district. The commentary is poor but this is still a great way to see the old city lit by floodlights. The open-top bus tour is shut in the monsoons.

By foot

Shriti Tyagi of **Beyond Bombay Tours** (98677-64409, beyondbombay@gmail.com; Rs 2, 000 upwards) organises tours of art galleries, landmarks featured in *Shantaram* and food places. **Bombay Heritage Walks** (98218-87321, info@bombay heritagewalks.com, Rs 1, 500 for 3 people) organises walking tours of heritage areas, usually with an emphasis on architectural details, around Fort, Banganga, Bandra and Khotachiwadi. Deepa Krishnan of **Mumbai Magic** (98677-07414, Rs 700-Rs 1, 500) holds two-hour walks through Fort, with handouts, a tea break and a souvenir, for two to six people. Customised tours of Chor Bazaar, Bhuleshwar, the Kala Ghoda art district, Elephanta Island and Mumbai's largest slum, Dharavi, are also available. **Reality Tours** (2283-3872, Rs 400 upwards) organises slum tours of the city and claim that 80% of its profits go to non-profit organisations.

By boat

Harbour cruises (Rs100 onwards) from Apollo Bunder in Colaba take leisurely rounds of the sea and offer views of the skyline, the docks and little neighbouring islands. The **Taj Mahal Palace hotel** (6665-3255; see p77), ever the purveyor of posh extras, also has a luxury yacht available for hire for up to ten people if you book two days in advance of your trip.

By cycle

Odati Adventures Private Limited (97696-79802, Rs1, 500 upwards) takes you on a pedal-powered tour of Fort, Ballard Estate, Town Hall, Chhatrapati Shivaji Terminus, Marine Drive, Nariman Point and Colaba, pausing to learn about the city's history and development. Tours are usually conducted on weekends and take about half a day. More sedate, and ideal if you want a break from the city (and its heavy traffic), the company also organises cycling tours in North Mumbai, where cyclists pedal along the coast and pass fishing villages.

GETTING AROUND

The intense traffic, crowds, noise, heat, shocking poverty and poor infrastructure can make Mumbai an exhausting and overwhelming city. Be gentle on yourself and don't try to do too much at once. Drink plenty of water and wear suitably light clothing and comfortable footwear that's suitable for uneven pavements. Some areas are best appreciated on foot (*see p55* **A Walking Tour of Fort**), but most of the time you'll find taxis much easier and a relatively cheap way to get around. Getting out to the suburbs is almost always faster by train, but if you can't face those packed carriages, you'll find it isn't that expensive to go by cab. Many street and place names have been officially changed in the last 20 years but most locals still use the old names. New names are often not recognised, even by taxi drivers, so in our listings and maps we've given both where appropriate and a prominent nearby landmark to aid navigation.

Resources A-Z

TRAVEL ADVICE

For up-to-date information on travel to a specific country – including the latest on safety and security, health issues, local laws and customs – contact your home country government's department of foreign affairs. Most have websites with useful advice for would-be travellers.

AUSTRALIA
www.smartraveller.gov.au

CANADA
www.voyage.gc.ca

NEW ZEALAND
www.safetravel.govt.nz

REPUBLIC OF IRELAND
foreignaffairs.gov.ie

UK
www.fco.gov.uk/travel

USA
www.state.gov/travel

ADDRESSES

Addresses usually begin with the flat number of the building or the housing compound, followed by the name of the house or building, followed by the street number and finally the street name and neighbourhood, with an E or W in brackets indicating whether the address is on the eastern or western side of the local railway line. For example, 31 Pluto Building, 54 Turner Road, Bandra (W). Addresses also often contain a reference to a local landmark such as 'opposite Mahalaxmi Racecourse', and a Mumbai postal code, locally called a 'pin number', which is a six-digit number beginning with 4.

AGE RESTRICTIONS

The legal age for drinking varies according to the drink. You have to be 21 to drink beer or wine, and 25 for spirits. In practice, proof of age is rarely asked for. The age of sexual consent is 16; the driving age is 18. It's illegal for shopkeepers to sell cigarettes to anyone under 18, but this too is rarely enforced.

ATTITUDES & ETIQUETTE

Mumbaikars are usually very warm and hospitable towards foreign visitors. Shaking hands is the common greeting, but Indians also touch their palms together in front of the chest and say the Hindi greeting '*Namaste*', or '*Namaskaar*' in Marathi. This can be a more appropriate way to greet the elders and women from traditional families.

Mainstream society does not look fondly on the idea of a man greeting a woman who is not his wife with a kiss, even on the cheeks, although many upper-class Mumbaikars will have no problem with it – stick to shaking hands and *Namastes* if in doubt. Be aware that some Indian men labour under the idea that Western women are more open to casual sex than their Indian counterparts. This is unlikely to cause serious problems. Still, women travellers should be careful of sending out the wrong signals.

Mumbai is a fairly liberal city and you will see women dressed in a variety of styles. Dress for the occasion: if you're going to a nightclub or a posh restaurant then a tight skirt or a skimpy top is fine; but if you're going for a bus ride or a walk on the beach then dress more conservatively if you don't want to be the focus of a thousand stares. When visiting religious sites, both men and women should cover their arms and legs, and remove their shoes before entering. Don't forget to cover your head before entering a Sikh *gurdwara* or a mosque.

Punctuality is not considered a great virtue in India and you can often expect to be kept waiting, but conversely, although Mumbaikars are in general a friendly lot, this is a big, crowded city and they don't have time to waste on niceties – when people turn up they get on with it. You may be surprised at the cursory, sometimes rude way in which Mumbaikars deal with servants, wait staff and other people working in service jobs – 'pleases' and 'thank yous' are often not bothered with. On trains, buses and in traffic, Mumbaikars are cut-throat in jostling for an inch of space. Queuing does happen at railway stations, bus stops and banks, but is not universal – just as on the road, the biggest and fastest gets to the front first.

COURIERS & SHIPPERS

Prices vary considerably, but the price of sending a 5kg package from India to the UK or North America is around Rs 6,000 inclusive of service tax and fuel charges, subject to customs.

BLUE DART

Ground Floor, Khaitan Bhavan, Jamshedji Tata Road, opposite Satyam Collection, Churchgate (2282-2495, www.bluedart.com). Churchgate station. **Open** 10am-8pm Mon-Sat. **Credit** MC, V.

DHL

Worldwide Express, 145A Embassy Centre, Jamnalal Bajaj Road, Nariman Point (2283-7179/7189, www.dhl.co.in). Churchgate, CST stations. **Open** 11am-8pm Mon-Sat. **Credit** AmEx, DC, MC, V.

FEDEX

Shop No.4 Kuber Complex, Opposite Laxmi Industrial Estate, New Link Road, Andheri, (6698-0000, www.fedex.com/in). Andheri station. **Open** 9am-9.30pm Mon-Sat. **No credit cards**. Call 2571-4444 to arrange a pick up.

CUSTOMS

Personal items can be brought in duty-free as long as they will be consumed or taken out of the country upon return. Up to 200 cigarettes or 50 cigars or 250 grams of tobacco and up to two litres of spirits or wine are permitted. For a complete list of duty-free rules see www.cbec.gov.in/travellers.htm.

DISABLED

Bad pavements, heavy crowds and intense traffic all make Mumbai a challenge for travellers with disabilities. There is no legislation making it mandatory for shops, restaurants, hotels or office buildings to offer wheelchair access, and most do not. Nor do any of the city's public transport systems offer disabled access.

DRUGS

Cannabis and other recreational drugs are illegal in India, and penalties for possession are severe, with prison terms of up to ten years. But that hasn't hampered a widespread drug culture across Mumbai's social classes. Hashish, locally known as *charas*, is more common and popular than grass (*ganja*) and finds its way into the city from Himachal Pradesh and Kashmir. In Colaba, tourists are likely to be approached by dealers peddling hash and heroin, and occasionally cocaine.

ELECTRICITY

The Indian domestic electric supply is 230-250V; 50 Hz UK appliances work with just a basic adaptor, but US 110V appliances will need a transformer as well. The plug sockets are round.

EMBASSIES & CONSULATES

Australia *36 Maker Chambers VI, 220 Nariman Point (6669-2000). CST or Churchgate stations.* **Open** 9am-5pm Mon-Fri.
Canada *Sixth Floor, Fort House, 221 DN Road, Fort (6749-4444). CST or Churchgate stations.* **Open** 9am-5.30pm Mon-Thur; 9am-3pm Fri.
Israel *16th Floor, Earnest House, NCPA Marg, Nariman Point (2282-2822). CST or Churchgate stations.* **Open** 9am-5pm Mon-Thur; 9am-3pm Fri.
Italy *First Floor, Kanchenjunga, 72 Pedder Road (2380-4071/ http://consmumbai.esteri.it). Grant Road station.* **Open** 10am-1pm Mon-Fri.
South Africa *Gandhi Mansion, 20 Altamount Road, Cumbala Hill (2351-3725/3726). Grant Road station.* **Open** 8.30am-5pm Mon-Fri.
United Kingdom *Second Floor, Maker Chambers IV, 222 Jamnalal Bajaj Road, Nariman Point (6650-2222,www.ukindia.com). CST or Churchgate stations.* **Open** 8am-4pm Mon-Thur; 8am-1pm Fri.
USA *Lincoln House, 78 Bhulabhai Desai Road, Breach Candy (2363-3611,http://mumbai.usconsulate.gov). Grant Road station.* **Open** 8.30am-5pm Mon-Fri.

EMERGENCIES

To report an emergency, dial 100. For more information, consult www.mumbaipolice.com.
Ambulance *102 (Rs 200) and 1298 (Rs 600-Rs 1,500).*
Children distress line *1098*
Fire Brigade *101.*
Mumbai Police *100.*
Senior citizen helpline *1090.*
Women's helpine *103.*

GAY & LESBIAN

Gaybombay *www.gaybombay.org.* Gaybombay's aim is to create safe spaces for the gay community in Mumbai. It does this through its website, the gaybombay@ yahoogroups.com mailing list, regular meetings on the first, third and fifth Sundays of each month, parties, film screenings, treks and more.
Humsafar Centre *Girish Kumar (administrator), Post Box No. 6913, Santa Cruz (W) (2667-3800,2665-0547/www.humsafar.org).* **Open** noon-8.30pm Mon-Sat. Humsafar is India's oldest organisation set up for creating support systems for sexual minorities. Its particular focus is communication and support on HIV/AIDS for gay men. It has open events on the second and fourth Sundays of each month.
Lesbians and Bisexuals in Action (LABIA) *98332-78171, stree.sangam@gmail.com.* LABIA is a city group focusing on the issues of queer and trans-identified women. It has regular meetings and film screenings, brings out a magazine called *Scripts*, conducts actions on current issues relating to queer and trans-identified women, and networks with other activist groups.
Salvation Star *www.salvationstar.com.* A group that runs a monthly party event at a bar in South Mumbai, with a focus on trendy, global music.
Samabhavna Society *1800-222-199.* Samabhavna is involved with issues of human rights and advocacy for the LGBT community. It has an advocacy cell and a toll-free helpline (in English, Hindi and Marathi).
Symphony In Pink (SIP) *www.symphonyinpink.com.* Symphony in Pink is an online discussion group for women only, to discuss issues relevant to lesbian and bisexual women in Mumbai.

HEALTH

Accident & emergency

In case of accidents, call 102 or 1298. Use the name of the hospital if hailing a taxi.
Bombay Hospital *Bombay Hospital Road, New Marine Lines, near Metro Adlabs cinema (2206-7676,www.bombayhospital.com). Marine Lines station.*
Cumballa Hill Hospital & Heart Institute *93/95 August Kranti Marg, Cumballa Hill (2380-3336). Grant Road station.*
Jaslok Hospital *Pedder Road (2352-3333). Mahalaxmi station.*
JJ Hospital *Ibrahim Rehamatullah Road, Byculla (2373-5555). Byculla station.*
Lilavati Hospital & Research Centre *A791 Bandra Reclamation, Bandra (W) (2642-1111,2655-2222). Bandra station.*
PD Hinduja National Hospital & Medical Research Centre *Veer Savarkar Marg, Mahim (2445-2222,2444-9199). Mahim station.*

PHARMACIES

Open 24-hour

Bombay Hospital Pharmacy *Bombay Hospital, New Marine Lines (2206-7676 ext 356/252). Marine Lines station.*
Dava Bazaar *32 Kakad Arcade, near Bombay Hospital, New Marine Lines (2203-6238). Marine Lines station.*
Hospital Chemist *Prarthna Samaj, Harkishondas Hospital, near Opera House, Charni Road. (2386-9219,2389-5553). Charni Road station.*

Insurance

India has no reciprocal healthcare agreements with other countries and you should take out a medical insurance policy before you travel.

Vaccinations

The most common vaccinations recommended for travel to India are against hepatitis A, typhoid and diphtheria. You should also consider taking anti-malarial pills (*see* **Malaria**) during your stay. If you're planning a long visit or trips to far-flung rural areas you may require additional vaccinations such as rabies, tuberculosis, hepatitis B, yellow fever and Japanese encephalitis. Check with your doctor at least three months before you travel.

Water

Visitors should avoid drinking water straight from the tap. Always drink bottled water or water that has been filtered or boiled or both. The most popular brands of bottled water are Bisleri and Himalayan. Evian is available at high-end restaurants and hotels. Always check the seal – bottles are sometimes refilled with tap water by unscrupulous vendors. Avoid salads unless they've been washed with boiled water and decline ice that hasn't been made with filtered water. Cylindrical ice with a hole running through it is factory-made and generally safe.

INTERNET

There are cybercafés across the city, many in the Fort area in South Mumbai. Many hotels are hooked up, but usually at higher rates than those offered by cafés. Local service provider MTNL (www.mumbai.mtnl.net.in/instant) offers instant dial-up services from any landline using the user's phone number as the username and 'MTNL' as the password.

Asiatic cyber café
New India Assurance Building, next to Asiatic department store, Veer Nariman Road, Churchgate (no phone). Churchgate station. **Open** 10am-8.30pm Mon-Sat.

Satyam Infoline
Prem Court Compound, next to Samrat, Jamshedji Tata Road, Churchgate (98921-71047). Churchgate station. **Open** 9am-8.30pm Mon-Sat.

LANGUAGE

Mumbai is the capital of the state of Maharashtra, the dominant language of which is Marathi. Although Marathi is commonly spoken in Mumbai, the lingua franca across the city's mix of communities is a form of Hindi known as Bambaiyya Hindi, which comprises elements of Gujarati, Marathi, Hindi and English, and is a bastardised version of the pure Hindi spoken in North India. English is commonly spoken, sometimes mixed with Hindi and other languages in an argot known as 'Hinglish'. Most public signs and notices across the city, and travel announcements at train stations and airports, are given in English and Hindi. Although Mumbaikars always appreciate efforts by foreign visitors to speak in Hindi and other Indian languages, English is common enough to allow you to get by without them.

LEGAL HELP

For legal assistance, contact your consulate or embassy (*see left*) in the first instance.

MALARIA

Malaria is a potentially fatal disease that is spread by the bites of infected mosquitoes. Malaria-carrying mosquitoes breed in Mumbai and Goa around areas with stagnant water, particularly at construction sites. Around 14,000 people a year are infected with malaria in Mumbai, with the riskiest season being the monsoon, from June to September. The typical incubation period is one week to one month, but travellers can fall sick up to one year after being infected, often long after returning home from India.

Symptoms include fever, body aches, chills, sweating, exhaustion, headaches, nausea and vomiting. Typically, malaria attacks last between six to ten hours and repeat after a period of abatement. The onset of malaria can be difficult to spot because the initial symptoms are flu-like and the disease must be diagnosed by a blood test. Consult a doctor immediately if you develop malaria-like symptoms. Severe cases can lead to seizures, comas, fluid in the lungs, hallucinations, kidney failure, respiratory problems and death.

Your chance of becoming infected on a short holiday to Mumbai or Goa are low, but both the UK foreign office and the US state department advise travellers to protect themselves against infection with anti-malarial drugs. Recommended drugs for India include chloroquine (sold under brand names like Nivaquine and Avloclor), taken once a week. There are some chloroquine-resistant strains of malaria present in India, so you should supplement that with a daily dose of proguanil. Start taking your medicine one week before travel and for four weeks after you return. The more expensive Malarone, a new-generation anti-malarial drug, combines atovaquone and proguanil, and is taken daily with food or milk. Start taking it two days before travel and for a week after you return. Bring enough medicine to last the duration of your trip; drugs like Malarone are not easily available.

Some anti-malarial drugs are associated with mild side effects, including stomach pains, mouth ulcers, nausea, itchiness, vomiting, sleep disturbances and headaches. Try switching to a different type if you suffer heavy side effects. Some drugs are not recommended for pregnant women, those with medical problems like epilepsy or those taking other drugs – consult your doctor.

Also protect yourself by using an insect repellent like Odomos. Use insecticide sprays in your room, sleep under a mosquito net, keep windows closed at night and cover your arms and legs. Pyrethroid coils to burn are readily available in India under the brand name Tortoise, as are repellents that can be plugged into electrical sockets (Good Knight Activ+ is particularly effective).

MEDIA

Newspapers

Mumbai has a rambunctious daily press in several languages, and is home to India's oldest newspaper, the Gujarati-language *Bombay Samachar*, founded in 1822. Foreign visitors reading the English-language press are often struck by how flippantly the front pages of the city's broadsheets juxtapose political reportage with celebrity gossip; articles about Liz Hurley's shopping lists and Paris Hilton's latest exploits are common features in even the so-called quality press. The dumbing-down started about a decade ago, when the venerable *Times of India*, founded in 1838, decided to practise what it called 'aspirational journalism' and 'sunshine stories', focusing on beauty contests and society parties, allowing stories about poverty and infrastructure on to its pages only grudgingly.

Until a few years ago, the feisty *Indian Express*, which prides itself on its investigative stories, especially about official corruption, was the *Times*'s only real competition. The *Asian Age*, notable for its wide international coverage (reproduced mainly from the *New York Times*), is weak on local affairs. But 2005 saw the birth of two new newspapers. While the multi-coloured *DNA*, which stands for *Daily News & Analysis*, has seemed content to ape the *Times*'s infotainment model, the local edition of the Delhi-based *Hindustan Times* has won fans for putting serious issues back on the agenda. For many Mumbaikars, the long train journey home after work affords the opportunity to browse through one of the two afternoon tabloids (a broadsheet would be impossible to read in a cramped compartment): the nearly defunct *Afternoon Despatch & Courier* is mainly read by an older audience who have fond memories of its late founder-editor Behram Contractor, a man who fancied himself as an Indian Art Buchwald and went by the pen name Busybee. *Mid-Day*, meanwhile, is a zesty mixture of shocking crimes, political scandal and showbiz tattle. *Mumbai Mirror* is a gossipy tabloid that comes free with the *Times*.

Radio

It's expensive to start up a radio station and more so to keep it running, and private radio stations in India aren't allowed to broadcast news. As a result, Mumbai's young breed of FM stations has been unable to appeal to niche audiences. Most stations seek the widest audience by playing the same songs as their competitors. The FM stations in Mumbai are Radio City 91.1, Big 92.7, Red 93.5, RadioOne 94.3, Radio Mirchi 98.3, All India Radio Gold 100.7, Fever 104, the women-centric Meow 104.8 and All India Radio Rainbow 107.1. All play Hindi film numbers and some English pop.

Television

TV sets started appearing in India only in 1959, and it wasn't until the 9th Asian Games in Delhi in 1982 that colour TV was introduced. But it was only in 1992 that private channels were allowed. Until then, Indian viewers had to make do with the state-run Doordarshan channel, which had a strong focus on education and socio-economic development. New channels MTV, Star Plus, CNN, BBC and the Hong Kong-based Star TV gave Indians new options.

Zee TV, the first privately owned Indian channel, brought a bevy of regional channels. A few years later, Discovery and the National Geographic Channel came in. Star also expanded its bouquet, introducing Star World, Star Sports, ESPN and Star Gold, among others. Regional channels flourished along with a multitude of Hindi channels and a few English channels. By the end of the '90s, HBO and Cartoon Network had made their appearance, as had Nickelodeon. MTV, which had become an entirely Hindi music channel, introduced popular international music channel VH1 in 2005.

A boom in news broadcasting in 2003 has left the market crammed with nearly 20 news channels. Of these NDTV (with NDTV India in Hindi and NDTV 24x7 and NDTV Profit in English) employs the most recognisable and experienced faces in Indian broadcast journalism. CNN-IBN formed as a breakaway from NDTV in 2005, and Times Now, a collaboration between the Times Group (which owns the *Times of India*) and Reuters, has occasionally novice reporters and sometimes tacky graphics. Other channels such as Headlines Today rely heavily on sensational news. Regional news channels all follow Aaj Tak (India Today Group), the first 24-hour Hindi news channel.

In 2007, digital set top boxes were made compulsory in South Mumbai, ending the era of the cablewallah and ushering in crystal-clear television reception thanks to direct-to-home providers like Airtel, Tata Sky (whose remote looks exactly the same as every other Sky box in the world) and Zee's Dish TV, which gave viewers the choice of subscribing to any or all of the 250-300 channels available on Indian television – everything from Fashion TV to God TV.

MONEY

India's currency is the rupee (short form Rs, although one rupee is written Re 1), which comprises 100 paise (p). Coins come in 50p, Re 1, Rs 2 and Rs 5 denominations. Paper money comes in denominations of Rs 5, 10, 20, 50, 100, 500 and 1,000. At the time of writing the tourist exchange rate was approximately Rs 70 for £1, Rs 45 for $1 and Rs 61 for €1. Avoid black market money-changers – it's illegal and they are frequently scamsters looking to short-change their victims.

ATMs

Most banks have 24-hour ATMs, often marked by an 'ATM' sign. They can also be found in shopping malls and some train stations. They dispense rupees only. Some are only for customers of certain banks, so look for the symbol of your card company. Links with international networks like Visa and MasterCard's Cirrus are common. You may be charged a small fee. Many ATMs are guarded by watchmen, but exercise basic caution and discretion if withdrawing large sums.

Banks

The banks below have branches throughout the city (except Barclays).

Barclays
501/503 Ceejay House, Shivsagar Estate, Annie Besant Road, Worli (6719-6575/www.barclays.in). Lower Parel Station. **Taxi** Planetarium **Open** 9.30am-5.30pm Mon-Fri; 9.30am-1.30pm Sat.

Citibank
Bombay Mutual Building, DN Road, Fort (2269-5757,www.citibank.co.in). CST or Churchgate stations. **Open** 10.30am-2pm Mon-Fri.

HDFC
Ramon House, HT Parekh Marg, off Maharshi Karve Road, 169 Backbay Reclamation, Churchgate (6631-6000,2282-0282). Churchgate station. **Taxi** Aakashwani. **Open** 9.30am-5.15pm Mon-Fri.

HSBC
52/60 MG Road, Flora Fountain, Fort (4042-2424,6680-0001, www.hsbc.co.in). CST or Churchgate stations. **Open** 9.30am-5pm Mon-Sat.

Standard Chartered
23-25 MG Road, opposite VSNL, Fort (2204-4444). CST or Churchgate stations. **Open** 9am-6pm Mon-Fri; 9am-4pm Sat.

Foreign exchange

ABN Amro Bank
Sakhar Bhavan, near Oberoi Shopping Centre, Nariman Point (2281-8008,www.abnamro.com). Churchgate station. **Open** 10am-7pm Mon-Fri; 10am-3pm Sat.

Thomas Cook *Thomas Cook Building, 324 DN Road, Fort (2204-8556). CST or Churchgate stations.* **Open** 9.30am-6pm Mon-Sat.

Credit cards

MasterCard (MC) and Visa (V) are accepted at many shops, restaurants and hotels. Some will also accept American Express (AmEx) cards, while a rare few accept Diners Club (DC) cards. To report a lost or stolen credit card call these 24-hour helplines:
American Express *98926-00800.*
Diners Club *2834-4653.*
MasterCard *000-800-100-1087.*
Visa *000-117-866-765-9644.*

NATURAL HAZARDS

Mumbai's famously moderate weather has turned a little nasty in recent years. The days between April and June are increasingly scorching and the monsoon between June and September causes floods every year, while the 2007-'08 winter was the coldest in 50 years. Bring plenty of sunscreen, dress in a T-shirt and loose trousers to avoid sweat retention. Drink lots of water, but don't take it straight from the tap. Boil it first or buy bottled water. Mosquitoes are a problem in Mumbai due to the humid weather. Arm yourself with a repellent (like Odomos) and keep windows shut after sunset. For weather averages *see p237.*

OPENING HOURS

General stores open by 10am and close around 8pm. Days vary; many businesses remain open on Sundays. Many liquor stores are shut on Thursdays. Banks generally open at 9.30am and stay open till 5pm on weekdays. On Saturdays, banks close around 2pm and are closed on Sundays.

POSTAL SERVICES

Post is delivered once a day from Monday to Friday. The city's main post office, the General Post Office near Chhatrapati Shivaji Terminus in Fort, is open from 10am till 5pm from Monday to Saturday. Stamps can be bought from post offices and some general stores. Most post offices also rent out post office boxes for a minimum of six months (Rs 250). See www.indiapost.gov.in for other services. *See also p231* Couriers & shippers.
General Post Office *St George Road, behind Chhatrapati Shivaji Terminus, Fort (2262-0956). CST station.* **Open** 10am-5pm Mon-Sat.
Colaba Post Office *SBS Marg, Colaba (2215-3833). CST or Churchgate stations.* **Open** 10am-6pm Mon-Sat.

SAFETY & SECURITY

Mumbai is a remarkably safe city. Muggings, robberies and other serious crimes against tourists are rare, although pickpockets do operate in crowded areas. Still, it's always a good idea to take basic precautions, especially at night. Keep an eye on your luggage when travelling. In an emergency, dial 100. For up-to-date info on the latest news on safety and security, health issues, local laws and customs, contact your home country's department of foreign affairs. For the UK, see www.fco.gov.uk/travel. For the US, http://travel.state.gov. *See also p232* **Emergencies**.

SMOKING

Smoking in public areas is banned. Under Indian law, selling cigarettes to persons under the age of 18 is illegal.

STUDY

India follows a 15-year education format – four years of primary school, six years of secondary school, followed by two years of higher secondary education. This often precedes a three-year Bachelor's degree. Indian Master's degrees usually take two years. Student visas are granted for the duration of the academic course of study up to five years on the basis of letters of admission from the educational institution.

University of Mumbai
Founded in 1857, the Mumbai University offers a massive number of Master's and diploma courses, but it lags behind in teaching quality.
Fort Campus *Mayo Road, next to Mumbai High Court (2265-2825). CST or Churchgate stations.*
Vidyanagari Campus *Kalina, Santa Cruz (E) (2652-6091/6226). Santa Cruz station.*

Studying music

There are several institutions in Mumbai teaching Hindustani and Carnatic classical music.

Bharatiya Vidya Bhavan's Sangeet Vidyapeeth *KM Munshi Marg, near Wilson College, Girgaum, Chowpatty (2369-8085). Charni Road station.*
Fine Arts School of Music & Dance *Fine Arts Society, Fine Arts Chowk, near Chembur Flyover, RC Marg, Chembur (2522-2988, www.faschembur.com). Chembur station.*
Jazz India Vocal Institute *nmjazz@vsnl.com.*
Professor Deodhar's School of Indian Music *Mody Chambers, Pandit Paluskar Chowk (2382-1940). Churney Road station.*
Sangeet Mahabharati *A6, 10th Road, Juhu Scheme, Vile Parle (W) (2620-7283). Vile Parle station.*
University of Mumbai Department of Music *Vidyapeeth Vidyarthi Bhavan, B Road, Churchgate (2204-8665). Churchgate station.*

TELEPHONES

Dialling & codes

The country code for India is 91 and the area code for Mumbai is 022. To call India from abroad, dial the country code and drop the zero of the area code, followed by an eight-digit number, for example 91-22-2123-4567. To call a mobile phone, use only the country code, for example 91-22-98200-98200. You do not need to dial 022 from within the city except when dialling from a mobile phone. Mumbai landline numbers have eight digits. In 2002, MTNL, Mumbai's public sector telecom provider, added an extra '2' to the start of all landline numbers, but some people, websites and other sources of information still quote the old seven-digit numbers. Just add the '2' and the number should work. The area code for Goa is 0832, but if you're calling from a Mumbai landline, dial 95832. Private fixed phone service providers like Tata Indicom and Reliance Infocomm have eight-digit phone numbers beginning with 6 and 3. To find phone numbers, try these 24-hour directory enquiry services:
Just Dial *2888-8888, 2222-2222.*
MTNL directory equiry *197.*
Times Infoline *6700-5555.*

Calling long distance

Kiosks across the city marked 'STD' (Subscriber Trunk Dialling) and 'ISD' (International Subscriber Dialling) offer facilities to make calls around India and internationally. Rates depend on where you are calling from and at what time.

Public phones

There are numerous pay phones around the city and every second shop is likely to have one. Look for yellow 'PCO' (Public Call Office) signboards or small boxy red phones at street stalls and outside shops. Local calls cost Re 1 for 90 seconds.

Mobile phones

Contact your local mobile phone provider for details on roaming facilities in India. Mobile phones are widespread in India. Several providers offer SIM cards with pre-paid/top-up billing. To buy one, you'll need two passport-size photographs and a photocopy of your passport. If you use your phone outside Mumbai city limits, you will be charged roaming rates.

Airtel
Shop No. 4, Yusuf Building, Veer Nariman Road, next to Akbarally's, Fort (98920-98920). Churchgate or CST stations. **Open** 10am-8pm daily.

BPL
Ground Floor, Rajmahal, near Ambassador Hotel, Veer Nariman Road, Churchgate (98210-99800). Churchgate station. **Open** 9am-8pm Mon-Sat.

Vodafone
Shop No. 3, Indian Merchant Chambers Building, 76 Veer Nariman Road, Churchgate (98200-98200). Churchgate station. **Open** 10am-7pm Mon-Sat.

TIME

Indian Standard Time is GMT +5 hours and 30 minutes. India does not use Daylight Saving Time.

TIPPING

In restaurants, a 5 to 10% tip is appreciated, but not expected. Mumbaikars never tip in taxis and rickshaws.

TOILETS

There are two styles of toilets in use in Mumbai – the Western-style toilet and the Indian 'squat' toilet. Squat toilets usually have ribbed areas to place your feet; stand on them and sit with your back to the hole. Although squat toilets take a bit of getting used to, it's worth the effort as the lack of a seat makes them more hygienic to use. Traditionally, toilet paper is not used; Indians usually clean themselves with a mug of water using the left hand. Public toilets in Mumbai are rare and where they exist are poorly maintained and unhygienic. However, most major stores and malls keep their toilets clean.

TOURIST INFORMATION

Maharashtra Tourism Development Corporation
Madame Cama Road, opposite LIC Building, Nariman Point (2202-4627/7762/ www.maharashtratourism.gov.in). Churchgate station. **Open** 10am-5.30pm Mon-Fri; 10am-3pm Sat.

TOUTS AND SCAMS

Overall, Mumbaikars are warm and welcoming to foreign visitors and tourists will find it a friendly place to explore, but around tourist-heavy sites like Colaba Causeway and the Gateway of India you're likely to be zeroed in on by persistent hawkers, beggars and the odd hashish dealer, especially in winter – peak tourist season. Some visitors find being repeatedly offered drums and oversize balloons for a 'very good price' distressing and tiresome, but be philosophical and just accept it as the price of admission. And rest assured that while scammers and con artists do operate, muggings – of either tourists or locals – are very rare. So, while you might be ripped off by a cute 12-year-old asking you to buy her some powdered milk at a hugely inflated price, or an aspiring shoe-shine boy who just needs a hundred rupees to buy some polish and brushes, but you're unlikely to be robbed at knifepoint. Tourist hotspot Colaba is by far the worst spot for foreigner-focused hawkers and hustlers. If it's all getting a bit much, get out of Colaba for instant relief. If you go to Bandra, however, do watch out for the fake nuns 'collecting for the orphans'.

VISAS & IMMIGRATION

All foreign visitors to India require a visa except for citizens of Nepal, Bhutan and the Maldives. There is no provision for granting visas upon arrival in India and you should apply to the Indian embassy or high commission in your home country. Visitors planning to stay over 180 days must register with the Foreigners' Regional Registration Office within 14 days of arrival.

Depending upon the purpose of your stay in India, you should apply for one of the following visa categories: **Tourist** six months, multiple entry. Tourist visas are easy to get (proof of residence is often enough) but they cannot be extended or converted into other visa types; **Business** valid for one year or more, multiple entry. Applications should be accompanied by a letter from a sponsoring organisation indicating the nature of business, probable duration of stay, places and organisations to be visited; **Employment** valid for one to two years, multiple entry. Applicants are required to submit a copy of a contract of employment; **Student** valid for the duration of the academic course of study or for a period of five years, whichever is less. Proof of admission from an Indian educational institute is required. Student visas cannot be converted; **Transit** issued to transit passengers for a maximum of 15 days, single/double entry; **Missionary** valid for a non-fixed duration at the discretion of the Government of India, single entry; **Journalist** issued to professional journalists and photographers, usually for three months, single entry; **Conference** issued to attendees of conferences/ seminars/meetings held in India. Applicants are required to submit a letter of invitation from the conference organiser.

Temporary Landing Permits

Temporary Landing Permits can be granted to foreigners without visas coming to India in an emergency such as the death or hospitalisation of a relative. A cash payment of US$40 (Rs 1,600) is required. Permits can also be granted to transiting foreigners with confirmed onward journey tickets departing within 72 hours, but the immigration officer will retain the passenger's passport for the period. This facility is not available to citizens of Sri Lanka, Bangladesh, Pakistan, Iran, Afghanistan, Somalia, Nigeria and Ethiopia.

Foreigners' registration

Registration is compulsory for all foreigners intending to stay in India for more than 180 days. It should be done within 14 days of arrival.

Foreigners' Regional Registration Office
Third Floor, Special Branch Building, Badruddin Tayabji Lane, behind St Xavier's College, Fort (2262-1169). CST or Marine Lines stations.

WEIGHTS & MEASURES

India uses the metric system. Indians also commonly use the terms lakh for 100,000 and crore for 10,000,000. For example, 'Rs 1 million' is usually written as 'Rs 10 lakh', and 'Rs 1 billion' is written as 'Rs 100 crore'.

WHAT TO TAKE

Mumbai has a tropical climate, so pack light summer clothes, but also take a thin sweater or thick shirt for cool January and February evenings. Clothes and shoes are widely available at cheap prices but with a limited range in larger shoe sizes for men. The sun is bright and burning, so bring a hat, sunglasses and sunscreen. Open shoes or sandals are a good option, but closed shoes are a must if you're coming in the monsoon, between June and September, as is an umbrella (easy to purchase in Mumbai). Foreign tourists are notorious among Mumbaikars for looking unkempt and dirty; Indians always make an effort to look neat and you should dress smart when visiting an Indian home.

Many medicines are available in Mumbai over the counter without a prescription, so only bring specialised personal medication. Essentials include luggage locks (bicycle locks are good for securing luggage on long train journeys), a money belt, insect repellent, photocopies of important documents like passports, spare batteries and an electrical adaptor. You might also consider bringing candles, a penknife (put it in your check-in luggage), a phrasebook, toiletries, sanitary towels and tampons, as well as an anti-bacterial hand gel.

WHEN TO GO

Climate

The 'winter', from December to February, is generally considered the most pleasant time to visit Mumbai, when average daytime temperatures dip to around 24°C (75°F) with low humidity. It can get very hot and humid in April and May, when temperatures peak at 35°C (95°F). In June, the monsoon begins, bringing torrential rain and intermittent flooding across the city right through until September, with the heaviest rains in spurts in July and August. In October, the temperature and humidity rise again after the monsoon, cooling off by early December.

Public holidays

Visit www.rbi.org.in for a list of public holidays.

WEATHER AVERAGES

MUMBAI

	Max (°C)	Min (°C)	Rainfall (mm)
January	30.6	20.1	0.0
February	30.7	21.7	4.2
March	32.4	23.8	0.0
April	33.3	25.9	0.0
May	34.2	27.9	0.7
June	32.7	26.6	803.3
July	30.5	26.1	524.8
August	29.9	25.3	687.4
September	30.4	25.2	420.5
October	33.3	24.5	0.0
November	33.2	23.1	2.4
December	32.0	21.2	0.0

PANJIM

	Max (°C)	Min (°C)	Rainfall (mm)
January	33.4	20.2	0.0
February	32.7	20.6	0.0
March	32.6	23.5	0.0
April	33.8	26.3	0.0
May	34.1	26.2	93.8
June	30.4	24.8	1077.3
July	29.5	24.5	688.6
August	29.1	24.1	887.0
September	29.5	24.0	763.2
October	31.6	24.1	81.9
November	33.4	21.2	75.6
December	33.4	20.9	0.7

WOMEN

Mumbai's women are not shrinking violets. Many are independent, assertive and are strongly represented in senior roles in industry and other walks of life. Women generally earn the same salaries as their male colleagues, but the glass ceiling persists at high levels of government and the corporate hierarchy. Even so, the streets and public spaces of Mumbai are more male-dominated than would be expected in a free and equal society. The level of independence that Mumbai's women enjoy varies for different classes and ethnic groups and the conservatism is driven by family pressures rather than governmental disapproval or legislation.

Despite all the ever-present lurid Bollywood movie posters of skimpily clad women, conservative dress for women is the norm – short skirts and tight tops are generally the preserve of the upper classes, although jeans and T-shirts are the city's college student uniform. 'Eve-teasing' is how Mumbaikars refer to cat-calls, sexual harassment and worse by men, which occur with distressing frequency, although rapes and other sexual crimes are not as common in Mumbai as in other Indian cities. Foreign women are likely to be the objects of curiosity for some, and occasionally of lascivious attention; it's best to avoid short shorts and skirts or getting too flirty (*see p231* **Attitudes & etiquette**).

WORKING IN MUMBAI

Foreigners are not allowed to work in India without an appropriate visa. Employment visas should be applied for in advance and are issued only in the applicant's home country (*see left* **Visas & immigration**).

Further Reference

BOOKS

Fiction

Chandra, Vikram *Sacred Games* An enjoyable, if telephone directory-sized, cops-and-robbers thriller.
De Souza, Eunice *Dangerlok* A finely etched portrait of an ageing English Lit professor struggling with life in a distant Mumbai suburb.
Desai, Anita *Baumgartner's Bombay* A German Jew, who has long made a new life in Mumbai, runs into a wild hippie from his homeland.
Mistry, Cyrus *Radiance of Ashes* A young Parsi market researcher makes his way through the city's underbelly.
Mistry, Rohinton *Tales from Ferozeshah Baug, Such a Long Journey, A Fine Balance* and *Family Matters* explore the anxieties and joys of the city's diminishing Parsi community.
Nagarkar, Kiran *Ravan and Eddie* Mumbai's much-vaunted cosmopolitanism is stretched and tested in this brilliant novel, set in a tenement.
Roberts, Gregory David *Shantaram* An Australian convict finds redemption in this simplistic New Agey narrative, purportedly based on real life.
Rushdie, Salman *Midnight's Children, The Moor's Last Sigh* and *The Ground Beneath Her Feet* careen through Mumbai (with tangents shooting through time and space) as India's best-known writer pays tribute to the city of his birth.
Tyrewala, Altaf *No God in Sight* A cinematically constructed journey through the heart of the Muslim community of Central Mumbai.

Poetry

Chaudhuri, Amit *St Cyril Road and Other Poems* Reflections on Bandra's Roman Catholic community, and other meanderings.
Ezekiel, Nissim *Collected Poems 1952-1988* Ezekiel's poems in Indian English display a verbal litheness that could only have been inspired by multi-lingual Mumbai.
Kolatkar, Arun *Kala Ghoda Poems* One of India's most famous English-language poets looks out across the city's most famous square.
Subramaniam, Arundhathi *Where I Live* It's a 'city of L'Oreal sunsets…of septic magenta hairclips…of hope and bulimia', says the poet.

Non-fiction

Dalmia, Yashodhara *The Making of Modern Indian Art* A lavishly illustrated, incisive look at the painters of the Progressive Artists Group, who invented a new idiom in the early years of independence.
D'Monte, Darryl *Ripping the Fabric: The Decline of Mumbai and its Mills* An analysis of how the shuttering of Mumbai's textile mills has undermined the city's social and economic health.
Dwivedi, Sharada and **Mehrotra, Rahul** *Fort Walks* is an indispensable guide to the buildings of the Fort district and *Bangaga: Sacred Tank on Malabar Hill* is an illustrated history of the temple complex in Walkeshwar.
Garga, BD *So Many Cinemas* A superbly researched history of Indian cinema, supported by film stills from the earliest movies.
Guha, Ramachandra *A Corner of a Foreign Field: The Indian History of a British Sport* Set largely in Mumbai, this book is a social history of India, told through its favourite sport.
Gupt, Somnath *The Parsi Theatre: Its Origins and Development* A study of a 19th-century theatre form that established the conventions still followed in Bollywood films.
Hansen, Thomas Blom *Wages of Violence: Naming and Identity in Postcolonial Bombay* How the nativist Shiv Sena party unleashed fundamentalist forces that polarised India's most cosmopolitan city.
Hoskote, Ranjit *The Complicit Observer* A showcase of the work of Sudhir Patwardhan, who paints Mumbaikars travelling on the train, on the street and sitting in Irani cafés and who delights in finding the extraordinary in the mundane.
Kapoor, Shashi and **Gehlot, Deepa** *Prithwiwallas* The story of how India's most famous film family built the auditorium that is now at the centre of Mumbai's theatre scene.
London, Christopher *Bombay Gothic* A pictorial history of Mumbai's fascination with a style that had its origins thousands of miles away.
Manto, Sadat Hasan *Mumbai: Stars from Another Sky* A catty collection of pieces from the time when one of the greatest Urdu writers worked as a film journalist.
Masselos, Jim and **Fernandes, Naresh** *Bombay Then and Mumbai Now* A lavishly visual book about old and new Mumbai.
Mehta, Suketu *Maximum City* A painstakingly researched book about the numerous worlds that make up Mumbai.
Michell, George *Elephanta* A guide to the sixth-century rock-carved caves on the island just off Mumbai.
Moraes, Dom *A Variety of Absences* The shimmering memoirs of the famous poet and journalist.
Neuwirth, Robert *Shadow Cities* An American writer takes up residence in shanty towns on four continents, Mumbai among them.
Patel, Sujata and **Thorner, Alice** *Bombay: Metaphor for Modern India* and *Bombay: Mosaic of Modern Culture* are collections of academic articles that examine the city's past – and make prescriptions for its future.
Pinto, Jerry and **Fernandes, Naresh** (editors) *Bombay Meri Jaan* An anthology of writing and poetry about India's most vibrant city. (*See p29* **Mumbai Today**)
Prakash, Gyan *Mumbai Fables* A charming story about Mumbai's history, its ideas, its people and its scandals.
Ramani, Navin *Bombay Art Deco Architecture: A Visual Journey (1930-1953)* A fascinating survey of some of the city's finest art deco buildings, the picture-led book is also an excellent introduction to the ideas of the art deco style.
Seabrook, Jeremy *Life and Labour in a Bombay Slum* The author finds optimism amidst the squalour of Mumbai's shanty colonies.
Sharma, Kalpana *Rediscovering Dharavi: Stories from Asia's*

Largest Slum A study of life in the district that has come to symbolise the urban policy that ensures that half of Mumbai's population has no hope of moving out of slums.
Zaidi, S Hussain *Black Friday: The True Story of the Bombay Bomb Blasts* A journalist's pacy reconstruction of the conspiracy that resulted in the explosions that killed 257 in March 1993.

History

Dwivedi, Shardha and **Mehrotra, Rahul** *Bombay: The Cities Within* An immensely readable tale of how seven malarial islands grew into a major metropolis, with lots of pictorial evidence.
Edwardes, SM *Gazetteer of Bombay City and Island* The ultimate administrators' handbook to the city, completed in 1909, has sections on the city's history, trade patterns, headgear, and even lists of distinctive hawkers' cries.
Farooqui, Amar *Opium City: The Making of Early Victorian Bombay* Opium, as much as cotton, boosted Mumbai's fortunes, says the author.
Marg Publications *Bombay to Mumbai: Changing Perspectives* An eclectic selection of articles, including pieces on early photography in Mumbai, 19th-century homes and the city's art deco architecture.
Menon, Meena and **Adarkar, Neera** *One Hundred Years, One Hundred Voices. The Millworkers of Girangaon: An Oral History.* A compelling history of how tumultuous changes in Mumbai's mill district shaped events across India.
Tindall, Gillian *City of Gold: The Biography of Bombay* A delightful stroll through the city's British history, told with a novelist's eye for detail.

FILM

See also p41 **Bollywood**.
Aar Paar (1954) 1950s tragedy king Guru Dutt directs as well as stars as a working-class taxi driver.
Boot Polish (1954) Prakash Arora tells the story of Ratan Kumar and his sister, who survive on the streets of Mumbai by scrabbling for food and coins at railway stations.
Taxi Driver (1954) Chetan Anand's rambling tale of the relationship between taxi driver Dev Anand and runaway singer Kalpana Kartik is a grand excuse to shoot Mumbai's urban vistas.
Mr and Mrs '55 (1955) Made by Guru Dutt in the decade when the post-independence bubbly still hadn't gone flat, this is a satire on the feudal upper classes.
Shree 420 (1955) Raj Kapoor's guileless tramp trips into Mumbai singing. The poor welcome him with open arms but he loses his way and starts working for a businessman who wants to raze the slum where his comrades and lady-love Nargis live.
CID (1956) *CID*'s magic lies in its taut storytelling, business-like characters and snappy editing. Plus, this Bollywoodian film noir story has the unofficial Mumbai anthem: 'Yeh Hai Bombay Meri Jaan'.
Chhoti Si Baat (1975) Basu Chatterji paints Mumbai as a truly romantic city, full of possibilities and a love of life. Amol Palekar's Arun meets Prabha every day at the bus stop. He's madly in love but has no confidence until he takes courtship lessons from a retired colonel.
Ardh Satya (1983) Govind Nihalini's gritty cop story takes on a debate over violence, authority and control, with a hard-edged story unfolding through the eyes of a Mumbai police inspector, played by Om Puri.
Jaane Bhi Do Yaaro (1983) In this cult slapstick satire, directed by Kundan Shah, two bumbling photographers stumble on to a scam being hatched by corrupt builders and municipal officials, and embark on a series of madcap adventures to unearth the truth.
Saaransh (1984) Possibly Mahesh Bhatt's best film, and one of the few Hindi movies to explore the Shiv Sena's reign of terror in the city.
Salaam Bombay! (1988) Many Mumbaikars hate this movie, and dismiss it as urban exotica, but Mira Nair's debut is a moving portrait of the city's underbelly, seen through its street children, whores and pimps.
Tezaab (1988) N Chandra's movie is a great visual dictionary for the city: it has street lingo, gangster brawls, tough love and hip-shaking songs. Anil Kapoor plays Munna, an aspiring naval officer whose journey to gangsterhood is told in flashback.
Parinda (1989) A successful assimilation of the Hollywood film noir genre, *Parinda* remains Vidhu Vinod Chopra's most evocative film and one of the most well-crafted gangster films in recent times.
Salim Langde Pe Mat Ro (1989) Saeed Mirza tackles issues faced by Mumbai's marginalised Muslims in this beautifully shot movie, set in the teeming alleys of Central Mumbai.
Bombay (1995) One of the few films to look squarely at the 1992-93 Mumbai religious riots, Mani Ratnam's love story has been dissected and dissed for its portrayal of events and characters – for example, the violence in the film is always initiated by a Muslim.
Rangeela (1995) Light at heart and on the feet, *Rangeela* is Ram Gopal Varma's ode to the magic of the movies.
Satya (1998) Through the character of Satya, a man with no background who emerges from the stone corridors of Chhatrapati Shivaji Terminus into the arms of the underworld, Ram Gopal Varma trawls through shoot-outs, betrayals and revenge. Bloody good fun, and a modern classic.
Munnabhai MBBS (2003) *Munnabhai MBBS*, a comedy about a street thug who teaches doctors a thing or two about treatment, isn't the first film to put Mumbai's street lingo into a film script. But it is one of the few Hindi films to use the language almost as a living, breathing character.
Taxi No 9211 (2006) A rich brat (John Abraham) and a working-class taxi driver (Nana Patekar) collide in this imitation of *Changing Lanes*.
Black Friday (2007) A fast-paced yet detailed adaptation of S Hussain Zaidi's book about the 12 March 1993 bombings across Mumbai.
Guru (2007) A hagiography based on the life of Dhirubhai Ambani, a businessman who came to Mumbai with nothing and founded one of India's biggest corporations.
Metro (2007) The lives of several characters intersect in this ensemble about life in a modern Indian metropolis.
Kaminey (2009) A gritty and comical story of identical but estranged twins whose lives get intertwined by a stash of cocaine hidden in a guitar.
Little Zizou (2008) This slice-of-life comedy is set in Mumbai's Parsi community and features a cross-section of lovable eccentrics.
Luck By Chance (2009) A movie about the movie business, seen through the eyes of two struggling actors.
Sankat City (2009) Small-time car thief Guru finds a suitcase containing millions of rupees – and then loses it.

Content Index

INDEX

Venue Index

Kanheri Caves, Borivali. *See p70.*

Advertisers' Index

Please refer to the relevant pages for contact details.

Maps

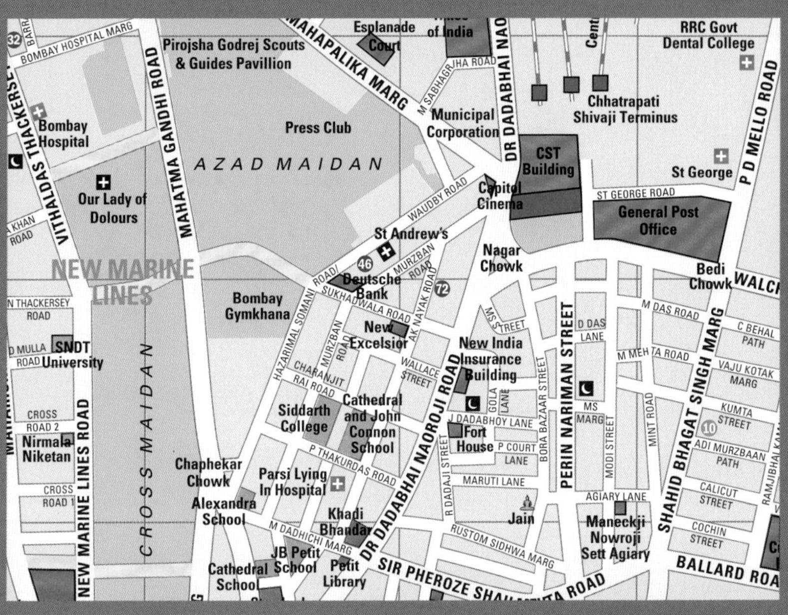

Place of interest and/or entertainment . . .
College/Hospital/University . . . .
Railway station/Bus depot . . . .
Ruins area . . . .
Parks . . . .
River . . . .
Beach . . . .
Main road . . . .
Pedestrian road . . . .
Airport . . . .
Church . . . .
Temple . . . .
Synagogues . . . .
Hospital . . . .
Post office . . . .
Mosque . . . .
Tourist information . . . .
Area name . . . . FORT

Mumbai Overview

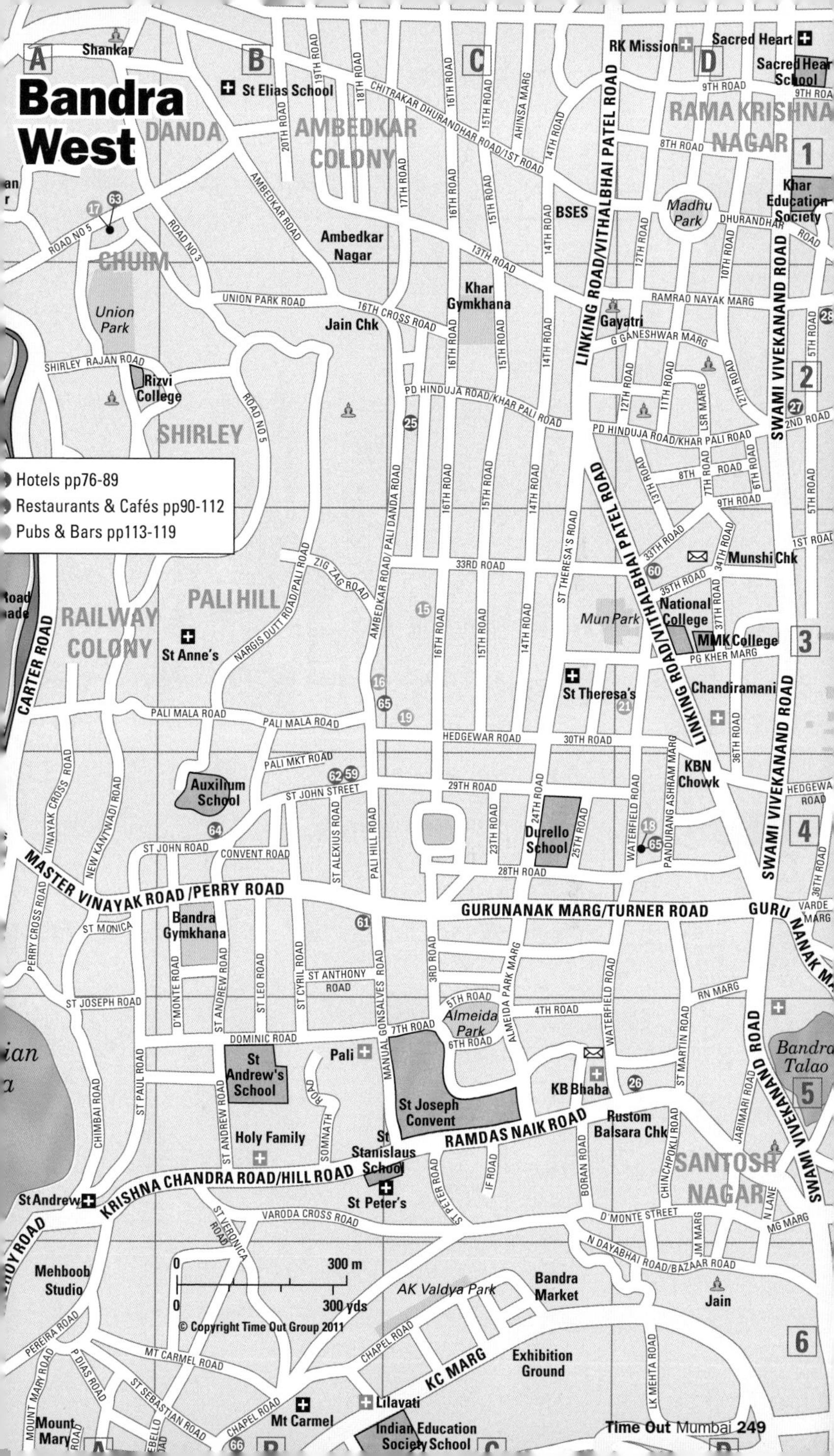
Bandra West
A
B
C
D
1
2
3
4
5
6
Hotels pp76-89
Restaurants & Cafés pp90-112
Pubs & Bars pp113-119
Shankar
St Elias School
RK Mission
Sacred Heart
Sacred Heart School
DANDA
AMBEDKAR COLONY
RAMA KRISHNA NAGAR
CHUIM
Union Park
SHIRLEY
PALI HILL
RAILWAY COLONY
SANTOSH NAGAR
Ambedkar Nagar
Khar Gymkhana
Jain Chk
BSES
Madhu Park
Khar Education Society
Gayatri
Rizvi College
Munshi Chk
Mun Park
National College
MMK College
St Anne's
St Theresa's
Chandiramani
KBN Chowk
Auxilium School
Durello School
Bandra Gymkhana
Almeida Park
St Andrew's School
Pali
St Joseph Convent
KB Bhaba
Rustom Balsara Chk
Holy Family
St Stanislaus School
St Peter's
St Andrew
Bandra Talao
Mehboob Studio
AK Valdya Park
Bandra Market
Jain
Exhibition Ground
Lilavati
Mt Carmel
Mount Mary
Indian Education Society School
CHITRAKAR DHURANDHAR ROAD/1ST ROAD
LINKING ROAD/VITHALBHAI PATEL ROAD
SWAMI VIVEKANAND ROAD
ROAD NO 5
ROAD NO 3
AMBEDKAR ROAD
UNION PARK ROAD
16TH CROSS ROAD
SHIRLEY RAJAN ROAD
PD HINDUJA ROAD/KHAR PALI ROAD
RAMRAO NAYAK MARG
G GANESHWAR MARG
DHURANDHAR ROAD
AHINSA MARG
ZIG ZAG ROAD
NARGIS DUTT ROAD/PALI ROAD
AMBEDKAR ROAD/PALI DANDA ROAD
ST THERESA'S ROAD
33RD ROAD
PG KHER MARG
CARTER ROAD
PALI MALA ROAD
HEDGEWAR ROAD
30TH ROAD
29TH ROAD
28TH ROAD
PALI MKT ROAD
ST JOHN STREET
ST JOHN ROAD
CONVENT ROAD
ST ALEXIUS ROAD
PALI HILL ROAD
WATERFIELD ROAD
PANDURANG ASHRAM MARG
MASTER VINAYAK ROAD/PERRY ROAD
GURUNANAK MARG/TURNER ROAD
VINAYAK CROSS ROAD
NEW KANTWADI ROAD
PERRY CROSS ROAD
ST MONICA
ST JOSEPH ROAD
D'MONTE ROAD
ST ANDREW ROAD
ST LEO ROAD
ST CYRIL ROAD
ST ANTHONY ROAD
MANUAL GONSALVES ROAD
3RD ROAD
ALMEIDA PARK MARG
4TH ROAD
5TH ROAD
6TH ROAD
7TH ROAD
DOMINIC ROAD
RN MARG
ST MARTIN ROAD
ST PAUL ROAD
CHIMBAI ROAD
SOMNATH ROAD
RAMDAS NAIK ROAD
KRISHNA CHANDRA ROAD/HILL ROAD
IF ROAD
ST PETER ROAD
BORAN ROAD
CHINCHPOKLI ROAD
JARIMARI ROAD
N LANE
MG MARG
VARODA CROSS ROAD
ST VERONICA ROAD
D'MONTE STREET
JM MARG
N DAYABHAI ROAD/BAZAAR ROAD
PEREIRA ROAD
P DIAS ROAD
MT CARMEL ROAD
ST SEBASTIAN ROAD
MOUNT MARY ROAD
CHAPEL ROAD
KC MARG
LK MEHTA ROAD
0
300 m
300 yds
© Copyright Time Out Group 2011

Arabian Sea
B ROAD
Jai Hind College
Govt Law College
S DEORA MARG
IM CHAMBER ROAD
Western Railway Headquarters
Churchgate Station
CROSS MAIDAN
Cathedral School
JB Petit School
M DADHICHI MARG
Khadi Bhandar
RUSTOM SIDHWA MARG
COCHIN STREET
New Customs House
SPROTT ROAD
Naval Museum
BALLARD ROAD
See p253
SIR PHEROZESHAH MEHTA ROAD
Standard Chartered Bank Building
DN ROAD
JANMABHOOMI MARG
NANUBHAI LANE
BANAJI STREET
CAWASJI PATEL ROAD
Universal Building
SA BRELVI ROAD
HOMJI STREET
Monetary Museum
Old RBI
MINT ROAD
New RBI
Govt of India Mint
BALLARD ESTATE
MARINE DRIVE/NETAJI SUBHASH CHANDRA BOSE MARG
VEER NARIMAN ROAD
A Holkar Chowk
Bhika Behram Well
Flora Fountain
R Poddar Chowk
VEER NARIMAN ROAD
Horniman Circle
Asiatic Society
Brabourne Stadium
Main Gate
Eros Cinema
New India Assurance Building
HOMI MODI STREET
St Thomas Cathedral
MUMBAI SAMACHAR MARG
DINSHAW WACHHA ROAD
IM CHAMBER ROAD
JAMSHEDJI TATA ROAD
JTS MALANI MARG
OVAL MAIDAN
High Court
ELDON ROAD
MAHATMA GANDHI ROAD
M SHETTY MARG
FORT
GREEN STREET
BANK STREET
SHAHID BHAGAT SINGH MARG
BABUBHAI M CHINAI
KC & HR College
UNIVERSITY ROAD
ASH LANE
MEADOWS STREET
AMBALAL DOSHI ROAD
BSE
DALAL STREET
Mumbai University
Rajabai Clock Tower
N MOTAWANI ROAD
KALA GHODA
Collector Central Excise
Advani Chowk
CHURCHGATE
MAHARISHI KARVE ROAD
KARMAVEER BHAURAO PATIL MARG
JB MARG
ROAD NO 3
WIAA Chowk
SAI BABA MARG
MASTER ROAD
FULLER ROAD
DR VB GANDHI ROAD
MADAME CAMA ROAD
CRESCENT ROAD
JD DARUWALA MARG
LIBRARY MARG
David Sassoon Library
K DUBASH MARG
Kenneseth Eliyahoo
Sessions Court
Elphinstone College
Jehangir Art Gallery
Mantralaya
St Andrews
Lion's Gate
SIR DORAB TATA ROAD
BARRISTER RAJNI PATEL MARG
VIDHAN BHAVAN MARG
Old Secretariat
Institute of Science
Prince of Wales Museum
Bombay Natural History Society
VK SHAH MARG
Inox
Vidhan Bhavan
Vidhan Chowk
Nariman Building
Municipal Children's Park
MADAME CAMA ROAD
NGMA
SP Mukherjee Chowk
DOCKYARD
NCPA MARG
National Centre of the Performing Arts
Nariman Point
JAMNALAL BAJAJ ROAD
Maker Chamber III
YB Chavan Auditorium
Anne's School
Campion School
YMCA
NARIMAN POINT
Mittal Tower
Regal Cinema
SHIVAJI MARG
COOPERAGE ROAD
Cooperage Maidan
QUEEN'S ROAD
NPA Marker Garden
Raheja Centre
FREE PRESS JOURNAL
H BHOSLE ROAD
WODEHOUSE ROAD
CONVENT ST
BATTERY ST
STEVEN ST
LANSDOWNE RD
TULLOCH ROAD
N F STREET
MLA Hostel
MSLTA
J & M Convent
Holy Name
Royal Bombay Yacht Club

Colaba to Churchgate

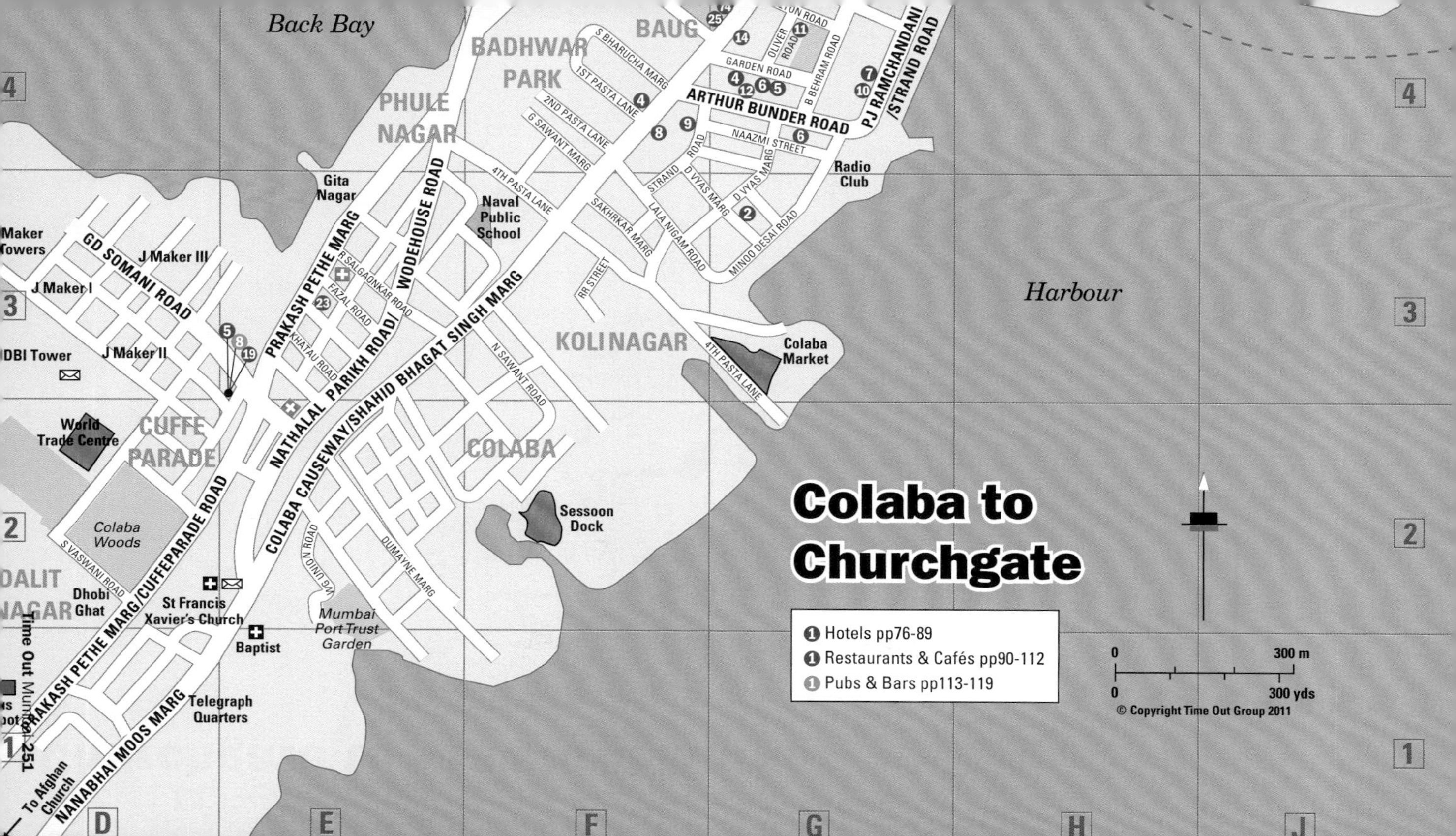

Churchgate to Crawford Market

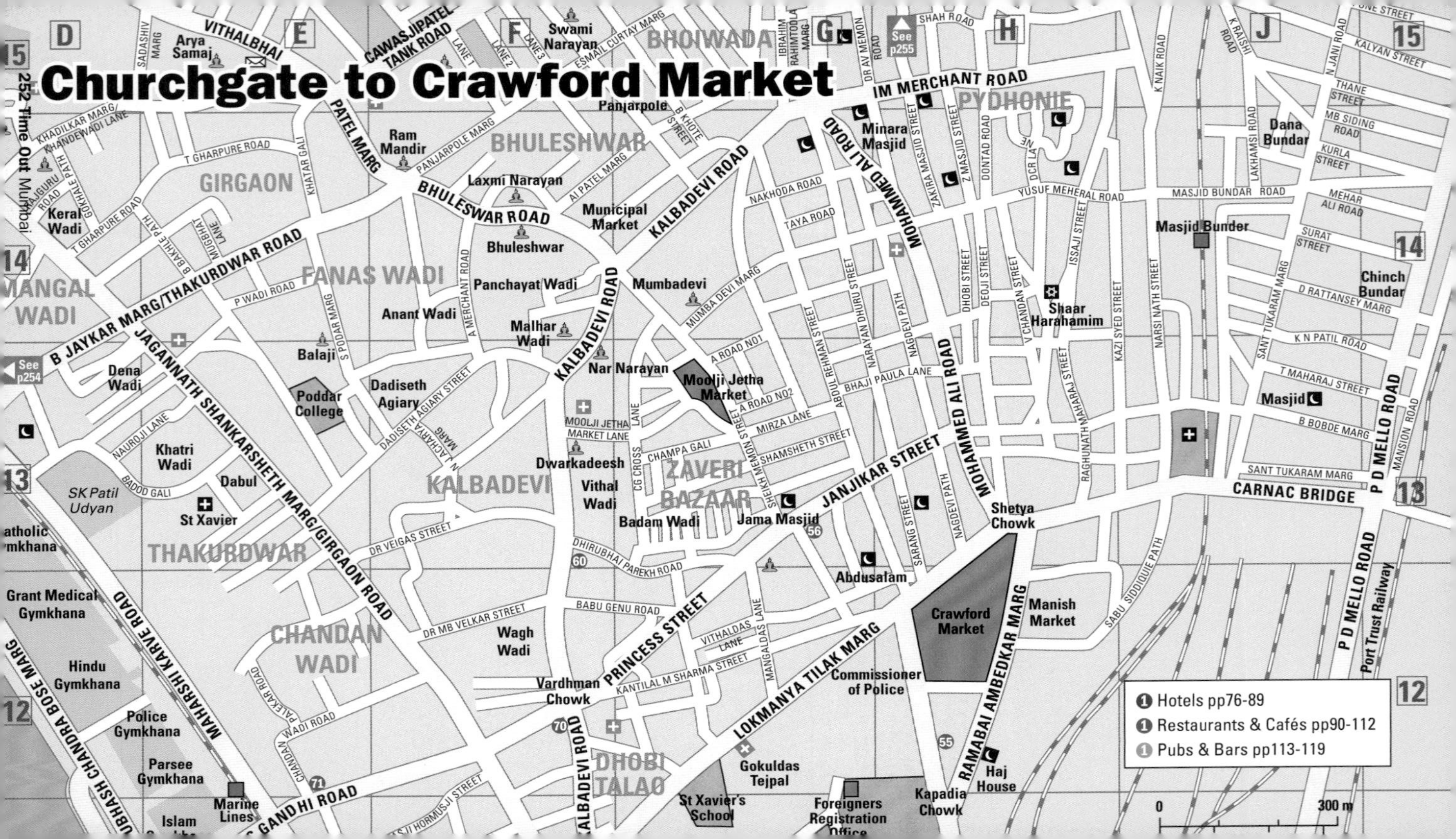

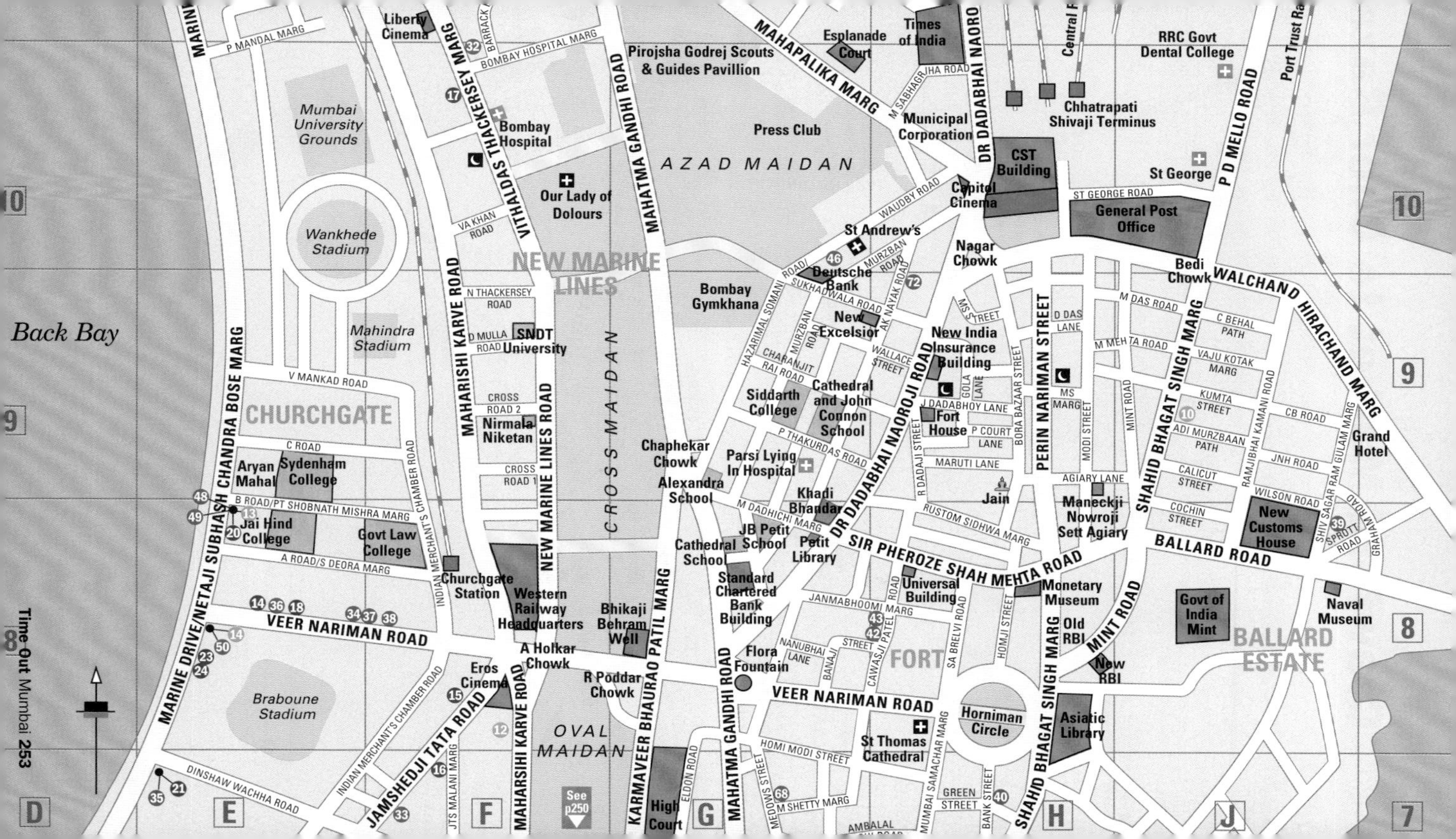

MARIN
P MANDAL MARG
Liberty Cinema
BARRACK
BOMBAY HOSPITAL MARG
VITHALDAS THACKERSEY MARG
Bombay Hospital
MAHATMA GANDHI ROAD
Pirojsha Godrej Scouts & Guides Pavillion
MAHAPALIKA MARG
Esplanade Court
Times of India
JHA ROAD
M SABHAGR
DR DADABHAI NAORO
Central R
RRC Govt Dental College
Port Trust Ra
P D MELLO ROAD
Mumbai University Grounds
Press Club
Municipal Corporation
Chhatrapati Shivaji Terminus
CST Building
St George
AZAD MAIDAN
Our Lady of Dolours
VA KHAN ROAD
WAUDBY ROAD
Capitol Cinema
ST GEORGE ROAD
General Post Office
Wankhede Stadium
St Andrew's
Nagar Chowk
NEW MARINE LINES
MAHARISHI KARVE ROAD
N THACKERSEY ROAD
Bombay Gymkhana
ROAD/ MURZBAN ROAD
Deutsche Bank
72
Bedi Chowk
WALCHAND HIRACHAND MARG
HAZARIMAL SOMANI MARG
SUKHADWALA ROAD
AK NAYAK ROAD
MS STREET
D DAS LANE
M DAS ROAD
C BEHAL PATH
Back Bay
Mahindra Stadium
D MULLA ROAD
SNDT University
CROSS MAIDAN
MURZBAN ROAD
New Excelsior
New India Insurance Building
M MEHTA ROAD
VAJU KOTAK MARG
V MANKAD ROAD
CROSS ROAD 2
CHARANJIT RAI ROAD
WALLACE STREET
DR DADABHAI NAOROJI ROAD
BORA BAZAAR STREET
PERIN NARIMAN STREET
MINT ROAD
SHAHID BHAGAT SINGH MARG
KUMTA STREET
RAMJIBHAI KAMANI ROAD
CB ROAD
CHURCHGATE
NEW MARINE LINES ROAD
Nirmala Niketan
Siddarth College
Cathedral and John Connon School
GOLA LANE
J DADABHOY LANE
Fort House
P COURT LANE
MS MARG
MODI STREET
ADI MURZBAAN PATH
SHIV SAGAR RAM GULAM MARG
Grand Hotel
C ROAD
Aryan Mahal
Sydenham College
CROSS ROAD 1
Chaphekar Chowk
Parsi Lying In Hospital
P THAKURDAS ROAD
R DADAJI STREET
MARUTI LANE
JNH ROAD
CALICUT STREET
Alexandra School
Khadi Bhandar
Jain
AGIARY LANE
Maneckji Nowroji Sett Agiary
WILSON ROAD
B ROAD/PT SHOBNATH MISHRA MARG
M DADHICHI MARG
RUSTOM SIDHWA MARG
COCHIN STREET
New Customs House
SPROTT ROAD
GRAHAM ROAD
INDIAN MERCHANT'S CHAMBER ROAD
Jai Hind College
Govt Law College
JB Petit School
Cathedral School
Petit Library
SIR PHEROZE SHAH MEHTA ROAD
BALLARD ROAD
MARINE DRIVE/NETAJI SUBHASH CHANDRA BOSE MARG
A ROAD/S DEORA MARG
Churchgate Station
Western Railway Headquarters
Standard Chartered Bank Building
Universal Building
Monetary Museum
Govt of India Mint
Naval Museum
JANMABHOOMI MARG
VEER NARIMAN ROAD
Bhikaji Behram Well
KARMAVEER BHAURAO PATIL MARG
HOMJI STREET
Old RBI
MINT ROAD
BALLARD ESTATE
A Holkar Chowk
NANUBHAI LANE
BANAJI STREET
CAWASJI PATEL STREET
Flora Fountain
FORT
SA BRELVI ROAD
New RBI
Eros Cinema
R Poddar Chowk
MAHATMA GANDHI ROAD
Braboune Stadium
INDIAN MERCHANT'S CHAMBER ROAD
JAMSHEDJI TATA ROAD
MAHARSHI KARVE ROAD
OVAL MAIDAN
Horniman Circle
Asiatic Library
ELDON ROAD
HOMI MODI STREET
St Thomas Cathedral
MUMBAI SAMACHAR MARG
DINSHAW WACHHA ROAD
JTS MALANI MARG
See p250
High Court
MEDOWS STREET
M SHETTY MARG
GREEN STREET
BANK STREET
AMBALAL
D E F G H J
7 8 9 10

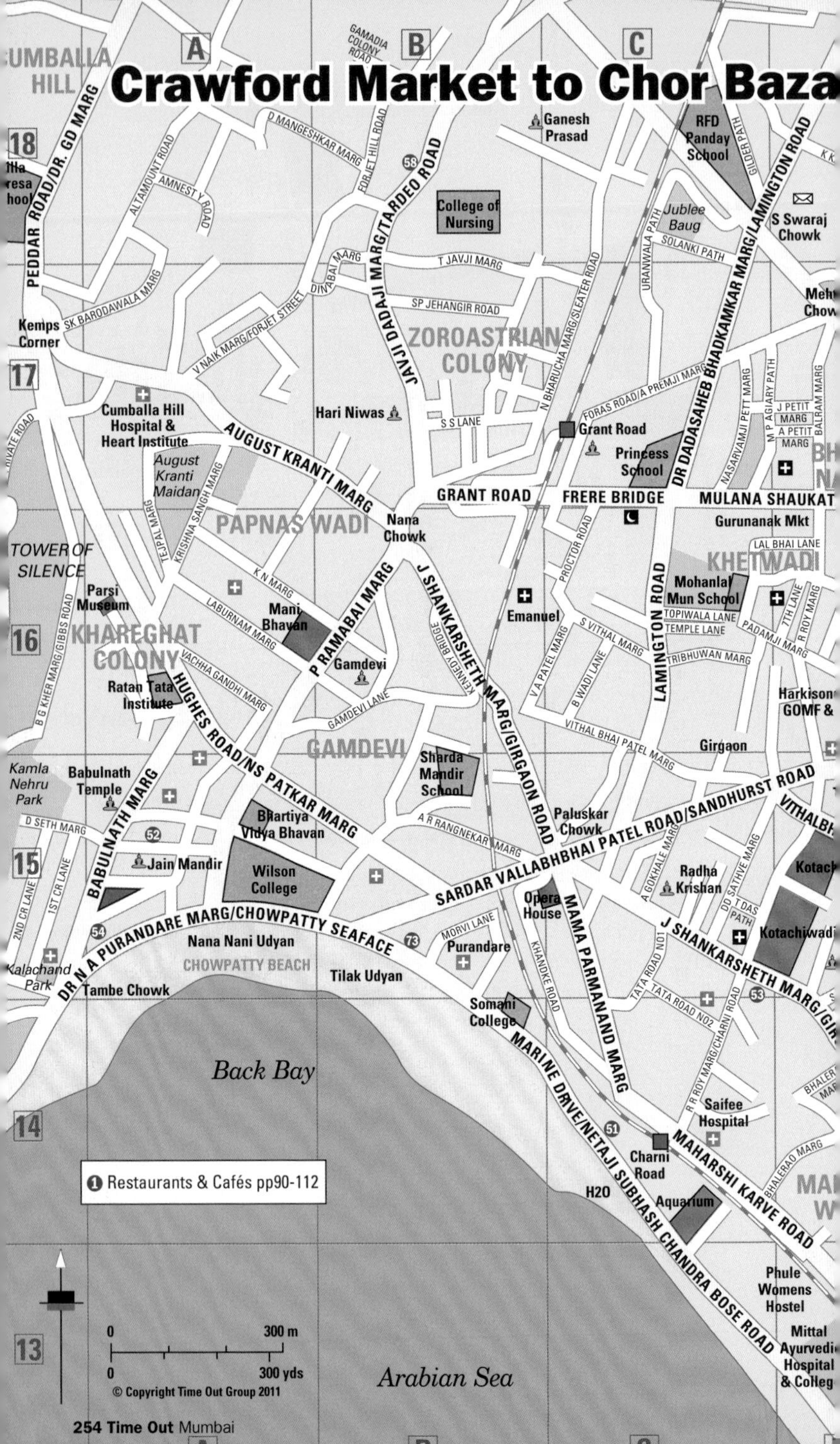

Crawford Market to Chor Baza
A
B
C
CUMBALLA HILL
PEDDAR ROAD/DR. GD MARG
D MANGESHKAR MARG
FORJET HILL ROAD
GAMADIA COLONY ROAD
JAVJI DADAJI MARG/TARDEO ROAD
Ganesh Prasad
RFD Panday School
GILDER PATH
DR DADASAHEB BHADKAMKAR MARG/LAMINGTON ROAD
ALTAMOUNT ROAD
AMNESTY ROAD
College of Nursing
Jublee Baug
SOLANKI PATH
URANWALA PATH
S Swaraj Chowk
T JAVJI MARG
SP JEHANGIR ROAD
N BHARUCHA MARG/SLEATER ROAD
SK BARODAWALA MARG
Kemps Corner
V NAIK MARG/FORJET STREET
ZOROASTRIAN COLONY
FORAS ROAD/A PREMJI MARG
Cumballa Hill Hospital & Heart Institute
Hari Niwas
S S LANE
Grant Road
Princess School
AUGUST KRANTI MARG
August Kranti Maidan
GRANT ROAD
FRERE BRIDGE
MULANA SHAUKAT
NASARVAMJI PETT MARG
M P AGIARY PATH
J PETIT MARG
A PETIT MARG
BALRAM MARG
PAPNAS WADI
Nana Chowk
TEJPAL MARG
KRISHNA SANGH MARG
Gurunanak Mkt
LAL BHAI LANE
KHETWADI
TOWER OF SILENCE
PROCTOR ROAD
K N MARG
P RAMABAI MARG
J SHANKARSHETH MARG/GIRGAON ROAD
Parsi Museum
Mani Bhavan
Emanuel
LAMINGTON ROAD
Mohanlal Mun School
TOPIWALA LANE
TEMPLE LANE
PADAMJI MARG
7TH LANE
R ROY MARG
KHAREGHAT COLONY
LABURNAM MARG
KENNEDY BRIDGE
S VITHAL MARG
V A PATEL MARG
B WADI LANE
TRIBHUWAN MARG
B G KHER MARG/GIBBS ROAD
VACHHA GANDHI MARG
Gamdevi
Ratan Tata Institute
HUGHES ROAD/NS PATKAR MARG
GAMDEVI LANE
VITHAL BHAI PATEL MARG
Harkison GOMF &
Girgaon
GAMDEVI
Sharda Mandir School
Kamla Nehru Park
Babulnath Temple
BABULNATH MARG
D SETH MARG
Bhartiya Vidya Bhavan
A R RANGNEKAR MARG
Paluskar Chowk
SARDAR VALLABHBHAI PATEL ROAD/SANDHURST ROAD
VITHALBH
52
Jain Mandir
Wilson College
A GOKHALE MARG
Radha Krishan
DD SATHVE MARG
D T DAS PATH
Kotach
2ND CR LANE
1ST CR LANE
Opera House
MAMA PARMANAND MARG
J SHANKARSHETH MARG/GI
Kotachiwadi
54
DR N A PURANDARE MARG/CHOWPATTY SEAFACE
Nana Nani Udyan
73
MORVI LANE
Purandare
KHANDKE ROAD
TATA ROAD NO1
TATA ROAD NO2
53
Kalachand Park
Tambe Chowk
CHOWPATTY BEACH
Tilak Udyan
Somani College
R R ROY MARG/CHARNI ROAD
Back Bay
MARINE DRIVE/NETAJI SUBHASH CHANDRA BOSE ROAD
BHALERAO MARG
Saifee Hospital
51
Charni Road
MAHARSHI KARVE ROAD
H2O
Aquarium
1 Restaurants & Cafés pp90-112
Phule Womens Hostel
Mittal Ayurvedi Hospital & Colleg
0
300 m
0
300 yds
Arabian Sea
18
17
16
15
14
13

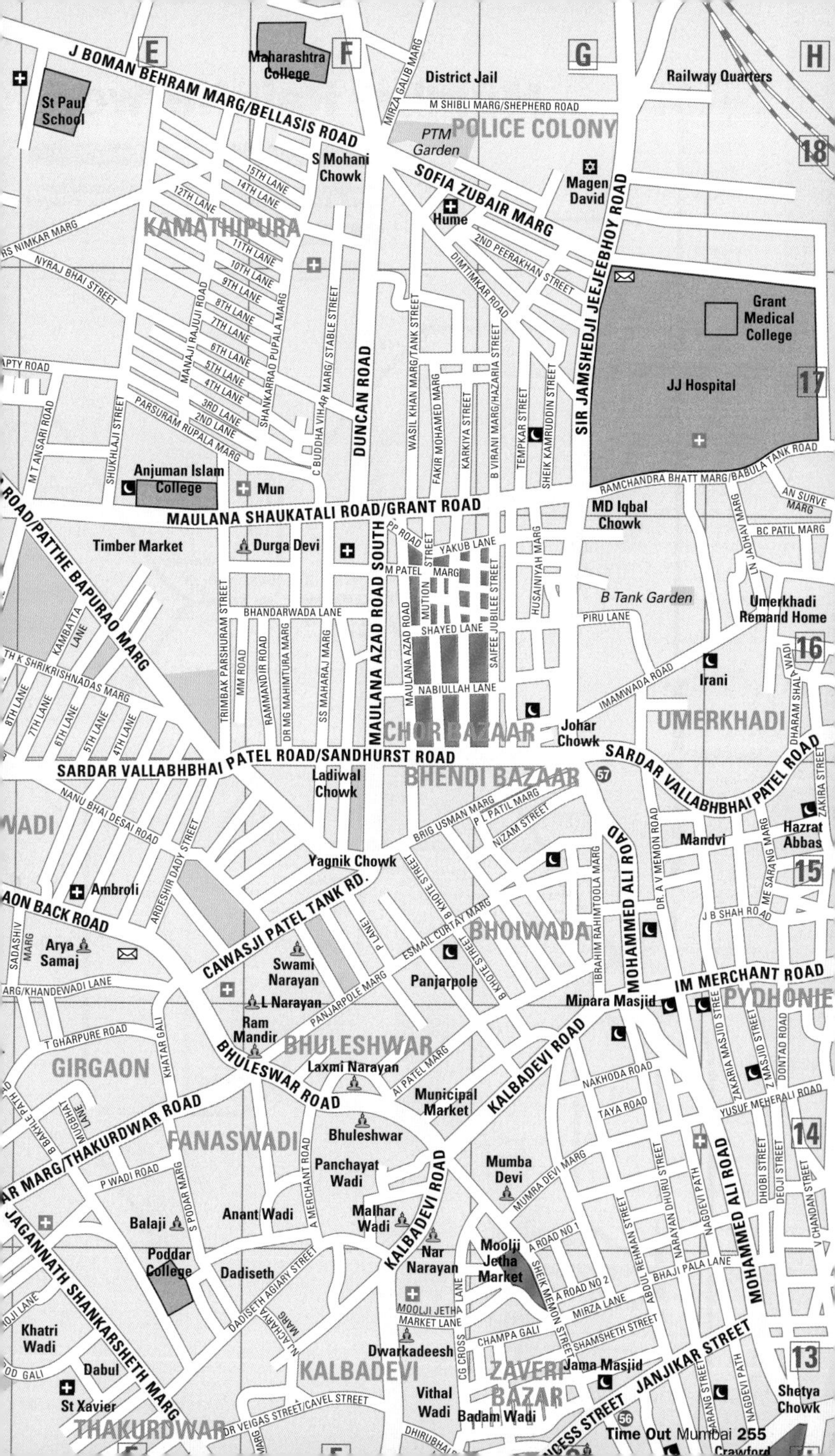
E
F
G
H
J BOMAN BEHRAM MARG/BELLASIS ROAD
Maharashtra College
St Paul School
District Jail
Railway Quarters
M SHIBLI MARG/SHEPHERD ROAD
MIRZA GALIB MARG
POLICE COLONY
PTM Garden
18
S Mohani Chowk
SOFIA ZUBAIR MARG
Magen David
Hume
KAMATHIPURA
15TH LANE
14TH LANE
12TH LANE
11TH LANE
10TH LANE
9TH LANE
8TH LANE
7TH LANE
6TH LANE
5TH LANE
4TH LANE
3RD LANE
2ND LANE
2ND PEERAKHAN STREET
DIMTIMKAR ROAD
SIR JAMSHEDJI JEEJEEBHOY ROAD
Grant Medical College
JJ Hospital
17
NYRAJ BHAI STREET
MANAJI RAJUJI ROAD
SHANKARRAO PUPALA MARG
C BUDDHA VIHAR MARG/ STABLE STREET
DUNCAN ROAD
WASIL KHAN MARG/TANK STREET
FAKIR MOHAMED MARG
KARKIYA STREET
B VIRANI MARG/HAZARIA STREET
TEMPKAR STREET
SHEIK KAMRUDDIN STREET
PARSURAM RUPALA MARG
SHUKHLAJI STREET
M T ANSARI ROAD
Anjuman Islam College
Mun
RAMCHANDRA BHATT MARG/BABULA TANK ROAD
AN SURVE MARG
MAULANA SHAUKATALI ROAD/GRANT ROAD
MD Iqbal Chowk
BC PATIL MARG
LN JADHAV MARG
ROAD/PATTHE BAPURAO MARG
Timber Market
Durga Devi
PP ROAD
YAKUB LANE
M PATEL MARG
MUTION STREET
B Tank Garden
Umerkhadi Remand Home
BHANDARWADA LANE
PIRU LANE
HUSAINIYAH MARG
KAMBATTA LANE
TRIMBAK PARSHURAM STREET
MM ROAD
RAMMANDIR ROAD
DR MG MAHIMTURA MARG
SS MAHARAJ MARG
MAULANA AZAD ROAD SOUTH
MAULANA AZAD ROAD
SHAYED LANE
SAIFEE JUBILEE STREET
NABIULLAH LANE
Irani
IMAMWADA ROAD
16
DHARAM SHALA WADI
TH K SHRIKRISHNADAS MARG
8TH LANE
7TH LANE
6TH LANE
5TH LANE
4TH LANE
CHOR BAZAAR
Johar Chowk
UMERKHADI
SARDAR VALLABHBHAI PATEL ROAD/SANDHURST ROAD
Ladiwal Chowk
BHENDI BAZAAR
57
SARDAR VALLABHBHAI PATEL ROAD
ZAKIRA STREET
WADI
NANU BHAI DESAI ROAD
BRIG USMAN MARG
P L PATIL MARG
NIZAM STREET
DR. A V MEMON ROAD
Mandvi
Hazrat Abbas
ARDESHIR DADY STREET
Yagnik Chowk
IBRAHIM RAHIMTOOLA MARG
MOHAMMED ALI ROAD
ME SARANG MARG
15
Ambroli
CAWASJI PATEL TANK RD.
B KHOTE STREET
ESMAIL CURTAY MARG
J B SHAH ROAD
AON BACK ROAD
BHOIWADA
SADASHIV MARG
Arya Samaj
Swami Narayan
P LANE 1
Panjarpole
IM MERCHANT ROAD
ARG/KHANDEWADI LANE
L Narayan
PANJARPOLE MARG
Minara Masjid
PYDHONIE
T GHARPURE ROAD
Ram Mandir
BHULESHWAR
KALBADEVI ROAD
GIRGAON
KHATAR GALI
BHULESWAR ROAD
Laxmi Narayan
AI PATEL MARG
Municipal Market
NAKHODA ROAD
ZAKARIA MASJID STREET
Z MASJID STREET
DONTAD ROAD
TAYA ROAD
YUSUF MEHERALI ROAD
B BAKHLE PATH
MUGBHAT LANE
AR MARG/THAKURDWAR ROAD
FANASWADI
A MERCHANT ROAD
Bhuleshwar
14
P WADI ROAD
S PODAR MARG
Panchayat Wadi
Mumba Devi
MUMRA DEVI MARG
Anant Wadi
Malhar Wadi
KALBADEVI ROAD
ABDUL REHMAN STREET
NARAYAN DHURU STREET
NAGDEVI PATH
MOHAMMED ALI ROAD
DHOBI STREET
DEOJI STREET
V CHANDAN STREET
JAGANNATH SHANKARSHETH MARG
Balaji
Nar Narayan
Moolji Jetha Market
A ROAD NO 1
Poddar College
Dadiseth
DADISETH AGIARY STREET
SHEIK MEMON STREET
A ROAD NO 2
BHAJI PALA LANE
MIRZA LANE
JAMSHETH STREET
OJI LANE
Khatri Wadi
VJ ACHARYA MARG
MOOLJI JETHA MARKET LANE
LANE
CG CROSS
CHAMPA GALI
SHAMSHETH STREET
Dwarkadeesh
13
Dabul
KALBADEVI
ZAVERI BAZAR
Jama Masjid
JANJIKAR STREET
NAGDEVI PATH
SARANG STREET
OD GALI
St Xavier
DR VEIGAS STREET/CAVEL STREET
Vithal Wadi
Badam Wadi
CESS STREET
56
Shetya Chowk
THAKURDWAR
DHIRUBHA
Crawford

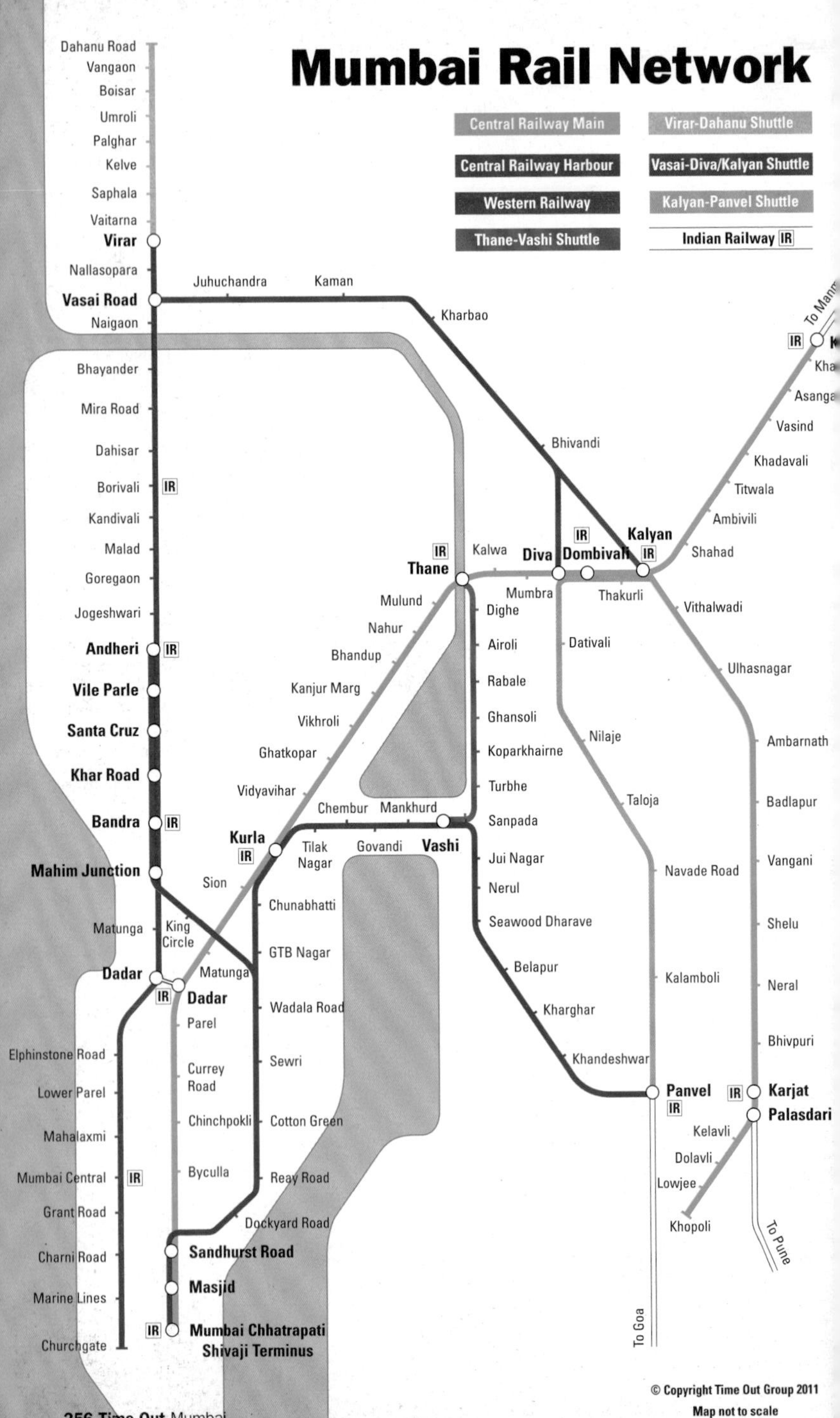
Mumbai Rail Network
Central Railway Main
Virar-Dahanu Shuttle
Central Railway Harbour
Vasai-Diva/Kalyan Shuttle
Western Railway
Kalyan-Panvel Shuttle
Thane-Vashi Shuttle
Indian Railway IR
Dahanu Road
Vangaon
Boisar
Umroli
Palghar
Kelve
Saphala
Vaitarna
Virar
Nallasopara
Vasai Road
Naigaon
Juhuchandra
Kaman
Kharbao
Bhayander
Mira Road
Dahisar
Borivali
Kandivali
Malad
Goregaon
Jogeshwari
Andheri
Vile Parle
Santa Cruz
Khar Road
Bandra
Mahim Junction
Matunga
King Circle
Dadar
Elphinstone Road
Lower Parel
Mahalaxmi
Mumbai Central
Grant Road
Charni Road
Marine Lines
Churchgate
Bhivandi
Thane
Kalwa
Diva
Dombivali
Kalyan
Mumbra
Thakurli
Mulund
Nahur
Bhandup
Kanjur Marg
Vikhroli
Ghatkopar
Vidyavihar
Kurla
Sion
Matunga
Dadar
Parel
Currey Road
Chinchpokli
Byculla
Sandhurst Road
Masjid
Mumbai Chhatrapati Shivaji Terminus
Tilak Nagar
Chembur
Govandi
Mankhurd
Vashi
Chunabhatti
GTB Nagar
Wadala Road
Sewri
Cotton Green
Reay Road
Dockyard Road
Dighe
Airoli
Rabale
Ghansoli
Koparkhairne
Turbhe
Sanpada
Jui Nagar
Nerul
Seawood Dharave
Belapur
Kharghar
Khandeshwar
Panvel
Dativali
Nilaje
Taloja
Navade Road
Kalamboli
To Goa
Vithalwadi
Ulhasnagar
Ambarnath
Badlapur
Vangani
Shelu
Neral
Bhivpuri
Karjat
Palasdari
Kelavli
Dolavli
Lowjee
Khopoli
To Pune
Shahad
Ambivili
Titwala
Khadavali
Vasind
Asangaon
© Copyright Time Out Group 2011
Map not to scale